UZBEKISTAN

1
*Ossuary from the vicinity of Samarkand, clay, moulded and fired. On the long sides
depiction of a Zoroastrian fire altar flanked by a priest (right) and an assistant (left). Both
wear masks covering mouth and nose so as not to defile the sacred flame with their breath.*
H: 75 cm, W: 52 cm, D: 24 cm
7th/8th century
Registan Museum, Samarkand

Heirs to the Silk Road

UZBEKISTAN

Edited by Johannes Kalter and Margareta Pavaloi

with contributions by
M. Pavaloi, H. Gaube, G. Kurbanov, K.J. Brandt, H. Halm, T. Leisten, K. Rührdanz, J. Kalter,
A. von Gladiss, G. Helmecke, M. Zerrnickel, G. Dombrowski, R. Eisener, J. Stadelbauer

Thames and Hudson

First published in Great Britain in 1997
by Thames and Hudson Ltd, London

First published in the United States of America in 1997
by Thames and Hudson Inc., 500 Fifth Avenue, New York, New York 10110

By arrangement with Edition Hansjörg Mayer, London

Library of Congress Catalog Card number: 96-62027

British Library Cataloguing-in-Publication Data
A catalogue record for this book is available from the British Library

ISBN 0-500-97451-9

Translated from the German by Stefan B. Polter

Printed and bound by Staib+Mayer, Stuttgart

Contents

2
Street scene in Samarkand with Registan Square in the distance, about 1900.

ЎЗБЕКИСТОН РЕСПУБЛИКАСИ ПРЕЗИДЕНТИ

Сопроводительное слово
к открытию выставки
"Наследники Шелкового пути"

Дорогие друзья!

В день открытия в Штутгарте выставки "Наследники Шелкового пути" позвольте сердечно приветствовать всех посетителей этой выставки. Верю, что проведение этого мероприятия даст возможность народам наших стран лучше узнать друг друга.

Узбекистан - одно из древнейших государств Центральной Азии, имеет многовековую историю.

Великий Шелковый путь, который проходил по территории Узбекистана на протяжении столетий, был местом соприкосновения великих цивилизаций Китая, Индии, Ближнего Востока и Европы. Древним народам, населявшим эту землю, удалось синтезировать их величайшие достижения и создать свою, неповторимую по красоте культуру. Открытия мыслителей и ученых, рожденных этой землей, золотыми буквами вписаны в историю мировой науки и культуры. Величие и совершенство архитектурных памятников Самарканда, Бухары и Хивы по-прежнему поражают мир.

Обретение независимости позволило вернуться к истокам нашей культуры. В них мы черпаем силы в осуществлении глубоких преобразований общества. Этому же должна способствовать реализация грандиозного проекта восстановления Великого Шелкового пути - экономического и культурного моста между Востоком и Западом.

Рукописи и изделия из бронзы, ганча, фарфора и слоновой кости, представленные на стендах этого музея, дадут возможность соприкоснуться с самобытной культурой и историей нашего народа. Надеюсь, что это поможет Вам лучше понять нас, создаст условия для дальнейшего расширения узбекско-германского сотрудничества, укрепления взаимовыгодных контактов, откроет новые пути к дальнейшему улучшению отношений между народами Узбекистана и Германии.

Пользуясь случаем, хочу выразить искреннюю благодарность устроителям этой прекрасной выставки.

Желаю посетителям выставки, жителям Штутгарта и всему немецкому народу благополучия и процветания.

Ислам Каримов
Президент Республики Узбекистан

город Ташкент,
26 июня 1995 года
I-585

Preface

The publication of "Uzbekistan – Heirs to the Silk Road" gives me the opportunity to welcome all readers. I believe that this book is a splendid chance for people of many nationalities to become better acquainted with Uzbekistan and her culture.

Uzbekistan is among the most ancient countries of Central Asia, and her history spreads over many centuries.

The great Silk Road which passed through Uzbekistan, brought into contact the high cultures of China, India, the Near East and Europe. The ancient peoples who had settled in the region were able to adapt these cultures' greatest achievements and at the same time to foster and develop the beauty of their own culture. The discoveries and inventions of the scientists and scholars who were sons of this soil are recorded in golden letters in the history of the world's sciences and cultures. The greatness and perfection of the architectural monuments of Samarkand, Bukhara and Khiva continue to amaze the world.

Since Uzbekistan gained her independence, we have been able to return to the sources of our culture. These sources provide us with the strength to realise the far-reaching changes in our modern society. The publication of this book about the great Silk Road, the economic and cultural bridge between East and West, forms part of this endeavour.

The manuscripts and objects of bronze, stucco, ceramic and ivory discussed and illustrated here provide a document to the special culture and history of our people. It is my sincere hope that they help towards a better understanding of our culture, the establishment of closer contacts between Uzbekistan and Europe and the opening-up of new relationships between Uzbeks and Europeans.

I am very grateful to the authors, editors and publishers of this book. To all its readers I extend best wishes for happiness, health and good fortune and would regard it as a great pleasure if this book provides an inspiration to visit the Republic of Uzbekistan.

Islam Karimov
President of the Republic of Uzbekistan

Acknowledgements

The German edition of this book was published to accompany the exhibition "Erben der Seidenstraße - Usbekistan" first shown at Stuttgart then Berlin and Rotterdam. Both exhibition and book include objects from the Republic of Uzbekistan.

We would first like to thank H.E. the President of the Republic of Uzbekistan, Islam Karimov, and H. E. the President of the Federal Republic of Germany, Roman Herzog. Both contributed significantly to this project. We are very grateful to the UNESCO for its institutional support by including our project in its Silk Roads Project. This assistance was arranged through the good offices of T. Höllmann, member of the International Consultancy Committee of the Silk Roads Project. D. Diène, coordinator of the Silk Roads Project and director of the Division for Intercultural Projects, actively supported our work. We are grateful to both.

We are specially indebted to the Minister of Culture of the Republic of Uzbekistan, E.K. Khaitbaev, the responsible departmental head, Mr. Usmanov, and the Ministry's staff as well as to the directors of the museums and institutes involved. In particular we would like to thank the directors of the Khamza Institute of Fine Arts, the Museum of Fine Arts and the Museum for Applied Arts in Tashkent, the Registan Museum in Samarkand, the Museum in the Ark in Bukhara and the Museum in the Ark in Khiva. We would also like to thank all those who supported our work in Uzbekistan and provided information and hospitality.

The embassy of the Republic of Uzbekistan in Bonn was interested in our project from the very beginning. We thank H.E. Ambassador Fasayev and his staff.

Without the assistance of the German embassy in Tashkent communication with our Uzbek colleagues and a host of technical and organisational details would have been impossible to manage. We thank H.E. Ambassador K H. Kuhna and his staff.

We are grateful to the following persons and institutions for contributing loan objects and photographs:

J. Allan, R. Barnes, Department of Eastern Art, Ashmolean Museum, Oxford; G. Shaw, M.I. Waley, A. Teh Gallop, Oriental and India Office Collections, British Library, London; S. Canby, Department of Oriental Antiquities, British Museum, London; M. Meinecke, V. Enderlein, A. von Gladiss, G. Helmecke, Museum für Islamische Kunst, Berlin; M. Yaldiz, Museum für Indische Kunst, Berlin; H. O. Feistel, Staatsbibliothek, Berlin; K. Helfrich, G. Dombrowski, C. Müller, Museum für Völkerkunde, Berlin; W. Böhning, Völkerkundemuseum der J.U.E. von Portheim-Stiftung, Heidelberg; E. M. Hoyer, Mr. Thormann, Museum für Kunstgewerbe, Leipzig; J. Frembgen, Museum für Völkerkunde, Munich; V. Himmelein, M. Honroth, Württembergisches Landesmuseum, Stuttgart; and private collectors in London, Esslingen, Frankfurt, Hamburg, Heidelberg, Karlsruhe and Sindelfingen. Our collections of Islamic art and ethnographic material benefited over the years from the support of Mr. J. Drechsel, to whom we would like to express our gratitude.

Our thanks also go to our colleagues K. Helfrich and G. Dombrowski (Museum für Völkerkunde, Berlin) and H. van Reedijk and C. Huygens (Museum voor Volkenkunde, Rotterdam) for their interest and efforts to present the exhibitions at their museums.

In spite of their other obligations, many colleagues agreed to contribute articles for this book. Their names can be found on the title-page. In addition, some helped to write the plate captions, and many gave valuable advice. We regret that it was not always possible to include all the suggested illustrative material, and some articles had to be slightly shortened. We are grateful for these contrubutions and for the understanding shown.

The names of all photographers appear in the picture credits. The main work fell upon I. Hermann, and to him and all those not mentioned here by name we extend our thanks. We are also grateful to the translator, Stefan B. Polter.

We further wish to thank the Board of the Daimler-Benz AG. and our contacts there for financial support towards the realisation of this exhibition and publication.

Several of our colleagues at the Linden-Museum helped during the preparation of this book (M. Zerrnickel, K.J. Brandt and G. Kreisel). For their help with the organisation, typing and text processing we also wish to thank U. Knöpfle, S. Mayer, I. Müller, I. Schneider, R. Tomaschewski and B. Wolfrum.

Should this list of acknowledgements be incomplete, we offer our sincere apologies and would plead that nobody is perfect but God.

Stuttgart, September 1996

Johannes Kalter
Margareta Pavaloi

(Note on the plate captions: Where no owner is mentioned, the object comes from the Linden-Museum, Stuttgart.)

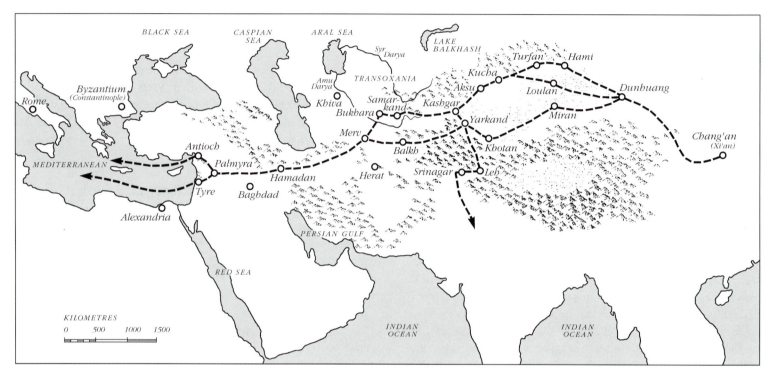

3
[Main routes of the Silk Road]
Rome, Byzantium (Constantinople), Mediterranean, Antioch, Tyre, Black Sea, Caspian Sea, Red Sea, Aral Sea, Khiva, Transoxiana, Samarkand, Balkh, Bukhara, Merv, Persian Gulf, Lake Balkhash, Indian Ocean, Kashgar, Kucha, Yarkand, Khotan, Kilometre.

Introduction

The Republic of Uzbekistan is one of the successor states of the Soviet Union in Central Asia – a very recent creation, barely seven years old. Although nowadays little is known about the region, yet once it was the heartland of the caravan routes – generally called the Silk Routes – which connected Europe with East Asia. Our book is an invitation to a journey through time, to an exploration of the multifaceted history and the diverse forces that shaped the cultural heritage of modern Uzbekistan.

It all began with silk, this most precious of all textiles. The story of how the first silks reached Europe will be told later. But it was the quest for its country of origin and the silk trade along an intricate transcontinental network of caravan routes – which was christened the Silk Road only in the last century – that first triggered an interest in this region, the size of which was only vaguely known and which for a long time did not even have a proper name.

Knowledge about the region only grew gradually. There was a general idea about the vast lands of Central Asia lying beyond Persia and India, with high mountain ranges and dangerous deserts which had to be traversed to reach China, the home of silk. For most of the time we are dealing with in the present book, people were hazy about where Europe ended and Asia began. The merchants travelling the caravan routes mainly distinguished between safe and unsafe, fertile and barren stretches of their journey. Means of travel, movement of populations, trade relations, climate and historical forces as a shared experience provided a sense of community, while religions, social systems and cultural traditions acted as differentiating factors. Long-distance trade created a sense of interdependence despite the huge differences of geography and diversity of cultures.

The trading routes of the Silk Road passed directly through the heartland of Central Asia – or Turkestan, as it was later called – and thus also through the region of modern Uzbekistan, whose cities were vital entrepots.

Although the ultimate terminals of the trade routes lay in China and the Levant, the lands they crossed were not simply so many way-stations, so many stop-overs on a road from A to B. The opening of these transcontinental passages were to have great historical and cultural consequences. It was through them that the various regions of Central Asia established links to the major civilisations of China and India, of Persia and the Mediterranean. All these cultures to a greater or lesser extent, influenced and shaped the regional characteristics of modern Uzbekistan. The Silk Routes therefore represent not only a spacial dimension but also provide a gateway to the history of a huge area in all its geographical and cultural diversity. These trading routes remained active over hundreds of years, accurately attuned to the various peoples and cultures and dependent on the rise and fall of empires, the migration of populations, the vicissitudes of history.

When in the early sixteenth century the Uzbeks, a people linguistically belonging to the East Turkish family of languages, became the dominant force in the homeland of the former Timurid empire, trade along the Silk Road had dimished to a trickle. Although commercial relations with India and Iran and to a modest extent also with China and Ottoman Turkey were still maintained, the grand transcontinental trading which connected China and the Mediterranean and for more than a thousand years had been the economic mainstay of the region, had practically become a thing of the past.

Turkestan, as the region was later to be called, soon found itself caught in a pincer movement between the forces of czarist Russia expanding southward, a strong Shiite Iran as well as Mughal India and China. By the end of the seventeenth century the small khanates, successor states of the Uzbek Shaibanid empire, had become largely isolated.

The khans in their modest principialities tried to emulate the great Timur in their building programmes and in court ceremonies. The craftsmen kept the legacy of the Silk Road alive by their choice of form and ornamentation. The majority of the illustrated objects dates from the time of the Uzbek khanates and comes from the area of present-day Uzbekistan.

Ceramic designs show a mixture of Chinese, Iranian and indigenous styles, while metalwork in addition takes up elements from the Indian subcontinent. The most distinctive regional type of textile, ikat cloth of silk or silk and cotton, is decorated with East Asian and Central Asian features in equal measure. The large silk embroideries called *suzani* from Bukhara and Nurata frequently display Mughal influence, while those from Samarkand have a more East Asian appearance.

Between the seventeenth and the mid-nineteenth century Turkestan almost vanished from Europe's sight. The main keepers of the material traditions of the Silk Road were the large cities in present-day Uzbekistan. The survival of this legacy lay not only in the hands of the Uzbeks and Tajiks (who spoke an East Iranian language), but also of some hundred different peoples, of which the most important were the Kazakhs, Kirghiz, Karakalpaks, Turkmens, Persians, Arabs, Tatars and Kalmucks. This multi-ethnic society in the true sense of the word originated and sustained a specific culture whose creativity and dynamics are reflected in its arts and crafts, the typical boldness and colouration of which sometimes jars on Western sensibilities.

Turkestan took in a major stretch of the Silk Road network, and thus Uzbekistan in the middle of Turkestan was of central importance for those trade routes and shared much of its long and eventful history.

In antiquity, at the time of Alexander the Great and his successors who founded the Graeco-Bactrian empire, the region was called Transoxiana, 'Land beyond the Oxus'. The easternmost point of Alexander's campaigns (4th century B.C.) was Fergana. Hellenistic elements entered not only Graeco-Bactrian art but also the Buddhist art of Gandhara, and can still be found in the folk art of the Swat valley in Pakistan.

Some two hundred years after Alexander, a Chinese envoy on a secret mission to secure allies against the Huns reached our region and discovered the famous 'blood-sweating' Fergana horses. For the Chinese, always in desperate need of good horses, the discovery was immensely valuable, and from their attempts to safeguard a steady supply evolved the trading network of the Silk Road.

In late antiquity urban culture in the region was heavily influenced by Iran. The steppes were ruled by equestrian nomads, by Sakas, Parthians and Huns and from the sixth century also by Turks. As varied as the ethnic make-up were the religious affiliations. There were Buddhist temples and monasteries, Zoroastrian fire altars, Nestorian churches as well as Jewish and Manichaean communities, and the shamanistic practices of the nomads of the steppes and deserts, some of which survived until the sixteenth century.

In the eighth century Arab troops on horseback conquered the region which thus became part of the Islamic world and once more was known as Mā warā `an-nahr, the 'Land beyond the River (Oxus)'. An event of great political and cultural significance was the battle near Talas in 751, when Muslim troops stopped the expansionist drive of Tang China, thereby establishing the border between the Islamic and Chinese spheres of influence. Among the Chinese captives were some versed in paper-making. Soon the world's first paper manufactory outside China was set up in Samarkand, for a long time the most famous of its kind. From here paper started its triumphant spread across the globe, first passing through the countries of the Near East and arriving in Central Europe during the fourteenth century. For the development of science and civilization paper was as important as the later invention of printing by Gutenberg in Mainz.

From 819 to 899, the Land beyond the River was ruled by the first dynasty of Iranian origin, the Samanids. Their capital Bukhara became a brilliant cultural centre. It was here that the revival of Iranian literature started, while the sciences also were encouraged. One of the greatest Muslim physicians, ar-Razi (865-925), whose writings on medicine were also used in the Western world for centuries, dedicated his works to a Samanid ruler. Within a courtly environment were produced some of the most delicate Islamic ceramics and metalworks ever made. The famous tomb of the Samanid ruler Isma`il is the earliest example of Islamic commemorative architecture. The Samanid period has often been called Central Asia's golden age.

There was a second glorious era during the classic period of Islam which concerns us here, namely the reign of Timur (1336-1405) and his heirs. His campaigns brought him to Mesopotamia, Syria, Anatolia and India. At the height of his power his rule extended from the Mediterranean to the Indus. He transformed Samarkand into a splendid capital for his vast empire. The Bibi Khanum mosque and the Gur-e Mir mausoleum bear witness to his building activites. From his conquests he brought back craftsmen and artists from all parts of the Islamic world. He and his art-loving heirs founded ateliers specialising in book-production, and the ceramic and metalworking arts experienced their last flowering. With the death of Timur's last direct descendant in Herat in 1506, historical developments took a turn which finally led to the situation that confronts us today.

The young Republic of Uzbekistan has started on a quest for the origins of her cultural identity. We would like to regard this publication as a small contribution to this endeavour. Realisation of our project would not have been possible without the many kindnesses shown to us by the people of Uzbekistan, by those who demonstrated their skills and talked about their profession and by those whose hospitality we enjoyed, and we extend our thanks in particular to the many anonymous artists who produced the objects presented in this book.

Stuttgart, September 1995
Johannes Kalter, Margareta Pavaloi

4
Caravan outside the walls of Khojent, about 1900.

Prologue

Margareta Pavaloi

A journey like the one we are about to undertake along the Silk Roads to the heart of Central Asia is, among many things, a confrontation with the phenomenon of time. History in particular is not a regular uniform flow of time, but combines diverse forms of concepts and experiences of time (for the following, cf. Chaudhuri 1985).

We normally understand historical time as a sequence of years associated with certain events which provide the building-blocks of factual historiography. This temporal chain of events produces the markings to guide us through history. But there exists another history where time moves almost imperceptively and change comes about much more slowly, a history of endless repetition or cyclical recurrence. This experience of time pertains to the evolving relationship of man with his environment, the formation of social organisation and traditional culture, and here the markers so important for a history of facts and events appear as accidental and random occurrences, as abrupt or even chaotic alterations. Both forms of time sometimes coincide and at other times are experienced with a delay, but finally converge in the shaping of a process we call cultural history. On our journey we shall meet both forms of time as we make our way through a factual and cultural history towards the present, the state of modern Uzbekistan.

The convergence of these two forms of time results in a development which is of much import in the region that concerns us, namely a tendency towards uniformity and integration. Regions formerly separate and independent and with their own characteristic traditions become part of a larger cultural entity. For this development, in addition to crucial historical events, two factors are important, religion and trade.

The role played by Christianity in the West was played in Central Asia first by Buddhism and from the mid-eighth century by Islam with its astonishing success as a religion, a political force and a way of life, which made the region of modern Uzbekistan part of the Islamic world. Another factor with decisive effects on this region were the migratory movements of the Central Asian nomads and their foundation of great military empires; and furthermore the ever-present political and cultural presence of China should never be overlooked.

What role was played by trade, especially by long-distance trade, within this complex pattern of interrelationships and how did it influence the course of history?

Trade, and participation in long-distance trade in particular, has always been a characteristic expression of the political strength of empires and cultures, a measure of their 'international' significance and a sign of their social, political and economic capabilities. Although in pre-industrial times people more or less depended on the food they grew themselves, they were not necessarily satisfied with the clothes and objects for everyday use they could produce under their own roof. Those everyday objects – clothes, vessels, tools, arms and even food –, by being produced by special techniques and invested with artistic imagination and skill, acquired the status of luxury articles. They became symbols to define rank, wealth and status within the community, and because of their exoticism aroused the envy of neighbouring societies.

Exchange of such goods involved a complicated process. Various types of barter came into play as well as social conventions, ritual uses and financial considerations. Perhaps the biggest problem to overcome was space, the sheer distance between producer and consumer. Furthermore, the existence of such long-distance trade, a veritable 'international' movement of goods and people, then as now highlights the role and importance of a money economy (money in various currencies as a medium of exchange). Prices reflected the demand for and admiration of specific products.

Long-distance trade was not only a complicated operation but also one inherently fragile. Fortune and failure were directly linked to geography and climate, factors which are beyond human control. The presence or absence of technological and practical capabilities, of competence in communication and logistics were further decisive factors. The vagaries of war and famine and the rise and fall of empires often deeply impinged on the fate of cities, commercial communities and all those who were either producers of goods or intermediaries in trade transactions.

Transcontinental trade also depended on the existence and vitality of urban centres embedded in an environment that provided a certain amount of surplus and raw materials. In addition, long-distance trade was not viable without some preconditions being fulfilled transcending political and cultural boundaries: security along the highways, effective 'national' legal procedures and a socially acceptable system of profit distribution.

Over the centuries the transcontinental trade evolved into a highly organised operation. There were highways for caravans to travel from one end of Asia to the other. And there were byways branching off from cities, which served as intermediate stops on shorter journeys, connecting them with a hinterland where people lived almost oblivious of those great arteries.

The starting-point of what was probably the world's longest trading route was the Levant with its great ports. The first major stage was Baghdad, where caravans from Iran, India, Central Asia and China met. From Baghdad a shorter route led through fertile Khuzistan to the ports along the Persian Gulf, and a longer route overland, which was the main transcontinental link and led past several way-stations to the major cities of northern India and to the Great Wall of China. This longer route in fact consisted of several alternative roads, the famed Silk Roads – which could equally well be called the Cotton Roads, since silk, although the most valuable good transported on this route, was by no means the only one.

Leaving Baghdad, the first major stop of the caravans bound for India and Central Asia was the old Iranian city of Hamadan; a second stage led to Nishapur or Mashad. The road then passed the Elbrus range between the arid Iranian plain and the wet grain-producing regions around the Caspian Sea. The terminal of the second stage gave a choice of three routes, one to India via Balkh, Kabul, Multan, Lahore and Delhi, another one a loop connecting Herat, Kandahar, Ghazni and Kabul, and a third, the Trans-Asian route to China.

While individual European and Middle Eastern travellers and merchants bound for China had no choice but to traverse the highway from one end to the other, the trade caravans usually shuttled only between the more important entrepots. Bukhara and Samarkand, situated on the major crossroads of the transcontinental routes, were the common terminals for caravans departing from Aleppo and Baghdad. Here they would meet with merchants arriving from Turfan, Kashgar, Yarkand and Khotan.

Beyond Samarkand and Kashgar the caravans had a choice of three different routes, a long-established southern one, a more recent northern one, and a third one crossing the steppes. The first route ran along the southern rim of the Taklamakan desert, passed several oasis towns and continued via Yarkand, Khotan and Miran to Lake Lopnor and on to Dunhuang where it joined the northern route for Chang'an. Lopnor was a staging-post for travellers bound for the Turfan oasis.

Marco Polo relates that caravans used to rest at 'Lop' to prepare for the crossing of the Taklamakan. The crossing took about thirty days, and although there were occasional watering-holes, provisions, including water, for both men and beasts had to be obtained beforehand.

This older southern route was later abandoned for reasons which are not entirely clear. Among the suggested causes may have been climatic changes resulting in the drying-out of oases as well as political disturbances.

Later the northern route became the most heavily frequented one. It crossed the southern ranges of the Tianshan (Chin. 'heavenly mountains') to Kashgar, passed Aksu, Kucha, Turfan and Hami and from there led through the Gobi desert to various Chinese border towns. Both the southern and northern routes were arduous on account of mountain ranges and deserts and needed much preparation and planning.

There was a third route called the 'steppe route', its main difficulty being the prevailing political constellations. It ran north of the Tianshan from Urumchi to Usu (these are modern approximations of the sites of the ancient way-stations) whence one branch continued across Dzungaria and the Kazakh steppes and the other led to Kuldja (modern Yining) and the Ili valley.

If peace reigned on the steppes or the area was controlled by strong rulers, caravans from Samarkand would take the northern route through the Zeravshan valley to China. At Turfan, Urumchi and other oasis towns of Central Asia the Chinese and Islamic worlds came into close contact. The men professing the 'Great Religion' found it easy to get along with the merchants belonging to the 'Small Religion', as they called Islam. From the tenth century Islam appeared among the steppe population and in the Tianshan valleys. By the time the Ming dynasty acceded to the Chinese throne in the fourteenth century, Islam had become an important political and social power. Many commercial enterprises in northern China belonging to converted Muslims were engaged in trade along the Silk Roads. Although they were ranked socially lower than the Confucians, their trading activities were not obstructed by the bureaucracy.

The real key to success in the Central Asian caravan trade, however, were the diplomatic and military relations between the Chinese empire and the rulers of the Turkic and Mongolian nomad tribes which controlled crucial stretches of the routes. It has to be remembered that the histories of China, northern India and the Middle East were more than once dramatically changed by nomad invasions from Central Asia. Relations with Central Asia were strengthened by dynasties of Turkic, Mongolian and Turco-Mongolian extraction which kept close links with their homeland. Thus the first Mughal emperor, Babur, was homesick for the Fergana valley for the rest of his life, and his heirs resided in marble palaces in spirit akin to light and airy tents rather than to sturdy houses.

Horses from the northern steppes were everywhere in great demand. Along the Ili and Fergana valleys a strong, resilient and shomewhat shaggy breed was raised for the stables of Chinese and Indian rulers, who were much concerned about the fighting power of their cavalries. The horse trade remained important for the survival of the Silk Roads long after the secrets of silk production had become known beyond the Great Wall and silk stuffs were being produced at many cities outside China, and when maritime trade across the Indian Ocean began to replace the overland trade.

5
Bridge built in the reign of Timur.

15

Long-distance trade on the Silk Road was always dependent on accurate information about the current geographic, climatic and political situation. To lead a caravan of a thousand camels across the Gobi, the Tianshan or the Taklamakan required high levels of discipline, teamwork, logistics and security. The position of the caravan leader resembled that of a ship's captain. His reputation (and remuneration) rested on his knowledge about the best available routes and his ability in handling men and beasts. For the duration of the journey he decided on the number and condition of the animals to be packed with goods and where and when camp was made. The main camel driver often substituted for the cook, and his cry "Let's have tea!" signalled the near end of the rest and the resumption of the journey. These conventions were still in place in 1926, when Owen Lattimore joined a caravan through the Gobi desert.

Loss through enemy attacks were a constant worry, and before a caravan set out, it was imperative to obtain the best available information about the political situation and security along the proposed route. A town in ruins or under siege could proof fatal to the entire caravan. This could happen even during the best of times. When Ibn Battuta arrived at Bukhara in 1333, the city lay in ruins. This had been the work of Genghis Khan's army and had occurred during a period when under the 'Pax Mongolica' the situation in the steppe regions had been unusually peaceful.

As the members of a camel caravan were usually a very mixed lot, certain social niceties and conventions had to be observed to accomodate different requirements and religious customs and thus to minimise areas of conflict. The presence of an international group of merchants, financiers, money-changers and private travellers in a city indicated not only its strategic location but also a favourable political situation and competent management of urban affairs. Those were preconditions for the flourishing of long-distance transport, and any disturbances had immediate repercussions, often resulting in a rerouting of the lucrative caravan trade.

The cities along the caravan route controlled the flow of goods in Eurasia. They supplied various indispensable services: brokers to set up contracts and guarantee delivery; markets to sell and buy goods of every description; banking houses to supply credit and bills of exchange, making money transactions both simpler and safer. One could obtain horses and pack-animals, and the caravanserais offered lodgings, stables and stores for merchandise. Only a well-organised city was able to present solutions to the manifold logistical problems of long-distance trade. In the end, however, the most important factor for a flourishing economy was political stability, and this was the hardest precondition to fulfil and the easiest to go awry.

6

*Bactrian camel with rider and groom, buff-coloured pottery with three-colour glaze (*sancai*)*
in yellow, brown and green.

The exceptionally large moulded figure of camel and rider shows very careful and detailed
modelling. The bearded rider with strong hooked nose is not a Chinese but presumably
comes from Central Asia or even further west. His peaked cap likewise is un-Chinese. In
his right hand he probably held the reins or a riding crop. The groom is disproportionally tall
and was probably not part of this group, since he must also have held reins and it is unlikely
that the animal had two reins. The groom's facial features with heavy eyebrows, deep-set eye
sockets and a hooked nose are also un-Chinese. His costume of a short coat with very wide
lapels is of Persian cut. His head is covered, however, with a Chinese futou *kerchief typical*
of the Tang period.
H: 88 cm, L: 71 cm (camel), H: 64 cm (groom)
China, first half Tang dynasty (618-907)
Museum für Völkerkunde, Berlin

The Old Silk Road

Transoxiana from the Fourth Century B.C. to the Eigth Century A.D.

7
The Great Wall of China near Beijing.

8

Model of a watch-tower, buff-coloured pottery with silvery oxydised green lead glaze.
*The large model of a two-storey watch-tower (*dianlou *or* wanglou*) constructed from several separate parts comes with twelve small figures, whose exact position cannot be reconstructed but who probably stood either on the balustrades or the galleries. We very often find figures with cross-bows arranged along the galleries, indicating the defensive character of such towers (see ill. 81). Having been buried in the earth for centuries, the original green lead glaze has oxydised to show a bright silvery surface.*

Such models of watch-towers used as burial objects are realistic representations of the original wooden structures with mud-covered walls and panels which have long since disappeared. They now give us an idea of how the wooden architecture of Han times must have looked like. Watch-towers were usually erected as part of large fortified farmsteads and were used as lookouts and defenses against attackers, mostly marauding nomad horsemen from the steppes. The upper storeys were narrower than the base. They provided the model for the pavillons and Buddhist pagodas of later times.
H: 108 cm
China, Eastern Han period (25-220)

How It All Began ...

Margareta Pavaloi

A century before the birth of Christ an adventurous young Chinese traveller called Zhang Qian set out across China on a secret mission to the then remote and mysterious regions of the west. Although the immediate purpose ended in failure, it proved to be one of the most important journeys in history, for it was to lead to China discovering Europe and the birth of the Silk Road. Zhang, who was renowned for his strength and daring, was sent on his trail-blazing journey by Wu, the Han emperor, who found himself facing increasing harassment from China's ancient foes, the Xiongnu. These warlike people, Huns of Turkic stock, were eventually destined to appear in Europe as the ravaging Huns of our own history books. Their raids on China had begun during the period of the Warring States (481-221 B.C.) and in 221 B.C. Shi Huangdi, the first emperor of the Qin dynasty, had built the Great Wall in an effort to keep them out.

Emperor Wu, or the Son of Heaven as he was officially known, had learned from Hun captives that some years earlier they had defeated another Central Asiatic people, the Yuezhi, made a drinking vessel from the skull of their vanquished leader and forced them to flee far to the west, beyond the Taklamakan desert. There, he was informed, they were waiting to avenge their defeat, but first sought an ally. Wudi immediately decided to make contact with the Yuezhi with the aim of joining forces with them and making a simultaneous attack on the Xiongnu from both front and rear.

9
Sasanian-Chinese textile fragment. Woven silk.
H: 4.5 cm, W: 25.0 cm
'Schiupang', Bulayiq, 8th century
Museum für Indische Kunst, Berlin

10
Textile fragment. Silk tapestry with lion decoration, woven silk.
H: 8 cm, W: 10 cm
Khocho, Ruin K, 9th century (?)
Museum für Indische Kunst, Berlin

11
Textile fragment. Kesi (slit tapestry weave) technique, woven silk.
H: 5 cm, W: 7 cm
Khocho, Ruin K, 9th century (?)
Museum für Indische Kunst, Berlin

12
Horse with saddle and harness. Buff-coloured pottery with traces of painting.
H: 28.8 cm, L: 30.2 cm
China, Tang dynasty (618-907)

He therefore sought a suitable volunteer for this dangerous mission – dangerous because an emissary from China to the Yuezhi would first have to travel through Hun-held territory. Zhang Qian, an official of the imperial household, volunteered and was accepted by the emperor. In the year 138 B.C. he set out with a caravan of one hundred men determined to run the Hun gauntlet. But in what is now Gansu they were attacked by the Xiongnu and the survivors taken prisoner, remaining captive for ten years. Zhang was well treated, however, and even provided with a wife. With the aim of eventually making his escape and continuing his journey westwards, he managed to retain Wu's ambassadorial token – a yak's tail – throughout his captivity. One day, after their captors had allowed them more and more liberty, Zhang and the remnants of his party managed to slip away and set out once again on their mission.

They finally reached the territory of the Yuezhi (who later became the Indo-Scythian rulers of north-west India), only to discover that in the years that had passed since their defeat by the Huns they had become prosperous and settled and had lost all interest in avenging themselves on their former foes. Zhang remained with them for a year, gathering as much information as possible about them and other tribes and countries of Central Asia. While journeying home through Hun territory he was captured again. As luck would have it, civil war broke out among his captors, and in the confusion he managed to escape once again. Finally, after thirteen years away, and long assumed to be dead, he reached Chang'an, the Han capital, to report to the emperor. Of his original party of one hundred men only one, besides himself, reached home alive.

The intelligence that Zhang Qian brought back – military, political, economic and geographical – caused a sensation at the Han court. From his emissary the emperor learned of the rich and previously unknown kingdoms of Fergana, Samarkand, Bukhara (all now in Uzbekistan) and Balkh (now in Afghanistan). Also for the first time the Chinese learned of the existence of Persia and of another distant land called Lijian. This, present-day scholars believe, was almost certainly Rome. But of more immediate importance was the discovery in Fergana of an amazing new type of warhorse which, Zhang reported, was bred from 'heavenly' stock. Fast, large and powerful, these were a revelation to the Chinese whose only horses at that time were the small, slow, local breed today known as Prejevalsky's Horse, and now only to be found in zoos.

Emperor Wu, realising that the Fergana horses would be ideal for cavalry against the troublesome Huns, was determined to re-equip his army with them. He sent a mission to Fergana to try to acquire some, but it was wiped out on the way there, as were successive missions. Finally a much larger force, accompanied by vets, was sent to lay siege to Fergana. However, the inhabitants rounded up their horses and drove them into the walled city, threatening to kill themselves and the horses if the Chinese army came any closer. At last an honourable surrender was arranged and the Chinese left for home with their chargers.

Greatly pleased with his emissary who had shown such determination on this epoch-making journey, Emperor Wu bestowed on him the title 'Great Traveller'. Many further expeditions followed, for Wudi was now determined to expand his empire westwards. One of these was again led by Zhang, this time in 115 B.C. to the Wusun, a nomadic people who lived along the western frontier of the Xiongnu, whom Wu hoped to gain as allies against the Huns. Again Zhang failed to enlist their aid, for they were too afraid of their powerful neighbours and China seemed far off. Not long after his return from this mission, the Great Traveller died, greatly honoured by his emperor, and still revered in China today. He could fairly be described as the father of the Silk Road.

It is hardly possible to better this (slightly modified) description by Peter Hopkirk of the beginnings of the Silk Road (Hopkirk 1980:14–17).

But in particular the Son of Heaven loved the horses from Kokand (Boulnois 1964:29). The reason was partly pragmatic. Han China with its imperial ambitions and constant fighting against the nomadic peoples to the north needed warhorses in great numbers. Shodding had not yet been invented, and although the small Mongolian horse was suitable for light cavalry, it was not strong enough to carry a fully armed and armoured rider over long distances. Its hooves were soft and quickly wore down. The horses of Kokand and Fergana were a different breed, larger, more powerful and with stronger hooves and capable of covering a thousand li in a day. Chinese records tell us that these horses sweat blood and are descended from the breed of heavenly horses (Boulnois 1964:20). And the report continues: "In the country of Kokand there are high mountains. The horses living there cannot be captured. Therefore at the foot of the mountains one sets loose mares who have a coat striped like a tiger's, so that they mate with the stallions from the mountains. The mares then throw foals secreting a bloody sweat. They are called 'foals of the heavenly race'" (ibid.).

The 'heavenly horses' fascinated not only the Son of Heaven, but also the sculptors and artists of the Han and Tang periods who immortalised them for our benefit. The most splendid example is the bronze 'Flying Horse' made some two thousand years ago and excavated by Chinese archaeologists on the Silk Roads in 1969 at Wuwei in Gansu province.

Emperor Wu was determined to secure access to the homeland of the 'heavenly horses' and to establish trade routes via Sichuan through Turkestan to Bactria. After their victory over the Huns the government established the province of Chiu-ch'üan ('well of wine') as a link with the lands of the north-west. For the same reason embassies were once again sent to An-hsi, Chiao-chih and the other countries (Boulnois 1964:27).

The Chinese missions to Central Asia mainly brought back horses. The gifts they took with them primarily consisted of silk which seemed the most obvious choice, as silk was used in China to pay wages and taxes and the government was reluctant to export metal money. Besides silk, the 'western lands' were eager to obtain weapons.

Only in 60 B.C. did the Chinese gain full control over both the southern route across the Tianshan ('heavenly mountains') and Pamirs as well as the northern route. The post of 'Protector General of the Western Region' was established, who was to keep a watchful eye on the neighbouring peoples. For the Chinese, Central Asia in the first century B.C. consisted of a multitude of petty states, some of which seemed to have a population of no more than a few hundred families.

Emperor Wu was the first Chinese emperor to send delegations to Persia, and the Persians – or more precisely, the Parthians – in return sent an embassy which presented the emperor with the personal gifts of an ostrich egg and a troupe of jugglers. These first contacts of 115 or 105 B.C. were later continued through the establishment of trade relations. Some historians argue that these relations constituted a regular commercial link between China and Persia. Once the Persians started buying Chinese silks, it did not take long for the Romans to become acquainted with the precious material.

For a long time the Romans were convinced that silk grew on trees. The Chinese did nothing to disillusion them, since it went some way to safeguard their monopoly on silk production and export. The Parthians, through whose lands the trade was carried out, also saw little reason to pass on information about the technical aspects of silk production, as they – like every subsequent dynasty that ruled over parts of the Silk Road – made a hefty profit from the silk trade.

The first Roman contact with this exquisite textile was not particularly propitious, however. Marcus Licinius Crassus, triumvir, consul and governor of Syria, was eager to follow in Alexander's footsteps and repeat his victories in the East. In 53 B.C. he commanded seven legions against the Parthians across the Euphrates. But it was not the news of victory or defeat what truly struck the Romans at home, but a purely coincidental event, the discovery of silk. The Romans learned about it at the same time as they heard of Crassus's defeat.

The Parthian warriors proved a frightening experience for the Romans, with the ghastly noise of their tambourines and war-cries and their trick to seemingly retreating and then suddenly turning in the saddle and letting loose a rain of arrows on the pursuing legionnaires – the famous Parthian shot. But an even greater shock were the large brilliant banners they suddenly unfurled and which completely disoriented the soldiers and made them flee the battlefield. It was one of the heaviest defeats in Roman history. According to the historian Florus, those gold-embroidered banners were the first silks the Romans ever laid eyes on.

For the next few hundred years the Romans were in the grip of a veritable silk fever, and they could never get enough of this wonderful material. The cool fabric, 'light as the clouds' and 'transparent as glass', was called sericum, from 'Seres', the Latin name for China. A search was started to find out were this precious material originated, because the Romans were sure that the Parthians were incapable of producing such fine fabrics.

It was to take six hundred years before the western world discovered the secrets of silk production. According to tradition, it was a Chinese princess who in 420 or 440 smuggled the secret out of China by hiding some silkworm eggs in her coiffure – an example of what today would be called 'technology transfer'. A marriage to the ruler of Khotan had been arranged, and the princess felt she could not do without silken stuffs so far from home. At first production must have been modest. Later, after Nestorian monks had brought silkworm eggs hidden in a walking-stick

from Central Asia to Byzantium, the Chinese silk monopoly was truly broken.

The caravans carried not only silk along the Silk Roads – metal, porcelain, spices and medicinal herbs were also profitable trade goods. And the Chinese not only appreciated glass but also Western textiles, especially Persian and Syrian brocades and cloth from Byzantium. Interest in Western 'exotics' was at its height during the Tang dynasty (618-907), when textiles, music, dancers, entertainers, myrrh, fruit (e.g., pomegranates) and much else was brought to China. Some Chinese cities held large communities of foreign merchants, in particular from Sogdiana, as we know from letters by Sogdian traders. It was only after the decline of the Tang dynasty and the victories of Arab armies in Central Asia that trade with the West slowly dried up and China again was closed to the West.

"The Caravanserai of the Gods"

Boulnois' phrase is very evocative of the fact that other 'goods' besides silk travelled along the trans-Asian highways, namely 'goods' of a literary, aesthetic and religious nature. The various creeds which took root in the regions traversed by the highways impressed themselves, each in its own specific way, on the arts and *Weltanschauung* of Central Asia and China.

The first religion to reach China via Central Asia was Buddhism. Founded by Gautama Buddha (c. 563-483 B.C.) in northeastern India, it became the official religion for almost the entire country after the conversion of King Ashoka in the third century B.C. Legend has it that Chinese interest in Buddhism was first aroused by the Han emperor Ming (58-75 A.D.), who in a dream saw the Buddha surrounded by a bright halo. However that may be, there is no doubt that Buddhist monks and pilgrims were already travelling the Silk Roads by that time.

The spread of Buddhism into Central Asia originated in the Buddhist kingdom of Gandhara in the northwest of modern Pakistan. There, an artistic synthesis had already been created from the Buddhist art of the Kushan period and the Greek heritage of the Graeco-Bactrian empire founded by Alexander's successors. Among the most impressive innovations of this synthesis are the portraits of the Buddha dressed in robes of typically Greek drapery and with classical Greek features. Indian influence is more subtle and shows in the long earlobes and heavy half-closed lids, the gestures and Buddhist symbols. The fusion of the two styles produced works of art whose beauty has lost none of its appeal for the modern observer.

Under the Kushan, a dynasty tolerant about religious matters and the existence of different religions within its realm, Buddhism spread to Bactria, Sogdiana and Khorezm, previously a stronghold of Zoroastrianism. The expansion of the new faith with its two main schools of Mahayana ('Great Vehicle') and Hinayana ('Small Vehicle') Buddhism and some minor sects, brought about the building of monasteries, temples and cave sanctuaries. These were decorated with wall paintings and sculptures commissioned by the ruling houses, leading local families and prosperous businessmen.

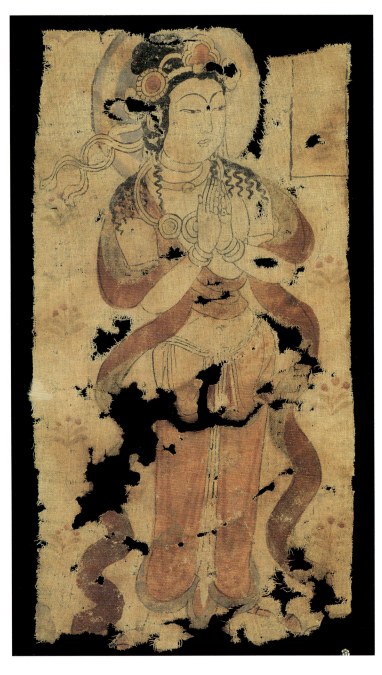

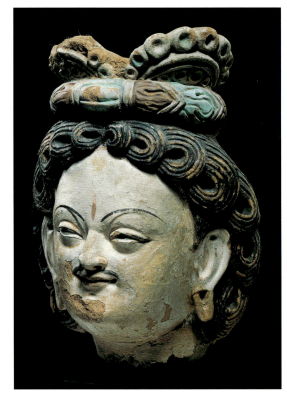

14

Head of a Bodhisattva. Clay, moulded and painted.
The shape of the face, the hand-modelled nose, the leftward gaze and the slightly asymmetric lines of the painted eyebrows emphasise the portrait-like character which is further enhanced by the curiously shaped locks and the hair ornament. The colouration is characteristic of the early phase of the first Indo-Iranian style. We may assume that the facial features correspond to those of the native population.
H: 27 cm
Kizil, Cave of the Statues, 6th century
Museum für Indische Kunst, Berlin

13

Temple banner with Bodhisattva. Painting on ramie.
The simply executed stencilled drawing shows Chinese influence both in the brushwork and the modelling of the figure which reflects the aesthetic ideals of the Tang period. The use of stencils in temple workshops was necessary because of great demand and adherence to strict iconographic rules.
H: 51.5 cm, W: 22.5 cm
Turfan area, 8th/9th century
Museum für Indische Kunst, Berlin

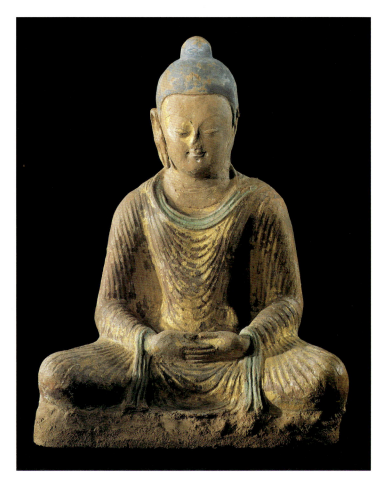

15

Meditating Buddha. Clay, moulded and painted.
This Buddha figure originally stood in a temple niche. The broad features with the high and strongly curved eyebrows, heavy eyelids und small expressive mouth are typical of Chinese Buddhist art.
H: 43.3 cm
Khocho, Temple W, 8th century
Museum für Indische Kunst, Berlin

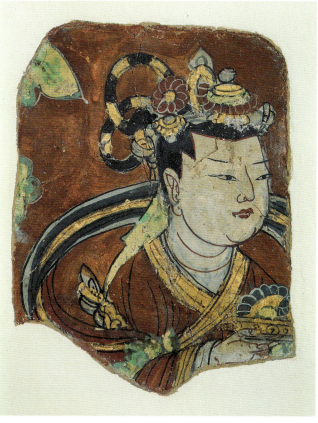

16
Small head of a female deity. Clay, moulded and air-dried.
The elegant modelling of the face with its dream-like smile and the hairstyle combed back
and surmounted by a head-dress is characteristic of the work of Indo-Iranian artists,
indicating that not only Chinese artisans were active in the Turfan region.
H 16.8 cm
Chikkan Köl, 9th century
Museum für Indische Kunst, Berlin

18
Group of donors (?). Secco wall painting.
The fragment shows two pairs of figures, the men wearing strange hat-like head-dresses, the
women being remarkable for their high coiffures arranged with bands and decorative combs,
their neck jewellery, plunging neck-line and high waist-line of their full-length garments.
While the female faces are without expression, the figure on the left has the face of an old
man. Facial features, costume and head-dress seem to belong to a specific people (Uighurs?)
or region.
H: 48.5 cm, W: 37.8 cm
Shorchuk, Kirin cave, 7th/8th century
Museum für Indische Kunst

17
Female deity with a bowl of flowers. Secco wall painting.
The deity's elaborate coiffure and fluttering scarf are eye-catching.
H: 19 cm, W: 15 cm
Sengim, terrace of Temple 10, 9th century
Museum für Indische Kunst, Berlin

Many wall paintings include portraits of the donors, men
and women, who through their patronage hoped for
prosperity in this life and merits in the next.

Besides holy scriptures the travelling monks carried
ritual objects and works of art which the people of Central
Asia and China found curious and attractive. Like other
religions, Buddhism made use of art and architecture to
illustrate and explain religious concepts. Along the Silk Road
a new artistic style developed which is sometimes called
'Serindian', although it was based on a synthesis more
complicated than the geographical names 'Seres' and 'India'
imply. Buddhism and Buddhist art were influenced by many
of the diverse regional cultures they encountered on their
long way to China.

19

Head of a Buddha. Schist.
The hair covering the topknot in wave-like strands is typical of late Gandhara style. The long pierced earlobes signify that Prince Gautama Shakyamuni divested himself of all heavy jewellery before setting out on the path of enlightenment and becoming the Buddha.
H: 46 cm
Pakistan, Gandhara region, 2nd/3rd century

Along the northern route, for example, two regions were particularly influential, the area around Kucha where the older Western style predominated (c. 500–700), and around Turfan with its more recent Eastern style (c. 650–950). Typical examples of the 'Western School' can be found, for instance, on the walls of the cave temples at Kyzyl. Because of its many Indian and Iranian elements it is called 'Indo-Iranian'. Indian influence is noticeable in the composition of Buddhist narrative scenes and the facial expressions of Buddha portraits, while Iranian elements can be found in the details of the hair ornaments of Bodhisattvas and the patterns of the robes, some of which can be traced to motifs found on Sasanian textiles. Chinese influence on the 'Eastern School' is easily recognisable in the facial features and style of dress. In addition, some elements of old Turco-Mongolian origin can be identified.

The works of art discovered in cities abandoned more than a thousand years ago, are interesting not only for their contribution to the history of religion. They also represent invaluable documentation about the cultural environment in which they were created.

The Teachings from the West

Manuscripts discovered at the ancient sites show even more clearly than other types of objects that Buddhism was not the only religion to reach Central Asia and China from a westerly direction. Zoroastrianism, Nestorian Christianity and Manichaeism were also present. Numerous Manichaean manuscripts, some with beautiful miniatures, were found in and around Khocho, the ancient Uighur capital. Proof that all these religions were actually represented in China is provided by an edict of 845, which proscribed foreign religions. Three 'barbaric' doctrines were singled out: Buddhism, Nestorianism and Zoroastrianism.

Further evidence of Nestorianism in China is supplied by the famous stele at Xi'an, which suggests the existence of a substantial Christian community at the time. The Nestorians had emigrated to Central Asia and China after the orthodox church in Syria had pronounced them heretics.

Christianity was known in China as the 'School of Light' in contrast to Zoroastrianism, the 'School of Fire'. The missionary activities of Nestorians and Zoroastrians were terminated by the proscription, when two thousand priests and monks were defrocked, a small number compared to the 260 500 Buddhist monks and nuns who suffered the same fate (Boulnois 164:199). The edict had serious consequences for the fortunes of Christianity in China. When an emissary of the catholicos returned from China around 980, he reported that he had encountered not a single Christian soul. Only after the Mongolian conquest did Christians return to China. At least the Franciscan William of Rubruck, who was dispatched to the court of the Mongol khan by the king of France, Louis IX, in 1252 (earlier than Marco Polo) and who left us the first description by a European of Central Asia in the time of the Mongols, was able to meet fellow Christians.

Zoroastrianism was already well-established in Central Asia by the time Buddhism arrived. Its founder, Zoroaster, was himself probably a native of Central Asia, where the religion remained alive long after the arrival of Islam, particularly in Khorezm. It was strongest in pre-Islamic Persia, where the Sasanians patronised it and proclaimed it the offical state religion. In China, however, the 'School of Fire' was less successful than Christianity; it remained almost exclusively a religion of foreigners and made very few converts among the Chinese.

More successful was Manichaeism, the 'School of the Two Principles', even though to Chinese eyes it must have appeared at least as strange as Zoroastrianism. Manichaeism combined elements of both Zoroastrianism and Christianity. It was characterised by a strict dualism based on two pre-existent and irreconcilable principles comparable perhaps to the dichotomies of Good and Evil and Light and Darkness of Zoroastrianism. After its proscription in Persia in the third century, Manichaeism found a new home in Sogdiana, and from the eighth century onwards the Uighurs became its greatest followers in Central Asia. Manichaeism flourished until well into the tenth century. Its success is attested to by numerous manuscripts and wall paintings. Chinese attitudes towards Manichaeans depended mainly on the state of their relationship with the Uighurs, who in turn were crucial for the operation of the Silk Road trade. After the tenth century Manichaeism had to make way for Islam in western Central Asia and for Buddhism in the eastern part of the region.

The art and culture of the Silk Roads found its finest expression during the Tang dynasty, China's golden age. The decline of this great dynasty was the beginning of the end of trade along these routes. The demise was a long and complicated development caused by political as well as climatic factors. Many of the oases dried out and the desert slowly engulfed the towns and monasteries. The Muslim advance put paid to Chinese ambitions in the 'western lands', and the spread of Islam drove Buddhism from the 'eastern lands'. Some cities along the Silk Road developed into important commercial centres of the Islamic world, while others descended into provicialism or were abandoned and disappeared under the sands of the Taklamakan and Gobi for centuries. Their rediscovery in the nineteenth century makes for a dramatic and fascinating tale.

The Rediscovery of the Silk Roads

By the time European interest began to concentrate on Central Asia in the nineteenth century, the Silk Roads had long become pure legend. Their rediscovery was as much an accidental by-product of political manoeuverings as their inception had been. Again we find an adventurous young man on a secret mission making his way across the snow-covered passes of the Karakoram towards a 'no-man's-land' in Central Asia. He was an Indian by the name of Mohamed-i-Hameed who had orders from the Queen of England to explore the oases of the Taklamakan. His superiors in London and Calcutta had chosen him for the same reason the Chinese emperor Wu once chose Zhang Qian – because he seemed a suitable candidate for a dangerous assignment. It would have been too risky to send a British officer to this

21
Ruins of Gaocheng on the northern Silk Route.
China, Xinjiang province, near Turfan

22
Grottoes at Bezeklik.
China, Xinjiang province, near Turfan

20
Stupa-shaped reliquary. Grey schist, turned.
H: 27 cm
Pakistan, Gandhara region, c. 3rd/5th century

23

Seated Buddha with gesture of Fulfilling of the Vow, Yungang grottoes near the ancient Silk Route.

China, Shensi province, near Datong

25

Head of a brahmin. Secco wall painting.

The temples at Bezeklik are among the most important sites in the Turfan area. Temple 9 is especially famous for its interesting wall paintings. This head of a brahmin with lively features, flowing hair and full beard is a good example of Indian influence in the art of the Silk Route.

H: 20 cm, W: 15.5 cm

Bezeklik, Temple 9, 7th/8th century

Museum für Indische Kunst, Berlin

24

Buddha flanked by his favourite disciples. Sculpture and wall paintings, "Caves of the Thousand Buddhas".

Tang dynasty (618-907)

China, Xinjiang province, Dunhuang

26

Head of an elderly brahmin. Clay, traces of paint.

This head of a brahmin shows realistic calm and sombre features. Buddhists regarded brahmins as infidels, and they are usually portrayed with very animated expressions which makes them look as if engaged in lively debate.

H: 26.8 cm

Shorchuk, Nakshatra cave, 8th century

Museum für Indische Kunst, Berlin

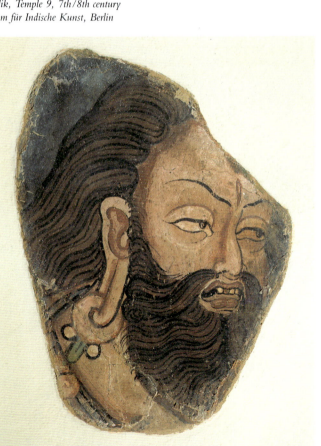

27

Three Manichaean women. Secco wall painting.
Both the style of painting and the blue background of this fragment recall Manichaean
manuscript illustrations, as do the coiffure with parted hair and the single lock hanging in
front of the ear. The head-dress consists of a diadem-like band of rolled-up white cloth with
a framed disc at the centre, perhaps a symbolic representation of the sun and moon. The
jewellery consists only of earrings.
H: 27 cm, W: 22 cm
Khocho, near Ruin K, 8th/9th century
Museum für Indische Kunst, Berlin

28

Fragment of a Manichaean illuminated manuscript. Ink, colour pigments, gold dust on
paper.
The upper part of the illustration shows two priests in white ritual garb and high head-
dresses, and beneath a group of laymen in colourful dress.
H: 29.4 cm, W: 19.0 cm
Khocho, temple, 8th/9th century
Museum für Indische Kunst, Berlin

area between the Russian and Chinese borders, both for reasons of personal safety and for political considerations. Russian expansion into Asia was increasingly regarded by Britain as a possible threat to its Indian possessions, and so it was necessary to obtain as much reliable information as possible about potential approaches by an enemy force. It was the high tide of the 'Great Game', as this conflict of interest between Russia and Great Britain was called, a time when both countries were busy securing their footholds in Asia and expanding their spheres of influence. During the early phase of the 'game' exploration of the terrain was of prime importance.

In the 1860s, Captain T.G. Montgomerie of the Survey of India, the body responsible for mapping the whole of British India and beyond, had hit upon a brilliant idea – the use of natives, in this case Indians, for clandestine mapping expeditions to dangerous areas, i.e. Turkestan, since he had noticed that Indians and particularly merchants passed freely backwards and forwards across those northern borders. So Mohamed-i-Hameed was chosen and set out for Yarkand. On his way back, however, he fell ill and died. As it was first rumoured that he might have been murdered, possibly by enemy agents, the government of British India ordered an investigation. Civil-Assistant William Johnson, who had been entrusted with the investigation, finally ruled out this suspicion. He even recovered Hameed's notes and observations and passed them on to Montgomerie. Among the papers Montgomerie came upon a note giving a hint of a possibly existing route through the Taklamakan desert, which had previously been regarded as nothing more than a legend. The note concerned the site of old Khotan, which long ago had been swallowed up by the sand. During a later expedition Johnson could substantiate the information. Not only had he seen brick tea dug from the ancient desert sites – although it had passed its sell-by date by a wide margin, it was still in great demand – but had also caught sight of some of the ruins. He reported that the location of the buried cities was known to a few persons who kept it secret in order to enrich themselves, for instance by digging for gold coins. Such intrepid forays into unknown territory were undertaken not only by British colonial officers but also by merchants and private travellers, who went to Turkestan by order of their governments, out of personal interest or adventurousness, and supplied much important information.

Nearly another thirty years went by before such scattered information was given serious attention. By then the Great Game had run its course and the colonial powers no longer sent agents to Turkestan but scholars. Earlier indications that the fabulous ghost towns of the Taklamakan might be more than wild imaginings had by then been almost forgotten. Most archaeologists had not bothered to follow them up, being more interested in gaining laurels for their relatively new academic discipline by digging up the recently discovered great civilizations of the Near and Middle East. The first to become alert were Indologists investigating a fragment of a manuscript from Kucha which had arrived in India. Written in Sanskrit on birch-bark and dating from the fifth century, it was earlier than any known text from India herself.

While the philologists were still hotly debating the significance of this discovery, in late 1895 the Swedish geographer Sven Hedin set out for an expedition to the 'buried cities' of the Taklamakan. He was one of a new breed of scholars – Aurel Stein, the first archaeologist of the Silk Roads, was another – who had appeared in Europe in the later 19th century. They typically combined romanticism with a large dose of courage, a love of adventure and a serious scientific outlook. Although himself not an expert in archaeology, art history or the history of religion, Hedin recognised the importance of the ruins and artefacts he discovered. His mapping of the Inner Asian deserts was not superseded until the advent of satellite reconnaisance.

In the spring of 1900, the Hungarian-born British archaeologist (later Sir) Marc Aurel Stein was impatiently waiting for the thaw to clear the passes leading to Inner Asia, so that he could start on his first expedition. With him the scientific exploration of the Silk Roads really took off. On his expeditions he never was afraid of difficult situations and hardships. He took with him two pack-mules carrying photographic plates, endured frost-bitten toes and explained to his Chinese companions that in an emergency porridge was good enough even for the Chinese, claiming the authority of an ancient text he had just excavated. For his return journeys he likewise used mules and camels to carry the precious finds he brought back under dramatic circumstances to India and England, where they can be admired today in New Delhi and at the British Museum. The great archaeologist Sir Leonard Woolley once described

29

Robert Shaw (centre) with companions, a photograph taken on his return from Kashgar and Yarkand, 1868-1869.
Shaw was one of the first Englishmen to reach eastern Turkestan. The coat he wears was a gift of Ya'qub Beg, the khan of Kashgar (cf. ill. 494). This coat as well as others he acquired are now in the Ashmolean Museum, Oxford. The photograph was discovered by Dr R. Barnes, who is working on the Shaw collection, while researching at the British Library's Oriental and India Office Collections, London.

Stein's expeditions as "the most daring and adventurous raid upon the ancient world that any archaeologist has attempted" (Hopkirk 1980:68). Stein is most famous for his explorations at Khotan on the southern branch of the Silk Road, his discovery of the cave temples at Dunhuang (1906-1909) and his excavations at Loulan and Turfan (1913-1915).

Others were soon to follow him. The treasures London had acquired were envied by Paris, St Petersburg and Berlin. Colonial Europe now decided to send scientific expeditions to Turkestan.

The race for archaeological sites along the Silk Road started in earnest in 1902, and the major participants were the Russian scholars Dmitri Klementz and the Beresovsky brothers from the Academy of Sciences in St Petersburg,the French sinologist Paul Pelliot from the Ecole Française d'Extrême-Orient in Hanoi, the American archaeologist Langdon Warner from the Fogg Art Museum at Harvard, the somewhat mysterious Japanese Count Otani, and Albert Grünwedel and Albert von Le Coq from the Berlin Museum für Völkerkunde. Sometimes cooperating with each other, but mostly in fierce competition and with methods and on a scale almost unbelievable today, they took home with them manuscripts and works of art in such numbers that the museums of their respective home countries together hold nearly as many objects as one can see at the sites themselves. The outbreak of the First World War put a sudden stop to these explorations. In 1930 the Americans and Japanese also had to give up, and for the time being the region was closed to foreigners.

The treasures held by the Museum für Indische Kunst in Berlin were brought back from four Turfan expeditions organised by the Department of Indian Art at the Museum für Völkerkunde between 1902 and 1914.

The scientific evaluation of the material from the four expeditions as well as accounts of the travels and travails involved, were published mainly by the two expedition leaders Grünwedel and von Le Coq. Grünwedel was a recognised authority on the Buddhist art of India and Tibet and a somewhat retiring scholar. Von Le Coq, on the other hand, was dynamic, urbane and full of initiative, and had been a successful businessman before he began to study Oriental languages at the age of forty and to work at the Museum. The two men of such different dispositions found it sometimes hard to work together, but the results of their combined endeavours are quite remarkable. Research of the prime material, which is still continuing, has produced highly important insights into that unique fusion of the most diverse influences and styles, the art and culture of the Silk Roads. Perhaps nothing better encapsulates the character of this region as a pivot of the Indian, Chinese, Western Asian and Near Eastern world than the fact that the manuscripts now at Berlin were written in no less than seventeen languages and twenty-four different scripts.

30
Sir Aurel Stein's caravan crossing the dunes of the Taklamakan Desert south of the Tarim river.

31
Sir Aurel Stein (centre) with his Indian and Chinese companions and his dog Dash II during his second expedition in the desert north of Chira.

32
The members of the third German Turfan expedition (December 1905-April 1907). Middle row, left to right: Pohrt, Bartus, Grünwedel (seated), von Le Coq.

33
Female head. Fragment of a sculpture, clay modelled in Graeco-Bactrian style.
H: 17 cm
Surkhan Darya, Dal'verszintepa, 1st/2nd century
Khamza Institute of Fine Arts, Tashkent

Uzbekistan and Its Neighbours in Pre-Islamic Times

Heinz Gaube

First of all we have to realise that for Western scholars Uzbekistan is virtually terra incognita. Until some years ago it was the domain of a Soviet archaeology and history based on ideological premises and ignorant of important post-1917 literature, which was therefore unable to play a part in international academic discussions, save in a few exceptional cases. Knowledge of Western languages deteriorated, the illustrations accompanying scholarly contributions were more than inadequate, and a constructive engagement with Western interpretations and new research models was almost non-existent. There was an abyss between scholars writing in Russian and others writing in Western languages, and there were only a few colleagues from East Germany, in particular B. Brentjes, who succeeded in establishing some kind of bridge. For this reason any attempt to provide an overview of the pre-Islamic history of Uzbekistan and its neighbouring territories for the time being must remain rather fragmentary. Much will be done in the next decades to adjust balances and provide greater detail. We nevertheless offer a first beginning based on many sources.

The Region

Uzbekistan is the centre of a region where the cultures of the Eurasian forest and steppe belt to the north, extending from the Danube to the western boundaries of China and encompassing Central Asia, China, North India and Iran, have encountered each other since time immemorial and created a synthesis which gave birth to its distinct culture, art and history. It therefore makes little sense to discuss Uzbekistan within the narrow confines of her present-day borders. Uzbekistan reflects the quintessential characteristics of the history and material culture of that larger cultural area to which it belongs.

This is primarily the case with Sogdiana, the land along the Zeravshan river with its famous oasis towns of Samarkand and Bukhara, today the geographical centre of the country. It is less true for the area north of the Jaxartes (Syr Darya) focussing on the oasis of Tashkent, the capital of modern Uzbekistan, and for the Fergana Valley southeast of the river – and hardly true at all for the mysterious Khorezm in the northwest along the lower reaches of the Oxus (Amu Darya), a culture area south of the Aral Sea cut off from its neighbours by deserts. We have to take account of all these areas and also of the regions to the north and south of the Hindu Kush, parts of Tajikistan and Afghanistan, for otherwise the history of Uzbekistan would be unintelligible.

We should treat Uzbekistan neither in isolation nor see her as a collection of fertile strips of land alongside several large rivers. The legendary Silk Road linking China and the Mediterranean, crossed the country: The northern branch ran across the steppes north of the Aral and Caspian Seas, the central branch passed through Uzbekistan to Iran and continued westwards, and the southern branch ran through Uzbekistan down to the Indus Valley and from there across the Indian Ocean and the Red Sea to Egypt. None of these highways could bypass Uzbekistan or her northern periphery; and along each of them the ancestors of the modern inhabitants of Uzbekistan were busy as intermediaries, organisers and profiteers in both financial and cultural terms.

Early written sources and the death of the Persian King of Kings Cyrus near Tashkent in about 530 B.C.

The earliest extended description in a Western language of the region was given by the Greek historian Herodotus (d. about 430 B.C.). In the *Histories* (Book I, 201-14) he tells us about an event that had happened some hundred years earlier: the death of the founder of the Persian empire of the Achaemenids, the first world empire in history, Cyrus II or 'the Great' (559-30 B.C.):

"After the conquest of Assyria, Cyrus' next desire was to subdue the Massagetae, whose country lies far to the eastward beyond the Araxes ... Some suppose them to be of Scythian nationality ... Like the Gyndes, which Cyrus divided into three hundred and sixty channels, the river Araxes rises in the country of the Matieni. It has forty mouths, all but one issuing into swamp and marshland, where men are said to live who eat raw fish and dress in seal-skins ... At this time Tomyris was queen of the Massagetae, having succeeded to the throne on her husband's death ... Cyrus ... turned to open force, and advancing to the Araxes began his assault upon the Massagetae by bridging the river for his men to cross and constructing upperworks on the ferry boats. While these works were still in hand, Tomyris sent him a message: 'King of the Medes,' it ran, 'I advise you to abandon this enterprise, for you cannot know if in the end it will do you any good. Rule your own people, and try to bear the sight of me ruling mine.' ... The queen, on hearing that Cyrus ignored her terms, engaged him in the field with all the forces she possessed ... There was a long period of close fighting with spears and daggers, neither side being willing to retreat. Finally, however, the Massagetae got the upper hand, the greater part of the Persian army was destroyed where it stood, and Cyrus himself was killed."

Cyrus was the first Persian King of Kings to meet his death in the northeastern Iranian borderlands. The same happened to the last ruler of the dynasty, Darius III (336-30 B.C.), and to two Kings of Kings of the Sasanian dynasty, Peroz (457-84 A.D.) and Yazdegerd III (632-51), again the last monarch of this dynasty. This shows that Uzbekistan and the adjoining lands to the south and southwest played a direct role in Iranian history. Since ancient times the Iranians called the region Turan or Aniran, 'not Iran' or the world beyond Iran.

Many elements of Iran's historical traditions are connected with Turan. There is some indication that

Zoroaster, the prophet of the one god Ahuramazda, came from present-day Uzbekistan. Parts of the Iranian national epic, the *Shahnama*, have been identified as referring to Turan. The same applies to parts of the *Avesta*, the holy scripture of the Zoroastrians, members of the pre-Islamic religion of Iran. According to some sources, the region was also host to a pre-Persian, i.e. pre-Achaemenid kingdom of Arians (i.e., Iranians) during the seventh century B.C.

Cyrus met his death near Tashkent, in Turan or Aniran. If we take Herodotus literally, however, this happened somewhere west of the Caspian Sea. The great historian needs to be read with caution, but his is the best and most comprehensive account we have about the early Persians. The only other sources come from later Roman historians and geographers, who include scattered information culled from lost writings by Greek authors contemporary with the Persian era, i.e. the period before Alexander the Great (336–23 B.C.).

The peoples of Uzbekistan and adjoining regions in the first millennium B.C.

Herodotus's subject in the *Histories* is the struggle between the Persians and the Greeks. He provides a description of the Persians and their neighbours, their history and form of government to the best of his knowledge. This includes a list (Book III, 89-94) of twenty satrapies or provinces as they existed under Darius I (522-486 B.C.); Bactrians are mentioned as belonging to the twelfth satrapy, the Sakas and Caspians as making up the fifteenth and the Parthians, Khorezmians, Sogdians and Arians the sixteenth satrapy. Except for the Caspians, these peoples inhabited Uzbekistan and the surrounding lands during the mid-millennium, partly as nomads and partly as settlers; the Sakas were identical with the Massagetae or at least formed a sub-group.

The Bactrians lived north of the Hindu Kush around Balkh in modern Afghanistan and Tajikistan, the Sakas around Tashkent and to the north of it, the Parthians west of the Bactrians, the Khorezmians south of the Aral Sea, the Sogdians close to the Zeravshan and the Arians south of the Parthians and west of the Bactrians around modern Herat in Afghanistan.

Darius I, with Cyrus II the greatest of Achaemenid rulers, left an inscription at Bisutun near Kermanshah in western Iran which records the names of all his subject peoples; the list again includes the Parthians, Arians, Khorezmians, Bactrians, Sogdians and Sakas (Scythians). Furthermore, the staircase of his throne-room (Apadana) at Persepolis near Shiraz in southwestern Iran was decorated with reliefs of nearly all these peoples, assembled probably for a New Year's audience, ethnically identified in fine detail and depicted with gifts typical of their different countries.

The members of the Saka/Scythian delegation from the region north of Tashkent, are shown with pointed 'Scythian' headgear, distinctly hooked noses, long pointed beards and 'Uzbek' physiognomies (ill. 37). They are dressed in riding clothes reaching down to the knee, and narrow trousers. Their leader carries over the left shoulder a bow in a bow-

34

Side view of an ossuary with Zoroastrian motifs (cf. ill. 1), the cone showing a female deity (the Iranian goddess of fertility Anahita?)
H: 75 cm, W: 52 cm, L: 24 cm
7th/8th century
Registan Museum, Samarkand

35

Head of Alexander the Great, marble.
H: 14 cm
Egypt, Damanhar (Nile Valley), 3rd century B.C.
Württembergisches Landesmuseum, Stuttgart (ex Sieglin collection)

36

Head of Alexander the Great with 'elephant cap'. Cast bronze fitting. Personification of the city of Alexandria?
H: 5.5 cm
Hellenistic-Roman
Württembergisches Landesmuseum, Stuttgart

case and a sword on his right. Four members of his delegation are dressed in similar fashion and carry the same type of sword. Their gifts consist of a horse, golden necklaces in Scythian animal style and robes, cloaks and trousers.

The faces of the Sogdians living south of the Sakas are depicted quite similarly, but their noses are less pronounced and their beards longer, and their headgear is a cap with a bulge where the hair is tied in a knot (ill. 38). They wear baggy trousers under their cut-away riding coats, and on their left carry bows in bow-cases. They offer weapons (a sword and battle-axes), jewellery similar to that of the Sakas and a horse of a breed obviously different from the Sakas': presumably a horse from Fergana.

The Bactrians appear much more 'Iranian' (ill. 39). Their hair is simply held by a band. Under a garment similar to that of the Sakas they wear calf-length riding breeches. They lead a 'Bactrian' two-humped camel and bear metal vessels as New Years' gifts for the King of Kings (Shahanshah).

The Parthians, who were then probably living northwest of the Bactrians, also bring a two-humped camel (ill. 40). They come bare-headed, their dress much like that of the Sakas. Their gifts again consist of vessels; it remains unclear whether it was the contents or the vessels themselves which was the actual tribute.

Strangely enough, the Khorezmians are not depicted on the Persepolis reliefs. Although they appear as throne bearers on Darius's tomb relief in Naqsh-e Rustam near Persepolis dressed similar to the Sogdians, they are not found – at least according to experts at Persepolis – on the Apadana reliefs.

Their habitat was the northwest region of modern Uzbekistan, and, being an oasis at the mouth of a river, this part of the country followed a separate historical development right up to the twentieth century as the khanate of Khiva and even today constitutes a distinct cultural entity within Uzbekistan. The history of pre-Achaemenid Khorezm is still littered with question marks. Archaeologists have found traces of living conditions before the first millennium B.C. corresponding to what Herodotus says about the Massagetae: that they lived in marshlands and ate fish. Herodotus's statement about Cyrus dividing the Gyndes, i.e. the Oxus (Amu Darya), into three hundred and sixty channels, has also been confirmed by archaeological evidence. In fact, not Cyrus but the Khorezmians themselves in pre-Achaemenid times constructed complex canal systems along the lower reaches of the Oxus and created a sophisticated oasis culture at the river-mouth characterised by strange housing estates arranged by clans or tribes, at least according to scholarly interpretation. These communal living quarters were sometimes more than thousand metres long and only slightly less wide, and have been tentatively identified as folds where animals were kept, with long, corridor-like rooms along all four sides as accomodation for thousands of people.

It is not impossible that a passage in the *Avesta* refers just this type of building (Vendidad II, 33-8): "Then Yima built a wara, each side as long as a riding course, for people

37

The delegation of the Scythians (Sakas). Relief with depictions of tribute bearers on the staircase to the great audience hall in the palace of Darius in Persepolis, before 486 B.C.

38

The Sogdian delegation.

39

The Bactrian delegation.

40

The Parthian delegation.

41
Part of a belt buckle. Polished bone engraved with a battle scene.
H: 11.0 cm, W: 13.5 cm
Orlat necropolis, 1st/3rd century
Khamza Institute of Fine Arts, Tashkent

42
Part of a belt buckle. Polished bone engraved with a hunting scene.
H: 11.0 cm, W 13.5 cm
Orlat necropolis, 1st/3rd century
Khamza Institute of Fine Arts, Tashkent

to live in; a wara ... as a fold for animals. He made the water flow there ... There he constructed living quarters consisting of a house, bastions and a farm – a settlement closed on all sides."

Given the source of this quotation, we may infer something about the religious situation in Uzbekistan during the first millennium B.C.: The religion and myths of the inhabitants of this part of Central Asia were somewhat alike to those of the pre-Zoroastrian Iranians as recorded in the *Avesta*. Deities both natural and utilitarian were venerated, and fire played an important part in ritual: many excavated complexes have been interpreted as fire altars.

Alexander the Great's invasion also took him to Uzbekistan, where he established his headquarters at Maracanda (Samarkand). Here he was visited by the king of Khorezm accompanied by fifteen hundred nobles who surrendered and offered military assistance against the peoples living north of Khorezm. If a Khorezmian delegation is indeed missing among the Persepolis reliefs, the explanation may be that this part of Uzbekistan had already become largely independent from Achaemenid rule late in Darius's I reign, when the reliefs were executed. Perhaps the same progressive independence explains the fact that whereas Herodotus mentions Khorezmians among Darius's I troops in the battle of 494 B.C. against the Greeks (*Histories* VII, 66), they do not appear in Arrian's description of the decisive battle between Alexander the Great and Darius III at Gaukamela in 331 B.C. (*Anabasis* III, 1).

The Greek kingdom in Bactria (3rd century B.C.- 2nd century A.D.)

Alexander declined the Khorezmian king's offer of military support, because he first wanted to move against India, so that after the conquest of Asia, as he saw it, he would be able to attack from the west the Scythians, inhabitants of the Eurasian forest-and-steppe belt, and subdue them. Thus no alliance was concluded between Greeks and Khorezmians against the Indo-Arian nomads then living to the north of Uzbekistan. But among the Greeks in Alexander's army there were some who chose not to return to Greece after the death of their leader at Babylon in 323 B.C.

Alexander's successors in the east, his generals Seleucus and Ptolemy, divided their legacy among themselves, Ptolemy (323-285) taking Egypt and parts of Syria, and Seleucus (312-281) ruling over Syria north of the Litani river and the whole remaining eastern region as far as modern Uzbekistan. His rule and that of his successors over Uzbekistan and her neighbouring lands did not last very long. Under Antiochus II (261-36) the Seleucids lost Bactria and Sogdiana. From modern Uzbekistan the Parthians drove a wedge between Bactria, Sogdiana and Iran (where Seleucid rule lasted longer), isolating Bactria and Sogdiana from the West. From their earliest capital Nisa in present-day Turkmenistan the Parthians eventually wrested control of the whole of Iran and modern Iraq from the Seleucids and became a dangerous adversary of the Romans until 225 A.D., when Ardashir, the first Sasanian king (225-39),

defeated Artabanus, the last king of Parthia, and founded the Sasanian empire (225-642).

In the Parthians' slipstream, so to speak, who had driven a wedge between the Seleucid empire in Iran and the western lands and Central Asia, a Greek kingdom evolved in Bactria, whose art and culture was to have a lasting influence in North India, Afghanistan and Uzbekistan and her neighbours. Greeks from Alexander's army who had decided to stay in Bactria, founded a state which was rediscovered by archaeologists only fairly recently. For more than a hundred years there flourished in Bactria a Greek culture far from the Mediterranean producing, in combination with Iranian culture elements, a highly creative synthesis, documented by excavations at Aï Khanum in northern Afghanistan. Hellenistic concepts of town planning were introduced into the region, where even before the advent of the Greeks settlements laid out in regular grids of insulae had been known, as excavations in Khorezm show. The minting of coins on the Greek model was introduced and was later to influence Sogdian and Khorezmian coinage; in Bactria and among its northern and southern neighbours the Greek script was used for centuries side by side with the Aramaic script introduced by the Achaemenids (the latter proving in the end the more resilient, since nearly all Central Asian scripts were derived from it) – to mention but two examples of the influence of the Graeco-Bactrian interlude.

43
Head of a warrior with the typical Saka leather cap. Clay, moulded and painted.
H: 10.5 cm
Kizil, penultimate cave before the pass, 7th century
Museum für Indische Kunst, Berlin

A Hoard of Graeco-Bactrian Coins at the State Museum of Art and Architecture, Bukhara

Golib Kurbanov

In April 1983, the State Museum of Art and Architecture received a number of Graeco-Bactrian silver coins from two teachers at the Bukhara highschools nos. 22 and 23, A.W. Miller and S.I. Tkatshev. The two visitors had found the hoard at the building site of the Dzhandar Canal (in 1983 still called the Sverdlovsk Canal) which passes through the "Pravda" kolkhoz eight kilometres southwest of Bukhara. Part of the treasure was scattered on the ground and the rest contained in a not particularly large pear-shaped clay vessel thrown on the wheel, and a broken handle. The broken piece as well as the lower part of the vessel were light brown, whereas the upper part showed a reddish brown, suggesting uneven firing.

Two years later A.W. Miller, who was interested in local history, found a further eight coins of the hoard at the same spot. It is very likely that the hoard had been part of the Takhmach tepe which had been levelled in September/October 1982 to supply earth for the construction of the canal.

Subsequently a team of archaeologists from the State University at Bukhara and the Bukhara Museum of Local History undertook some not very extensive excavation work and found in the upper layers remains of rooms dating from the eleventh/twelfth century. On the eastern slope of the tepe a stratigraphic exploration of four square metres was undertaken, which covered the entire culture level. This level was seven metres high and dated from the second/first century B.C. to the fourth century A.D.

The hoard includes coins from the reigns of three Graeco-Bactrian kings. Some of the earliest coins date from the time of the founder of the Graeco-Bactrian kingdom, Diodotus I, and are ascribed to two different reign periods. The first period (256-46) is represented by four tetradrachms still bearing the name of the Seleucid king Antiochus II.

Obverse: head of Diodotus I with diadem turned right.
Reverse: Zeus turned left, an eagle at his feet, with an aegis and Perun, the god of thunderstorms.

Three coins with ⩑ one with ⟰

Legend: **ΒΑΣΙΛΕΩΣ ΑΝΤΙΟΧΟΥ**
Diameter: 24-27 mm
Weight: 15.8-16.4 g

The second reign period of Diodotus I (after 246) is represented by a single tetradrachm with the same design as those described above.

Monogram: ⟰ diameter: 25 mm   weight: 16.5 g

Coins showing Diodotus are rather rare in Central Asia. The Amu Darya hoard included Diodotus tetradrachms with the names of Diodotus and Antiochus. At Sharinau in both 1963 and 1978 a single tetradrachm with Diodotus's portrait was found inscribed with the name of Antiochus.[1]

The majority of coins were tetradrachms with the head of Euthydemus I, all of one type.

Obverse: head of Euthydemus with diadem turned right.
Reverse: Heracles sitting on an omphalos or a pile of stones with a wavy club in his right.
Legend: **ΒΑΣΙΛΕΩΣ ΕΥΘΥΔΗΜΟΥΑ**

The rim shows various monograms.

Diameter: 24-30 mm
Weight: 15.4-16.7 g, but three coins weighing 12.5 g, 13.6 g and 14.7 g, respectively.

There are certain differences between the coins. On the obverse the portraits show the emperor at different ages, some as an adolescent, some as a young man and others at a mature age. This probably reflects the main minting periods of Euthydemus's reign.

On some coins the design and iconography of Heracles is rather unusual, and we also note a number of curious monograms. On coins with the young Euthydemus Heracles is shown in his typical pose, sitting on a ledge and resting his club on a pile of stones. On coins with the mature Euthydemus, however, he is shown sitting on an omphalos covered with a lion pelt, with one end of the club leaning against his right knee.

The monograms are very unusual. The trident shape is typical of the early period, although there are some coins with a more delicate pattern found behind the seat (no. 7). The monograms of the middle period also are in a different position, namely to the right behind the inscription. The main monogram of the third period links the two letters rho and kappa (no. 6). One also finds some monograms typical of the early period, perhaps indicating that they were produced at the same mint. A coin with the portrait of the young Euthydemus and a monogram also bears a symbol resembling the letter ny below the figure of Heracles.

Among the single coins from the hoard are commemorative medals from the later period, minted by Agathocles in honour of Antiochus and Enthydemus.

1. Obverse: head of Antiochus turned right.
    Legend: ΑΝΤΙΟΧΟΥ ΝΙΚΑΤΟΡΟΣ
    Reverse: Zeus walking to the right with Perun, an
    aegide in his hand and an eagle at his feet.
    Legend: ΒΑΣΙΛΕΥΟΝΤΟΣ ΑΓΑΦΟΚΛΕΟΥΣ ΔΙΚΑΙΟΥ
    Diameter: 31-32 mm
    Weight: 16.2 g
2. Obverse: head of Euthydemus turned right.
    Legend: ΕΥΘΥΔΗΜΟΥ ΘΕΟΥ
    Reverse: Heracles sitting on a rock.
    Legend: ΒΑΣΙΛΕΥΟΝΖΟΣ ΑΓΑΦΟΙΥ
    Diameter: 28-29 mm
    Weight: 16.4 g

Medals of this type have been known for some time,
although so far none had been discovered in Central Asia.[2]
They are important for dating the hoard, because they are
among the most recent coins. Like the reign periods of all
Graeco-Bactrian rulers, that of Agathocles can be dated only
approximately and is usually given in the 170s or 160s B.C.
This would suggest that the hoard was buried some time
between the mid and early second century B.C. It is entirely
possible that it originally came from a considerable distance,
and if so, one should probably date the hoard some decades
later.

At the time of writing the hoard has only been
published in preliminary reports.[3] Two hypotheses are put
forward:

1. The hoard was assembled in the locality where it was
found and thus documents the circulation of actual money in
the Bukhara oasis during the late third and first half of the
second century B.C.[4]

2. The hoard has to be understood as buried treasure
and not as evidence of the circulation of Graeco-Bactrian
money in the oasis.[5]

Further and more comprehensive research on the silver
tetradrachms in the museum at Bukhara will be necessary to
find out more about the ancient history of Bukhara.

44

Graeco-Bactrian silver coins.
From the Bukhara hoard which included 58 tetradrachmas of the kings Diodotos I,
Euthydemos, and Agathokles. The value of four drachmas according to the Attic standard of
c. 16.5 gm silver was the main currency throughout the Hellenistic world. Even in classical
times the silver content of four tetradrachmas was checked by cutting, and this indicates a
certain wariness in Transoxanian trade relations of this medium of exchange still relatively
new about 200 B.C. Earlier coins still show the name of the Seleucid king Antiochos II,
but the portrait is of his Bactrian governor Diodotos I (see the coins in the second row), who
later by adding his own name signified his independence.

45

The majority of coins from the Bukhara hoard were tetradrachmas of Diodotos I, c. 250-
230 B.C. (top and middle row), and of Euthydemos I, c. 230-200 B.C. (bottom row).
The portraits show a pronounced realism, and the changing features of Euthydemos I from
youth to old age are particularly poignant. Except for some very early and very late
examples, the reverse shows a seated Heracles, tutelary deity of the first Bactrian kings. Zeus
hurling thunderbolts (ill. 44, bottom row left) appears on more recent coinage dating from
the reign of Agathokles, c. 190-180 B.C., which depict the descent of the royal Bactrian
house from Alexander the Great and the Seleucids.

1   *Sedevry drevnego iskusstva i kultury Tadzhikistana* (Masterpieces of Ancient
    Tajik Arts and Crafts). (Exhib. cat., Moscow, 1983), 72.
2   Gardner, P. "On some coins of Syria and Bactria." *Numismatic Chronicle*
    (1880):2-3. Lahiri, R. *Corpus of Indo-Greek Coins* (Calcutta, 1965), 65, pl.
    I.10, II.1. Francfort, H.P. "Deux nouveaux tetradrachmes
    commémoratives d'Agathocle." *Revue numismatique*, 6th series, 17
    (1975):19-22.
3   Rtveladse, E.V., and M.I. Niyazova. "Pervuj klad greko-baktrijskich
    monet iz Bukhary" (The first Graeco-Bactrian hoard at Bukhara).
    Obscestvennye nauki v Uzbekistane (Tashkent) 6 (1984):54-6. Kurbanov,
    G.N., and M.I. Nijazova. *Katalog greko-baktrijskich monet iz fondov
    Bukharskogo muzeja* (Catalogue of Graeco-Bactrian Coins in Bukhara
    Museums). Bukhara, 1989.
4   Rtveladse and Niyazova, 57-8.
5   Zeimal, E.V. "Iz istorii kollekzij drevnich sredneaziatzkich monet v
    muzejnych sobranijach Uzbekistana" (On the history of the collections
    of ancient Central Asian coins in the Bukhara museum). *Numizmatika
    Uzbekistana* (Tashkent 1990):16.

The advance of the steppe peoples: the Kushan (2nd century B.C.- 2nd century A.D.)

The Graeco-Bactrians already had made forays into north India between 190 and 170 B.C.; at the end of the second century B.C. they were pushed in that direction again by invaders from the north, and then slowly moved beyond the light of history. Northern pressure on Bactria had its origins in conflicts along China's western border. The Chinese drove the 'Huns', who had threatened her borders, to the west and in about 214 B.C. started to build the Great Wall as a protection against Eurasian nomads. The question whether the Huns in general and these 'Huns' in particular ethnically belonged to the 'Europoid' or 'Mongoloid' branch is still under debate. What is certain is that all textual evidence produced by the 'Hun' groups advancing from the northeast into Iran until well into the sixth century is written in Iranian languages. This indicates that they or at least the elite or at the very least the scribes were 'Europoid' just like the 'Arians', who during the second millennium B.C. migrated from Central Asia to India and Iran and have defined the characteristic culture of Pakistan, India and Iran ever since.

Population movements between China and the northeastern frontier regions of Iran induced the Sakas to move from northern Uzbekistan to the area in southeast Iran named Sistan (i.e. Sakestan) after them, and new tribes called 'Yuezhi' in Chinese sources, to advance from the north in the direction of Bactria. In 176 B.C. they had been driven westwards by the Chinese and formed a confederation of five tribes which soon after established themselves in the region north of the Oxus. According to a Chinese source dated 128 B.C., five 'nations' were at the time living in the vicinity of Uzbekistan; one of them was a settled culture and boasted more than seventy towns, of which some had up to hundred thousand inhabitants.

This number is certainly too high; it is doubtful, though not impossible that the statement refers to the Yuezhi confederation as a whole. Be that as it may; one tribe of the Yuezhi which became known in history as the Kushan, gained pre-eminence and in the early first century A.D. conquered Bactria and soon afterwards parts of North India.

The Kushans came into a region with a Graeco-Bactrian culture incorporating Iranian elements. Their nomadic origins are reflected in their dress. A statue in half relief found at Mathura (North India) of the greatest Kushan ruler, Kanishka (about 132-150), shows him dressed in a long coat over a richly decorated costume and in trousers reaching down to the ankles (ill. 48). A similar half-relief figure perhaps of the same ruler from Surkh Kortal in present-day northern Afghanistan wears the same sumptuously decorated costume under a coat and wide trousers of the same length.

The excavations at Surkh Kortal have thrown much light on Kushan language, religion and architecture during Kanishka's reign. An Iranian fire temple of Hellenistic appearance has been unearthed, and in its vicinity a Buddhist

46-47
Small comb. Ivory, polished, carved and engraved.
Depictions of a lady making her toilet and a lady riding an elephant.
H: 9.2 cm, W: 7.8 cm, Surkhan Darya, Dal'verzintepa, 2nd/3rd century
Khamza Institute of Fine Arts, Tashkent

sanctuary presumably of the same date. For it was under Kanishka that Buddhism began to spread from India via Central Asia to China, although the king himself probably adhered to a pre-Zoroastrian Iranian faith. This can be deduced from surviving inscriptions at Surkh Kotal written with Greek letters in an Iranian-'Bactrian' language, where water and the Iranian god Mihr play a prominent role.

This may have been Kanishka's private religion (or that of his family), but for political or other reasons he became a patron of Buddhism. With him began the flowering of Buddhism in Central Asia, of which various Buddhist temples and monasteries in southern Uzbekistan and further east bear witness. How firmly established Buddhism was in Uzbekistan or at least south of Sogdiana, is indicated by the fact that the Barmecides, the famous family of viziers who served the 'Thousand-and-One-Nights' caliph Harun al-Rashid (786-809), descended from hereditary Buddhist priests at Bactra (modern Balkh), the capital of Bactria.

The application of Kushan Graeco-Bactrian artistic traditions to Buddhist imagery resulted in the birth of Buddhist art. This first manifestation is known as the art of Gandhara after an region between the sources of the Ganges and the Indus, where Indian substance acquired Hellenistic form. To oversimplify: The image of the Buddha is of Greek origin. The folds of his garments as well as the various postures and gestures of other figures of the Buddhist pantheon can only be understood as derivations of the Graeco-Bactrian style created during the Kushan period.

Given their nomadic background, the Kushans were knowledgeable about the regions between China and the West. It is thus not surprising that they should also engage in trade relations between China and the West, established long before their arrival at various times by various peoples. While they helped Buddhism to find its way eastwards along the Silk Route, they also managed to profit from trade running in the opposite direction. Their conquests in India should also be seen in this light. Earlier commercial traffic between China and the West went either through the steppes north of the Caspian Sea or – and more importantly – via Parthian Iran. Now the Kushans diverted a considerable amount of this trade east of Iran towards the south and the Indian Ocean, whence Chinese goods (and by no means only silk) left the ports for Egypt and the Mediterranean. Monetary policy reflected this mercantile orientation of the Kushan rulers. For their gold and silver currency they adopted the Roman standard of coinage, while their copper currency was convertible into Chinese copper currency.

One of the important intermediaries of the trade along the Silk Road were the Sogdians. It seems that by the second century A.D. there were Sogdian merchants in almost every important town in China, as a happy discovery made by Sir Aurel Stein in 1907 suggests. Sir Aurel, Hungarian by birth and an Indologist with a degree from Tübingen University, came upon a bundle of letters in a tower along the Great Wall, addressed by the Sogdian merchants residing in China to their business partners back in Samarkand. They date from either 196 or 311 and include descriptions of life in China, reports on purchases and instructions about their disposal at home.

48
Statue of the Kushan ruler Kanishka (130-150 A.D.).
Mathura Museum

Sasanians and Huns (3rd–7th century)

Soon after the Sasanians in about 225 had brought an end to more than four hundred years of Parthian rule and set up a new centralised Iranian state with a similarly controlled 'state church' of Sasanian-Zoroastrian character in the West, they applied the same principles to their conquests in the East. Either under Ardashir I (225-39/41), the founder of the dynasty, or his son Shapur I (239/41-72), the Sasanians conquered the northern parts of the Kushan empire, "Sogdiana and Tashkent up to the mountains of Kashgaria" (i.e., the region east of Tashkent); these military exploits were recorded by Shapur I in a long inscription at Naqsh-e Rustam near Persepolis in three languages, Parthian, Middle Persian and Greek. Henceforth Bactria and its neighbouring territories were ruled by a Sasanian *kushanshah*, a position often filled by the crown prince. We know their names from Kushano-Sasanian coins struck at Merv, Herat, Balkh and other cities. Khorezm is not mentioned in this inscription, nor have any Kushano-Sasanian coins minted there come to light. This would indicate that it was not directly subject to Sasanian rule.

But new pressure was exerted from deep inside Central Asia against Sogdiana, Bactria and eastern Iran. Again the reason for this westward migration of nomadic peoples was unrest along China's western borders. In 350 the Sasanian king Shapur II (309-79) had to break off his campaign against the Romans (Byzantians) when the northeastern borders of the country were threatened by invading nomads. These were the Chionites, the Middle Persian term for 'Huns', and the king remained on their territory and that of the Eusenos (i.e., the Kushans) right through the winter of 357 (Ammianus Marcellinus XIV:3 and XVI:9).

In 359 Shapur II once more moved against the Byzantians. Now his troops included Chionites under their king Grumbates (ibid., XVII:6). So between 357 and 359 his former enemies must have turned into allies. Shapur seems to have been unable, however, to completely subdue the Chionites and had to make concessions to them, for shortly after 360 Kushano-Sasanian coinage disappears, and Kushano-Sasanian coins minted at Balkh, instead of showing the name of the Sasanian *kushanshah*, now bear the name 'Kidara'. This date, if not before, marks the beginning of 'Hun' rule over Uzbekistan and her borderlands, again with the exception of Khorezm, which seems to have retained some sort of independent status.

For the next two hundred years Sogdiana and Bactria were under the overlordship of one or another group of 'Hun' origin (so-called 'Iranian Huns'). They seem to have ruled with a light hand, and were careful not to exploit the natural resources to such an extend as to endanger the primarily agrarian economy of Sogdiana and her neighbours. Very little is known about the relations between the 'Hun' rulers and the native sub-commanderies of Sogdian and Tokharian/Bactrian stock ('Tokharian' being a later term for Bactrian, primarily used in Oriental sources), but we may assume that a fruitful symbiosis between the newly-arrived Iranians and the Iranians already settled in Sogdiana and Tokharia/Bactria was soon established.

Some of the immigrating Iranian 'Huns' have been identified by name. Most prominent among them according to historical documents were the Hephtalites (Arab. Haiyatila), who twice succeeded in defeating the Persian Sasanians, and who may even have been able to advance into their heartland during a period of internal weakness and rule it for some years; they later appear as allies of the Persians along the Byzantine border. All this happened during a dark and crisis-ridden period of Sasanian rule in Persia.

King Peroz of Persia (457-484) twice undertook campaigns in the northeast to drive the Hephtalites from his borders. The first campaign ended with his capture and release in return for large tribute payments, the second with his death. His son and successor Kavadh (484–531), who as a hostage had grown up among the Hephtalites and married a daughter of their king, effected a conciliation with this powerful opponent in the east.

Arab sources based on pre-Islamic Persian material place the Hephtalites in Tokharia (i.e., Bactria) and supply lenghty descriptions of the wars between the Sasanians and Hephtalites. Procopius (active before 560) recounts in very similar fashion the wars between the Persians and Hephtalites. He also provides some ethnographic details (I:3ff.): "The Ephthalitae are of the stock of the Huns in fact as well as in name; however they do not mingle with any of the Huns known to us, for they occupy a land neither adjoining nor even very near to them; but their territory lies immediately to the north of Persia ... they are not nomads like the other Hunnic peoples, but for a long period have been established in a goodly land. ... They are the only ones among the Huns to have white bodies and countenances which are not ugly ... they are ruled by one king, and since they possess a lawful constitution, they observe right and justice in their dealings both with another and with their neighbours, in no degree less than the Romans and Persians."

These 'noble savages', presented by both Procopius and the Arab historians presumably in too positive a light, for some two hundred years decided on the external affairs of Sogdiana and her neighbours, whereas domestic policies seem to have been in the hands of a native aristocracy of landowners and merchants.

Sogdiana during the last centuries before the arrival of Islam (5th-8th century)

In 484 the Sasanian king Peroz died fighting the Hephtalites. His son Kavadh, faced with a serious domestic crisis, was forced to ask the Hephtalites and others for assistance, and it was only Peroz's grandson Khusrau I (531-79) who succeeded with the help of a new power emerging in the region north of the Hephtalites, the Turks, to finally defeat the Sasanians' old enemy.

About the early Turks little is known. Their origins have obviously been glamourised by some scholars. Around Mongolia and further northwest (to put it very simply), a tribal community must have emerged during the fifth century, which, following a nomadic pattern, first had to pit itself against everyone else, then succeeded in establishing a territory of its own and from this base became a dominant influence on the post-Islamic history of Central Asia, Iran and countries further west. To use concepts like 'unity' or even 'nation' in connection with the early Turks and to say anything more specific would be rash or misleading. We have a few names, vague geographical identifications and some isolated historical facts like the Turkish-Byzantine coalition against the Sasanians of about 568, which tend to become burdened with a surfeit of interpretations, some scholars going so far as to suggest wide-ranging economic factors at work, namely the silk trade between China and the Mediterranean.

Better to admit that we know next to nothing about the early Turks, about their relations with China and with other barely defined Central Asian peoples, about their fortunes and their achievements. Clear literary evidence is lacking. It is of little help that the Orkhon inscriptions found far east of Uzbekistan, seem to point to a first organised Turkish statehood (or rather an approximation thereof, since we have to evaluate such concepts within a universal framework). The first and second Turkish kaghanates achieve prominence within our historical context during the end (or last flowering) of the Sasanians under Khusrau I and his campaign against the Iranian 'Huns'. And their importance becomes manifest in the Buddhist kingdom of the Uighurs in the Tarim Basin, for the Uighurs could claim a highly developed artistic sensibility, a language of their own and a remarkable measure of tolerance, as we know from the writings by members of other religions. A first merging on a personal human level between Turks and Iranians occured in Sogdiana. This process is reflected in Arab sources dealing with the last century of Sasanian rule, which frequently confuse Hephtalites and Turks. The Turkish term kaghan is often used to identify the ruler of the Hephtalites. So the Turks begin to play a part in the history of the Near East by the sixth century at the latest, and they have been doing so ever since.

After their victory, the allied Turks and Sasanians under Khusrau I (half Turk, half Hephtalite?) divided the Hephtalite lands among them, which meant that for several centuries the Uzbekistan region was under Turkish and not under Iranian domination, while Sasanians ruled in Bactria and a Turkish elite probably replaced the Hephtalites in Sogdiana.

These developments seem to have taken place peacefully. Like the Hephtalites before them, the Turkish conquerors probably mixed easily with the native population, as indicated by a document of the early eighth century for instance, where a Sogdian ruler grants permission to a Sogdian female to divorce a man with a Turkish name.

Before the Islamic conquest, which was mainly completed by the late eighth century, Sogdiana achieved an astonishing cultural flowering lasting several hundred years and producing probably the most impressive artistic objects of the East Iranian world. Without this culture supported by rich urban merchants and the squirarchy of village leaders, the *deghane*, we would have no documents about their lives and religion nor the Persian national epos, the *Shahnama*.

The wall paintings from temples, palaces and private houses (ills. 65-7) from Pendjikent near the Tajik/Uzbek border, and from Samarkand and Warakhsha near Bukhara give a particularly impressive insight into the sophisticated life-style of the time. The site of Pendjikent has been most thoroughly excavated. The city was surrounded by a wall, the streets followed a grid pattern, the city centre was occupied by a temple, and the ruler's palace was situated within a fortress on the outskirts.

The religious paintings show various deities, local variants of the pre-Zoroastrian Iranian religion which are heavily influenced by Indian painting, but the walls were also decorated with epic themes, battle scenes (including female warriors – we are here not far from the lands of the legendary Amazons), banquets, a state reception (at Samarkand), hunting scenes, pictures of musicians, of erotic encounters and much more. Furthermore, pieces of sculpture have survived made of stucco and plaster and of very delicately worked wood (ills. 49, 56).

49
Wooden sculpture from settlement III at Pendjikent, 6th/7th century.

44

Khorezm before the Muslim conquest (1st–8th century)

We already mentioned that because of its isolated geographical position, Khorezm developed along separate lines, and that a king of Khorezm paid a visit to Alexander the Great at Maracanda. At that time (fourth century B.C.) there existed numerous urban settlements as well as scattered homesteads while the earlier pen-like living quarters had disappeared.

In contrast to Sogdiana, which consisted of several smaller city states, Khorezm seems to have been ruled for centuries after Alexander's visit by a single monarch, identified on coins dating from soon after the introduction of minting (probably in the 1st century A.D.) as 'king' in a local variant of the Aramaic script.

The capital of Khorezm during the first three centuries B.C. was, according to some archaeologists, the settlement of Toprak-Kala inhabited until the sixth century (ill. 57). The city was secured by a wall, and at the far end of its main street with alleys leading off at right angles lay the (fire?) temple and the fortress, while beyond the walls were gardens and country houses.

Clay objects and fragments of wall paintings discovered in the fortress are related to Sogdian styles, but look more archaic and almost Parthian which is not surprising, given their early date. From excavated documents we see that detailed tax records were kept during the third and fourth centuries. The centralised administration during the first three or four centuries A.D. was also favourable for the development of an irrigation system which during this period reached its greatest extent and complexity.

Khorezm's urban culture seems to have gone into decline during the fourth century. Rural areas became more important. Castles and single farms multiplied while urban settlements shrunk and the central authority grew weak; this at least seems to be indicated by the fact that on coins the ruler is no longer simply called 'king', but 'lord (or king) of kings', if we interpret the new title 'MR'Y MLK' correctly.

Thus Khorezm was a fragmented country by the time of the Muslim invasion in the first half of the eighth century; on the other hand, a delegation from Khorezm was sent to China to ask for assistance in 741, the year of the decisive battle between Chinese and Arab troops in their fight for the region of Uzbekistan and her borderlands. According to Khorezm tradition, the Arab conquest was accompanied by a blood-bath, the destruction of Khorezm's historical literature and the extermination of its scholars.

It is difficult to say how much such accounts are coloured by the exaggerations of Khorezm scholars writing during the Middle Ages, when there was no shortage of them, and how much truth there is in the claim that Khorezm emigrants soon afterwards conquered the Khazar empire in the northwest, between the Black and Caspian Seas. As proof for this claim, coins of the Khorezm type are mentioned whose inscription is read as "Lord, king, blessed, Khazan". More persuasive is an eighth-century list of bishoprics of the Khazar-Jacobite Church, which mentions among the eight Khazar bishoprics a certain 'Khavalis', said to refer to Khorezm.

50
Bottle (rhyton) in the shape of a male head with long spout. Pottery, freely turned, modelled, fired, painted with a substance containing mica to produce a metallic appearance.
H: 21 cm
Kafirkala, southern Sogdiana, 7th/8th century
Registan Museum, Samarkand

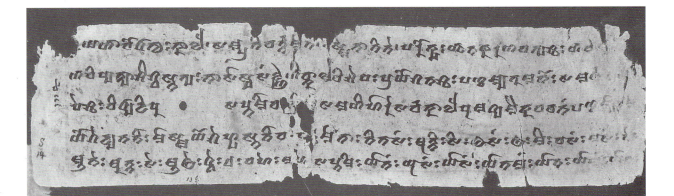

51
Sogdian manuscript, Vishesha-chinti-brahma-pariprichcha-sutra, ink on paper.
H: 15.3 cm, W: 25.5 cm
Shorchuk, Cave in the City, 8th century
Museum für Indische Kunst, Berlin

52
Page from a Sanskrit grammar. Ink on paper.
H: 6 cm, W: 24 cm
Sengim, stupa opposite the Nakshatra temple, 8th/9th century
Museum für Indische Kunst

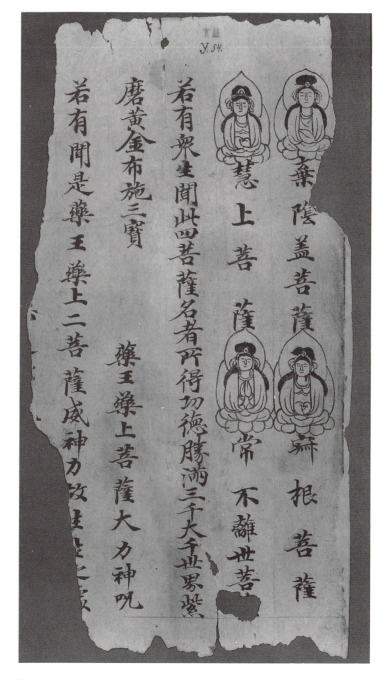

53
Text of a Syriac psalm. Ink on paper.
H: 9.0 cm, W: 28.7 cm
Bulayiq, 9th/10th century
Museum für Indische Kunst

54
Chinese scroll with Buddha images. Ink on paper.
H: 25.8 cm, W: 13.0 cm
Yarkhoto, 9th/10th century (?)
Museum für Indische Kunst, Berlin

55

Manichaean prayer in Uighur script. Ink on paper.
H: 34.5 cm, W: 20.3 cm
Khocho, Ruin K, 8th century
Museum für Indische Kunst, Berlin

56

Architectural fragment. Wood, carved, with late classical scroll ornament.
Pendjikent, 6th/7th century

57
Excavation site at Toprak-Kala.

58-63
Bactrian gold jewellery. 58-62 show the objects roughly to scale. 2nd century B.C.-2nd century A.D.

58-59
Necklaces with pendants. The scorpions with turquoise inlay and the agates presumably were regarded as amulets.

60
Earrings, chased.

61
Leaf-shaped pendants for necklaces, cut and chased.

62
Plaques for sewing on garments in typical Central Asian fashion.

63
Belt with typical late classical scroll design.
L: 90 cm, W: 30 cm (clasp only)
6th/7th century A.D.
Private collection, Karlsruhe

50

64
Small comb (front and back). Ivory, cut, engraved,
painted with a bird and the portrait of a lady.
H: 5.2 cm, W: 5.5 cm
Kampyrtepa, 1st/2nd century
Khamza Institute of Fine Arts, Tashkent

65
Banqueting scene. Wall-painting.
The young man wears a head-dress and the coat-like garment with belt typical of the region.
A fruit bowl with a melon and peaches or apricots is set in front of him, and he is being
offered a rhyton. (Fruit from Central Asia was a choice delicacy in China and the Islamic
world.) These drinking horns with an opening small enough to close with a finger were
known already in pre-Christian times and apparently were still used in Central Asia on
festive occasions in the eighth century.
Pendjikent, object XXIV/1, 7th/8th century

66
Horsemen. Wall-painting.
Afrasiab, 7th century

67
Hunting scene. Wall-painting.
The nobleman (?) in Indian dress on an elephant is hunting leopards. The painting shows
not only Indian but also Sasanian elements, for instance in the fluttering bands of the
diadem.
Varaksha, 7th/8th century

51

68

Large mirror. Bronze with figural design in relief.

The back of this large mirror shows the two Daoist deities Xiwangmu (Queen Mother of the West) and Dongwanggong (Royal Ruler of the East) with a two-wheeled carriage drawn by five horses and opposite two rows of seven and five horses respectively with seven bird-like creatures behind them. The rather deep relief is surrounded by a band with inscriptions about the peaceful times, good wishes for the population, abundant harvests and everlasting happiness for futuregenerations, phrases found similarly on numerous mirrors of the same period. The outer band shows stylised dragons.

The actual mirror surface on the front originally was highly polished, and like most mirrors is slightly convex. Bronze mirrors have been part of Chinese tomb furnishings since the early 1st millennium B.C., and became an almost indispensable accessory during the Han period (206 B.C.-A.D. 220). At first the front was decorated with a flat design usually of cosmological and religious symbols, but from the late Han period onwards shows figures in high relief of mythical animals, legendary creatures, immortals and Daoist deities, as on this example. (See also ills. 83-86)

D: 23 cm

China, Eastern Han dynasty (25-220)

China and the West

Klaus J. Brandt

China's contacts with the West were at first limited to the countries just beyond her borders, and consisted mainly in military actions to safeguard her territory and to a lesser extent in economic and commercial relations. Something of a special case were the journeys of Chinese pilgrims to the Buddhist centres in India, Central Asia and Sri Lanka during the fourth to ninth centuries.[1] These journeys were almost without exception of a private nature and without official backing, sometimes undertaken clandestinely and even in the face of downright condemnation by the emperor.[2] In addition to Buddhist scriptures the pious travellers brought back Indian texts on astronomy and astrology, on mathematics, physics and medicine.

The next phase, now officially sanctioned, of China's interest in Western things – apart from military and trade matters – only developed during the late Ming (1368-1644) and the first half of the Qing dynasty (1644-1911), when Jesuit priests, scholars, artists and scientists were called to China, some of them even acting as advisers to the emperor.

The lack of interest shown by official China towards the West or rather towards the world beyond her frontiers generally, has its roots mainly in the traditional ethnocentric Chinese view of her position in a global context; that the situation has changed little in the meantime is clearly expressed in present-day official designation as *Zhongguo*, the Central Nation. The concept of the world as surrounded by four oceans and ruled by the Chinese emperor, the Son of Heaven, dates at least from the third century B.C. China is situated at the centre of this world, surrounded by countries inhabited by strangers and 'barbarians'. Just as China lies at the centre of the world, so does her culture present the centre of civilisation, her benefits and wise rule extended by the emperor to the less privileged barbarian nations around it.[3] Consequently her foreign relations were conceived in tributary terms, with other countries forced to accept the suzerainty of imperial China and to send tribute missions to the court in acknowledgement.[4] This approach determined China's relations with the outside world and remained effective right until the end of the Chinese monarchy in 1911.

China's first documented contacts with the West, i.e. with Central Asia and regions further west, such as Transoxiana between the Oxus and Jaxantes, date from the first half of the Western Han period (206 B.C.-8 A.D.), when she discontinued her pacification policy towards the northern steppe peoples united under the tribal confederations of the Xiongnu. Under Maodun (209-174) the Xiongnu empire extended from the Baikal and Balkhash lakes in Mongolia southwards almost to the 40th parallel. Although China had pursued a policy of appeasement since about 200 B.C., sending them not only silk, money, wine and foodstuffs but also royal princesses, the Xiongnu continued their ferocious raids into North Chinese

69
Neighing horse. Grey pottery with reddish loess incrustations.
The unusually large figure is assembled from two separate parts, the head and neck and the main body. It comes from Sichuan province in southwest China, where since Han times a type of horse was bred more wiry and muscular and with a longer neck than the Mongolian type then common.
H: 100 cm, L: 60 cm
China, Eastern Han dynasty (24-220)

70
Horse with saddle. Grey pottery.
This model shows the typical squat Mongolian pony, a tough and undemanding animal resembling in general respects the wild horse (Equus przewalskii). Its head is relatively large, the mane sticks up and the tail is powerful.
H: 34.2 cm, L: 43.7 cm
China, Western Han dynasty (206 B.C.- 8 A.D.)

71
Horse with lifted foreleg. Buff-coloured pottery with straw-coloured, brown-speckled glaze.
This tall type of horse with long neck and rather small head is the result of cross-breeding Arab horses imported from Central Asia and the Fergana Valley with the squat native Mongolian type.
H: 58.5 cm
China, Tang dynasty (618-907), before 756

72
Ox-cart. Pottery with traces of cold painting.
The two-wheeled covered cart with driver is drawn by a sturdy ox, the horn-shaped yoke connecting the shafts resting on its neck. This type of construction of cart and yoke and including high wheels with spokes for lightness and easily detachable hubs (the latter a Chinese invention of the late Shang period, 17th-11th century B.C.) is still in use today. It shows a concept for carriages that had been in use at least since the Eastern Zhou period (770-221 B.C.) which was well thought-out and could be little improved upon.
H: 21.5 cm, L: 41.5 cm
China, Six Dynasties period (220-589), c. 5th/6th century

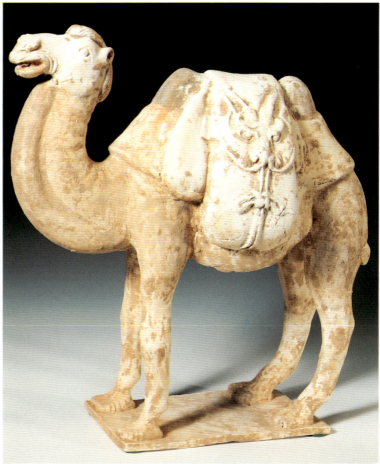

74
Ox-cart. Buff-coloured pottery with traces of paint.
H: c. 30 cm, L: 44 cm
China, early Tang dynasty (618-907), 7th century

73
Pack-camel. Buff-coloured pottery with traces of cold painting.
The camel standing on a flat plate carries a large saddle-bag decorated with a horned dragon's head (?) to ward off ghosts and demons.
H: 33.8 cm, L: 33.2 cm
China, 1st half Tang dynasty (618-907)

provinces.5 Successful campaigns into Xiongnu territory initiated by Emperor Wu (141-87) finally in 41 B.C. split the Xiongnu federation into an aggressive northern branch and a peaceful southern one – the latter allied with China and inhabiting Inner Mongolia – and put an end to the Xiongnu menace. The campaigns begun under Wu in 133 B.C. brought Chinese troops as far west as the Tarim Basin and beyond; at first the aims were mainly defensive and preventive but eventually turned to conquest.

Chinese expansion into Central Asia and the West had been triggered by Emperor Wu and his successors' quest to obtain horses, the almost legendary famous tall 'blood-sweating' breed from the Fergana Valley, to cross-breed them with the smaller Mongolian type which was hardy but not well-suited to carry the weight of a warrior in full armour. In 139 B.C. Emperor Wu sent Zhang Qian (d. c. 104), a high palace official, to the Yuezhi to persuade them to conclude an alliance against the Xiongnu. The Yuezhi, who spoke an Indo-Iranian language and were known to the Greeks as 'Indo-Scythians', had been driven by the Xiongnu from modern Gansu province through Central Asia to Bactria south of the Amu Darya (Oxus). Although the Yuezhi were too much afraid of the Xiongnu to accept Zhang Qian's proposition, and his journey proved a most arduous one – he only returned to China in 126 B.C., thirteen years after his departure – he did not come back empty-handed. Not only had he reconnoitred a route to the West and discovered the breeding area of the 'blood-sweating' horses, but had also collected information about countries far away in the west and opportunities for trading Chinese goods. On his travels, Zhang Qian had followed ancient trade routes which later became famously known as the Silk Road.7

This general term for the almost nine-thousand-kilometre-long overland road connecting China with the West was coined by the German geographer Ferdinand von Richthofen (1833-1905) appropriately enough, since silk was the most important and probably most profitable item moving along this highway.8 It would be more accurate in fact to talk of 'Silk Roads', since the east-west transverse frequently branched off to the north and south; there was a further 'silk road' running southwest from China via Sichuan province to Burma (the Burma Road), and another one from the upper reaches of the Amu Darya via the Hindu Kush and northern India to the Pakistan coast and on from the Indus delta to northwest India and the Gulf of Cambay near modern Bombay. The terminals of the main east-west transverse were the city of Chang'an, the Chinese capital during the Western Han (206 B.C.-8 A.D.) and Tang (618-907) dynasties, and the Levant, especially the ports of Antioch (Antakya), Tyrus (Tyr) and Alexandria as well as Byzantium (Istanbul).9

The most dangerous and difficult passage of the Silk Road was across the Tarim Basin, where it split into a northern and southern route along the foothills of the Tianshan and Kunlun ranges respectively, traversing the notorious Gobi desert and the even more terrible Taklamakan and crossing either the Pamirs or Hindu Kush by passes completely blocked during the winter months. To natural obstacles including boiling heat, freezing cold and blinding sand-storms were added human ones in the shape of robbers and troops engaged in local wars. The journey could only be undertaken by convoys of caravans providing mutual assistance and in relatively peaceful and well-ordered times. A measure of security along the Silk Road existed after Emperor Wu's successful campaigns in the late second century B.C., during the third to sixth centuries, when non-Chinese dynasties ruled this northern part of China, and during the Tang dynasty.

North of this route across the Tarim Basin ran the 'steppe route', winding its way through a narrow passage between the foothills of the Altai and Tianshan and along the Dzungarian valley via Urumchi, Alma-Ata and Frunze and ending at the Caspian Sea. Although much easier in topographical respects, this route had serious drawbacks both because of the presence of nomad horsemen and the absence of settlements providing lodgings for man and beast and markets for restocking and trade. This northern route played an important role since prehistoric times, however, not only as a commercial link, but also for the exchange of ideas and techniques running both ways. It was presumably used for trading silk – with the Scythians as intermediaries – even before the Han dynasty, as the discovery of silk remains scattered across a vast area would suggest: They have been found in tombs of the fifth century B.C. in Pazyryk in the Altay mountains, in late Hallstatt-period and Celtic graves of the seventh to fifth century in Germany and in roughly contemporaneous tombs along the middle Volga reaches, on the Crimean and in the vicinity of Athens. The fact that this northern route and other parts of the Silk Road were frequented in pre-Christian times is further substantiated by recent excavations of fortified towns dating from the eighth to third century B.C. – contemporaneous with the Achaemenid empire (559-330 B.C.) – along the western section of this highway in western Turkestan, the territory of the present-day republics of Turkmenistan and Uzbekistan.10

The 'steppe route' was presumably also the main silk-trading artery for the various tribes of nomad horsemen of northeast Asia who received enormous amounts of silk from the Chinese either as conciliatory 'gifts' or in exchange for horses so desperately needed by the Chinese army. The silk-for-horses exchange was a constant feature of Chinese foreign relations from the Han to the early Ming period: The Han dealt with the Xiongnu and Xianbei, the Northern Qi, Sui and Tang with various Turkic peoples including the Uighurs, the Song with the Khitan and Tanguts, and the Ming with the Mongols. This highly valuable barter of silk for horses interfered with the purely commercial trading relations practised along the ancient silk routes and undermined them. In the north the large profits of the middlemen remained in the hands of the nomad horsemen, resulting in a drain on the Chinese economy and a deterioration of the finances of the oasis towns. In the fourth and fifth centuries some nations and great trading centres like Sogdiana and Khotan sought to make up for the scarcity of silk and the fluctuations in the Chinese supply by establishing their own silk manufactories.11

Besides silk, the more important goods carried westwards along the silk routes included woven and embroidered silk products as well as undyed textiles and silk yarn, ceramics, lacquerware, tea, steel, bronze mirrors from the Han to Tang periods, and from other parts of the Eurasian continent and southeast Asia precious stones, pearls, ivory, spices and medicinal items, rare woods, perfume and incense; eastwards went glass, gold and silver vessels and jewellery, precious textiles of wool and cotton and much more from the eastern Mediterranean and Iran. In addition, new plants and fruits like sesame, grapes, garlic, walnuts, cucumbers, figs as well as western music, dance and musical instruments were introduced from the West via Central Asia, while peaches, pears and oranges were first grown in China and disseminated via 'silk roads' to Central Asia, India and further west.

At the same time the silk roads acted as transmission belts for Buddhism on its way to China, and also for other religions like Islam, Nestorianism and Manichaeism, to mention only the most important.

Within a broader context, however, the intermediary role of the silk routes was much more important in respect to ideas and information than to material goods. We shall mention a few of the inventions and techniques originating in China and passing to the West through the good offices of Arab countries: Silk technology, paper manufacture, book printing, gunpowder, the magnetic compass with needle, treadle loom, water-powered spinning-mills and piston bellows, porcelain manufacture, the collar harness and stern-post rudder, and the concept of segmental arches for bridge-building.[12] There is indeed a host of inventions and discoveries developed and perfected in China centuries and even millennia before they appear in the West.[13]

The Silk Road again became an important trading link between China and the West with the establishment of the Tang dynasty, when the political and cultural influence of the Chinese empire reached its greatest extent since Han times, spreading in the west across Central Asia including the Tarim Basin and northern Afghanistan to the borders of modern Iran, in the north temporarily to Mongolia, in the south to the northern parts of Vietnam and in the east and northeast to Manchuria and north Korea. This came as a result of a highly successful military and diplomatic policy during the first decades of the new dynasty. A system developed by the Han was revived, namely to garrison militia along the borders who farmed the land so as to be largely self-sufficient and less of a burden on the exchequer.

The expansionist wars were fought with tremendous losses among the Chinese adult male population. But the Tang also enjoyed long periods of peace and an extraordinary flowering of culture and the arts which reached its high point during the long reign of Emperor Xuanzong (712-756). The disastrous rebellion (754-763) of one of his favourites, the general An Lushan, born near Bukhara of a Turkish mother and Sogdian father, started the slow but inexorable decline of the dynasty. The rebellion was only put down with the help of Uighur cavalry, who despite their rich rewards, continued well into the ninth century to

75
Pole-caps of a horse-drawn carriage. Bronze with silver inlay.
The four cylindrical pole-caps together form a set and are richly decorated with silver inlay. The design on the broad bands shows highly stylised dragon motifs and delicately scrolling spirals. The top has a design of broad lobes and spirals. The larger caps are fashioned with four hard-edged discs separated by grooves which may have served as fastenings for cords holding parasols or an awning.
All caps carry a four-character inscription inlaid with silver wire and read as Lingli Guo Min. The first two characters are a place name probably referring to a small town in Shaanxi province, while the other two characters give the name of the owner.
H: 7.7 and 4.0-4.1 cm
China, Western Han (206 B.C.- 8 A.D.)

76
Belt or crown. Chased silver with design in high relief.
This large silver object was most probably a belt or crown originally placed in the tomb of an empress or imperial princess.
The belt with lobed profile broadening in the middle is made of strong sheet silver and decorated with engraved and chased designs in high relief. The centre shows a flaming wish-granting jewel surrounded by five stylised wave-like clouds. Two long-tailed phoenixes, usually symbols of the empress, fly towards the jewel, while the remaining surface is decorated with a further ten paired clouds. The background is embellished with an engraved scroll pattern and dense ring punches. The border consists of a row of single chased dots. With an unusually large diameter and relatively slight curvature this object, which was tightened with a silk cord or something similar tied to the bridges on the narrow ends, is more likely to be a belt fastened around the waist of the deceased rather than a crown.
H: 15.0 cm, D: 37.5 cm, L: 51.5 cm
China, Liao dynasty (907-1125)

77
Groom. *Buff-coloured pottery with three-colour glaze (sancai).*
The figure, formed from two moulds, of a bearded horse or camel groom (originally holding reins in his right fist) is dressed in a coat covered with a three-colour glaze of honey-brown and two shades of green. The facial features, dress and hair-dress identify the small figure beyond doubt as a foreigner, a member of the large group of people from Central Asia and the Near East travelling to China and famous and much in demand for their skill in handling horses and camels. They were either in Chinese employ or looked after the camels and horses of trade caravans.
H: 32.1 cm
China, Tang dynasty (619-907), probably 7th century

78
Groom. *Buff-coloured pottery with three-colour glaze (sancai) in brown, blue and light yellow.*
The facial features and pointed cap of this burial figure identify him as a native of Central Asia or lands further west. He originally held the reins of either a mount or a pack-animal.
H: 19 cm
China, 1st half Tang dynasty (619-907)
Museum für Völkerkunde, Berlin

79
Figure of a warrior with shield. Grey pottery with traces of coldpainting.
The fine modelling of the armour and shield provides a good illustration of the equipment of Chinese foot-soldiers of the time.
H: 33 cm
China, Northern Wei dynasty (386-534), 5th/6th century

80
Figure of a warrior. Buff-coloured pottery with small traces of cold painting.
The figure in full armour with realistically modelled details was taken from a mould. It shows traces of the original cold painting and like the preceding figures served as a tomb furnishing.
H: 60.5 cm
China, Tang dynasty (618-907), 7th/8th century

81
Model of a watch-tower. Reddish pottery with silvery iridescent green lead glaze.
The model of a two-storey watch-tower is placed in a deep bowl symbolising a pond and decorated with plainly modelled ducks, frogs, turtles and fishes. At the corners of both balustrades stand archers with cross-bows at the ready. On the upper story two men play at a board-game with two others watching. (See also ill. 8)
H: 90 cm, D: 65 cm (bowl)
China, Eastern Han dynasty (25-220)

82
Two small flower-shaped bowls. Chased and partly gilt silver with scroll and flower designs.
The two small bowls with a rather high foot are designed in the shape of a flower, the outlines of the leaves, filaments and centres chased in relief. The bowl on the right is in the shape of a flower with six rounded petals, while the one on the left has six bracket-lobed petals and lancet-shaped leaves. Both shapes are presumably meant as stylised plum blossoms, even though the real flower has only five petals.
H: 5.1 and 5.7 cm, D: 9.3 and 9.5 cm
China, Southern Song dynasty (1127-1279)

descend on Chinese cities and whole regions purely for plunder. Some years before the outbreak of the rebellion, Chinese troops had suffered a decisive defeat against an Arab army at the Talas river south of Alma-Ata in 751, resulting in the Islamisation of Central Asia and the loss of Chinese influence in the region and control of the Silk Road.

From the late eighth century onwards, maritime trade therefore gained in importance. It was much greater in quantity than the overland traffic and also much less costly and dangerous. The main trading route ran from the South China Seas to the Persian Gulf and the east coast of Africa or via the Red Sea to the Mediterranean, taking advantage of the dominant monsoons according to the principle 'southwards in winter and northwards in summer'. Since the ships were principally staffed by Persians, the lingua franca of maritime trade was Persian; on the silk routes it had been Sogdian until the thirteenth century, when Persian took over here as well. The largest ships to anchor at ports along the South China coast, primarily at Canton (Guangzhou), came from Sri Lanka; they were up to sixty-five metres long and carried some six to seven hundred men, both crew and passengers. The Arab boats departing from the Persian Gulf were considerably smaller.[14]

The Tang period is characterised by a very un-Chinese cosmopolitan outlook and tolerance towards foreigners and their religions and culture, and was eager to adopt and adapt their art and fashion, their customs and achievements. There were substantial colonies of foreigners in the capital Chang'an and all the major cities and ports; according to the Arab traveller and merchant Abû Zaid the city of Canton was host in the ninth century to some 120.000 foreign traders and employees.[15] Despite this general tolerance which, for instance, allowed the foreign colonies a certain degree of self-government and extraterritorial jurisdiction, there were also repeated irritating moves to limit the free movement and trading activities of foreigners.[16] The loutish behaviour of Uighurs living in Chang'an was one of many factors leading to the outbreak of xenophobia in China in the mid-ninth century, the banning of certain religions and the persecution of Buddhists in 845.

With the Song dynasty (960-1279) all tolerance towards or even interest in foreign things vanished completely. Foreigners were now regarded with suspicion and considered a threat. Such changed behaviour can surely be explained largely by the fact that large parts of China during these centuries were ruled by non-Chinese dynasties. The Liao dynasty (907-1125) of the Khitan held sway over Peking (Beijing) and lands to the north, the Tangut Xixia dynasty (982/1032-1227) and the Jurchen Jin dynasty (1115-1234) over the northwest, the latter, having vanquished the Liao in 1119, advancing as far south as the Huai river, so that the Southern Song from 1227 were left with a truncated China, whose new capital was Lin'an (modern Hangzhou). Instead of waging costly wars the Southern Song preferred to buy peace with so-called 'reparations', sending large amounts of silk and silver to the Liao, Xixia and Jin rulers.[17]

The Xixia empire of the Tanguts was conquered shortly before his death in 1226/27 by Genghis Khan, the Great

Khan of All Mongols, and his successor in 1234 defeated the Jin dynasty, forcing the Song court to flee and re-establish itself at Lin'an. Only in 1279, after decades of laying siege to the Southern Song and after the suicide of the last emperor, did the Mongol forces succeed in capturing the rest of China. Some years before, in 1271, Qublai Khan (1215-1294) had proclaimed the Yuan dynasty (1271/79-1368) with Datu or Khanbaliq (modern Beijing) as its capital.

For most Chinese, this period of foreign rule brought increased compulsory labour, serfdom and brutal exploitation. Only trade and commerce were allowed to flourish, and many Western merchants travelled to China, among them Marco Polo. The huge extent of Mongol conquests and nation-building from China to eastern Europe, the Near East and the southern coast of the Mediterranean made possible the re-opening of regular trading relations between East and West and, equally importantly, safe passage along the Eurasian highways. From 1340 domestic unrest was fuelled by economic mismanagement, palace intrigues and natural catastrophes, leading eventually to the fall of the Mongol Yuan dynasty and the establishment of the Ming dynasty by Zhu Yuanzhang, a former Buddhist mendicant monk.[18]

Before the Song period (960-1279) China did not have her own ocean-going merchant vessels, and it seems that Chinese traders only in ninth or tenth century began to travel on chartered boats as far as India.[19] Improvements in maritime navigation, especially the development of the magnetic compass, were responsible for a decisive shift towards sea-borne trade and away from the overland silk routes, again unsafe after the fall of the Yuan and now fading into insignificance. Commercial goods travelled mainly by sea, being carried in ever-larger ships which were relatively fast and safe.

Under Emperor Yongle (1403-1423), China became the greatest sea power in Asia and perhaps the world. He initiated seven large-scale maritime expeditions under the command of the Muslim eunuch Zheng He (1371-1435), each of several years' duration, which visited altogether more than fifty countries in Southeast Asia, India, along the Persian Gulf and the coast of East Africa. The rationale of these expeditions has never been satisfactorily explained, but their purpose seems to have been less the establishment of new trade relations and more a 'showing the flag' to demonstrate China's might to far-away countries. In 1435 these expeditions were suddenly discontinued, probably for financial reasons.[20]

Asia and China had much to offer which the West either lacked or was long unable to produce itself, while Asia and China themselves had almost everything they needed. Furthermore, China had little tradition of seafaring, her economy always having been based primarily on agriculture. Almost every war the Chinese fought aimed either at unifying the country or at safeguarding this unity and defending her imperial power. Only rarely were wars directed towards expansion and conquest, even these mainly instigated by non-Chinese rulers on the throne.

83
'TLV' mirror with the four directional animals. Bronze.
The name of this type of mirror derives from the peculiar elements on its back shaped like the letters T, L and V. The broad rim shows stylised scroll or dragon designs interspersed with the animals of the four directions, the turtle or 'Black Warrior' of the North, the phoenix or 'Vermilion Bird' of the South, the 'Blue Dragon' of the East and the 'White Tiger' of the West.
D: 12.7 cm
China, Western Han dynasty (206 B.C.-A.D.8)

84
Mirror with lion and grape designs in high relief, bronze.
This small but heavy mirror with a silvery gloss has a knob for fastening a silk cord in the centre in the shape of a bear and surrounded by a broad band showing five lions among grapes and scrolls, and another narrower band with eleven different kinds of birds again among grapes and scrolls.
D: 12.7 cm
China, Tang dynasty (618-907)

85
Bronze mirror with the twelve animals of the zodiac in relief around a central scroll design.
D: 15.8 cm
China, Sui dynasty (581-618)

86
Eight-lobed thick bronze mirror.
The high relief decoration shows two lions and two phoenixes between highly stylised hibiscus scrolls, and along the lobed rim lingzhi fungi of immortality (?) alternating with butterflies, an auspicious symbol.
D: 13.6 cm
China, Tang dynasty (618-907)

87
Large low bowl with sea-green celadon glaze, light grey porcelain-like stoneware.
The large heavy bowl is decorated in the well with a moulded dragon design and along the sides with a carved scroll pattern. This type of massive celadon bowls was a popular item for export to Southeast Asia and Muslim countries in the West.
H: 8.4 cm, D: 35.1 cm
China, Longquan (Fujian province), Yuan dynasty (1271-1368)

88
Two plates. Impressed plant and butterfly designs and three-colour glaze (sancai) in white, honey-brown and green, reddish buff-coloured and high-fired pottery.
The small eight-lobed plate is decorated in the centre with a stylised lotus blossom surrounded by green-glazed waves, and the central design of the large plate also shows a flower motif inside a ring of waves.
D: 13.8 and 22.8 cm
China, Liao dynasty (907-1125)

89
Rooftile with figure of a horse. Reddish-grey pottery with dark green and yellow lead glaze.
Such rooftiles with plastic decoration of mythical motifs were supposed to ward off evil. The horse riding on a cloud presumably refers to the heavenly horses of Chinese mythology (see also ills. 90, 91).
H: 36.45 cm, L: 31 cm
China, late Ming dynasty (1368-1644)
Museum für Kunsthandwerk, Leipzig

90
Decorative tilework with a lion. Reddish pottery with yellow and dark green lead glaze.
The forward-lunging lion or fo dog on a high rectangular base decorated with a cloud motif
in relief, holds a ball between its paws, and perhaps served as a rooftile of a palace or temple
roof or as the finial of a so-called 'shadow wall' (yingbi) meant to deflect evil spirits and set
parallel to the entrance, thereby also barring the view into the interior.
H: 48.8 cm, W: 20.0 cm, L: 63.5 cm
China, probably 1st half Ming dynasty (1368-1644)

91
Head of a dragon with gaping mouth. Reddish pottery with light brown and light green lead
glaze.
Such lion-like heads of dragons with ferocious mien served as finials on gables and were
thought to ward off evil spirits and thunderstorms.
H: c. 25 cm, W: c. 25 cm
China, Southern Song/Yuan dynasty (1127-1279/1271-1368), c.13th century

Chinese imports well into modern times mainly consisted of luxury goods and curios, for which demand was limited to a very small elite. Foreign goods were often valued only for their exotic appeal and were usually considered inferior to domestic products both in design and craftsmanship.

The re-evaluation of Chinese traditions and values by the Song scholar-officials with a concomitant anti-foreign bias provided the intellectual and sentimental basis for the chauvinist and isolationist policies of the Ming and Qing dynasties (1369-1911). That brilliant period of internationalism, of tolerance and lively interest in foreign things and ideas during the first half of the Tang dynasty, so fruitful in many ways, unfortunately remained a rare experiment and unique episode in Chinese history.

1   The motivation for such journeys tended to be two-fold, as both true pilgrimages in the sense of visiting sacred sites, but also aiming to acquire Buddhist texts at their source in India, Central Asia and Sri Lanka. For the problems of translating and editing Buddhist scriptures for Chinese readers, cf. Gernet 1983:191-195.

2   This was the case, for example, with the sixteen-year journey (629-645) of the monk Xuanzang, who left China clandestinely against the wishes of the imperial court to visit Central Asia and India. He was the greatest of all translators of Buddhist texts into Chinese. A year after he returned to China one of his disciples, basing himself on his master's travel notes, wrote the *Da Tang xiyuji* (Record of a journey to the west during the Tang dynasty), which includes much information about the countries Xuanzang passed through and is today one of the prime sources for the history of those parts of the world. The same can be said about most of the travel literature composed by these pilgrims, such as the *Fuguoji* (Record of Buddhist lands) or *Faxian zhuan* (Faxian's record), a detailed description by the monk Faxian of his journey (399-414) through more than thirty countries in Central Asia, India, Sri Lanka and Sumatra. See Gernet, 1983:191-3, 235-6.

3   Cf. Kuhn 1993:57-58.

4   The Chinese term for tributary states is *fan*, literally 'frontier, boundary wall, defense, hedge', indicating what the Chinese considered to be their main function. Ideologically speaking all foreign countries were seen as a defensive barrier, and *fan* became synonymous with everything foreign and beyond the Chinese borders. On the rituals of a foreign emissary's audience with the Chinese emperor, see Schafer 1963:27, 285 n.166.

5   Los Angeles 1994:55. For the hard-won Chinese victory over the Xiongu, see Gernet 1983:107-9.

6   These wars of conquest were often organised on a grand scale. The first expedition against the Xiongnu in 133 B.C. involved an army of three hundred thousand soldiers with waggons, cavalry and field kitchens. See Gernet 1983:108-16, 120. When the small principality of Khojent in the Fergana Valley refused to deliver the required stallions and mares, Emperor Wu is said to have sent an army of sixty thousand troops with a hundred thousand oxen, thirty thousand horses and ten thousand pack animals against them. Although this gained the Chinese some three thousand stallions and mares in foal, less than a thousand survived the treck to Chang'an, and only ten thousand troops returned home. See Boulnois 1964:30-32.

7   On his second journey in 115 B.C., Zhang Qian crossed Dzungaria and visited the land of the Wusun tribe southeast of Lake Balkhash, which also was famous for its horse-breeding; see Gernet 1983: 109, 118, and Boulnois 1964:19-26.
    The 'blood-sweating' horses of Fergana, mentioned already by Herodotus, seem to have been infected by a parasite (Parafiliaria multipapillosa); see Schafer, 1964:58-70.

8   Ferdinand Freiherr von Richthofen. China: Ergebnisse eigener Reisen und darauf gegründeter Studien, vol. 1. Berlin, 1877.

9   During the Eastern Han dynasty (25-220) and the following centuries until the Sui and Tang, the eastern terminal was at Luoyang, capital of the Eastern Han.

10 Nishikawa and Ueda 1988:18. Lapis lazuli from Afghanistan appears in Egypt as early as the third millennium B.C.; see Kuhn 1993:59. For much earlier sites revealing silk fragments presumably of Chinese origin, see Los Angeles 1994:19, and Eggebrecht 1994:199.

11 Nishikawa and Ueda 1988:21.

12 Kuhn 1993:14-15.

13 See Gernet 1983:65, 68, 125-6, 265; Eggebrecht 1994:25, gives a list of major Chinese inventions followed by detailed discussions on pp. 7-164, 176-222.

14 On maritime trade and the size of ships, see Schafer 1963:11-13.

15 Ibid., p. 282 n.65.

16 See ibid., pp. 20-25.

17 For details about Chinese 'reparations' laid down in the peace treaty with the Tanguts after the war of 1040-44, see Pjotrowskij 1993:51.

18 See Goepper 1988:86-100.

19 Schafer 1963:12, 49.

20 Goepper 1988:103-4.

92
'The Capture of Baghdad by Mongol Troops'. Painting on paper.
H: 37.2 cm, W: 29 cm

Early 14th century
Staatsbibliothek, Berlin; Preußischer Kulturbesitz, Orientabteilung, Diez A, fol. 70, p. 7
Illustration from the Universal History of Rashid al-Din

Central Asia in Islamic Times

Eigth to Fifthteenth Century

The Land Beyond the River: Islam in Central Asia

Heinz Halm

The Arab-Islamic conquest

Māwanā `an-nahr, "what is beyond the river", was the name the Arabs gave to Transoxiana, the land beyond the Oxus river, of which they first became conscious after the Muslim conquest of the Sasanian empire. The Arab-Islamic conquest of the Iranian highlands originated in the two military camps at Kufa and Basra on the Euphrates, established in 638 and 640, respectively. The Arab troops stationed in these two cities seem to have pursued their conquests independently of each other and without the general supervision of the caliph at Medina. During the years 651-2 Arabs from Basra ensconced themselves at Merv (modern Mary in Turkmenistan), situated in the oasis formed by the branches of the Murgab river, and consolidated their rule through agreements with the regional Iranian nobility, the barons (*deghān*) and margraves (*marzbān*) of the former Sasanian empire. The Arab garrison at Merv, the ruins of which even today are an impressive sight, was the military base for the Muslim conquest of Central Asia. Still in the seventh centuries more than fifty thousand families of soldiers from Kufa and Basra are said to have settled in the five towns of the oasis; the number may be an exaggeration, but there is no doubt that Merv constituted an important Arab colony. In 676 some four thousand men arrived from Basra, among them a cousin of the Prophet, Qutham ibn al-`Abbas, whose alleged tomb at Samarkand is still venerated today.

Since ancient times the rural and urban cultures living beyond the Oxus - called 'Jayhun' by the Arabs and 'Amu Darya' by the Iranians - were influenced by Iranian politics and civilisation. The languages of the settled population likewise belonged to the Indo-Iranian family: Tokharian was spoken along the middle reaches of the Oxus, in the region of Tajikistan and northern Afghanistan; Khorezmian along the lower Oxus reaches, in the area of modern Urgench and Khiva; and Sogdian in the Zeravshan valley, where Bukhara and Samarkand lie. The titles of the rulers of these cities were also Iranian: the 'king' (khshêd, modern Pers. shāh) of Sogd, the 'master' of Bukhara (Bukhār-khudā), the 'king' of Khorezm (Khwārizm-shāh). Tashkent (Turk. 'city of stones') at that time bore the Iranian name Chāch (Arab. Shāsh), and even today in Samarkand, Bukhara and Tashkent there is an old core of Iranian ('Tajik') speakers.

But even at the time of the Muslim conquest there was a Turkish element from Central Asia - the dominating one in modern Uzbekistan - among the local population, and not only among the steppe nomads; it seems likely that the Bukhār-khudās despite their Iranian appellation, were of nomad Turkish descent. The quest of nomad rulers to achieve control over the cities and establish their own dynasties which partook of the civilisation of settled cultures,

is a constant feature not only of the history of Central Asia but also of Iran.

By 667 the south bank of the Amu Darya with the bridgeheads at Zamm and Amol were under Arab occupation, with Tirmidh (modern Termez) added in 676. This provided the base for attacks against Bukhara, Samarkand and Khorezm which finally lead to the conquest of 'what is beyond the river', a campaign led by Qutaiba ibn Muslim, general to Caliph al-Walid I (705-715). Prince Peroz, a grandson of the last King of Kings Yazdegerd III, after attempts to regain the land of his fathers with Chinese support, went into exile in China. In 709 the Arabs captured the citadel of Bukhara and in 712 Samarkand, while in Khorezm the native dynasty remained in power, although under Muslim suzerainty.

With the Arabs came Islam. At the same time as the caliph completed the Umayyad mosque in Damascus and the Aqsa mosque in Jerusalem, Bukhara in 713 and Samarkand slightly later acquired mosques, of which nothing remains today.

The state religion of the Sasanians, Zoroastrianism, had to make way for Islam and so had Buddhism, at the time still widespread, its grand centre at Balkh (nau bahār, 'new monastery'; ancient Bactra) in northern Afghanistan destroyed by the Arabs as early as 661; it is worth recalling that Bukhara derives its name from vihara, the Sanskrit word for 'monastery'. Other religious communities were tolerated, such as the Nestorian Christians, which survived for several centuries, and the Jews, whom we find to this day in various localities, for instance in Bukhara.

The forays to Tashkent, Khojent and into the Fergana Valley, undertaken in 713-4 by Qutaiba ibn Muslim in his late years, defined the eastern-most limit of the Arab-Islamic expansion into Central Asia; here the empire of the caliph came up against China's sphere of interest. Yet in vain did the ruler of Tashkent call for Chinese support against the Arabs; China, being herself engaged in a war with the Tibetans, was unable to repulse the Muslim advance. From 713 the caliph sent several embassies to the Chinese court. During the 740s the Chinese attempted to re-establish their power as far as Tashkent, but in 751 in the battle at Athlakh near the town of Taraz (Talas), Muslim troops inflicted a decisive defeat on the Chinese. The battle was significant not only politically but also in terms of cultural history: According to the historian Tha`alibi, the Arabs not only made captives but also discovered paper-making facilities among the army's equipment together with expert personnel and took both to Samarkand. For some time Samarkand enjoyed a monopoly on paper-production, but eventually the secrets of the craft reached Baghdad, since 762 the new residence of the caliph; and within a short period the new writing material displaced papyrus and vellum, a technological revolution whose significance for the development of civilisation cannot be overestimated.

Under the Baghdad caliphate of the Abbasids (749-1258), whose original power base had been Merv, the cities of eastern Iran (Khorasan), Khorezm and Transoxiana grew into centres of Islamic culture. The native population of

Iranian and Turkish origin became part of this culture; Qutaiba had already included many of the aristocrats in the army roll (dīwān) of the Iranian military. The Islamisation of Central Asia seems to have taken only a short time, and with it came the Arab language as a medium for the dissemination not only of the religion, but also of science and learning; and the names of Muslim scholars who during the Middle Ages studied in Bukhara and Samarkand is indeed legion.

The most momentous invention to reach the West via the caliphate empire besides paper-making we owe to a man from Khorezm: In about 820 Mohammed ibn Musa al-Khwarizmi (d. c.845) wrote the earliest Arab treatise on calculations using 'Indian' numerals, which we call 'Arabic'. Although not his invention, he helped to spread the technique: Translated as *De numero Indorum* in Spain into Latin in the twelfth century, his book introduced the West to the numerals we use today as well as to the nought and calculations with place values. The word 'algorithm', meaning mathematical operations such as addition and multiplication, derives from 'Algorismi', the Latinised form of the author's name. 'Algebra' comes from the title of another of his writings; *al-gabr* or *al-gebr* means 'to reset', originally used for resetting bones, but later also for the setting of a mathematical equation. A monument to al-Khwarizmi in Urgench reflects the policy of the Soviet authorities to celebrate the historical secular achievements of Islam in Central Asia, while discouraging its religious traditions (ill. 93).

The Samanids

The Land beyond the River as part of the caliphate of Baghdad, only acquired its own distinctive character in the ninth and tenth centuries under the Samanids, a dynasty of governors. Its founder Saman, an Iranian nobleman from the north of modern Afghanistan, had converted to Islam; his four grandsons served the caliph al-Ma'mun (813-33) as governors of Herat, Samarkand, Fergana and Tashkent; Nasr ibn Ahmad (864-92), the son of the governor of Fergana, in 875 was made governor of all Transoxiana. Until 999 the Samanids, bearing the title of amīr (military commander) and having a status somewhat akin to margraves, governed the northeastern frontier region of Islam in the name of the caliph. The rise of this dynasty exemplifies the integration of a native aristocracy into the higher echelons of the Arab-Islamic empire. At their court, Persian - now in its New Persian form - for the first time since the Arab conquest again became the favourite language of poets. Like the poets Rudaki and Daqiqi the great Firdausi, creator of the Persian national epic, the *Shāhnāma* (Book of Kings) with its nearly sixty thousand verses, had begun his career under the Samanids.

Two of the major scientists of the time also were born on Samanid territory. In 980 Ibn Sina (Latinised 'Avicenna') was born near Bukhara (d. 1037 in Hamadan, west Iran), his father probably Persian, although he himself wrote in Arabic. He studied at Bukhara during the time of the Samanid emir Nuh II ibn Mansur (976-97), and from his recollections we

93
Statue of Musa al-Khwarzemi (d. 845), Urgench.

94
Statue of Ibn Sina (b. 980), Bukhara.

95
Statue of the poets Nawa'i (1441-1501) and Jami (1414-92), Samarkand.

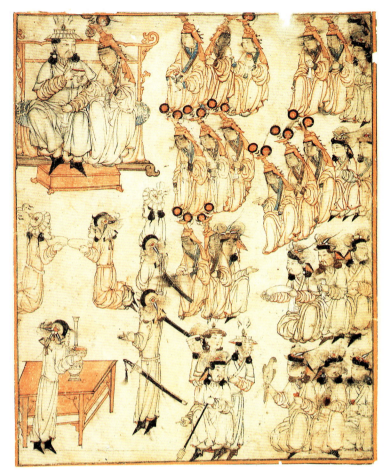

96-98

'Illustrations of Mongol State Council Meetings Presided over by the Grand Khan and His Main Wife'. Painting on paper.

Illustrations from the Universal History of Rashid al-Din, vizier of the Mongol ruler Ghazan Mahmud (1295-1304) and his brother and successor Olghaitu Chudabanda (1304-1360). The illustrations were executed by Mongol, Uighur, Persian and Turkish artists, all members of different religions.

The custom to produce visual records of political events has a long history. The ceremonial accompanying Mongol council meetings was very strict and highly complicated and remained a model for a long time; both Timur and the Manchu (Qing) emperors of China used it as a point of reference. Certain features like the ceremonial baldachin above the throne with the Great Khan's cushion, the seating plan for the princes and princesses and the procedure for presenting gifts were adopted by successor dynasties. Clavijo, who travelled to Samarkand as an ambassador of the Spanish king (1403-6), has left us a description of the ceremonies attending his reception at Timur's court. Emissaries and guests, for example, had to step forward two by two, kneel down and then down the cup of wine or fermented mare's milk which had also been offered to the ladies.

The high headgear with a veil touching the shoulders, a fashion among married upper-class Mongol women until the 17th century, was already described by Zhao Hong in 1221: "The wives of the tribal leaders wear the gugu head-dress. [The support] is made of wire … It is some three feet long, covered with brocade worked in red and blue and embellished with pearls and gold." Clavijo mentions an identical headdress worn by Timur's main wife as well as Timur's own large hat with precious stones.

Early 14th century

Staatsbibliothek, Berlin; Preußischer Kulturbesitz, Orientabteilung, Diez A, fol. 70, pp. 10, 22, 23

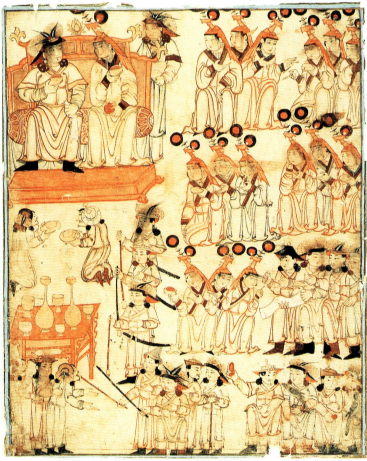

99

'Harried Horses'. Painting on paper.
This leaf from Rashid al-Din's Universal History *exemplifies the typical Mongol style. Its forms and colours combine elements of Islamic western Asian styles with Central Asian and Far Eastern painting traditions. The figures and landscape show a certain spatial depth, and the depictions after nature appear very life-like.*

H: 37.2 cm, W: 29.0 cm
Early 14th century
Staatsbibliothek, Berlin; Preußischer Kulturbesitz, Orientabteilung, Diez A, fol. 70, p. 19

100

'Autumn Landscape with a River'. Painting in the Chinese manner on paper.
After the mid-14th century the influence of Chinese painting becomes more pronounced and examples of painting 'à la Chinois' multiply.

H: 19.2 cm, W: 28.1 cm
Saray Album, mid-14th century
Staatsbibliothek, Berlin; Preußischer Kulturbesitz, Orientabteilung, Diez A, fol. 71, p. 10

learn that the city's book-market was second to none. The young scholar was allowed to use the emir's library which was housed in several rooms, each devoted to one subject, where the books were kept in chests. His most famous medical work, the *al-Qānūn fī t-tibb* (The Canon of Medicine), known in the West as the *Canon Avicennae*, remained a standard textbook well into the seventeenth century (ill. 94).

The other famous scholar of the period was al-Biruni (973-c.1050), born at Kath in Khorezm on the right bank of the Amu Darya not far from modern Urgench. As with Firdausi and Ibn Sina, his career was spent far away from home; like Firdausi he served Sultan Mahmud of Ghazni, accompanying him on his Indian campaigns. Al-Biruni knew Sanskrit and was familiar with the history, thought and science of India like no other Muslim scholar, and his works are an inexhaustible source about the subcontinent (ill. 95).

At their capital Bukhara the Samanids have left us an impressive mausoleum, probably built under Emir Isma`il (892-907) and one of the earliest surviving examples of Islamic architecture in Central Asia (ill. 110). Another monument from Samanid times, the recently discovered mausoleum of Arab Ata at Tim dated 978, is remarkable for its octagonal dome as a transitional concept in the evolution from cube to cupola, an important stage in the development of Islamic architecture (ill. 117).

The Turkish 'Khans from the North'

In 992 Bukhara was taken - not for the first time, as we have seen - by a man from the steppe. Bughra Khan - his Islamic name was Harun or Hasan - was the leader of a confederation of Turkish nomads from the northern steppe; his grandfather had already adopted the Muslim faith. The dynasty he founded is called 'Karakhanid' because many of its members used this title; in Turkish, kara means both 'black' and 'northern'. In 999 the Karakhanids finally succeeded the Samanids, and their rule, which ended in 1211, extended as far south as the Amu Darya. The massive brick caravanserai of Ribat-e Malik (before 1078) on the road between Samarkand and Bukhara bears witness to the flourishing trade conducted along the Silk Road. In Bukhara itself some impressive buildings of this period have survived, in particular the Great Mosque (Pers. kalān, huge) of 1127-9 (ill. 120), and the small Maghak-e Attari (Pers, 'Tomb of Attari') mosque with its richly decorated façade also of the twelfth century. Outside the city at the place where the open-air celebratory prayers were held (Arab. *musallā*, Pers. *namāzgāh*) at the end of the fasting period Ramadan and during the month of pilgrimage, presided over by the ruler himself, the *qibla* wall, indicating the direction of Mecca, with the prayer niche (*mihrāb*) of 1119 is still standing.

Besides these architectural remains, the legacy of the Karakhanid period survives in the form of two precious literary documents, the earliest books written in Turkish. In 1069 the treasurer Yusuf Khass Hajib, following Persian precedent, produced for his sovereign a 'mirror for the prince' called *Qutadghu Bilik* (Auspicious Knowledge

Wisdom), and Mahmud al-Kashgari from Kashgar, which together with Bukhara and Samarkand was one of the Karakhanid capitals (now in the Chinese province of Xinjiang), compiled the earliest Turkish dictionary, the *Dīwān-e lughāt-e Turk* (Compendium of the Languages of the Turks), in 1073-7.

The rule of the Karakhanids in Bukhara and Samarkand came to an end in 1211, when the neighbouring shah of Khorezm occupied the towns along the Zeravshan. The Khorezmshahs - a dynasty, also of Turkish descent, since about 1077 - began to extend their territory very energetically from the early thirteenth century onwards. Their troops threatened India in the east and Anatolia in the west and occupied the Land beyond the River. Surviving from their short period in power are the impressive mausolea of the Khorezmshahs at their capital Gurganj (modern Kunya-Urgench) south of the Aral Sea.

Transoxiana as part of the Mongol empire

Early in 1220 Genghis Khan with his Mongolian troops crossed the Syr Darya at Otrar; in March Bukhara admitted him through her gates, as did Samarkand soon afterwards. Khojent was taken and then Gurganj, and the last Khorezmshah made his escape westwards and died on an island in the Caspian.

The invasion of the pagan Mongols in the thirteenth century brought ruin to the Land beyond the River, which was the first Islamic country to fall into their hands. Although the Mongol rulers soon adopted Islam and like other conquerors from the steppes, adapted to the *dār al-Islām*, Transoxiana lost its significance during the twelfth and thirteenth centuries, the political and cultural centres of the Mongolian era having moved elsewhere.

With the capture of Baghdad in 1258, Iran and Iraq became provinces of an Asian empire greater than any the world had seen before, whose capital since 1264 was at Khanbaliq (modern Beijing). For all the devastation wrought upon the Near East by the Mongolian conquest, one should not forget that the splendour of the late thirteenth and fourteenth centuries owed very much to the Pax mongolica. During this time trade between China and the Mediterranean along the Silk Road probably reached its greatest extent, and the first Europeans made their way overland to Central Asia: Giovanni di Piano Carpini in 1245-7 at the behest of Pope Innocent IV, the Dominican friar André de Longjumeau in 1249 and the Franciscan friar William of Rubruck in 1253-4, the latter two as emissaries of King Louis IX of France; the merchants Maffeo and Niccolò Polo left in 1262 and for three years lived in Bukhara, while Niccolo's son Marco set out from Venice in 1275 and only returned in 1292.

The Mongol empire established by the Great Khan Khubilai (1259-1294) and under the direction of the central government in Beijing, finally disintegrated in the fourteenth century into its earlier constituent parts, which the Mongols called *ulus*, a term sometimes confusingly translated as 'horde'. It is a corruption of Turkish *ordu* (troops, army) and various Turkic peoples from Central Asia. The three main successor states soon fell under the influence of the more sophisticated Islamic civilisation, and their rulers all eventually adopted the Muslim faith: the Golden Horde with their urban centres along the Volga (Kazan, Saray Berke close to modern Volgograd, and Astrakhan); the Iranian-Iraqian empire of the Ilkhans centred in western Iran (Tabriz, Maragha, Soltaniyeh); and in Transoxiana 'Chagatai's Horde', in Turkish also called *ulugh ev* (great house). Genghis Khan's second son, Chagatai (d. c.1241), and his successors, whose heartland remained the steppe country along the Ili river (north of modern Alma-Ata in Kazakhstan), for a long time retained their nomad traditions and their pagan creed; they delegated the government of urban centres like Bukhara and Samarkand to members of the native Muslim elite. How little the Mongols at first valued cities was clearly demonstrated by Khan Buraq, whose preparation for a campaign against an Iran ruled by fraternal Mongols included plundering cities in his own realm. During the Iranian counter-attack in 1273-4 Bukhara was again looted and demolished, lying in ruins until 1282. So it is not surprising that the Arab traveller Ibn Battuta, a native of Tangier, on his visit to the residences of Khan Tarmashirin (1326-34) at Samarkand and Bukhara, was shocked about the ruinous state of the cities of the Land beyond the River.

More than a century of Mongol rule in Transoxiana left a legacy of two major features. One was linguistic: Because the armies of Chagatai and his successors also included a majority of Turks, the shift from Iranian to Turkic languages accelerated, having already begun in pre-Islamic times. This was especially the case in rural areas, and in consequence most of the old village names in Central Asia mentioned in Arabian sources from before the Mongol invasion, do not appear on any modern map, because they have been replaced by Turkish ones. Persian continued to be used for a time – and has not completely disappeared even today – as the language of city-dwellers and for written texts; but eventually it was supplanted by Turkish or rather 'Chagataian' and was finally accepted even by poets and writers as their favourite medium.

The second surviving legacy from Mongolian times was its impact on religious life. The period of Mongol invasions and destruction with its daily experience of misery and death, encouraged a strong revival of the mystic strands of Islam, of Sufism or Dervishism (the word derives from Arab. *sūf*, wool, a reference to the woolen garb of ascetics, and from Pers. *darwīsh*, a poor man or beggar). The individual religious experience acquired with the assistance of a spiritual teacher (*pīr*) now complemented the great emphasis on ritual and regulation (*shari`a*) of traditional Islam. During the period of Mongol domination the mystic movements coalesced to form organisations akin to religious orders (Arab. *tarīqa*, path), meeting regularly for communal devotions (dhikr) in their own meeting places (Pers. *khāneghā*,

sites with glamorous memorials. A typical example of such mausolea is the tomb of the mystic master Saifuddin Bakharzi (1189-1260) outside Bukhara, which consists of two domed buildings, the actual mausoleum with the cenotaph and a visitors' hall (*ziyārat-khāne*) for the pilgrims. The great reverence paid these tombs of holy men can be gauged by the surrounding cemeteries; in Bukhara, for instance, right next to the mausoleum of the saint, the Mongol khan Buyan Quli (d. 1358 in Samarkand) built himself a tomb decorated with a splendid faience façade. From about 1300 the Chagatai rulers had increasingly come under Muslim influence, especially after they had moved their residence to Nakhshab (modern Karshi), southwest of Bukhara. One of the last Chagatai khans of Transoxiana was a patron and protector of the Sufi master Baha'uddin Naqshband (1317-1389), whose mystic teachings are followed to this day by the well-connected and influential dervish order of the Naqshbandi.

Timur and the Timurids

The fall of Khan Tarmashirin in 1334 led to three decades of war and anarchy, while the Mongol khans and the Turkish emirs fought each other. One of the Turkified local dignitaries was the emir of Shahr-i Sabz (Green City), Taraghai, to whom in 1336 was born Timur (Turk. *temür*, iron), also known as Tamerlane (Pers. *Timur lang*, Timur the Lame). During the second half of the fourteenth century Timur succeeded not only in rebuilding Chagatai's disintegrated *ulus* but also to make Transoxiana the centre of a huge, though hastily-assembled empire stretching from Ankara in the west to Russia in the northwest and Delhi in the southeast. His victorious campaigns – benefiting partly from the internal weakness and decline of the surrounding empires – have made Timur's name a synonym for furious destructiveness. But as in the case of the Mongol invasions, so here destruction was soon followed by a period of efflorescence. Timur himself was eager to bring artists and artisans to Transoxiana, by force, if need be. The great Timurid buildings at Shahr-i Sabz, Samarkand and Bukhara determine the character of these cities to the present day. In Samarkand Timur built the monumental mosque of Bibi Khanum and his own mausoleum Gur-e Mir (Tomb of the Emir). On a visit in 1403-4 the ambassador of the king of Castille, Ruy Gonzales de Clavigo, thought the palaces and gardens of Timur's birthplace Shahr-i Sabz so magnificent that he compared them to Paris.

Timur himself was a pious man and patron of the dervish orders and he must be credited for firmly rooting Islamic culture in Transoxiana. He was a thoroughly urbanised cultured Muslim with few ties to the ways of the steppe, but still felt it necessary to legitimise his rule by marrying two Chagatai princesses, a fact which provided his successors – among them the Mughal ('Mongol') emperors of India – with a rightful claim to be the heirs of Genghis

101
'Siege of a City'. Painting on paper.
Miniature from a late Timurid Shahnama.
H: 31.3 cm, W: 24.0 cm
Iran, 15th/16th century
Private collection, Frankfurt

103
'Timurid Nobleman'. Painting on paper, unfinished.
The costume shown in this miniature combines urban and nomadic elements.
H: 26 cm, W: 14 cm
Iran or Central Asia, c. 1425-50
Staatsbibliothek, Berlin; Preußischer Kulturbesitz, Orientabteilung, Diez A, fol. 73, p. 9,1

102
'Mongol Horseman in a Rocky Mountain Landscape'. Painting on paper.
H: 19.5 cm, W: 15.7 cm
Saray Album, mid-14th century
Staatsbibliothek, Berlin; Preußischer Kulturbesitz, Orientabteilung, Diez A, fol. 71, p. 28,1

104
'Stag Couchant'. Pen drawing.
The position of the stag is highly reminiscent of the ancient 'animal style' of the steppes.
H: 14.5 cm, W: 21.5 cm
Iran, c. 1400-50
Staatsbibliothek, Berlin; Preußischer Kulturbesitz, Orientabteilung, Diez A, fol. 72, p. 10

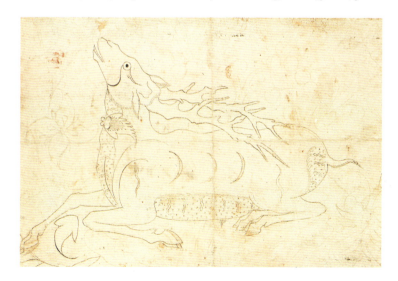

Khan. His huge empire did not survive his death in 1405 for long. Under his son and successor Shah Rukh (1405-1447), Herat became the capital; Transoxiana fell to his grandson Ulugh Beg.

With their patronage of religion, literature and science and art and architecture, the Timurids in Transoxiana, eastern Iran and northern Afghanistan produced one of the most splendid periods in Islamic history; Timurid art was further developed in Mughal India, founded by the Timurid Babur. Innumerable buildings decorated with faience and stucco and books with miniatures and calligraphy have survived from the period. The Shah-e Zinda necropolis near Samarkand with more than a dozen faience-decorated mausolea of the fourteenth and fifteenth centuries presents a unique ensemble of Timurid architecture (ills. 137-43). Ulugh Beg, himself a serious astronomer, built an observatory on a hill near Samarkand, of which the sextant built of stone with a radius of forty metres still exists (ills. 105-7). To advance Islamic scholarship, Ulugh Beg in 1417 founded a madrasa ('place of study' or collegiate mosque) in both Samarkand and Bukhara, huge rectangular buildings with a spendid entrance façade, and two storeys with cubicles for the law students placed around an inner courtyard (ill. 109). The madrasa as an institution spread from Transoxiana to the entire Islamic world; the earliest establishment of this type is recorded for Bukhara in 937. These institutions relied on the income derived from endowments (waqf) by wealthy donors, and this paid for the upkeep of the buildings, the teachers' wages, paper and ink and often also for grants to the students. Until the twentieth century the madrasas remained the most important educational institutions in Transoxiana. To gain an insight into their organisation, one need only visit the Mir-e `Arab madrasa at Bukhara, where even under Soviet rule successive generations of Islamic clerics were trained for work all over Central Asia.

The Timurids were great connoisseurs of the art of the book; book-bindings, calligraphy and miniatures of outstanding quality were produced under their patronage. The poets Jami (1414-1492), the last to write classical Persian poetry, and his friend and patron, the vesir Mir `Ali Shir Nawa'i (1441-1501), who wrote in Chagadai-Turkish, were active at the Timurid courts. Written in the same language were the memoirs of Babur (1483-1530), that adventurous Timurid prince, who after failing to retain Fergana and establish himself in Samarkand, tried his luck in India, where he founded the Mughal empire. Literary Chagatai is closely related to modern Uzbek and the (New) Uighur of the Turkic population in the Chinese province of Xinjiang.

The Uzbek empire

At the end of the fifteenth century, the Timurids were succeeded by the Uzbeks or Özbeks who gave their name to the new state. A confederation of nomad Turkish tribes under a leader of Mongol Genghiskhanid descent and calling itself Özbek, had already moved into the steppes between

105
Observatory of Ulugh Beg (1428/9), Samarkand.

106
Sextant of the observatory.

107
Observatory of Ulugh Beg (reconstruction after Pugachenkova)

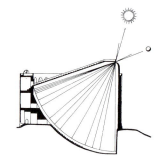

the Syr Darya and Amu Darya in 1430. The power vacuum created by the declining Timurid empire encouraged the tribal leader Muhammad Shaibani in 1500 to take possession of Samarkand, Bukhara and Karshi, Tashkent and the Fergana Valley and finally Khorezm in 1505; this region roughly coincides with the territory of modern Uzbekistan. From 1501 Safawid Iran slowly evolved in the southwest, while north of the Syr Darya the Kazakh people began to emerge as a political entity; thus were the outlines of modern Central Asia formed. Although Shaibani died in the battle against the Iranian shah `Ismail near Merv in 1510, he had managed to prevent the Iranian advance into the Land beyond the River. This also had religious consequences: With the encouragement of the ruling house, for the next two centuries Iran was dominated by Shiites, while in Central Asia the majority of Muslims were Sunnis.

The cultural achievements of Timurid Transoxiana continued after the accession of the Uzbek Shaibanids, as can be seen from its architecture and the miniatures produced by the Bukhara school during the sixteenth century; the rulers also patronised Chagatai literature. The great khan `Abdullah II (1583-98) was succeeded by his brother-in-law Jani Beg; the Janid dynasty (1599-1785) made Bukhara their capital. Khorezm with its new capital at Khiva remained in the hands of a collateral branch of the Shaibanids, while the Fergana Valley under the khan of Kokand became independent in around 1700. The three khanates were to remain the major political players in Central Asia until the arrival of the Russians.

Both Samarkand and Bukhara owe some of their distinctive architectural features to the systematic building programmes of the Janids. Thus in Samarkand under Imam Quli Khan (1619-36) the Shir-dar ('House of the Lion') madrasa was erected in 1619-39 opposite Ulugh Beg's madrasa (ills. 109, 109a, 127), and Bukhara acquired in 1620-3 the enchanting ensemble of Lab-e Khawz ('at the edge of the pond'), its tea-houses shaded by ancient trees forming the centre of the Old Town to this very day. Khan `Abdulaziz (1647-80) completed the two school buildings of Samarkand's Registan ('sandy place') Square with its resplendent Tela-kari ('gold-covered') mosque (ill. 109), and in 1652 built another college opposite the Ulugh Beg madrasa in Bukhara. These and other grand seventeenth-century buildings cast doubt on the popular theory of Transoxiana's rapid economic decline under the Uzbeks, although in the long run the discovery of a passage to India in 1497-8 probably did much to bring an end to trade and prosperity along the ancient overland routes.

The last dynasty of the Bukhara khanate were the Mangits. Originally nomad chieftains along the lower reaches of the Amu Darya, around 1700 they rose to become majordomos of the Janids, succeeding them in 1785. While Great Britain was strengthening her influence in Kashmir and Afghanistan, Russia sought to gain a foothold in the three Uzbek khanates. Shortly before Russia forced the khan of Bukhara to accept her protection in 1868, the Hungarian Arminius Vambéry, disguised as a dervish, visited Bukhara and Samarkand (1863); his *Travels in Central Asia* in 1863,

published in English in 1864, provides a final glimpse of the independent Uzbek khanates – a thrilling and entertaining story.

Kokand, having fiercely resisted all Russian advances, was annexed in 1876, while the more accomodating khanates of Bukhara and Khiva were allowed to remain Russian protectorates; their end only came in 1920 in the wake of the Russian Revolution.

108
Astrolabe. Brass, cast and engraved.
Scale: c. 1:1
Bukhara, 16th/17th century; acquired by Rickmers in the 1890s.
Museum für Völkerkunde, Berlin, Rickmers Collection

109
Registan Square, Samarkand. The square is among the largest and most impressive open spaces of the Islamic world. The buildings date from various periods. The earliest building is the madrasa of Ulugh Beg (left), constructed in 1417-20. The central building is the Tela-kari ('gilded') madrasa, built in 1646-60. On the right is the Shir-dar ('House of the Lion') madrasa, commissioned by the Uzbek leader Jalangtush and constructed under the supervision of the architect Abu al-Jabbar in 1611-36.

109a
Wall-tiles, Shir-dar madrasa.

Islamic Architecture in Uzbekistan

Thomas Leisten

The main focus of our discussion will be the origin of the types of architecture and architectural decoration to be found in Uzbekistan, and we shall point out wherever possible whether they derived from older local traditions, constituted new developments or were dependent from prototypes established in other parts of the Islamic world.

Although the first Muslims arrived in the region of present-day Uzbekistan already in the late seventh century on military reconnaissance and eventually as conquerors, few records exist about the early building activities of the invaders and no material evidence has survived. The latter fact is mainly explained by the three most commonly used building materials, all of them highly perishable: unfired, sun-dried mud bricks; *terre pis*é, where earth, often mixed with water, is rammed into a wooden form as a time-saving method to construct walls; and timber, mainly used for supports and roof beams.

Before fired bricks became more commonly used during the tenth to eleventh century, buildings deteriorated rather quickly and frequently were further endangered by deliberate demolition in times of war. Mediaeval sources already mention the repair of city walls or the complete rebuilding of structures that had only been erected a few years before. In contrast to the situation in arid desert regions, in this area mud-brick buildings have always needed constant care. While mud bricks were inexpensive and could be produced very quickly, wood was such a valuable material that time and again buildings were demolished so that their beams and carved pillars could be re-used in the construction of new palaces, mosques and madrasas. So fire, demolition and wilful destruction together with the inherent frailty of the material were the reasons why it is extremely rare to find Islamic buildings with wooden furnishings in Uzbekistan earlier than the fifteenth century.

Certainly the towns along the Silk Road and big cities like Bukhara and Afrasiab (Old Samarkand) must have dazzled and inspired the Muslim invaders with their great number of religious and secular buildings. Although nothing remains of Uzbekistan architecture from the first two centuries of Muslim rule, it can safely be said that there was no immediate radical change in the appearance of the cities. Any democraphic shift of the local population due to the influx of Arab and Central Asian troops stationed in the garrisons was probably negligible. Patronage of artists and craftsmen remained locally based, and although they converted to Islam, customers are unlikely to have changed their long-established fashions and aesthetics. Even religious architecture was slow to change: For a considerable time the places of worship of various other confessions remained standing side by side with the new Islamic mosques. Abu Bakr Muhammad an-Narshakhi from the vicinity of Bukhara in about 332 (943/4 A.D.) mentions a *but-khane* (presumably

110
So-called 'Mausoleum of the Samanids' (early 10th century), Bukhara.

111
Fragment from the mihrab of the mosque at Afrasiab (Old Samarkand). Cut stone.
H: 45 cm, W: 54 cm
Second half 8th century
Registan Museum, Samarkand

112
Architectural fragment. Wood with a design executed in oblique carving style.
H: 22 cm, W: 44 cm
Samarkand (?), 12th century
Registan Museum, Samarkand

113
Architectural fragment of a window from a building close to the Afrasiab mosque. Sandstone with carved relief.
H: 105 cm, W: 86 cm
Late 12th/early 13th century
Registan Museum, Samarkand

a Buddhist pagoda), which had been built by a Chinese princess in the Bukhara suburb of Ramitin shortly before the Muslim invasion as still standing three hundred years later at the time of writing. He also records the existence of ancient Zoroastrian fire temples in Ramush and Bukhara and churches of Nestorian Christians, suggesting the survival of pre-Islamic traditions well into Islamic times.

The constant threat of attacks by Turkish nomads from the northern steppes and deserts necessitated the building of strong fortifications for settlements and cities. Even after the Samanid emirs in Transoxiana had switched from a defensive to an aggressive policy in the ninth century, their military campaigns against the Central Asian Turks being combined with slave-raiding, all cities were furnished with strong fortifications or at least a citadel. It must have been an impressive feature, for the accounts by Arab and Persian geographers and others invariably begin by describing the fortifications in almost stereotype phrases. Excavations in modern times have confirmed the great age of such protective walls and castles. In mediaeval literature their construction is sometimes ascribed to such legendary figures as Afrasiab, the founder of Bukhara, or one of the pre-Islamic 'Lords of Bukhara'. Besides the standard city fortifications, both Bukhara and Samarkand were surrounded by great walls. The huge 'Kanpirak' wall of Bukhara with a length of two hundred and fifty kilometres enclosed the entire oasis city together with the outlying towns, agricultural areas and irrigation systems. The wall had been built in pre-Islamic times but began to deteriorate after the invasion; it was repaired at the instigation of the population by the governor of Khorasan, Abu l-`Abbas al-Fadl Sulaiman at-Tusi, in the late eighth century. After the Samanids consolidated their position in the tenth century and the nomad threat receded for the time being, the wall became obsolete and fell into disrepair. Remains of the impressive mud-brick construction can still be seen west of the city.

Tomb architecture also remained linked to pre-Islamic customs for a time. At Paikand (modern Karakul) on the banks of the Amu Darya, corpses from Bukhara received communal burial in a domed building used as a burial house (*gur-khane*) as late as the tenth century. Such mass burials recall the charnel-houses of the Zoroastrian creed, but the people buried at Paikand were almost certainly Muslims. Similar edifices elsewhere in Iran would suggest that part of the population, although converted to Islam, continued to practise earlier burial customs.

From early times Muslim rule found visible expression in the erection of mosques. At first built on empty plots outside the town and close to the garrison, mosques were later established on the sites of older places of worship, either by converting such buildings or erecting new ones on the same spot, partly perhaps to give the newly converted population a sense of continuity and show respect for traditionally venerated ground. Documentary evidence shows that large towns and even some smaller ones were provided with a mosque to conduct Friday prayers for the whole catchment area. Unfortunately, information is lacking about the specific appearance of these great mosques. The

Arabic pattern introduced in the conquered territories provided for a walled courtyard with a number of attached buildings for ritual ablutions and a hypostyle prayer-hall. It seems reasonable to assume that these early mosques looked not much different from the Friday mosque to be seen in Khiva. Although it only dates from the late eighteenth century, some of the richly carved wooden pillars of the prayer-hall are as early as the tenth or eleventh century. The almost rectangular prayer-hall has a brick wall and 212 pillars, each cut from a single trunk, with a globular end resting on a stone base and decorated capitals, and supporting a flat wooden roof. The construction from an assembly of parts dating from various periods is a traditional feature of the region, where the earliest mosques were built from the pillars and beams of tumbledown palaces; and indeed we know that for the Khiva mosque pillars from old buildings at Kath were used.

One of the earliest extant examples of Islamic architecture in Uzbekistan is at once a masterpiece: the mausoleum of the Samanid dynasty in Bukhara from the early years of the tenth century. The purity of its forms and its unique decoration have made it probably the most famous early monument in Uzbekistan. When it was built it lay outside Bukhara in the precinct of Naukande village, presumably part of the extensive garden of the ruling house. Down to the present century it was the focal point of a large cemetery, because a visit to the mausoleum and burial in its vicinity were regarded as auspicious acts by mediaeval and early modern Bukharans.

From the outside the building presents itself as a cube of rather modest size (roughly 35 feet square) built with fired bricks and covered by a dome. Visually the weight of the base is tempered somewhat by the slight upward tapering of the walls. Verticality is also emphasised by the integrated round pillars at the corners. On each side an entrance leads into the hall with two more recent cenotaphs. The transition zone from square base to circular dome has squinches inside, while on the outside it is indicated by a graceful miniature gallery of round arches. The single-shell hemispherical cupola is moved back considerably from the top edge of the base and appears rather insignificant; nothing yet foreshadows the important role accorded to the dome in later centuries. Another feature is worth mentioning: The four small cupolas in the area between base and dome, which relate to the corner pillars and seem to continue their upward surge past the band of round arches, are not found again in later architecture. Both these and other architectural features probably derive from pre-Islamic buildings in Sasanian Iran. This applies in particular to the most remarkable element of the mausoleum, namely the four entrances, one on each side. This design, called *chahar-taq* ('building with four arches') in Persian, is often connected with Sasanian fire temples in Iran.

The Samanid mausoleum and its architectural peculiarities show that Islamic architecture consciously made use of earlier traditions which, however, had existed in a different context; the notional translation of a fire temple into a mausoleum exemplifies the great flexibility and

114
Window shutters or part of a ceiling. Wood, iron fittings, coffered star design.
H: 106 cm, W: 78 cm
Khiva, 17th century (?)
Museum in the Ark, Khiva

115
Tile. Green glaze, carved design.
H: 19 cm, W: 20 cm
Samarkand, 12th/13th century

81

116
Taq-e Furushan caravansarai (16th century), Bukhara.

117
`Arab Ata mausoleum (dated 979), Tim.

120
The Kalan minaret (1168), Bukhara.

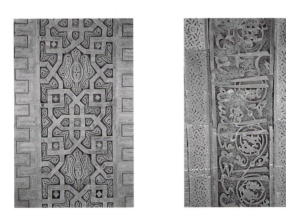

118
Detail from the façade of the central mausoleum at the necropolis of the Karakhanid dynasty, Uzkand, c. 1100.

119
Detail of an epigraphic frieze in thuluth from the façade of the mausoleum on the right from the same necropolis, dated in accordance with 1187/8.

creative power of Islamic architectural concepts. The decoration of the exterior and interior surfaces with differently textured bricks and panels of carved or decoratively arranged bricks represents the highest standards of the time. Its appeal rests solely on the play of light and shadow, whereas later times would make use of a much broader spectrum of decorative techniques such as calligraphy and colourful glazes. The precision with which the bricks have been arranged into mainly abstract and only occasionally floral patterns, suggests that this technique evolved over a lenghty period before it could be handled with such consummate skill. And indeed it would seem that the Samanid mausoleum at Bukhara marks the summit and at the same time the turning-point of this specific type of ornamentation. It was to remain the most important decorative technique in the region for several centuries until superseded by terracotta and stucco carvings, colourful glazed bricks and painted tiles. On the other hand, no monument of the period ever equalled the variety of patterns and their archaic expressiveness of this splendid example of Samanid architecture.

The next important monument to survive is again a dynastic mausoleum, the `Arab-Ata tomb at Tim (ill. 117). It dates from the second half of the tenth century and is thus only sixty years later than the Samarid mausoleum, with which it shares some features but also shows remarkable new developments. The building is again completely square and accented by integrated corner columns. But whereas each side of the Bukhara mausoleum had the same status, the `Arab-Ata has a high screen-like wall on the side looking at the lost mediaeval settlement at the bottom of the valley (now vanished). This is the first appearance in Islamic architecture of the *pishtaq* or monumental portal, which was to become one of the most characteristic elements of Central Asian and Iranian architecture. But again its origin is pre-Islamic, a similar type of façade having been reconstructed by archaeologists working on tomb monuments near Bukhara of the second century A.D.

The *pishtaq* at Tim presents itself as a kind of frame for the single ogee-shaped entrance to the tomb. Two medallions flanking the tip of the arch mark the visual middle line of that section of the façade to which the *pishtaq* acts as a frame. Finally the entrance has three niches with multi-lobed arches, known from buildings of a similar nature erected a hundred years earlier in Syria and Iran. The horizontal termination of the *pishtaq* is lost, and would probably have extended its height by about one metre. The dome which starts to draw in after about seven metres, originally was presumably invisible behind the *pishtaq* of at least nine metres.

The interior, although rather plain, also shows some interesting new features. Opposite the entrance we find a *mihrab* or prayer niche. The niche is of course a standard feature of mosques indicating the direction of Mecca and of prayer, but it also appears more frequently from the tenth century in mausolea, the `Arab-Ata being the earliest known example. This fact is all the more remarkable since orthodox Islam prohibits any kind of veneration of the dead, being

121
Tile fragments. Glazed earthenware, dark blue painting on white ground with red-brown contours and applied sheet gold.
10.1 x 8.0 cm, 17.5 x 10.5 cm
Termez, 15th century
Museum für Islamische Kunst, Berlin

122
Tile. Glazed earthenware with relief decoration, painting of cobalt and turquoise blue on white ground, clear transparent glaze, overglaze lustre decoration.
The framing inscription (only partly read) in thuluth names the Timurid sultan Abu Sa`id Bahadur Khan (d. 1469) as the building's patron and Nusra as the calligrapher.
H: 29.5 cm, W: 18.0 cm Uzbekistan (?), dated A.H. 860 (A.D. 1455/6)
Museum für Islamische Kunst, Berlin

123
Star-shaped tile. Glazed earthenware, low relief design, painted in red, blackish brown, white and gold over a turquoise-coloured glaze.
It presumably comes from a palace. The dragon motif derives from Chinese models of a snake-dragon with feet, a design introduced to Central Asia during the Mongol invasion.
21 x 21 cm Iran, Kashan, lajvardina ware, 13th century

particularly opposed to ritual prayer in cemeteries and at the grave. The presence of prayer niches in mausolea should not be taken as an indication of heterodox practices, however, but presumably rather as symbolising the piety of the patron and the deceased.

Instead of the hemispherical squinch we encountered at Bukhara, here for the first time a tripartite solution for the transition between square base and circular dome has been attempted by the construction of two spherical triangles. From this tentative beginning one of the most important decorative features of Islamic architecture was to develop, namely the *muqarnas*, the 'stalactite' or 'honeycomb' ornament or vaulting made up of small concave elements. These corner solutions are imitated by trefoil niches above the four walls. As at the Samanid mausoleum, corner solutions and niches are separated by slim decorative columns.

Besides the spectacular employment of a *pishtaq* for the main façade, the patterns of shaped brickwork also played an important role in visually structuring the building and its decoration. For the various decorative bands of the *pishtaq* bricks cut into smaller sections were used, while the remaining wall surfaces received an appealing texture simply through brick panels set on edge. The inscription in relief against background scrolls, running at right angles along the outer edge of the *pishtaq*, is also of terracotta. It is among the earliest surviving examples of the use of Arabic calligraphy on an Islamic building in Central Asia. It was meant to inform the visitor of the social position of the deceased and the dates of his birth and death; the introductory quotations from the Koran were seen as a promise for the deceased and an exhortation to the living. The inscription begins on the lower right with the formular "In the Name of God, the Merciful, the Compassionate" and continues with a Koran verse (sura 2, 281): "And fear a day wherein you shall be returned to God, and every soul shall be paid in full what it has earned; and they shall not be wronged." The lost horizontal band presumably gave the name of the deceased together with his titles. Fragments of this together with the date of completion (September/October 979) appear at the end of the vertical lettered band.

From somewhat later times a type of building has survived that greatly enriches our knowledge about the Islamic architecture of Central Asia. The Ribat-e Malik at Karmina on the Silk Road between Samarkand and Bukhara is an example of the caranvanserais along the trade routes which provided protection, accomodation and provisions for travellers and their animals. Such *ribats* were built and maintained by the local rulers, and they often included troops to escort the travellers for the next stage of their journey. In regions exposed to the threat of marauding nomads, the function of the *ribat* oscillated between that of a caravanserai and a fortress, and tellingly enough the term covers both meanings.

The walls of the Ribat-e Malik, intimidating and defined by massive bulges, emphasise the fortress-like character of the compound measuring eighty-four by eighty-six metres. The four high corner towers reflect the custom to furnish rectangular buildings with a tower at each corner, but probably could also be used as outlooks. Such towers accompanying buildings of various types, were to become a leitmotif of Central Asian Islamic architecture.

Immediately behind the splendid *pishtaq* and the entrance one came upon domed storage halls and a courtyard for the pack-animals. Separated from this part on the north side were the actual living quarters for the travellers, arranged around an arcaded courtyard. Although the inscription over the entrance does not give the founder's name, he is assumed to have been the Karakhanid Shams al-Mulk Nasr ibn Ibrahim (1068-80). Excavations brought to light not only coins and ceramics but also the remains of an older structure of the tenth century, possibly also serving as a caravanserai, so that the present building is probably only a Karakhanid restoration.

During the eleventh and twelfth centuries the art of monochrome brick- and terracotta-carving was at its height. Its development during this period can be followed at a complex of three adjoining mausolea situated in Uzkand at the eastern end of the Fergana Basin. At the time Uzkand was the capital of the western Karakhanid khanate; the mausolea are the remains of a larger necropolis for the khans. Although differing in size, the three monuments all follow the same plan, being square buildings with a dome and a projecting *pishtaq*. The central mausoleum presumably was built for one of the first Karakhanids and dates from the first quarter of the eleventh century. The tomb on the north (left) side dates from 1152, while that on the south side, measuring just eight by ten metres, is dated 1187/8. The geometric interlacing bands of terracotta tiles seen on the device framing the entrance of the central tomb foreshadow similar decoration found in Samarkand three hundred years later, where they are executed, however, with coloured ceramics. The northern mausoleum, dedicated to a khan who used a boastful 'Drinking Companion of the Caliph' as one of his titles, has similar decoration on the entrance frame, but the entrance niche is framed by a lively calligraphic frieze in naskhi, while at the top of the entrance were the titles of the Karakhanid founder written in stylised kufic. Due to considerable restoration, the original revolutionary concept of the decoration is hard to visualise today, with only a small fragment of glazed turquoise ceramics surviving in the tympanum above the entrance niche to aid our imagination. In the mid-twelfth century colour was added to the monochrome decoration, at first limited to turquoise glazes based on copper oxide and easy to achieve. The introduction of colour by means of glazed bricks and tiles brought about a complete reorientation of decorative schemes. Even though the devastating Mongol invasion early in the thirteenth century probably slowed down its development in Central Asia, yet a foundation for polychrome decoration had been laid during the twelfth century, so that it could flower brilliantly in Samarkand and Bukhara during the second half of the fourteenth century and become a characteristic feature of Islamic architecture in this region. The use of turquoise glazed tiles for the northern Uzkand mausoleum represents a first tentative exploration of this new scheme and style. Interestingly enough, the founder or architect of the southern mausoleum erected thirty-five years later ignored this innovation and based the decoration of the façade exclusively on the appeal of masterly carved terracotta panels embellished with a wide range of geometric and floral designs combined with calligraphy.

The architecture of the world conqueror: Buildings of the Timurid period

On the history of Central Asia and the Middle East since the late fourteenth century falls the light and shadow of the reign of Timur (1370-1405), a descendant of Genghis Khan and his dynasty. Like his Mongol predecessors, Timur was out to conquer the world, and his campaigns took him as far as Asia Minor and Syria in the west and India in the east. For his residences in his native Central Asia this ambition resulted in a building programme which completely refashioned the cities and the capital Samarkand in particular, enriching them with splendid monuments. For these projects he brought artisans - often simply by deporting them - from all parts of the Islamic world to wherever they were needed. In this period, the major cities of Central Asia must have looked like huge building sites, because at Timur's death very few of his projects had been fully completed. In Samarkand alone in 1404 some one hundred and fifty thousand labourers are said to have been at work, often living under the most primitive conditions. Timur himself was in charge of all the projects, and time and again we read about approved designs being torn down before or after completion. He was particularly concerned about the height of buildings, and sometimes disproportionally tall structures are something of a trademark of Islamic architecture under Timur and his immediate successors.

The speed with which buildings were erected meant that often materials were not properly prepared and walls not given time to settle. Very soon cracks would appear, and the building became hazardous and susceptible to earthquakes. From descriptions of Timur overseeing work at a building site and giving instructions we can safely assume that the monuments at Samarkand and Shahr-i Sabz, towering above the roof-tops like mountains, in terms of proportion, style and aesthetics owe a great deal to the world conqueror himself. And it is due to him that a unique mixture of styles, techniques and traditions resulted in monuments in Samarkand, Shahr-i Sabz, Bukhara and later in Herat in Afghanistan, which are among the most fascinating contributions to Islamic architecture. Even at the time writers, not usually given to pronouncements on architecture, remarked on a 'new style' which impressed everyone. This new style covered almost every aspect of a building, from the spectacular outsized dimensions to innovative techniques of decoration and design.

To get an idea of what Timur's buildings looked like we are not confined to the surviving structures, often much ruined yet still very impressive, but can also consult literary sources. The fact that the court was often residing at Samarkand or Shahr-i Sabz gave writers the opportunity to witness the building work in progress, and their descriptions including monuments long since gone complement the visual evidence. We even have a record of how a contemporary visitor from the West reacted to those splendid edifices: In 1404, one year before Timur's death, the ambassador of Henry III, King of Castile and Léon, Don

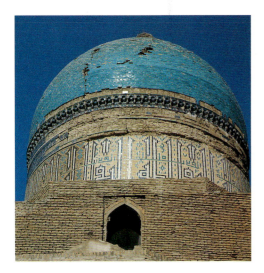

124
Dome of the Bibi Khanum mosque (1398-1405) with monumental kufic inscription, Samarkand.

126
Kukeldash madrasa (1560), Tashkent.
The design of interlacing stars on the entrance iwan *closely resembles the* iwan *of Ulugh Beg's madrasa at Samarkand.*

125
Timurid architectural decoration, Samarkand.

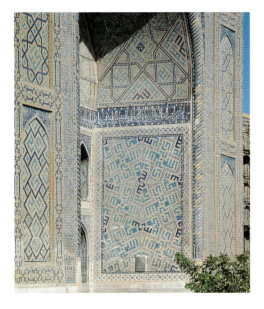

Ruy Gonzales de Clavijo, together with dignitaries from other countries, visited Samarkand and met Timur during various audiences and festivities. His observations are a valuable source on the new style of architecture. (Quotations are from: Clavijo, *Embassy to Tamerlane*, transl. Le Strange, 1928).

Clavijo devotes a long and detailed description to the city of Shahr-i Sabz, the mausoleum for Timur's ancestors and especially to the Aq-Sarai (White Palace), for which building began in 1379 and continued until Timur's death. Timur had been born near Shahr-i Sabz in 1336, and here, some fifty kilometres south of Samarkand on the other side of the Zeravshan mountains, lived his family and stood the graves of his forebears. As soon as he took over the reins of power he began to reshape the city which still bore its ancient name of Kish, into a residence with the programmatic name of Shahr-i Sabz, the Green City. The 'sight-seeing tour' of the city and palace elicited from the Spanish visitor exactly the response it was meant to evoke, and Clavijo was deeply impressed by the size, splendour and expense:

The next day which was Thursday the 28th of August at the hour of mid-day mass we found ourselves come near a great city which is known as Kesh. It stands in the plain, and on all sides the land is well irrigated by streams and water channels, while round and about the city there are orchards with many homesteads. … The city of Kesh is surrounded by an earthen rampart, having a very deep ditch crossed at the gates by draw-bridges. … There are throughout the city many fine houses and mosques, above all a magnificent mosque which Timur has ordered to be built but which as yet is not finished. In this mosque is seen the chapel in which his father's burial place has been made, and beside this is a second chapel now being built in which it is intended that Timur himself shall be interred when the time comes. They told us that when a month or so before the date of our arrival here Timur has entered Kesh he had been much dissatisfied with the appearance of this chapel, objecting that the doorway was too low and ordering that it should be raised; and it was on this alteration the builders were now at work. In this mosque too is seen the tomb of Prince Jahangir, the eldest son of Timur. The whole of this mosque with its chapels is very finely wrought in tiles that are of blue and gold, and you enter it through a great courtyard planted with trees round a water tank. Here daily by the special order of Timur the meat of twenty sheep is cooked and distributed in alms, this being done in memory of his father and of his son who lie here in those chapels.

On the following morning which was Friday they came and took us to see another great palace that was being built; and this palace they told us had been thus in hand building for the last twenty years, for though continually thus working day after day the builders were still at their work upon it. This palace of which we are now speaking had an entrance passage constructed to be of considerable length with a high portal before it, and in this entrance gallery to right and to left there were archways of brickwork encased and patterned with blue tiles. These archways lead each one into a small chamber that was open having no door, the flooring being laid in blue tiles. These little rooms are for those to wait in who are in attendance on Timur when he should come here. At the end of this gallery stands another gate-way, beyond which is a great courtyard paved with white flagstones and surrounded on the four sides by richly wrought arches, and in its centre is a very large water tank. This courtyard indeed may measure some three hundred paces in its width, and beyond it you enter through a very high and spacious gateway the main buildings of the palace. This gateway is throughout beautifully adorned with very fine work in gold and blue tiles, and over the entrance are seen the figures of the Lion and the Sun, these same figures being repeated over the summit of each of the arches round the courtyard, and this emblem of the Lion and the Sun was, they told us, the armorial bearing of the former lord of Samarqand. …

From this main portal of the courtyard just described you enter a great reception hall which is a room four square, where the walls are panelled with gold and blue tiles, and the ceiling is entirely of gold work. From this room we were taken up into the galleries, and in these likewise everywhere the walls were of gilt tiles. We saw indeed here so many apartments and separate chambers, all of which were adorned in tile work of blue and gold with many other colours, that it would take long to describe them here, and all was so marvellously wrought that even the craftsmen of Paris, who are so noted for their skill, would hold that which is done here to be of very fine workmanship. Next they showed us the various apartments where Timur was wont to be and to occupy when he came here with his wives; all of which were very sumptuously adorned as to floors and walls and ceilings. Many were the various grades of workmen still at work on building and adorning these palaces. We were shown in one that we visited a great banqueting hall which Timur was having built wherein to feast with the princesses, and this was gorgeously adorned, being very spacious, while beyond the same they were laying out a great orchard in which were planted many and divers fruit trees, with others to give shade. These stood round water tanks, beside which there were laid out fine lawns of turf. This orchard was of such extent that a very great company might conveniently assemble here, and in the summer heats enjoy the cool air beside that water in the shade of these trees. But such indeed was the richness and beauty of the adornments displayed in all these palaces that it would be impossible for us to describe the same adequately without much more leisure than we can here give to the matter. The mosque aforesaid and these palaces are a work that Timur has begun and is yet perfecting.

Today, almost nothing remains of the Aq-Sarai, and to retrace Clavijo's steps is impossible. Only one reminder – and a monumental one at that – of its former glory has survived, the *pishtaq* Clavijo mentions at the beginning of the quotation which is so deep it almost forms a hall, an architectural feature called an *iwan*.

But even the ruins are still impressive. The entrance was twenty-two metres wide, while its arch measured some forty to fifty metres in height. The *iwan* is flanked by two towers with a polygonal base and circular shaft. A spiral staircase inside the towers leads to rooms and corridors on several storeys, the door openings still visible from the back of the building. The structure was built of fired brick and completely covered with tile panels, mosaics of cut tiles and patterns produced by bricks glazed only on one side. To save on the elaborate and expensive mosaics which were placed at carefully chosen locations at eye-level and slightly above, the craftsmen produced tiles with polychrome decoration. Since

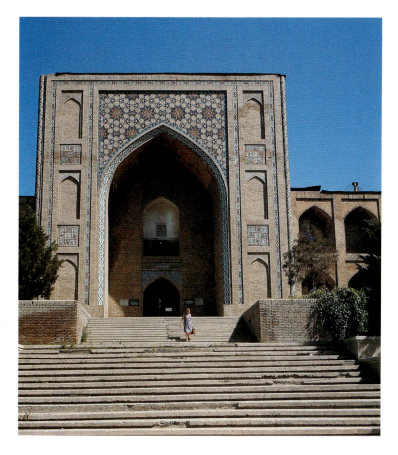

127
Detail of the façade of the Shir-dar madrasa at Samarkand (1619-35) showing tigers and a rising sun.

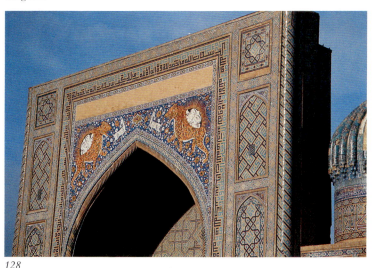

128
Koran lectern in the inner courtyard of the Bibi Khanum mosque, Samarkand.

coloured glazes because of their different compositions fire at different temperatures, polychrome designs tend to run. To avoid this effect, the potters used the *cuerda seca* technique, whereby the pigments are separated from each other by an oily substance mixed with manganese, which leaves a dark brown outline after firing.

The polychrome tiles and mosaic panels present the entire decorative repertoire of coloured tiles known at the time. Most of the bottom half of the portal is dominated by small-sized panels with floral patterns of leafy scrolls, flowers and rosettes. Between them appear calligraphic inscriptions in various scripts, suras from the Koran and pious phrases in long white or golden bands, medallions and cartouches. At a height of about twelve metres, where the minutely executed details are no longer visible to the naked eye, runs a border. Inside the *iwan* this is decorated with a delicate band of *thuluth* script, which includes the date of completion equivalent to 1396 A.D. On the towers the corresponding inscription in large old-fashioned kufic reads *as-sultan zill Allah*, "the sultan is the shadow of God". From the fact that the inscriptions on both towers are identical but of different length we can gather that they were produced freehand and not by stencilling. The towers and the (collapsed) vault of the *iwan* are covered by a slanting network of glazed brickwork. What at first sight appears to be a geometric pattern turns out to be another piece of calligraphy. This gives the name of the Prophet and of the so-called 'Rightly Guided' first four caliphs Abu Bakr, `Umar, `Uthman and `Ali – an indication of the patron's Sunni persuasion. Large-scale calligraphy produced by geometric patterns of carefully arranged brickwork had appeared some hundred years earlier and reached the height of its popularity in Timurid times.

The Aq-Sarai palace, built on a grandiose scale, was demolished only 150 years after its construction. A Shaibanid emir from Bukhara, jealous of the glamour and glory of the Timurids, ordered its demolition and re-used the bricks and tiles for his own buildings.

Southeast of the former palace grounds and close the the Great Mosque we find the building complex Clavijo identified as the mosque and mausoleum of the Timur family. Begun almost at the same time as the Aq-Sarai, it was still unfinished at the time of the Spanish ambassador's visit. The monumental, half-ruined brick structure of today represents only the northern wing of the planned Timurid mausoleum. The *Dar as-Siyadat* ('Palace of Power') complex included besides the Timurid tombs and Timur's own mausoleum a mosque, a dervish convent and a theological seminary, the buildings arranged around a big domed hall, the *ziyarat-khane*, for the devotions of visitors. The only surviving tomb, erected for Timur's son Jahangir, who died in 1376, can be found behind the massive southeastern pylon of the erstwhile entrance *pishtaq* and *iwan*. A cross-section of the mausoleum shows the complex tripartite construction of the dome. The actual tomb chamber above the crypt is enlarged by the cross-shaped addition of four niches, with ornate *muqarnas* (probably over a wooden support) at the transitional sections. Then the chamber expands to a height of 16.5 metres before the inward curvature of the cupola

starts at the squinches. But there is more to come. A cone-shaped second cupola rises above the smaller one and extends the height of the tomb to 27.5 metres. To minimise its weight, the second cupola has brick walls so thin that they had to be reinforced with internal bars. Although the shape of Jahangir's tomb is reminiscent of Iranian tower mausolea of earlier times, the ostentatious daring of the high cupola construction exemplies a characteristic streak in Timurid architecture.

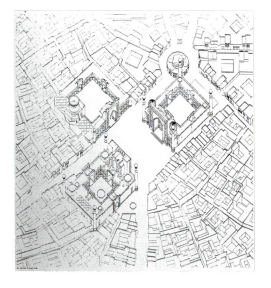

129
Plan of Registan Square, Samarkand. For identification, see ill. 109.

130
Gur-e Mir, Timur's mausoleum at Samarkand (1404).

133
Bibi Khanum mosque, plan.

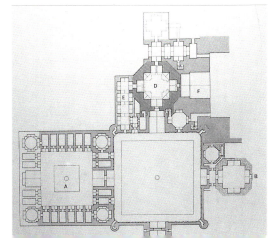

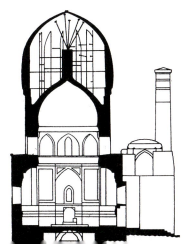

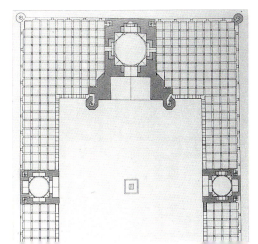

Like Shahr-i Sabz, Samarkand was also completely remodelled and its mediaeval layout obliterated. To handle the enormous trade the city was attracting because of its position between East and West and its function as the new capital, Timur had a large new bazaar built. A grand avenue was cut, running straight through the city from one end to the other. Behind the demolition teams came work gangs to erect standardised two-fronted shops inside the covered bazaar. Working day and night, building made rapid progress but had to be discontinued in winter 1404 before its final completion.

134
Tile mosaic, architectural fragment from the Mir-e `Arab madrasa, Bukhara. Glazed stone-paste with epigraphic band in thuluth *script.*
H: 60 cm, W: 48 cm
16th century
Museum of Fine Arts, Tashkent

135
Fragment of a tile. Glazed earthenware, carved design, kufic inscription on a scrolling background: "Sovereignty belongs to God"
L: 35 cm, W: 20 cm
Uzbekistan, second half 14th century
Museum für Islamische Kunst, Berlin

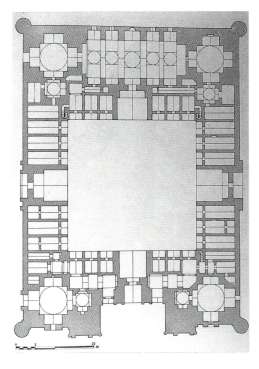

144
Ulugh Beg madrasa, plan.

At the centre of the new Samarkand Timur planned the city's main mosque, where the faithful assembled for Friday prayers and to hear the achievements of the ruler praised and God's blessing invoked. On the site of an earlier mosque the new building was erected partly from the spoils gathered during a campaign into India during Timur's late years. Extant inscriptions mention two dates, 1399 and 1404. In a rather unusual gesture, the mosque was dedicated to a woman, Timur's favourite wife Sarai Mulk ("Bibi") Khanum, a Mongolian princess. As was customary for all important buildings erected in the Islamic Middle Ages, an astrologer determined the most auspicious date for the laying of the foundation stone. In the *Zafarnama*, Sharaf ad-Din `Ali Yazdi gives a description of the building:

On the last Sunday of Ramadan 801 [1399 A.D.], at an auspicious hour and during the most benevolent constellation of the stars, skilled architects and experienced builders lay the foundation stone for this building. Five hundred stonemasons from Azerbaijan, Fars, Hindustan and elsewhere had been summoned to work on this mosque, not to mention the labourers who quarried the stones in the mountains and transported them to the city. Experts in diverse arts and in painting, each an outstanding member of his guild, were assembled at the residence from all corners of the earth. To convey the buildings materials to the site, ninety-five elephants had to be brought from India to Samarkand to roll the huge blocks along with the help of many people. Timur himself oversaw the work, assisted by his princes and emirs. While building was going on, Timur for a time stayed at the living-quarters of the near-by madrasa and those of the Tuman Aqa. The ceiling [of the mosque] rests on a timber structure supported on 480 columns of dressed stone. Each column is seven gaz [5.4m] high. The magnificent floor is covered with cut and polished marble slabs; the height from the floor to the ceiling is about ten gaz [7.2m]. The dome would rank supreme were it not

the Milky Way. Connected to the colourful façades, four minarets tower at the corners, their tops reaching for the sky. The Sufis send their call [for prayer] in the four directions. The sound of the great metal doors made from an alloy of seven metals, calls the faithful from all climes to the House of Islam. The walls of the dome's chamber are covered with calligraphy carved in stone. The pulpit is conspicuous for its particularly fine embellishments, and the prayer niche for its construction.

As with his other building projects, Timur interfered whenever he thought his architects failed to produce the required monumentality. This could have serious consequences for those in charge, as Sharaf notes: *When His Highness visited the Great Mosque which he had built, it was His Majesty's opinion that the portal erected during his absence was too low. He ordered its destruction and the building of a new one both bigger and higher. On account of the mistakes made in connection with the building of the portal, Khwaja Mahmud Dawud was retained for investigation.* Weakened by various illnesses and presumably fearing that he would not live to see Samarkand transformed into the capital of the world, Timur drove everyone to exhaustion. Clavijo gives an eye-witness account:

The Mosque which Timur had caused to be built in memory of the mother of the wife the Great Khanum seemed to us the noblest of all those we visited in the city of Samarqand, but no sooner had it been completed that he began to find fault with its entrance gateway, which he now said was much too low and must forthwith be pulled down. Then the workmen began to dig pits to lay the new foundation, when in order that the piers might be rapidly rebuilt his Highness gave out that he himself would take charge to direct the labour of the one pier of the new gateway while he laid it on two of the lords of his court, his special favourites, to see to the foundations on the other part. Thus all should see whether it was he or those other two lords who first might bring this business to its proper conclusion. Now at this season Timur was already weak in health, he could no longer stand for long on his feet, or mount his horse, having always to be carried in a litter. It was therefore in his litter that every morning he had himself brought to the place, and he would stay there the best part of the day urging on the work. He would arrange for much meat to be cooked and brought, and then he would order them to throw portions of the same down to the workmen in the foundations, as though one should cast bones to dogs in a pit, and a wonder to all he even with his own hands did this. Thus he urged on their labour: and at times would have coins thrown to the masons when especially they worked to his satisfaction. Thus the building went on day and night until at last a time came when it had perforce to stop - as was also the case in the matter of making the street - on account of the winter snows which began now constantly to fall.

The ruins of today still mark the original extend of this gigantic building, although only the parts constructed with brick remain, those of stone having disappeared. Of the columns, the marble wall panels and the tiled floors almost nothing survives save for a huge marble Koran-holder in the middle of the courtyard donated by Timur's grandson Ulugh Beg.

Theoretically the remaining structures could also be

towers - or in this case, minarets - with its deep *iwan* recalls
the portal of the Aq-Sarai in Shar-e Sabz. On the same axis
at the end of the seventy-six-metre long courtyard rises a
second large *iwan* between two minarets on an octagonal
basis. Behind it and invisible from the courtyard rose the
typical Timurid double-shell cupola on the high drum
Sharaf mentions. Decorated with a stepped *muqarnas* frieze,
the cupola seemed to bulge at the base before tapering. This
daring construction of the thin outer shell was only possible
by inserting supporting ribs which transferred the weight
and pressure on to the drum. The drum was embellished
with quotations from the Koran and repeats of the phrase
"Constancy rests solely in God!" made of tiles and glazed
bricks, while the ceiling showed floral paintings and traces of
arabesques made of gilded cardboard still in place early this
century. The decoration of the niche panels of the flanking
towers was of tiles and polychrome cut stone arranged like
tile mosaics.

145
Front hall of a mosque. Bukhara, about 1900.

146
Bukhara. Plan of the Old Town.

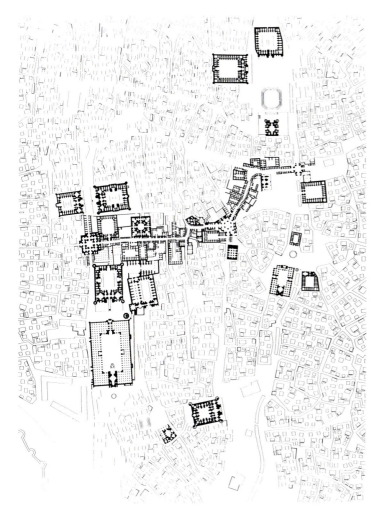

147
Bukhara. Map of the old city centre with the Kalan mosque.

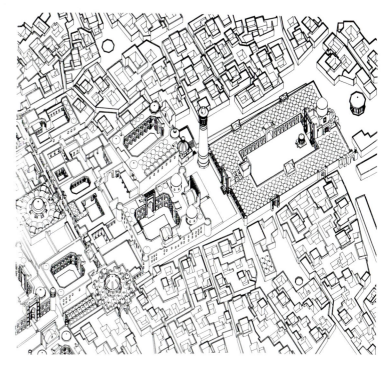

In the middle of each long wall was a small *iwan* with a domed hall, miniature versions of the great domed *iwan* giving the direction of prayer (*qibla*).

The mosque itself represented a type of architecture with pre-Islamic roots which had been formalised during the tenth to eleventh century in Iran and did duty for a great variety of Islamic representative building types. By Timurid times it had reached full maturity. While the typical Arabic mosque consisted of a courtyard-cum-prayer hall, the Iranian version of the so-called four-*iwan*-pattern was characterised by a covered hall placed in the middle of each wall and opening on to the courtyard. The roofed buildings between the *iwans* housed prayer rooms. This scheme turned the courtyard into the actual centre of the compound and removed the visual guideline of the layout, since all four sides looked basically similar. The Timurid solution was to provide the two main *iwans* with elongated façades like those of the Bibi Khanum mosque. This emphasised the axial orientation and broke the monotony of the courtyard area.

Like many of Timur's projects, the mosque probably was never completed, partly because of shoddiness during execution. Only a few years after Timur's death, falling brickwork became a hazard for the congregated faithful. It is also typical of this architecture designed as symbols of power that as far as one can tell from the surviving structures, the decoration of the exterior surfaces was almost finished while the interior was still under construction.

The most frequently visited building in Samarkand dating from Timur's time is the Gur-e Mir mausoleum. The popular misconception that this is the tomb he had built for himself is correct at least insofar as that Timur is buried here and not in the family mausoleum at Shahr-i Sabz, as he had wished. According to Sharaf's *Zafarnama*, Timur commissioned the building for his nephew and successor Sultan Muhammad when the latter returned to Samarkand in 1404 after spending six years away on military campaigns.

Only rarely did the ruler live in his palaces; usually he stayed at one of several gardens in the capital where tents and pavillons had been put up. Sharaf tells us:

His exalted Majesty moved to the Shemal Garden for several days ... There all the agas and noyans [headmen] assembled for the celebration of a royal wedding. Later the Buland Garden became a paradise with the arrival of the Radiant [i.e. Timur]. From this refreshing spot, where the body was strengthened by rays of vitality, he went to Samarkand and honoured the palace of the late prince Muhammad by making it his royal quarters. The order was given to erect a dome next to the said prince's madrasa to serve as the exalted burial place. Thus in the forecourt of the convent adjacent to the south portal a dome was built similar [in height] to the sky, its walls decorated with marble patterned with gold and lapis lazuli. A crypt for the burial of the deceased was built [below]; several chambers in the vicinity were pulled down so that a small paradise-like garden could be laid out.

According to the *Zafarnama*, the Gur-e Mir, the Aq-Sarai palace and the Great Mosque at Samarkand were all built at the same time. Their exterior decoration is indeed closely related. But first we shall turn to its architectural features. The mausoleum was erected at the southern end of an existing building. Shortly before, a madrasa had been built on the eastern side and a Sufi convent on the western side of a square courtyard. This courtyard was entered by a portal on the northern side decorated with some of the most splendid tile mosaics of the Timurid period. It was built in 1434 during the reign of Ulugh Beg and was the work of the master-builder or tile specialist Muhammad ibn Mahmud al-Isfahani, a native of western Iran. The portal also marks the abandonment of Timur's megalomanic projects by his successors. The mausoleum became the visual focus of the whole compound, being placed midway between the school and the convent. It is remarkable that entry was not along the liturgical axis but gained by way of a covered passage from the east. This passage-way in the east and a fronted building in the west obscure the fact that the building was originally conceived as an octagonal, while the interior was dominated by the four niches of the cruciform *ziyarat-khane*, the 'visitation' hall with the cenotaph placed above the underground crypt.

More than half of the building's total height of thirty-seven metres is taken up by the drum and dome. While in pre-Timurid times the usual canonic proportion of base to superstructure was 2:1, here the ratio between the three elements of base, drum and cupola is 1:1:1. This development can not solely be explained by Timur's ambition for ever larger and higher buildings. Already by the mid-fourteenth century domed monuments of stone with approximately similar proportions had appeared in Mamluk Cairo and occasionally in the Syrian area. It is highly likely that this Near Eastern concept reached Samarkand together with Syrian artisans. The dome of the Gur-e Mir is a masterwork. It is again constructed from two shells. The transition from the square plan to the pointed cupola is as usual effected by squinches and niches. Their prime function as structural elements is completely hidden by a decoration of *muqarnas* of very small niches (probably of wood or papier-mâché under a stucco layer). This interior cupola is of the same height as the drum. But the most spectacular achievement is the outer dome. It represents a further development of the *mihrab* dome of the Bibi Khanum mosque which because of the *muqarnas* frieze started with a slight bulge, continued vertically and then tapered to end in an obtuse angle. The Gur-e Mir dome also rests on a *muqarnas* frieze but then continues to form a pointed ogee arch, an effect further emphasised by the thick ribs of the roofing. A cross-section of the dome shows the complicated system of brick ribs and a fan-like arrangement of radiating beams that was necessary to stabilise the fragile outer dome which lacks its own support. How far this building prefigured the later tradition of 'melon domes' prevalent in Central Asia and Mughal India, is difficult to say, and we are equally in the dark about its prototypes, although smaller ribbed domes were built in Egypt and North Africa during the ninth to eleventh centuries and for a short while again in the early fourteenth century. Unlike most other domes, that of the Gur-e Mir was kept in good condition through the centuries because of the prominence of its situation, and it is therefore not inconceivable that it provided a major inspiration for other domed buildings.

148
Khiva. Hall of columns of the Friday mosque (at present a museum). The columns date from the 12th to 19th century.

The decorative scheme of the polychrome tilework is also traditional, but here it is very effectively used to provide an eye-catching appeal even from a distance. Grand cruciform and diamond-shaped designs along the ribs of the dome, contrasting friezes and bands and pious phrases of "Constancy is solely with God" and "Praised be God" in large decorative letters produce various visual stimuli, which are all the more striking because of their basic simplicity.

Funerary monuments form an important part of the legacy of Timurid architecture, because they ideally combine piety and great commemorative buildings. At the same time they were an expression of the power and godliness of the ruling house and its entourage. On this point, Clavijo provides a lively description:

On the Thursday week, which was the 30th of October, Timur betook himself from his camp in the Horde back to the city of Samarqand, taking up his residence in a certain place adjacent to the Mosque which he had lately ordered to be built. This Mosque was the place of burial of one of his grandsons. … Timur had loved this grandson greatly and in his remembrance had caused this Mosque to be built at his place of burial. To the palace adjacent thereto and but recently constructed Timur came that day, it being his intention to celebrate the consecration of his grandson's tomb by a feast, to which we as usual had been graciously invited. Then as we presented ourselves we were shown over that chapel, which was the place of interment of the Prince, and we found it square in plan and very loftily built. Both outside and in it was magnificently adorned in gold and blue tiles beautifully patterend, and there was much other fine work in gypsum.

Now when this Prince had died in the Turkish country, as above explained his body had been transported home to Samarqand for burial, and the city authorities had received command to erect this Mosque for his tomb. But recently Timur had come in from the Horde to view the building and he found that the chapel was not to his liking, holding that it was built too low. Immediately he ordered the walls to be demolished, and laid it on the architects that it should be rebuilt within ten days' time, under threat of a terrible forfeit to the workmen. Without delay the rebuilding was set in hand, day and night the work went on, and Timur himself already twice had come into the city to see what progress had been made, on which occasions he had caused himself to be carried in a litter, for at his age he could no longer sit on his horse. The chapel had now been completely rebuilt within the appointed ten days' time, and it was a wonder how so great a building could have been put up and completed within so brief a space.

Funerary monuments are especially valuable for charting the development of architectural concepts and in particular of decorative elements. For such an exercise, Samarkand is ideally suited. The Shah-e Zinda necropolis was probably first laid out in the ninth to tenth century around the tomb of the hero Qutham ibn al-`Abbas, said to have met his death during the Islamic conquest of Afrasiab. During the late thirteenth century most of the mausolea erected in the meantime were demolished and the area later remodelled to form a funerary road with tombs basically restricted to members of the Timurid dynasty and the highest officials. The remaining sixteen tombs can serve as a cross-section to illustrate the artistic development and experiments with various decorative techniques from the mid-fourteenth to the mid-fifteenth century. Particularly interesting are the cut and glazed tiles, star and flower medallions and inscriptions which, in combining polychrome with plastic features, are even more captivating than the flat painted tiles. The colouration consists mainly of various shades of blue and green, yellow, brown and red. As on some particularly precious panels at the Aq-Sarai in Shahr-i Sabz, here again we find gold painting in conjunction with inscriptions. All the mausolea are rather small buildings with this opulent decoration furthermore restricted almost exclusively to façades and the interior, so that the relation of costs and benefits was presumably relatively moderate. This consideration may help to explain why at the Aq-Sarai and Gur-e Mir relief tiles are rare or non-existent.

The madrasa of Ulugh Beg

After Timur's death his son Shah Rukh became ruler of Khorasan (northeastern Iran and western Afghanistan) and western Persia. In 1409 he made his son Ulugh Beg regent of Transoxiana with Samarkand as its capital. Ulugh Beg was not a builder of palaces and tomb monuments, but at least he finished and furnished some of the buildings Timur had begun. Himself an astronomer of repute, he had an observatory built for his own use near Samarkand in about 1420. He was also a patron of the sciences and built a madrasa and a Sufi convent on the Registan in the city centre. Ulugh Beg's madrasa, a centre for Koranic studies and Islamic law, is the earliest surviving example of a building type of similar form and function that was being built in Uzbekistan well into the eighteenth century. Its derivation from early Timurid architecture is obvious on account of its Iranian four-iwan layout and spectacular high portal with the resulting axial directedness and structural harmony. The high rectangular pishtaq frames a deep iwan-like ogee-shaped niche. As at the Aq-Sarai and Bibi Khanum mosque, the portal is flanked by minarets. The decoration uses various techniques designed to make the building look attractive from every distance: Big geometric patterns filled with calligraphic elements for the front and reveals of the portal, a delicate design of interlacing stars for the panel above the pishtaq opening made of tile mosaics and relief bricks, and very fine tile mosaics of cut and moulded ceramic tiles and

marble and alabaster panels near the actual entrance. The courtyard has a large iwan on each side. At the end of the axial aisle lies the madrasa. Except at this western end, originally there were doors on all sides leading to the rooms of the approximately one hundred students and their teachers living at the madrasa. The cruciform corner rooms probably housed lecture rooms, kitchens and the library.

Architecture in Uzbekistan under the Shaibanids and Toqay-Timurids

Building activity in the region remained lively under the Shaibanids, who in 1500 wrested control of Transoxiana from the last Timurid ruler and remained in power until 1598, and under their successors during the seventeenth and eighteenth centuries, the Toqay-Timurids. The Shaibanids made Bukhara their capital and graced it with representative buildings. During the sixteenth century a new bazaar was built, which only partly followed the traditional pattern of covered passages with shops on both sides, the main commercial thoroughfare having additional huge square or rectangular domed buildings housing up to sixty shops and workshops. At the same time the buildings - called taq (arch) or tim (shopping hall) - served as terminals for several streets, so that potential customers in large numbers passed through them. As was traditional, each building was occupied by a single trade or guild. Today the only indication of their original purpose are the old names, Taq-e Zargaran (goldsmiths' bazaar) and Taq-e Sarrafan (money-changers' bazaar).

Among the most important complexes in Bukhara remaining of this period are the Kalan mosque of 1514 and the madrasa Mir-e `Arab of 1535/6 opposite. The Kalan mosque is the successor of Bukhara's Friday mosque built by the Kharakhanids in the early twelfth century. The old minaret with its typical twelfth-century shaped tiles was left untouched by the Shaibanids. They also retained the Iranian ground-plan with its four iwans. The Kalan mosque was obviously modelled on the Bibi Khanum mosque in Samarkand. By making the two iwans at the entrance and the prayer-hall both wider and higher, the building axis pointing in the direction of prayer is clearly emphasised. The proportions and dimensions of the courtyard measuring seventy-seven by forty metres strengthen the visual impact of the dominating pishtaq in front of the prayer-hall. The side iwans, bereft of any liturgical function, are insignificant. All the halls surrounding the courtyard were originally domed - another feature recalling the Bibi Khanum mosque, which was still in use when the Kalan mosque was built. Here the transition zone is constructed in a way that evolved during the Timurid era and soon spread widely. The bridge between square base and circular dome is provided not by hemispherical squinches but by pendentives (spherical triangles). True to Timurid precepts, the cupola behind the prayer-hall's iwan rests on an extra-high drum and completes the tensile arch spanning the entrance and the hall.

Opposite the Kalan mosque lies the Mir-e `Arab madrasa, a memorial to the Iranian mystic Sayyid Mir

`Abdullah as-Sairami, who was active in Bukhara in the early sixteenth century. His tomb is situated in the *gur-khane* (burial house) beneath the northern turquoise cupola flanking the portal, its counterpart covering the *dars-khane* (lecture hall) of the madrasa. The custom of placing the tomb of the patron or namesake of a madrasa inside a domed chamber near the entrance is a Central Asian tradition of long standing, with archaeological evidence in Samarkand dating from the early eleventh century and later. A new feature of the whole complex is the erection of a second building as a mirror-image of the first, so that two *pishtaqs* confront each other. This conceit became very popular and of course was realised in Bukhara and Samarkand as well. At Samarkand the initiative was supplied by Ulugh Beg's madrasa of the second decade of the fifteenth century, from which developed the present-day lay-out of Registan Square. Between 1619 and 1636 the military governor Yalangtash built the Shir-dar madrasa opposite Ulugh Beg's madrasa for the imam Quli Khan, a member of the Astrakhanid dynasty. The architect, `Abd al-Jabbar, adopted the proportions and dimensions of his model built two hundred years earlier, but embellished the new madrasa even more profusely and produced even more dazzling architectural effects. Its present name 'Shir-dar' derives from a representation of two hunting tigers under a rising sun. The façade is very similar to its model down to small details, but the designs of glazed brick are even more dense and colourful, with orange, purple, lemon yellow and a violent green being added to the traditional palette.

Between the *pishtaq* and the corner minarets we again find two domes. High drums with calligraphic inscriptions of the Prophet's words support ribbed 'melon domes' terminating at an acute angle. Presumably out of the desire to obtain visual symmetry with the Timurid building opposite, the double row of arcades seen inside the mosque are not repeated on the exterior. Because the Shir-dar madrasa was conceived as a mirror-image of the Ulugh Beg madrasa, its mosque had to be placed at the front and not at the back, where it usually appears to indicate the direction of prayer (which in most Central Asian mosques is slightly out of true west).

Ten years after the completion of the Shir-dar madrasa, the Registan was completed by the addition of a third building, the Tela-kari mosque ('decorated with gold') to replace the Bibi Khanum mosque which by then had deteriorated so much as to be unusable. It was designed like a madrasa so as to harmonise with the two earlier buildings. The axial arrangement of the two main *iwans* was discarded and the south wing of the mosque supplied with a typical madrasa portal. The two rows of arcades along the front simulate students' rooms. On entering the courtyard, visitors had to turn left (west) to reach the prayer hall, which followed the familiar pattern by having a large cupola above the *mihrab* and smaller domes above the hall. Its interior and the ceiling of the cupola justify its name: Walls and arches are covered with a profusion of floral designs against a blue and white background, with leaf gold applied over wood and presumably also over cardboard.

Itshan-Qala at Khiva: A museum city of the nineteenth century

The Old Town at Khiva in northeast Uzbekistan is a superb illustration of the continuity in the region of architectural and artisanal traditions from the High Middle Ages right down to very recent times.

Although Khiva is mentioned by Persian and Arab geographers as early as the tenth to eleventh century, very few archaeological remains of this and later periods have come to light. The city is famous because of Itshan-Qala, the old quarter in the city centre which has been declared an open-air museum. It houses a complete ensemble of all kinds and types of buildings mainly from the eighteenth and nineteenth centuries, erected by the khans of Khiva which ceased to be part of a 'Khorezm emirate' in the seventeenth century and remained independent until the territory was occupied by Russian troops.

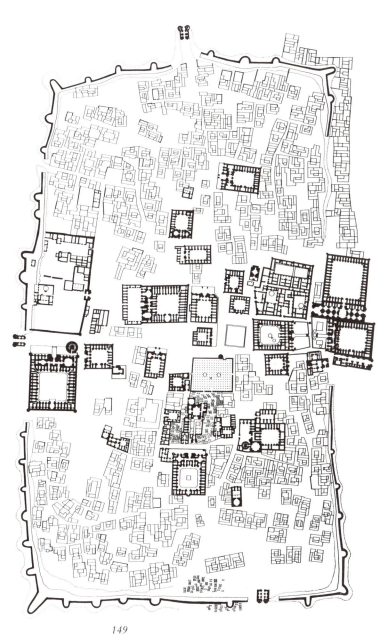

149
Khiva. Plan of the walled Old Town.

97

150-152
Khiva. Itschan-Qal`a: Inner courtyard and harem complex. The wall-tiles date from the 19th century.
The designs incorporate elements from different artistic traditions, for instance from East Asia (ill. 151) or from classic Islamic concepts with their severely geometrical interlacing star patterns (ill. 152).

153
Tile from the Ibadullah Chura complex (1918). Stone-paste painted in cobalt-blue under a transparent glaze. Although of relatively recent date, the spiral scrollwork clearly follows classic Timurid models.

154
Khiva. The Old Town.

155
Khiva. The unfinished mid-19th century Kalta Minar ('short tower') minaret was Muhammad Amin Khan's abortive attempt to build the highest minaret in the area.

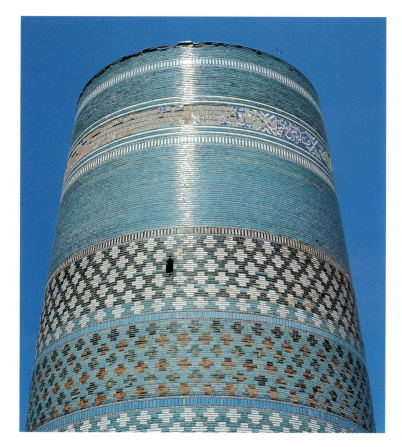

Today the visitor approaches the city on a road across numerous small canals fed by one of the branches of the Amu Darya. Driving past cotton fields, one eventually enters a green belt of gardens and small groves mentioned already by explorers in the last century. In his *A Ride to Khiva*, Captain Fred Burnaby of the Royal Horse Guards described his arrival:

We were now fast nearing Khiva, which could be just discerned in the distance, but was hidden, to a certain extent, from our view by a narrow belt of tall, graceful trees; however, some richly-painted minarets and high domes of coloured tiles could be seen towering above the leafy groves. Orchards, surrounded by walls eight and ten feet high, continually met the gaze, and avenues of mulberry-trees studded the landscape in all directions.

The town itself is surrounded by a second wall, not quite so high as the one just described, and with a dry ditch, which is now half filled with ruined débris. The slope which leads from the wall to the trench had been used as a cemetery, and hundreds of sepulchres and tombs were scattered along some undulating ground just without the city. The space between the first and seconds walls is used as a market-place, where cattle, horses, sheep, and camels are sold, and where a number of carts were standing, filled with corn and grass. Here an ominous-looking cross-beam had been erected, towering high above the heads of the people with its bare, gaunt poles. This was the gallows on which all people convicted of theft are executed.

...

It is difficult to estimate the population of an Oriental city by simply riding round its walls; so many houses are uninhabited, and others again are densely packed with inhabitants. However, I should say, as a mere guess, that there are about 25,000 human beings within the walls of Khiva. The streets are broad and clean, while the houses belonging to the richer inhabitants are built of highly polished bricks and coloured tiles, which lend a cheerful aspect to the otherwise somewhat sombre colour of the surroundings. There are nine schools: the largest, which contains 130 pupils, was built by the father of the present khan. These buildings are all constructed with high, coloured domes, and are ornamented with frescoes and arabesque work, the bright aspect of the cupolas first attracting the stranger's attention on his nearing the city.

Little has changed in the meantime except for heavy building around the old town centre. A look at the map shows that even in the nineteenth century Khiva possessed all the features of a traditional Central Asian city. Four gates guarded the two main intersecting thoroughfares. A domed building at the intersection, today serving as a market hall, is still called a *tcharsu* ('four directions'); such monuments marking the very centre of a city were also found at Samarkand and Bukhara. In addition there were the major religious, administrative and trading institutions, namely the most important mosque, the saints' tombs attached to the school buildings, the palace of the khan and market halls and caravanserais.

In the west, the rectangular fortifications were dominated by an elevated citadel, the seventeenth-century Kunya Ark ('old castle') with the residence of the khan, the garrison and mint. The central position is taken up by the audience hall, built during the first years of the nineteenth century in the shape of a two-pillared *iwan* opening on the courtyard. As in the Khiva mosque of the tenth/eleventh century mentioned earlier, the wooden pillars are richly carved and rest on stone supports, in this case of marble. The broad capitals terminating in a stylised decoration reminiscent of animal protomes continue local as well as Iranian traditions, which go back as far as the Achaemenid period. The tile panelling of the walls, on the other hand, derives from Timurid examples. The tiles made at Khiva in the mid-nineteenth century show a characteristic dense design of floral and geometric motifs. The decoration of the hall beyond the *iwan* resembles that found in the same location in Timurid and Shaibanid buildings and shows polychrome patterns carved from stucco, with golden designs especially prominent.

Opposite the citadel lies the earliest of the more than twenty madrasas surviving in Khiva. Founded by Muhammad Amin Khan in 1851, it is the largest (78m by 60m) and most richly endowed college for Islamic studies in Khiva. It fits in perfectly with the tradition of rectangular four-*iwan* compounds with a high *pishtaq* erected in Samarkand and Bukhara since the fifteenth century. Following a fashion of the seventeenth century, both the outer and inner façades have two-storeyed arcaded passages. In front of the portal we find the twenty-six-metre high stump of the Kalta-Minar, the remains of the abortive project of the khan to build to highest minaret of the region.

Broad bands of polychrome glazed bricks with cross and lozenge designs vaguely recall the friezes of bricks laid in concentric patterns of Bukhara's Kalan minaret made six hundred years earlier. A more direct inspiration presumably was the minaret of the Friday mosque of the late eighteenth century.

To the east of the mosque we find a number of buildings of various kinds from the time of `Ala' Quli Khan (1810-1838). Beyond the old city wall stands a huge caravansarai-cum-market begun in 1832. The market consisted of a double row of domed halls, which also served as a gateway through the remodelled city wall. To the south of this complex we find another religious building, a madrasa erected again by `Ala' Quli Khan. For this project, large parts of the Hodja Bardshiya mosque of 1688 were demolished, with its foundations used as the base for the new building. Although mosques and caravansarais served completely different functions, a glance at the plans of the two adjacent examples here in Khiva shows that they followed the same principles and differed only in details. This multi-functional aspect of Iranian architecture is typified by a rectangular ground-plan with towers at the four corners, a portal formed by a *pishtaq* and arcades with *iwans* serving as entrances leading to the rooms occupied by students or travellers. To the south of the madrasa was another combined gateway-cum-market structure, the Palwan-Darwaze (1832-5), its two towers controlling access to the city. Behind the two watch-towers was a single row of six domed halls with shops and a small public bath.

Khiva thus preserves much of its traditional features and affords the visitor with an illuminating insight into the structure of a Central Asian oasis town.

The Arts of the Book in Central Asia

Karin Rührdanz

As in other parts of the Islamic culture area, appreciation of books manifested itself in Central Asia through their artistic embellishments. At first the main interest had been in Koran manuscripts, but the arts of the book found their finest expression after the fourteenth century, when they were most importantly applied to the beautification of classical Persian poetry. From the stamped and gilded decoration of the cover, the carefully pressed paper, sometimes coloured or sprinkled with gold dust, the elegant calligraphy of the writing and the diverse ornaments in bright colours of the illumination to the illustrative miniatures, the outward appearance of the book was made to match the elaborate language of the text.

(Since it proved impossible to obtain a sufficient number of illustrations of Central Asian examples, we have included specimens from Timurid and Safawid art. – The editors.)

156
Miniature depicting simurghs.
H: 28 cm, W 28.5 cm
West Turkestan, 15th century
Museum für Kunsthandwerk, Leipzig

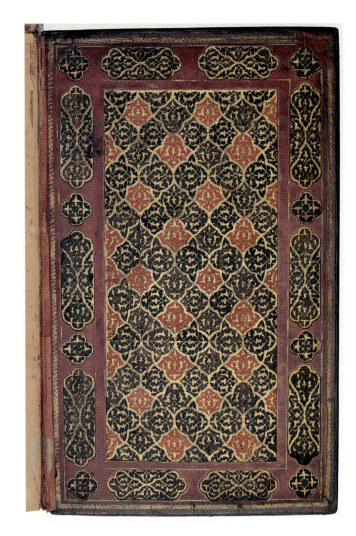

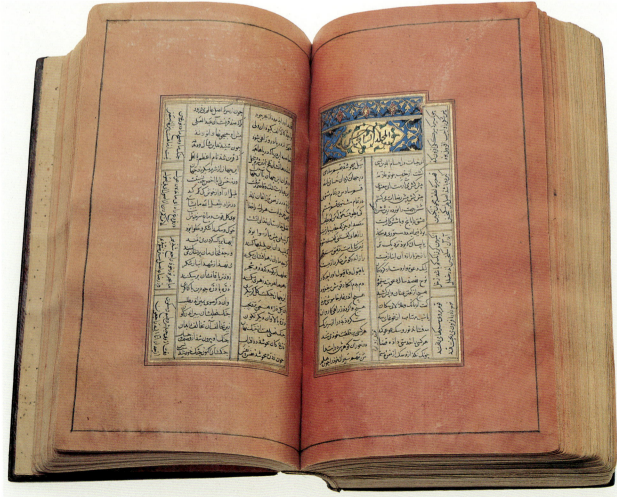

157-159

157-159
Carefully made copy of Jalal ad-Din Rumi's didactic poem Mathnawi-yi ma`nawi *with gold-stamped covers; the book is opened at the beginning of a chapter. The ornamental decoration on the inside cover is similar to that on Timurid carpets only known from miniatures. The calligrapher is named as Hasan ibn Ahmad al-Katib al-Ardistani.*
Iran, dated A.H. 866 (A.D. 1461)
H: 24.3 cm, W: 15 cm

160
Double page from a Timurid anthology of Koran suras. The designs in the margins were produced with stencils and shows flowering branches and bushes, cypresses, birds and antilopes.
H: 25 cm, W: 32 cm (open)
Central Asia, 14th/16th century

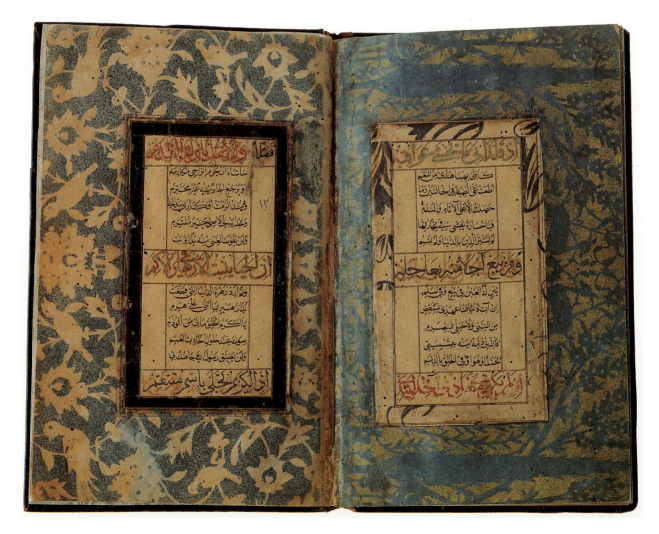

After the destruction caused by the Mongol invasion, the arts of the book in Transoxiana needed a considerable time to evolve. The nomadic background of the rulers of the thirteenth and fourteenth centuries did little for their appreciation either of the intricate multi-level style of Persian poetry or of books in general, and since urban life was slow to flower again, so was its influence on courtly culture. While in Iran book illustration developed as the most recent branch of the arts of the book and a new style of writing, the elegant cursive nastaliq, came into fashion, Transoxiana was only marginally influenced by these developments through the calligraphers, illuminators and painters Timur is said to have brought back from his campaigns. He was mainly interested, however, in arts which lent themselves to grandiose displays of power, and books did not benefit from this vision. His grandson Ulugh Beg, who ruled Timurid Central Asia from 1411 to 1449, was a more likely candidate to patronise an art which was based on a familiarity with classical Persian poetry and a fine sense for narrative details. But he also seems to have shown no interest in establishing a studio at Samarkand, whereas both his brothers possessed famous palace workshops at Herat and Shiraz. After the assassination of Ulugh Beg in 1449, the climate in Samarkand became even less favourable to the arts of the book.

Talented writers and artists flocked to Herat instead, where a splendid flowering of urban and courtly culture set in during the 1470s. The spiritual climate, defined by the philosophical, religious and poetical ideas of `Abd ar-Rahman Jami (1414-93) and Mir `Ali Shir Nawa'i (1440-1501), fostered an intellectualised Sufism which favoured philosophical knowledge instead of ritual and an active life in society instead of monastic contemplation, and regarded a thorough familiarity with the various arts as part of a person's quest for perfection. Since this time a growing number of the calligraphers known to us are members of highly respected families.

162
'Iskandar lifts the Khaqan of Chin from his saddle'. Miniature for Amir Khusrau Dihlawi's Khamsa.
c. 1670
Metropolitan Museum of Art, New York, Gift of Alexander Smith Cochran, 1913, 13.228.24, fol. 206b

161
Inkwell. Steatite, polished, cut and engraved.
The vessel in the shape of an eight-petalled flower has stylised plant designs on the outside and ribbed legs.
H: 5 cm
Samarkand, 10th century
Registan Museum, Samarkand

163
'King Jamshid writes his message on a rock'. Miniature for Sa'di's Bustan.
1616
Chester Beatty Library, Dublin, pers. 297, fol. 22a (with kind permission of the Trustees)

164
'Bizhan slays a Turan enemy'. Miniature for Firdausi's Shahnama.
First quarter 17th century
University Libraries, Princeton, Department of Rare Books and Special Collections, 59 G, fol. 1147b

Under the artists working within this favourable situation – foremost among them the painter Bihzad (d. 1535/6) – illustration achieved a standing equal to that of the text itself, as we can see from the choice of unusual subjects for illustrating popular texts and the new ideas and inventions for the visual interpretation of well-known themes. Whether the miniatures accompany the romantic poems of Nizami (1140-1202), Amir Khusrau Dihlawi (1253-1324/5) or `Ali Shir Nawa'i or the didactic and moralistic *Bustan* and *Gulistan* of Sa`di (c. 1189-1291), they tend to depict instances of decision-making, of moral trials, of intellectual and emotional and physical exertion, although the last only seldom and even then usually as a metaphor.

Herat's glory came to an end with the Shaibanid conquest in 1507, followed by that of the Safawids three years later and the subsequent decades of the struggle for Khorasan. Yet the brilliance of the era dazzled rulers from Istanbul to Bukhara who aspired to claim its inheritance. Among other things this meant enticing scholars, poets, artisans and artists from Herat to join their courts. Some followed the call with a view of a well-endowed position and favourable treatment, while others were forced to leave Herat in the train of the retreating Shaibanid army.

In Bukhara the patron of Timurid scholars and artists was Muhammad Shaibani's nephew `Ubaidallah, who ruled in Bukhara from 1512 to 1540 and in 1533 became the overlord of Transoxiana. His patronage was partly motivated by a desire to strenghten his claim to Khorasan, which he attempted to enforce during several campaigns. He captured Herat more than once, on one of these conquests (in 1528/9) taking the famous calligrapher Mir `Ali al-Husaini (al-Herawi) back with him. Yet in none of the manuscripts Mir `Ali then copied at Bukhara does the name of Khan `Ubaidallah appear. It seems that already in the 1530s he was working for the khan's son `Abd al-`Aziz (1540-50).

What for the father had been little more than a political expedient, for the son was a matter of genuine interest. Even before he succeeded his father in 1540, `Abd al-`Aziz had begun to set up a studio in Bukhara on the Herat model. In painting, continuity was guaranteed by artists like Shaikhzada who had worked in Herat as late as the 1520s. But this continuity was limited mainly to technical aspects. While Shaikhzada's work shows the tranquil harmony in composition, the elegant line, clear colour contrasts and fine detail characteristic of the Bihzad school, he has very little of its originality in the choice and execution of his subjects. He was followed by such painters like Mahmud Mudhahhib, `Abdullah and Shaikhum (or Shakhim), who were active in `Abd al-`Aziz's workshop under the supervision of Sultan Mirak *kitabdar* (head of the royal scriptorium). They enriched the spectrum of pictorial representations by the use of double spreads, which occasionally served original conceits like depicting a relation between cause and effect, but more commonly simply enhanced the decorative appeal.[1]

`Abd al-`Aziz's successors continued to keep the Bukhara workshop busy with commissions. Although competent in terms of technique, the illustrations are mainly repeats of Bihzadian compositions, simplified and adapted to

105

165
'Boat-trip on the Amu Darya'. Miniature.
H: 24.8 cm, W: 14.4 cm
Central Asia, 'Turkmen school', 15th/16th century

166
'Rustam's birth in the garden'. Miniature from a Shahnama.
H: 30.9 cm, W 20.3 cm
Central Asia, 'Turkmen school', 15th century

167
'Prince in a garden'. Miniature from a poetry album.
H: 19.7 cm, W: 12.6 cm
Central Asia, 'Turkmen school', 14th/15th century

168
'Four angels paying homage to the prophet Adam'. Miniature from a Persian work.
Central Asia, 'Turkmen school', 15th century

169
Page from a Sharafnama by Nizami. Gold-painted title, the border with half and quarter medallions in gold.
H: 21.2 cm, W 11.7 cm
Iran or Central Asia, 15th/16th century

170
'King Solomon as lord of the animals'. Miniature.
H: 25.9 cm, W: 15.7 cm
Iran, 16th century

new subjects. From the 1560s the narrative function of the miniatures was increasingly disregarded, making way for representations of single pictures. The illustrated manuscript had turned into an item with self-contained drawings.

On the other hand, numerous manuscripts produced in Bukhara and Samarkand during the second half of the sixteenth century document the proliferation of fine calligraphy. They give the names of many calligraphers, who are mentioned nowhere else, and indicate a flourishing urban profession working for a free market. The manuscripts often include illuminations of good quality. At the same time a type of decoration for the page borders evolved which became a characteristic of Central Asian manuscripts: Small cut-outs of various shapes were filled with coloured paper usually decorated with delicate scrolls and the adjacent area embellished with large scrolls or trellis patterns in gold painting on a coloured ground.

From the 1570s the quality of the illustrations increasingly deteriorated in relation to the other decorative elements of book design. But they at least permit us to conclude that by this time pictorial representations had become generally accepted as part of the arts of the book. It is indeed the weakness of such designs produced during the last quarter of the sixteenth century what indicates that illustrations were by then regarded as a crowning glory of book design and as highly desirable, even if they were of much lower quality than the calligraphy and illumination.

Partly responsible for this development was doubtless the waning interest in an art form which was hardly suitable for propagandistic purposes. Although a number of illustrated manuscripts were commissioned by `Abdullah Khan II (r. de facto 1557-, de jure 1583-98), his ambition was mainly directed towards the erection of new buildings in his capital. Despite such neglect, the production of illustrated manuscripts continued, being kept alive by patrons like `Abdi Khwaja, son of the illustrious Juibari shaikh Khwaja Kalan, for whom an illustrated copy of the *Majalis al-`ushshaq*, a collection of tales and legends about famous Sufis, was executed in 1597/8 (ill. 171). The manuscript is decorated only with a medallion with an inscribed dedication to the patron and an embellished headpiece (`unwan), but includes almost seventy second-rate miniatures.[2]

The discrepancy between the continuing demand for illustrated books and the rather poor quality of the Bukhara and Samarkand workshops finally led potential customers to take their custom elsewhere. Khorasan had always been synonymous with superior artistry, and if the painters did not come to Bukhara, the Bukharans had to go to the painters. Political developments proved favourable. The Uzbek advance into Khorasan and the conquest of important cities like Herat (1588) and Mashhad (1589) provided an opportunity especially for members of the military aristocracy stationed at those cities, to commission works from Iranian artists.[3] This resulted in a particular type of miniatures, a mixture of Khorasan styles with an Uzbek overlay in that the figures were shown in Uzbek dress.[4] The direct employment of Khorasan artists only hastened and deepened a development which had started sometime before.

The reaction of the book illustrators of Bukhara and Samarkand to this competition was a very limited and basically unsuccessful adaptation. The revival of miniature painting at the turn of the seventeenth century was mainly due to two artists, Muhammad Murad Samarkandi and Muhammad Sharif. They decisively broke with the traditions of Bukharan painting and fashioned a new starting-point on the basis of Khorasan styles practised in the 1580s and 1590s. It is possible that both painters had familiarised themselves with the new artistic developments during an apprenticeship in Khorasan commercial workshops, or they might have had the opportunity to study some of the imported manuscripts and single pictures, which would have given them the advantage of picking up elements of Khorasan painting and successfully adapt them for their own purposes. The earliest extant example of this change of direction seems to be Muhammad Murad's illustrations for a *Shahnama*, Firdausi's epic about the legendary and historic kings of Iran.[5]

The surprising aspect of these productions is the reappearance of typical elements of the Bihzad school, a feature already noticeable in some Khorasan paintings of the late sixteenth century. The new style is characterised by sinuous lines, sometimes soft, sometimes tensile, for the depiction of figures. A stronger focus on individual traits and expressive gestures is achieved by the same method used in Herat painting, namely by leaving the garments plain and unadorned. This was at first accompanied by a sparse indication of background, but gradually the paintings became more ambitious. The illustrations for a *Bustan* of about 1616 produced for a member of the leading Juibari family of Bukhara shows an architectural background with more detailed ornamentation and richer, albeit stylised natural life (ill. 163). A certain sense of depth is created by diagonals of the architectural structures and colour contrasts for the landscape background.[6] The mannerism of Herat painting of the early seventeenth century finds an echo in the soft, curving manner of Muhammad Murad, while Muhammad Sharif remains close to Timurid traditions with his strong emphasis on line and colour and a clearly structured composition.[7]

The Khorasan inspiration remains noticeable in Central Asian miniature painting until the 1620s, an example being a 1629 copy of the *Zafarnama*, Yazdi's history of Timur's exploits.[8]

At the same time the development of Central Asian miniature painting since the early seventeenth century experienced a further influence, this one emanating from the Mughal empire. The first flowering of Mughal art at the court of Akbar (1556-1605) stimulated artists to produce several simplified varieties of the Mughal style, the spectrum extending from works with strong Iranian influence to paintings showing the characteristic traits of pre-Mughal Indian art. Early work by the same artist who contributed to the 1629 Zafarnama appears in a *Shahnama* finished in 1600 at the Samarkand home of Mir Urtuq (ill. 164). He typically painted small figures in vigorous action against a barely structured background of pastel-coloured areas.[9] This 'Indian' treatment of space and colour is indebted to popular Mughal painting.

171
'Shah Shuja' watches the poet Hafiz'. Miniature from Husain Gazurgahi's Majalis al-
'ushshaq.
1597-8
University of Michigan, Ann Arbor, Special Collections Library, Abdul Hamid Collection,
Ms. 270, fol. 64b

172
'Humai faints on seeing Princess Humayun'. Miniature from Khwaju Kirmani's Khamsa.
1667-8
Museum für Islamische Kunst, Berlin

173
'Caravan and resting-place with yurts'. Miniature from a Shahanshahnama by Ahmad
Tabrizi copied by Muhammad Sa'id Hafiz al-Qari.
The foreground shows the camp with pitched yurts and a campfire, while in the background
a caravan with loaded pack-animals passes by.
H: 25.8 cm, W: 16.8 cm
Shiraz (?), dated A.H. 800 (A.D. 1397/8)
British Library, London, Or. 2780, fol. 44b

174
'Genghis Khan speaks in the Bukhara mosque'. Miniature from a Shahanshahnama by
Ahmad Tabrizi copied by Muhammad Sa'id Hafiz al-Qari.
The event depicted in the miniature probably never took place. The painting documents,
however, the key importance of Genghis Khan for the Timurid claims to legitimacy. Timur
based his right to rulership on his Genghid ancestry, and among other measures ordered that
the name of a descendant of Genghis be mentioned in the khutba (sermon) of the Friday
congregational prayer. For the same reason Timur took the Mongol title of kürägän (son-in-
law) when he married a princess of the Chaggatai dynasty.
H: 25.8 cm, W: 16.8 cm
Shiraz (?), dated A.H. 800 (A.D. 1397/8)
British Library, London, Or. 2780, fol. 61

175
'The construction of the palace at Khawarnaq'. Miniature from a Khamsa by Nizami
copied for Amir `Ali Farsi Barlas.
H: 25 cm, W: 17 cm
Herat (?), dated A.H. 900 (A.D. 1494/5)
British Library, London, Or. 6810, fol. 154b

111

Thus in contrast to the stylistic uniformity of the second half of the sixteenth century, the first three decades of the seventeenth are characterised by a variety of different approaches. The reason for this was not only the fact that a new beginning had been made which oriented itself on a number of different models. The early Janid period lacked a cultural centre which could have unified the development of styles. It appears that no palace workshop existed in the capital. Where the manuscripts mention the names of patrons, these mostly refer to emirs and *khwajas*, dignitaries of the influential Sufi order, and only very rarely to a Janid ruler.

The situation charged under `Abd al-`Aziz Khan (1645-81). His name is associated with a new style clearly different from the previous period. However, the name of one of its practioners, the painter Bihzad, already appears in a manuscript of 1627 copied for `Abd ar-Rahman, the *atalyq* (guardian) of Prince `Abd al-`Aziz.[10]

The father of the prince had taken up residence in Balkh in 1612, and the part of Janid territory under his supervision developed largely independent of the other part with its capital at Bukhara. Balkh, having already played a crucial role in contacts with Khorasan and the Mughal empire during the sixteenth century, now acquired an eminence equal to Bukhara. The illustrations accompanying a manuscript of Nizami's *Khamsa* commissioned by `Abd ar-Rahman *atalyq* are proof that miniature painting also evolved an independent style. All these artistic developments, whether at Balkh or Bukhara or Samarkand, fed on a creative interplay of Iranian and Indian influences. Three of the miniatures represent a highly idiosyncratic adaptation of the Herat style with extremely slim and elongated figures. Whereas these date from the time of the manuscript, the dating of Bihzad's contribution is less secure. It belongs to his early work and may well have been produced before `Abd al-`Aziz came to power in Bukhara. After an interruption of more than half a century, the Bukhara palace workshop was re-activated at such short notice that `Abd al-`Aziz probably did not start from scratch but had brought a few calligraphers and painters with him.

`Abd al-`Aziz Khan became a famous patron of artists and poets. Representatives of the new painting style include Farhad, Bihzad, Muhammad Muqim, Muhammad Amin, Muhammad Salim and Lachin. It received its classical formulation during the 1660s, an example being an illustrated copy of Khwaju Kirmani's *Khamsa*, a collection of romantic Sufi tales, dated 1667/8 (ill. 172).[11]

Under the supervision of the *kitabdar* `Abd ar-Rahman the manuscript was copied by the calligraphers `Arabshah and Barqi for `Abd al-`Aziz Khan. Although the illustrations were produced by Bihzad, Muhammad Muqim, Muhammad Amin and Lachin, they are surprisingly similar. The most common scheme consisted of a well-defined composition with clearly arranged elements. Light modelling was applied to figures and faces and parts of the architecture. Both the technique for suggesting plasticity and the frequently appearing towering rocks of the background derive from Mughal models. The bizarre shapes of the rocks as well as the figures dressed in Central Asian costume are typical features of miniatures of the `Abd al-`Aziz period. Although the style was much indebted to Mughal painting, its particular expression was partly due to local peculiarities, but more importantly to the juxtaposition of newly acquired elements with compositional schemes harking back to classical Timurid precepts. Unlike Safawid and Mughal painting, which also based itself on Timurid miniature painting, in Transoxiana this legacy remained much in evidence even during the second half of the seventeenth century. This also applies to the function of the images: While in the two other culture areas the single independent picture predominated, in Transoxiana the image remained linked to the text, to Persian literature, even if the interpretation tended less towards the idyllic and more to prosaic and action-filled scenes. The persistence of the textual link probably owed much to `Abd al-`Aziz's personal preferences; over the years he had a whole library of classical Persian poetry illustrated by the palace studio, including a collection of epics and Amir Khusrau Dihlawi's *Khamsa* (ill. 162).[12]

The khan was obviously not the only patron of the miniaturists, as is indicated by other manuscripts with only summarily executed illustrations presumably commissioned by less wealthy customers. Whether they were produced simultaneously with work for the palace or only date from after `Abd al-`Aziz's abdication and a less favourable artistic climate, is difficult to say because we lack inscribed dates. The accession of Subhan Quli Khan (1681-1702) spelled the end of royal patronage for the arts of the book and eventually of Transoxianian miniature painting altogether, although calligraphy and illumination of some distinction continued to be produced. This does not mean that interest in paintings and illustrated manuscripts completely disappeared, but what demand there was could be satisfied by the Indian market.

I would like to thank Professor Robert D. McChesney of New York University, who never tired answering my questions about Central Asian history, and Professor John Seyller of the University of Vermont, who supplied crucial information about the complex problems involving sub-imperial and popular Mughal painting. I also would like to thank the public and private manuscript collections for providing access to their holdings.

1   An example of double-spread miniatures by Mahmud Mudhahhib and `Abdullah is a *Bustan* completed in 1542 by Mir `Ali Herawi for `Abd al-`Aziz Khan; cf. Basil Gray and Ernst Kühnel, *Oriental Islamic Art: Collection of the Calouste Gulbenkian Foundation*, Lisbon 1963, no. 123. For a volume of Sufi poetry illustrated by the two artists together with Shaikhum and produced in 1549 for Mir `Ali under the supervision of the *kitabdar* Sultan Mirak, cf. Muhammad Ashraf, *A Concise Descriptive Catalogue of the Persian Manuscripts in the Salar Jung Museum and Library*, Hyderabad 1975, vol. 4:7-23.

2   Ann Arbor, University of Michigan Library, ms. 270 pers.

3   Among them were the three sons of Jani Muhammad, two of whom succeeded their father in the first decade of the seventeenth century to become the first rulers of the Janid dynasty. Documentary evidence shows that the eldest son, Din Muhammad, who lost his life during the Safawid reconquest of Herat in 1598, employed Herat artists; cf. Barbara Schmitz, "Miniature Painting in Herat, 1570-1640", Ph.D. diss., New York University, New York 1981:21, 55, 279-84, 324, 383f.

4   For single miniatures and illustrated manuscripts of this group cf. Basil W. Robinson, *Persian Paintings in the India Office Library: A Descriptive Catalogue*, London 1976, nos. 906f., 919f.

5   Institute of Oriental Studies, Academy of Sciences of Uzbekistan, Tashkent, ms. 1811; cf. Elmira M. Ismailova and Elena A. Poliakova, *Oriental Miniatures of the Abu Raikhon Beruni Institute of Orientology of the UzSSR Academy of Sciences*, Tashkent 1980, nos. 44f. The text had been copied by 1556/6, while the illustrations probably date from the late sixteenth century.

6   Chester Beatty Library, Dublin, pers. 297; cf. Arthur J. Arberry, et al., *The Chester Beatty Library: A Catalogue of the Persian Manuscripts and Miniatures*, Dublin 1962, 3:66f.

7   Cf. fol. 184a, cf. David James, *Islamic Masterpieces of the Chester Beatty Library*, London 1981: no. 29, fol. 159b. For a painting on the border of two sheets including a figure by Muhammad Sharif in the centre, cf. *L'Islam dans les collections nationales*, Paris 1977:199ff., no. 440 (Paris, Musée National du Louvre, A.O. 7109); see also Glenn D. Lowry et al., *An Annotated and Illustrated Checklist of the Vever Collection*, Washington, D.C., 1988:310f. (Arthur M. Sackler Gallery, Washington, D.C., S. 86.0304); for a colourplate, cf. Glenn D. Lowry with Susan Nemazee, *A Jeweller's Eye: Islamic Art of the Book from the Vever Collection*, Washington, D.C., 1988:67.

8   Institute of Oriental Studies, Uzbekistan Academy of Sciences, Tashkent, ms. 4472, especially fol. 181a; cf. Ismailova and Poliakova, no. 36.

9   Department of Rare Books and Special Collections, Princeton University Libraries, 59 G; cf. Mohamad E. Moghadam and Yahya Armajani, *Descriptive Catalog of the Garrett Collection of Persian, Turkish and Indic Manuscripts Including Some Miniatures in the Princeton University Library*, Princeton 1939:2f., no. 4.

10   *Khamsa* Nizami, Catherine and Ralph Benkaim collection; cf. *Sotheby's Catalogue of Fine Western and Oriental Manuscripts and Miniatures,* London, May 5, 1965, lot 177.

11   Museum für Islamische Kunst, Berlin, I. 1986.227.

12   Metropolitan Museum of Art, New York, 13.228.24; cf. Abraham V.W. Jackson and Abraham Yohannan, *A Catalogue of the Collection of Persian Manuscripts including also some Turkish and Arabic presented to the Metropolitan Museum of Art New York by Alexander Smith Cochran*, New York 1914:120-3, no. 15.

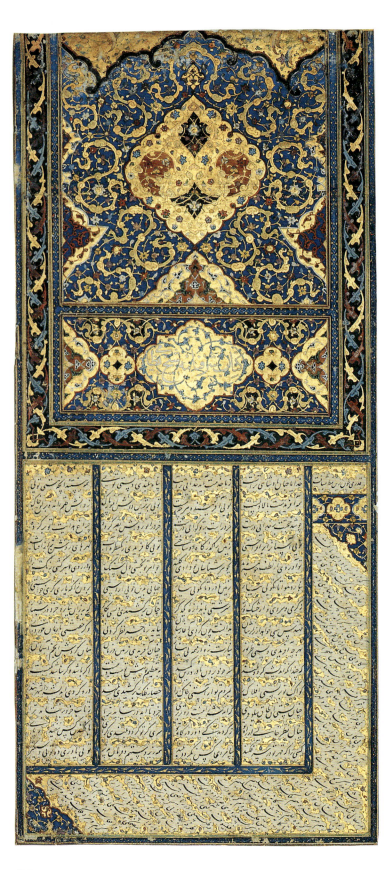

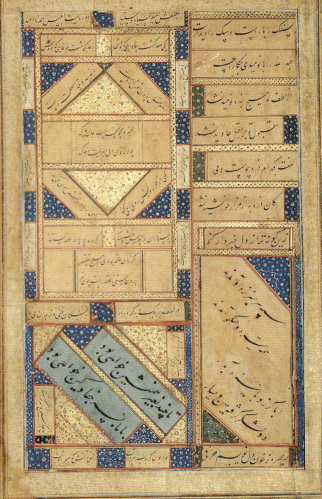

176
Leaf from a volume of poetry. Nastaliq in red, gold and white on a blue ground.
H: 14.9 cm, W: 9.4 cm Iran, 14th/15th century

177
Album leaf. Two columns, nastaliq, illuminated with flowering scrolls on a blue and gold ground.
H: 31 cm, W: 20.7 cm Iran, 15th/16th century

178
Illuminated title page of a Sharafnama by Nizami. Nastaliq, central medallion, orgival cartouche, scrolls and cloud-bands.
H: 26.5 cm, W: 12.1 cm Iran (?), 16th/17th century

179-180
Title page of a Koran and detail of the vase motif.
H: 53.5 cm, W: c. 60 cm (open)
Bukhara, dated 1785/6
Museum in the Ark, Bukhara

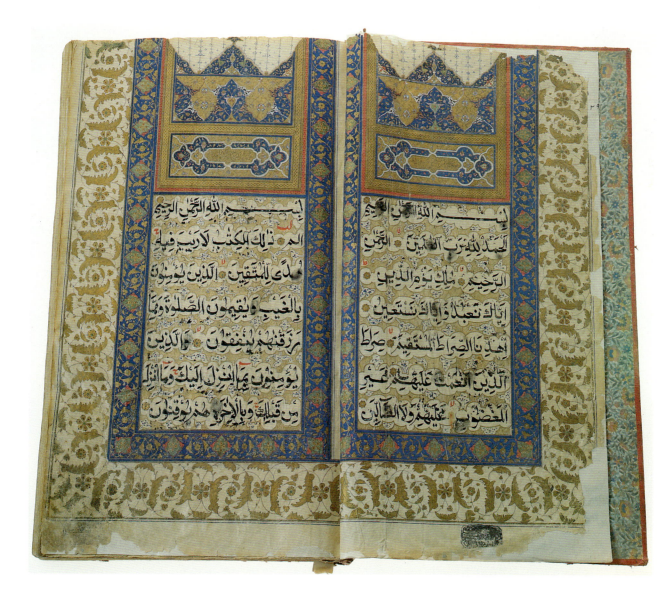

181
Storage jar. Unglazed pottery with cold painting in bone black. The designs along the horizontal bands include geometric patterns, animals (stags or ibexes?) and a four-wheeled waggon in a style reminiscent of rock paintings.
H: 111 cm
Northern Afghanistan, near Maimana, 10th century

Is There a Distinctive Central Asian Type of Islamic Art?

Johannes Kalter

For architecture, the answer to this question is a resounding 'yes'. The tomb of about 900 A.D. built for the Samanid Isma`il is the oldest extant Islamic funerary structure. It marks the beginning of a development which was particularly influential for Pakistan tomb architecture. A previous essay dealt with the distinctive building style of Timur and the Timurids, the most important remains of which are found in Samarkand and Shahr-i Sabz. But even in nineteenth-century Khiva new mosques, madrasas and a palace were being built with tile decoration incorporating Timurid elements and ornamental panels reminiscent of carpet designs from eastern Turkestan and the Caucasus, which are unique in the Islamic world. In the art of the book as well, Central Asia went its own way, whether one thinks of the Timurid school of painting at Herat or the Shaibanid school of miniature painting at Bukhara.

Here I shall therefore try to define a Central Asian style in the minor arts. The task is not made easier by the fact that most historians of Islamic art usually have treated Central Asia as something of an eastern extension of Iran, and that furthermore most objects in our public and private collections were acquired through the art market and not from controlled excavations. My aim is to identify typical elements of a Central Asian style on the basis of inscriptions or ephigraphic motifs and of certain 'domesticated' ornaments of Chinese or Indian origin. We shall then discover the existence of a distinctive repertoire of forms which, on the basis of our present knowledge, is unique to the Central Asian culture area.

The problems of attributing ceramic wares were brought a great step forward in the catalogue for the exhibition "Terres secrètes de Samarcande" of 1992. Until then Samanid ceramics produced between 873 and 999 had a very indistinct profile. The ceramic centres of the East Iranian Samanid dynasty were Nishapur and Afrasiab (Old Samarkand). Unlike Nishapur productions, the body of polychrome glazed wares from Afrasiab was often completely covered with designs. A common colour scheme of over-glaze painting included red, manganese brown, green and olive on a white slip, or white or light green painting on a dark brown or blackish brown slip. The bold kufic inscriptions on the inside of bowls or the outside of vessels have endings either wedge-shaped or showing a lively trefoil motif. On bowls with purely epigraphic decoration there is a pronounced difference between Nishapur wares, where manganese brown predominates, and Afrasiab wares, where the colour varies between manganese brown and red. Another typically Afrasiab feature is a sprinkling of small red flowers. From ninth/tenth-century Afrasiab we know green-glazed ceramics like the illustrated globular incense burner

with flattened shoulder and wide rim, which corresponds to contemporary metal shapes of the region (ill. 182). Another typical Central Asian feature are circular medallions filled with quartered plant motifs to suggest a Greek cross as on the illustrated relief tile from Samarkand (ill. 115). The bowl with the dynamic representation of a highly stylised peacock filling the entire interior exemplifies the difficulty of distinguishing wares from Nishapur and Afrasiab (ill. 200). The monumentality of the design and the yellow to olive-green colour of the framing surfaces together with information obtained from the previous owner suggest an eleventh-century Samarkand origin.

A unique example of Iranian ceramic design from the early Islamic period is provided by a group of vessels found in North Afghanistan in the region of Maimana close to the Amu Darya. One of the vessels shows along the shoulder and the lower part of the exterior fluting reminiscent of lotus petals, a feature also found on Samanid metalwork (ills. 183-7). A band of bold kufic inscription interspersed with circular medallions decorated with animal motifs recalls kufic inscriptions on early glazed Afrasiab ware. The base shows a leaf pattern, also in relief and again with the negative area suggesting a Greek cross. It could well be that the 'cross' pattern, which survives in present-day Central Asian art, refers to the four elements – fire, water, earth and air – and their corresponding directions. The blank area would then be the world tree or world mountain, the axis connecting the nether world with the world we live in and the heavens above. This ancient cosmology from northern Asia was presumably introduced to the region by the early Turks.

Also from Maimana comes a group of unglazed ceramics with manganese painting over the slip or cold painting, the pigments obtained from burnt bones. The most remarkable object is an eleven-centrimetre-high shoulder pot, presumably used as a storage vessel (ill. 181). The ornamentation of the upper half consists of horizontal bands with alternating designs of geometric and curvilinear motifs as well as representations of animals and carts reminiscent of rock paintings. We suggest a date of about 1000 A.D. The build-up and firing of such a large object required exceptional craftsmanship, although the decoration itself is surprisingly awkward.

For metalwork, a distinctive Central Asian style can be very clearly identified since the Timurid period. Probably the most outstanding example is the flattish copper bowl with traces of tin plating, the exterior completely covered with designs (ills. 188-90). This ornamentation is arranged in three horizontal bands, the top one showing a leafy scroll interspersed with endless knots, an auspicious symbol derived from Buddhist iconography frequently encountered in Central Asia and something of a leitmotif helpful for determining the place of origin. The second band is broader and contains an epigraphic frieze in 'speaking' naskhi. The terminations show faces, snake heads and birds. The third band is the broadest of all; it consists of a background of delicately engraved plant patterns with circular medallions enclosing a lute player, a man smoking a water pipe and another ladling water (symbolising Aquarius?), again

182
Censer. Glazed earthenware, bottle-green monochrome glaze, openwork incised decoration, glaze partly degraded, the lower part of the body with bold grooves. The type is also known from contemporaneous metalware.
H: c. 16 cm, D: 24 cm (body), 10 cm (bottom)
Afrasiab, 9th/10th century

183-187
Jug with handle. Unglazed pottery with moulded designs, freely modelled neck with flower-shaped rim and inset sieve. Along the shoulder and lower third of the body petal rosettes. The kufic inscription is interspersed with roundels showing hares, lions and sphinxes. The floral decoration on the bottom is arranged so as to form a Greek cross.
H: 21 cm
Northern Afghanistan or Central Asia, 10th/11th century

interspersed with alternating representations of endless knots and single letters ending in human and animals heads. The centre of the fully decorated bottom shows a lion depicted in a calligraphic manner within a typical Timurid interlacing band. The outer band on the bottom has a much defaced inscription and geometricised rosettes inside roundels. Here again the centre with its four arms corresponding to the four directions receives much emphasis. I am not aware of any other vessel with the same decorative scheme. It was probably made in Bukhara in about 1500. Some of the design elements reappear on the metalwork described further down.

Another object undoubtedly of Central Asian provenance – from sixteenth-century Bukhara, in fact – is a tin-plated sherbet bowl with a broad everted strengthened rim (ills. 191-92). The upper band is decorated with bold naskhi script, while the main design consists of cartouches with highly stylised vase motifs alternating with roundels enclosing Greek crosses and opposing fishes. The fishes and the script – monumental when compared to contemporary Iranian styles – cleary indicate its Central Asian origin.

The decoration of a tin-plated bowl consists of elements similar to those on the above-mentioned flattish copper bowl (ills. 196-97). The top band shows round and horizontal cartouches with suspended cartouches and half-cartouches enclosing antilopes and birds. Especially the quatrefoils superimposed on a square within the roundels point to a Central Asian origin, as do the endless knots suspended from the half-cartouches.

A detail of a wash bowl from eighteenth-century Khiva represents a good example of the survival of classical elements in late Central Asian metalwork (ill. 199). A pointed medallion with reliefwork is surrounded by an elegant spiralloid forked leaf scroll well-known from Timurid metalwork. The centre is emphasised by a lozenge and again shows four lotus blossoms arranged in the four directions; the tip consists of a merlon-shaped border enclosing floral motifs.

The most astonishing discovery during my search for examples of distinctly Central Asian minor arts was the alms-bowl of a dervish (ills. 193-95). On first sight there was nothing to distinguish it from dozens of similar objects I had handled. But the decoration turned out to be highly distinctive. The first remakable feature is the unexpectedly fluid and bold scroll on the top. The very broad inscribed border is also unusual. The main surface is covered with scrolling vines almost obscuring scenes with fighting animals recalling Timurid miniatures. The rounded front shows a lion killing an ibex with an antelope fleeing to the left, while the flat back has a lion killing an antelope and an ibex fleeing to the left. The clearest proof for its Central Asian origin, however, is the band covering the lower part of the body showing trefoils within bracket-lobed cartouches.

The small amount of Timurid jewellery we know mostly comes from Iran and is made of gold. Our silver plaque from Herat indicate its origin in Central Asia clearly through its main motif, a bracket-lobed cartouche with a geomteric design terminating in trefoils (ill. 198). It divides

188-190
Low bowl. Copper, traces of tin-plate. The decoration is arranged in three horizontal bands, the narrow upper border with scrolls and 'endless knots' and below a broad band with an epigraphic frieze in 'speaking' naskhi, the hastae showing human faces, snakes' heads and birds. The main band is decorated with auspicious knots and floral elements interspersed with roundels enclosing plants and human figures. The lip bears an inscription, the bottom is entirely covered with designs and shows calligraphy in the shape of a lion in the centre.
H: 9.8 cm, D: 27 cm (top), c. 22 cm (bottom)
Central Asia, Bukhara (?), 15th century
Private collection, Sindelfingen

191-192
Sherbet container. Tin-plated copper. Slightly everted strenghtened rim, upper band with epigraphic frieze in naskhi and below cartouches with vase motifs framed by opposed fishes and roundels with leaf scrolls.
H: 13.5 cm, W: 26.7 (top), c. 15 cm (bottom)
Central Asia, Bukhara, 16th century
Private collection, Sindelfingen

193-195
Alms-bowl. Carved coco-de-mer (Lodoicea seychellarum), iron attachments. The top with bold scrolls with trefoil motif, the semicircular front with a lion striking an ibex on the right and a fleeing antilope against a scrolling background on the left. The flattened back shows a lion striking an antilope and fleeing antilopes. The upper band bears an inscription in naskhi, the bottom shows typical Central Asian quatrefoils.
H: 12.5 cm, W: 25 cm, D: 11.7 cm
Central Asia, 15th century
Private collection, Sindelfingen

196-197
Cylindrical bowl (detail). Tin-plated copper. The bold scrollwork and in particular the four-petalled flower superscribed over a square (left) and the 'endless knots' suspended from cartouches suggest a Central Asian provenance.
Central Asia, Bukhara (?), 17th century
Private collection, Sindelfingen

198
Plaque. Silver, chased, engraved and pounced. The bracket-lobed quatrefoil in the centre and the joined trefoil motif divide the surface into four decorative fields showing hares above and lions below against a scrolling background.
Afghanistan (Herat) or Central Asia, 15th century
Scale: c. 1:1

the remaining surface into four fields decorated with two opposing hares above and addorsed lions below. Chinese influence on Timurid art is more clearly demonstrated on an alabaster plaque with two addorsed dragons in relief flanking a highly stylised floral motif (ill. 202).

At least from the eighteenth century onwards, there can be no question any longer about the existence of a distinctive Central Asian type of Islamic art. Until twenty years ago, large embroidered wall hangings and bed covers (*suzanis*) as well as ikat coats and ikat textiles used as wall hangings, could only be found in a few ethnographic collections. They have been appearing more and more frequently for the last ten years in catalogues of the major auction houses in London, Paris and New York under the heading 'Islamic Art'. Suzanis were produced solely in the area of present-day Uzbekistan and northern Afghanistan and cannot be mistaken for any other type of embroidery from the Islamic world. Even though every city and locality developed its own style, still they have so much in common that in a pile of textiles one can identify a suzani with closed eyes. This applies even more to Central Asian ikats, which can never be confused with ikats from any other part of the world because of the brilliance of their colours and their designs with their seemingly archaic patterns of cloud bands, sun motifs and trees of life and with representations of pomegranates and amulets. Regional metalwork since the seventeenth century, although yet little researched, is distinctive both in the profile of ewers and other vessels and in the ornamentation, which follows its own formal repertoire. So we may conclude that Central Asia or Turkestan developed its own characteristic style in all the important branches of Islamic art and crafts.

Finally I would like to offer the following proposition for further discussion: A distinctive Central Asia version of Islamic art can be first discerned, albeit vaguely, during the Samanid period. It evolved during the late Timurid period and is fully formed by the time of the Shaibanids. This finds its historical explanation in the fact that until Timurid times Central Asia (or what later was called Turkestan) was linked by trade routes with Muslim countries, but also with India and China, both empires heavily influencing the region during the rule of the Mongols and Timurids. In the early sixteenthth century, an Islamic nation-state of Shiite persuasion quickly established itself. Turkestan bordered on Iran and on the Muslim Mughal empire in India. Long-distance trade came to a halt. The area of modern Uzbekistan was ruled by the khanates of Kokand, Bukhara and Khiva, each a local cultural centre in its own right. Artists and artisans were cut off from contact with other Islamic regions. The repertoire of ornament and decoration retained numerous Timurid elements. On the other hand, older local traditions were further developed. These developments brought about the creation of a culture area with its own distinctive character, which despite manifold local variations clearly differs from Iranian art of the late Safawid and Qajar periods and from the art of Mughal India. I am aware that this sketch towards a definition of its special qualities leaves much to be desired. But my main aim was simply to contribute to a discussion which should treat the Islamic arts of Central Asia with the attention they deserve.

200
Bowl. Glazed earthenware, manganese-brown underglaze painting on a white slip showing a peacock.
H: 7.5 cm, D: 18 cm
Transoxiana (Afrasiab?), 11th/12th century

201
This detail from a jug with moulded decoration shows a pair of figures holding hands and dressed in a Central Asian costume of the 12th century.

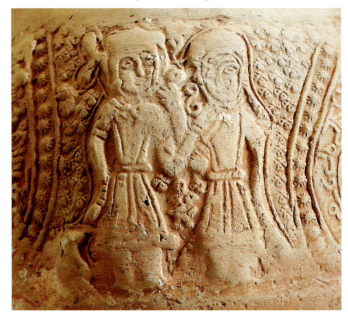

199
Ewer (detail). Engraved brass.
The quatrefoil arrangement of the peony flowers within the ogival medallion derive from traditional Timurid designs.
Khiva, 18th century

202
Plaque. Carved jade with a design of addorsed dragons.
Scale: c. 1:1
Northern Afghanistan or Central Asia, 14th/15th century

Islamic Metalwork from the Ninth to Fifteenth Century

Almut von Gladiss

When Henri Moser and Willi Rickmer Rickmers were visiting the cities of Central Asia in the late nineteenth century, the bazaars offered a wide variety of brass household wares, as the photographic evidence shows (Bukhara 1993, ills. 76, 77, 82). Bukhara's production of and trade in copper wares had a long history. From early Islamic times its metal bazaar had an excellent reputation after Ibn Hauqal had praised its great variety of brass and copper wares in the tenth century; as a merchant he had travelled the Islamic countries from Spain to Transoxiana, gaining a sound knowledge of the special goods of each region.

Moser and Rickmers acquired a large number of copper wares, some brand-new, others second-hand and some again centuries old. Two key works of eastern Islamic metalwork were also discovered at Bukhara: The 'Bobrinsky Bucket' dated equivalent to 1163 in the Hermitage was bought in 1885, and the pen-case dated equivalent to 1210 in the Freer Gallery of Art in Washington in 1928 (Veselovsky 1910; Herzfeld 1936). The latter piece has an inscription praising its owner Majd al-Mulk al-Muzaffar, grand vizier of the last Khorezmshah `Ala'uddin Muhammad, and was thus the property of a documented dignitary who is credited with the foundation of a library at Merv.

203
Tray. Silver, partly gilt.
H: 3.0 cm, W: 35.8 cm
Transoxiana (Bukhara?), 10th century
Museum für Islamische Kunst, Berlin

Central Asian silverwork

Few metal objects can be assigned a Central Asian origin on the evidence of their inscriptions. We therefore have to base our research on stylistic and technical features from objects discovered by accident or by controlled excavation. Of particular importance are discoveries of objects made of precious metals such as the silver bowl from a tomb at the Ljakhsh II necropolis, or the silver bowls from Chilek near Samarkand, which form part of a hoard (Zurich 1989, no. 49; Marshak 1986: 39, ills. 11-13). These bowls with thin walls were used as drinking vessels during banquets and come from pre-Islamic Central Asia. According to al-Tabari, in 752 the Arabs during a raid against a Sogdian ruler, seized a number of precious metal objects near Samarkand such as they had never seen before. The Muslim conquerors acquired a taste for luxurious tableware and made sure of a constant supply.

Central Asia had rich sources of precious metals. Gold particles carried in the Sughd and Amu Darya rivers were caught with sheepskins, several gold mines were exploited in Fergana, and there were silver mines in Transoxiana, near Ilaq in Uzbekistan, in the Talas valley in Kirghizstan, in the Pamirs in Tajikistan and near Panjshir and Jarbaya in Afghanistan, as described by travellers in the tenth century. The mining of silver was supervised by an official and part of the production retained by the State. During the tenth and eleventh centuries, silver from Panjshir and Jarbaya went to Balkh, and that mined in Transoxiana to Bukhara. The local rulers had well-filled treasuries, and silver provided the foundation of their political and economic power.

Silver coins were minted in large numbers, especially in Balkh and Bukhara, where mints had been established since the eighth/ninth century. The famous scholar al-Biruni from Khorezm writing in Ghazni early in the eleventh century, emphasised the commercial value of such metals. Central Asian silver coins were mainly used in foreign trade. Their geographical position gave the cities of Central Asia great opportunities for controlling the transcontinental trading routes, they themselves contributing in particular paper, textiles and silver vessels to the flow of goods. Silver coins and vessels were exchanged for furs, ores, precious stones and slaves from eastern Europe and the northern steppes. We get an idea of the great distances covered from Ibn Fadlan's account of his official journey from Baghdad via Bukhara, Khorezm and Turkish lands to the Bulghars of the Volga, which took nearly eleven months.

Trade relations are documented by numerous silver vessels which found their way to the Urals and Altay region, where they were used as votive offerings. But a more important indication of the significance of the Central Asian entrepots are the thousands of silver coins that reached Russia, Poland and Sweden. Of tenth-century Islamic coins found in these parts of Europe, more than sixty percent come from the mints at Samarkand, Bukhara and Tashkent.

They were minted by the Samanids, the dynasty ruling Central Asia during the ninth and tenth centuries as governors of the caliph in Baghdad. The Seljuq vizier Nizam al-Mulk, who spent many years in Central Asia, mentions the splendid tableware used at the Samanid court and the vessels of precious metal which the Samanid ruler Nasr ibn Ahmad distributed among his followers during a banquet held at Bukhara. Silver tableware continued to be regarded as a status symbol at Central Asian courts.

A magnificent example of the period is the octagonal silver tray from the Museum für Islamische Kunst in Berlin (ill. 203). It is the prototype of a shape which only occurs in eastern Islamic regions and is documented in several brass versions dating from the eleventh to thirteenth century. Most of the trays are rectangular, although a few square ones are known (Melikian-Chirvani 1982, nos. 28, 29), and are characterised by the sunken octagonal well, its shape in our case repeated by the rim. The silver plate was shallowly beaten and the design chased with variously shaped punches. In Central Asia embossing and engraving were two well-established decorative techniques mainly used for copper and brass objects, as we can see from trays found at Pendjikent and other sites in Tajikistan and Uzbekistan (Pugachenkova 1988, pl. 179; Kuwait 1990, no. 40; Leningrad 1985, no. 824).

The tray's main motif is the *senmurv*, the monstrous being from Persian fable; it appears on the central medallion and on four of the either smaller roundels. To the Sasanians, the senmurv was a symbol of power, and during the reign of Khusrau I it was also used for royal textile designs, as we can see on the Taq-e Bustan reliefs. Its survival among the neighbouring countries under Sasanian influence is documented by extant silk clothes and their representation on wall-paintings. The throne room of the Sogdian palace at Afrasiab (Old Samarkand), decorated shortly before the Arab conquest of the city, shows a royal reception, where one of the participants wears a costume with a senmurv design (Pugachenkova 1988, pl. 74). The motif was later applied by silversmiths who also adopted the medallion pattern from textile art. Painted vessels from Afrasiab show figural motifs arranged in similar medallion patterns connected by knots. They are decorated with *senmurv*-like figures, the curved elements on the creature's body forming part of a separate arrangement of forms (Paris 1992, nos. 200, 201, 225).

The continued relevance of the senmurv motif indicates a Samanid interest in the glorious past. The Samanids were proud of their aristocratic Iranian ancestry. The first documented member of the dynasty, Saman-khuda, was a *deghan* (landlord) from the Balkh region, who had converted to Islam in the eighth century in order to serve one of the last Umayyad governors of Khorasan. According to al-Biruni, the dynasty traced itself back to Bahram Chubin, leader of a revolt against the Sasanian king Hormizd IV in 590, who briefly occupied the throne before being forced to flee to Turkestan.

Like all post-Sasanian silver vessels in the Museum für Islamische Kunst, the tray was part of the Botkin collection exhibited in St Petersburg in 1911, which consisted of wares excavated in Russia during the nineteenth century.

The tray can be related to a small silver ewer in the Hermitage with a pattern of roundels filled with peacocks at the neck and body, and on the shoulder a blessing in kufic, suggesting a tenth-century date (Marshak 1986, ill. 128). The ewer was found at Perm and fits into a series of silver vessels unearthed at sites between the Aral Sea and the Urals. They have been assigned to Central Asia on the basis of Arabic inscriptions, which occasionally include the name of a documented person.

A silver tray measuring 37 by 24 cm excavated at Jamal-Nenzen near Tobolsk has a wide rectangular rim with an nielloed inscription, a dedication to a ruler of Khorezm south of the Aral Sea: "Blessing and power to the emir, our lord, the just king, the crown of the people and the light of the religious community, Shah of Khorezm Abi Ibrahim, Governor to the Commander of the Faithful [i.e., the caliph]" (Marshak 1986, ill. 140). This was a son of the Khorezmshah Altuntash, who had driven the Karakhanids from Bukhara in 1032 and soon afterwards died. The modest design heightened by niello consists of a small medallion of floral scrolls on a raised centre, and globular medaillons at the corners with birds recalling Sasanian depictions of pheasants or ducks.

A silver bottle (height 25 cm), also excavated in the Jamal-Nenzen area, shows an inscription in similar kufic style on the body, and on the shoulder a dedication with the name of the vizier Abu Ali Ahmad ibn Muhammad ibn Shadan against a background of scrolling vines (Marshak 1986, ill. 139). The vizier was stationed at Balkh in the 1030s and 1040s, and among his subordinates was the young Hasan Tusi, the later Nizam al-Mulk mentioned above. The bottle provides a reference for a number of silver objects found in the Urals region, including a second bottle, a cup with handle, a bowl and a ewer with a blessing over a scroll pattern with lobate vine leaves. The roundels are filled with scrolls or birds and animals such as lions and hares and occasionally with a bird of prey striking a hare or duck, a motif well-known from Sasanian designs. During the eleventh century Balkh, situated north of the Hindu Kush, was the leading centre of production, its silversmiths' quarter recorded by al-Baihaqi. On account of its long artisanal tradition we can assume that Samarkand as well was still producing silverware. Drinking cups of sophisticated design are mentioned in the contemporary literature, but the medium is not indicated.

A silver plate in the Linden-Museum presumably dating from the early twelfth century, also shows the traditional bird motif within roundels very popular in eastern Iran (ill. 204). The blessings inscribed between the medallions are written in clear angular kufic, the wedge-shaped endings ornamentally connected. The same unusual style appears on a brass bowl said to have been found at the site of Afrasiab (Melikian-Chirvani 1982, no. 25). A similarly shaped silver plate found at Sludka in the Perm area shows the same alternation of inscriptions and bird motifs, while the centre is decorated with a musician (Marshak 1986, ill. 141). In both cases the motifs are enhanced with niello (a silver sulfide paste), a standard decorating technique of silverwork produced in eastern Islamic countries since the eleventh century.

204
Plate. Nielloed silver.
H: 4.0 cm, D: 20 cm
Transoxiana (Samarkand?), about 1100

205
Amulet. Silver with copper inlay.
H: 21.0 cm, W: 19.5 cm
Transoxiana, 13th century

A silver bowl in the Linden-Museum is decorated with inlay, a technique rarely applied to precious metal (ill. 206). The blessings along the rim have copper inlay, and larger pieces of inlay are used for the crescents at the upper end of the ribs. The ribs themselves are covered with strange leaf patterns. Pre-Mongolian bronze bowls occasionally show comparable patterns reminiscent of calligraphy (Melikian-Chirvani 1982, no. 46), while the narrow bands of scrolls along the concave parts mainly appear on shaped ewers of the time. The Central Asian provenance is suggested mainly by the ribs of various designs, a feature as typical of mediaeval vessels as of Bukharan ewers of the nineteenth century.

Our silver bowl is a work of rare sophistication and incorporates inlay, a decorating technique established for bronzes which reached its first flowering at the time, when crescent moons of silver or copper inlay were also popular.

A copper-inlay crescent supplies the central motif of a silver amulet, its craftsmanship continuing the workshop tradition not only in technique but also in terms of style (ill. 205). The plain crescent at the centre of a star of arabesques is enhanced by the colour contrast between the two metals. The amulet owed its potency not only to its large size symbolising power but also to the precious substances it once contained.

The jewellery of wealthy citizens was comparatively plain, as we can see from two silver hoards found at Sidshak and Sayram Su. The hoard from Sidshak on the banks of the Chirchik, consisted of a pottery vessel holding eight bracelets, eight amulet containers, one earring, a pear-shaped pendant and twenty-seven beads. Their shapes, decorating technique, niello inlay and wire casing is very similar to the objects found at Sayram Su near Chimkent. This hoard, which had also been placed in a pottery vessel, was much

206
Bowl. Silver with copper inlay.
H: 11.5 cm, D 19.8 cm
Transoxiana, about 1200

larger and also included adornments for men, such as sets of belts. Both hoards included large numbers of amulet containers, an item which later became very popular in Central Asian jewellery. The Sayram Su hoard also comprised Buyid, Samanid, Ghaznavid and Ilkhanid coins minted between 949 and 1040, suggesting that it was buried in the mid-eleventh century. At Sidshak the above-ground remains also date from the eleventh century (Moscow 1991, nos. 729-36).

Central Asian copperwork

By early Islamic times the bazaars of Central Asia had a great variety of copperware on offer. The further development of urban lifestyles and increasing wealth extended the circle of patrons and customers. Utilitarian wares made from copper formed a basic part of urban Muslim households, both quality and quantity of the vessels regarded as a social indicator. Central Asia possessed rich copper deposits, the chief mining areas being Fergana and the headwater region of the Sughd. Since Samanid times copper-working was a highly productive craft in Bukhara and Samarkand. In the tenth century, al-Muqaddasi mentions copper lamps from Bukhara, copper vessels from Samarkand and copper weapons from Fergana among the goods exported by Transoxiana (Barthold 1958:235). Presumably the products were of superior quality and spread the reputation of the coppersmiths beyond the confines of the region.

A representative example of the copper lamps mentioned by al-Muqaddasi would be the lamp-stand in the Linden-Museum measuring 110 cm with the matching oil-lamp (ill. 207). In assigning it to Bukhara we base ourselves on a comparable but incomplete torch-stand in the Victoria and Albert Museum, which was acquired in 1903 from an art dealer with a suggested Bukharan provenance (Melikian-Chirvani 1982, no. 17). The Central Asian origin of this type of object is established by a base and shaft excavated at Afrasiab (Kondratieva 1961, pls. 3, 6).

The base with three legs has a dome with a ribbed rim like the torch-stand. The dome shows geometric lattice-work with palmettes, which is repeated along the shaft and the spherical elements. The lamp-dish has lattice-work along the ribbed rim, while the well is decorated with a band of leafy scrolls. The characterising feature is their mould-like execution. The lamp has three spouts and shows open-work leafy scrolls at the foot and cover which, instead of being concave like the above-mentioned decoration, are slightly convex. The finial of the cover is formed like a pomegranate, a shape used for the finials of handles on a type of ewer documented in Central Asia by examples in the

207
Lamp-stand with oil-lamp.
H: 110 cm
Transoxiana, Bukhara, about 1000

208
Vase. Bronze with copper inlay inscription in elongated kufic.
H: 24.5 cm, D: 19.5 cm
Transoxiana, 10th/11th century

209
Fragment of a bronze shaft.
H: 23.0 cm, D: 17.2 (bottom)
Transoxiana, 11th century

210
Vase. Bronze with copper rivets.
H: 19.5 cm, D: 17.0 cm (top)
Transoxiana, 10th century

Samarkand Museum and in Tajikistan (Marshak 1972, ills. 8-10; Pugachenkova 1988, pl. 180; Leningrad 1985, nos. 364-5). The handle of our lamp was surmounted by the figure of a bird which, on the evidence of the surviving feet, was much more elaborately worked than most of its known contemporary counterparts. Although the kufic inscription on the foot of the oil-lamp is as yet not completely deciphered, it seems to give no indication of the place of manufacture. The workshop responsible for this impressive object was obviously well-versed in bronze casting, and the model must have been of a material soft enough to be shaped with a cutter or spatula to produce the slight concavities and convexities.

During the tenth and eleventh centuries several stylistic elements evolved which were to survive into the nineteenth century: a certain sinuous line both in shape and decoration, open-work and the use of colour contrast, which on our lamp is exemplified by soldered copper disks near the spouts.

Two silver bowls found at Chilek already show ribs with spoon-like convexities which appear on a number of pre-Islamic bowls and cups found in southern Russia, Mongolia and China. The Linden-Museum has an eight-lobed cup, a bronze example from early Islamic times (inv. no. A 36613 L). Another vase-like vessel in the Museum shows very pronounced ribs and a wide splayed foot mirroring the mouth (ill. 208). The mouth and foot recall ceramic and metal shapes of the Tang dynasty. With its position along the great transcontinental trading routes, Central Asia was a meeting-point and melting-pot of very

diverse influences, so that the local craftsmen were able to offer their customers products inspired by various foreign models. An eleventh-century earthenware ewer excavated at Termez on the Amu Darya shows a similar shape, although much reduced in size because of the material (Moscow 1991, no. 538).

While the bronze vase is decorated along the mouth and foot with holes arranged to form rosettes, a vase-shaped stand (incomplete) shows pierced animal and plant motifs (ill. 209). A band of slightly concave heart-shaped palmettes runs around the body, while the open-work animal motifs appear along the shoulder. The rim of another vase in the Linden-Museum is decorated with cut-out geometric patterns (ill. 210). The surface of the body is enlivened with three bands of roundels either slightly concave or decorated with archaic knots. Set at regular intervals between the roundels are copper plugs driven through the bronze wall, while the above mentioned oil-lamp showed soldered copper disks on a recessed ground (ill. 207). The kufic inscription on the bronze vase (ill. 208) was enhanced by inlaid strips of copper sheet. Various methods to achieve polychrome effects were tried out before inlaid copper sheet became the most widely used technique from the twelfth century onwards.

Naturally enough, incense burners were perforated with large openings, as shown on an example in the Linden-Museum (ill. 212). Inside is a small hemispherical bowl for burning the aromatic substances. The body is decorated with large roundels filled with diagonal trefoil palmettes to form an elaborate lattice-work. Some Central Asian incense-burners are in the shape of birds or cats of prey. The upper section of such two-part burners, discovered by chance at Budrakh near Denau, consists of the head and body of a large feline, the neck decorated with an open-work scroll (ill. 213). A complete incense-burner of feline shape and signed by `Ali ibn Abi Nasr was found at Chulbuk in southern Tajikistan (Zurich 1989, no. 93). These are provincial productions compared to a cat-shaped incense-burner (height 45 cm) in the Hermitage, where the neck and body are decorated with an open-work pattern of cinquefoil palmettes rather similar to the design on the lamp-stand in the Linden-Museum (Kuwait 1990, no. 18).

Also from Budrakh comes a heavy mortar (height 20 cm) of the eleventh century and thus the earliest surviving metal example of a type of vessel common in the eastern Islamic world (ill. 214). Such bronze mortars, which slowly replaced the early Islamic stone mortars also documented for Central Asia (Afrasiab), were used for the preparation of drugs, condiments, pigments and perfumes.

The Budrakh mortar bears a three-line inscription in foliated kufic: "In the name of Allah, the Merciful and Compassionate, blessings to its owner." The cylindrical shape interspersed with bosses identifies our piece as a prototype of the high-quality mortars produced in the twelfth century, their widespread distribution suggesting a remarkable standard of living. They are usually supplied with two rows of globular bosses set either parallel or alternate (ills. 215, 216). A mortar from Uzbekistan is decorated with floral scrolls between the bosses (Pugachenkova 1965, ill. 243).

The mortar acquired by Rickmers in Bukhara shows a band of lozenge-shaped bosses found on numerous companion pieces, and copper inlay (ill. 216). The strips of copper sheet produce a solid frame for the various motifs including the ubiquitous birds (Westphal-Hellbusch 1974, no. 124), while the regular arrangement of silver wire emphasises the delicate weave-pattern. Mortars with inlaid decoration were widespread in pre-Mongol times. The British Museum holds a mortar with a weave-pattern similar to the one from Bukhara and a mark on the base known from Chinese bronzes of the Song dynasty, *zhi bao yong zhi* ('to be used as a treasure') (Barrett 1949, pl. 11). Contemporary sources note the presence in Samarkand of a large Chinese community.

Another type of vessel common to Central Asia is the bulbous bucket, the illustrated example having been found at Merv (ill. 219). It was presumably inspired by a Chinese Tang-dynasty shape, with examples in the museums at Samarkand, Tashkent and Akhabad suggesting Central Asian influence on its regional variations. The Linden-Museum holds a bucket of similar dimensions and is also decorated with the twelve zodiacal symbols within roundels (Stuttgart 1993, ill. 78). The motif is not uncommon and reflects a growing interest in astronomy, astrology and magic. The high detail was presumably influenced by contemporary manuscripts, now lost. On our specimen the zodiacal symbols are connected by a broad copper band forming knots between the roundels. The upper part of the body shows a copper-inlaid inscription against a background

matted by ring-shaped punches and covered with palmettes. The ribbed foot is a feature frequently encountered on Central Asian objects.

Some idea of the kind of customers for whom such buckets were produced is supplied by a companion piece in the Hermitage, dated equivalent to 1163 and acquired in Bukhara in 1885 (Veselovsky 1910; Kuwait 1990, no. 30). According to the inscription, the piece originally belonged to a trader from Zanjan in northern Iran, here praised as a "pride to merchants", a pious Muslim who had made the pilgrimage to Mecca and Medina. The percentage of those who had travelled to the holiest places of Islam was particularly high among merchants. With wealth came the obligation to perform the hadj, which was also an opportunity to trade sanctioned by the Koran. The bucket was richly inlaid with silver and copper by a craftsman from Herat recorded in the inscription, and its depictions of wine drinkers, musicians and backgammon players, the embodiment of sophisticated entertainment, reflect the aspirations of merchants who had made good.

Many of the most successful merchants in Muslim Central Asia came from Khorezm, where opportunities for far-flung trading ventures were especially rich. From literary sources we learn that merchants from Khorezm, conspicuous by their high fur caps, were represented in every town in Khorasan. They used part of their profits for educational purposes, and according to al-Muqaddasi there were few teachers of law, religion or philosophy who had no Khorezmians among their students. The main Central Asian centres of learning were Bukhara and Samarkand, and it is due to a high regard for the sciences that astronomical and astrological symbols and motifs were integrated into the decorative repertoire. In these grand cities, the costly bronze mortar became established as an important item for alchemical and pharmaceutical experiments.

Among the beneficiaries of this respect for learning were the makers of paraphernalia for the writing-desk, items which became a status symbol among scholars. Excavations at Afrasiab brought to light cylindrical ink-wells and a rectangular pen-case, variously fashioned from clay, glass and stucco. The earliest bronze ink-well was found at Nishapur and is probably of Central Asian origin (Allan 1982, no. 105), while writing implements found in Uzbekistan and Tajikistan date from the twelfth century (Pugachenkova 1961, pls. 195-7; Leningrad 1985, no. 779). In the eastern part of the Islamic world, these implements of bronze were the most prestigious objects for a discerning clientele served by master craftsmen.

A bronze pen-case found in 1887 on the site of an ancient castle on the south-eastern bank of the Aral Sea is inscribed with the maker's name, `Umar ibn al-Fadl ibn Yusuf al-bayya, 'al-bayya' indicating that he belonged to those highly respected merchants who according to surviving documents, were sometimes also in charge of quality control and trade supervision. The owner of the pen-case was one `Ali ibn Yusuf ibn `Uthman al-Hadji, presumably also a merchant, since that profession included a particularly large number of pilgrims (Giuzalian 1968, 95). The copper and

211

Plate. Cast bronze, engraved. After casting, the relief decoration was carved with a chisel or burin. The rather rough cast was enhanced with a thick layer of fire-gilding. The motifs of a ruler on horseback and sphinxes are unusual for metalware, but can be found on minai pottery of the late 13th/early 14th century. No similar gilt bronze object seems to be known.

D: 18.2 cm

Khorasan or Central Asia, 13th/14th century

silver inlaid pen-case is dated equivalent to 1148. A contemporary ink-well inscribed with the name 'Muhammad al-bayya' is further proof that particularly distinguished merchants also did business as craftsmen, but they mainly appear as customers and patrons on the occasional inscription. One major commission is a large late-fifteenth-century basin from Herat or Samarkand (Komaroff 1992, no. 37). Merchants knew about the merits of particular workshops and appreciated objects of fine quality for personal use.

The most famous pen-case from pre-Mongol times was acquired in Bukhara in 1928 and is now at the Freer Gallery of Art in Washington (Herzfeld 1936; Atil 1985, no. 14). It is dated in accordance with 1210-1 and originally belonged to Majd al-Mulk al-Muzaffar, Grand Vizier to the last shah of Khorezm. The shah, who had exchanged embassies with Genghis Khan and thereby had kindled the latter's interest in trade relations with Muslim countries, was held responsible for the murder of members of a Mongol trade caravan, which provoked the Mongol storm across Central Asia. The grand vizier, a bibliophile and founder of a library at Merv, died in 1221 during the capture of the city. The pen-case was presumably also produced at Merv, which was not only the hometown of its owner but also a centre for metalwork, reflected in the cognomen 'al-Marwazi' used by some artists. In this case, however, the artist was Shazi, who hailed from Herat. Like commercial traffic, itinerant craftsmen contributed to the dissemination of shapes and decorative techniques.

212
Censer. Cast bronze.
H: 13.0 cm, D: 15.2 cm (top)
Transoxiana, 11th century

During the second half of the twelfth century, Herat was the undisputed centre of inlaid metalwork, the great skill of its craftsmen documented, for instance, by the above-mentioned bucket of 1163 in the Hermitage. This type of decorative work was also popular among the rulers themselves, as a candlestick dated 1166 with a silver inlaid inscription to the Ghurid Abu l-Fath Muhammad shows (Stuttgart 1993, ills. 82-83). Contacts between the Ghurids and the Khorezm shah surely helped to spread the demand for inlaid metalwork; the fluctuating character of these relations is perhaps defined by the fact that Muhammad sent an embassy to the shah's court and Khorezm conquered the Ghurid heartland including Herat and Balkh in 1206.

Ribbed bowls like the one in the Moser collection (MK 158) with inlaid motifs in roundels recalling the symbolic animals of earlier silver flasks, were now produced in Central Asia. The large serving plates of Central Asia with ribbed body or rim and a simple engraved decoration (Sarre 1906, no. 13; cf. Martin 1902, pl. 30; Melikian-Chirvani 1982, no. 20; Paris 1992, no. 335; Leningrad 1985, no. 825) were supplemented and replaced by more elaborate examples with relatively thick inlay of copper and silver, as we know from discoveries made in western Turkestan (cf. London 1976, no. 185).

Meanwhile regional characteristics tended to be displaced by a mixture of stylistic elements from various directions. The development of a trans-regional style had been encouraged both by ordinary trade ware and the much-acclaimed gifts presented by embassies, their exotic appearance presumably inspiring much imitation. A large basin in the Samarkand museum, which recalls a type of vessel known from central Afghanistan, could thus conceivably have been produced in Central Asia (Paris 1992, no. 334). The central ornament shows an eight-petalled rosette with silver inlay surrounded by fishes, also with silver inlay and indicating the vessel's use as a water-basin. The fish motif also appears on ceramics from Afrasiab (Moscow 1991, no. 574).

A central rosette enhanced by silver inlay appears on numerous basins of the late twelfth century as well as on serving plates with typically Central Asian multi-shaped sides and on a basin with incurved rim in the Linden-Museum (ill. 220). The most remarkable feature are the two handles in the shape of human figures, which closely resemble objects excavated in Tadjikistan (Leningrad 1985, no. 778). The similarity in size, decorating technique and the hairstyle and posture of the figures raises the question of provenance. The practice of fashioning handles in a somewhat similar way is documented by an accidental discovery made at Budrakh of a handle surmounted by a feline head (ill. 217). The crudely finished handle has been dated to the eleventh century (Moscow 1991, no. 552).

Immediately after the Mongol conquest the Chinese monk Changchun, approaching via Talas, visited the cities of Central Asia. His account suggests that even two years after its capture by the Mongols, Samarkand was still a flourishing entrepot (Waley 1931:107). Genghis Khan had given permission to plunder Samarkand and Bukhara only once.

213
Part of a censer in the shape of a large feline head. Bronze.
5.5 x 4.0 cm
Transoxiana, Budrakh, 11th century
Khamza Institute of Fine Arts, Tashkent

214
Bronze mortar inscribed "In the name of God,
the Compassionate, the Merciful,
blessings on the owner".
20 x 20 cm
Transoxiana, Budrakh, 11th century

215
Bronze mortar with epigraphic bands, naskhi at the top and kufic at the bottom. Medallions
enclosing animal figures and a female bust.
11.0 x 12.7 cm
Transoxiana, 12th century
Private collection, Sindelfingen

216
Mortar. Bronze with copper inlay.
10.9 x 12.7 cm
Transoxiana, about 1200
Museum für Völkerkunde, Berlin

Changchun was surprised to see tableware for everyday use made of brass or copper, whereas in China these metals were reserved for ritual paraphernalia and ordinary wares were of porcelain. Among local ceramics he mentioned in particular a white ware which in China was highly esteemed and may have been produced at Samarkand by Chinese potters. Changchun remarks that "Chinese craftsmen are found everywhere" in Samarkand, their presence perhaps explaining the Chinese mark on the above-mentioned bronze mortar.

By the mid-thirteenth century the cities of Central Asia had regained their pre-Mongol cultural level. Samarkand continued to produce much metalwork, as suggested by excavations of Registan Square at the city centre, where the workshop of a coppersmith was discovered at a depth of eight metres below the present building level (Moscow 1991, nos. 682-90). On the evidence of the multitudious forms and designs it must have been active for several generations, the discovery of a silver coin from the reign of Timur (1370-1405) providing a reference point.

Among the earliest objects from the time of the Mongol conquest is a vessel with an animated inscription around the neck highlighted by silver inlay (ill. 223). Human faces engraved on the silver inlay recall a decoration popular in Central Asia in the early thirteenth century, which also appears on the above-mentioned pen-case. The inscriptions are separated by large knots with silver inlay, a traditional feature of Central Asian designs used to great effect, as on the bronze kettle with copper inlay (ill. 219).

While the vessel is Central Asian in form and design, other bronzes may be of Iranian origin. Among them are works of the late thirteenth and early fourteenth century which may have reached Samarkand as trade or booty. A silver inlaid fragment also has gold inlay, a type of decoration first found under the Mongol Ilkhan dynasty (Moscow 1991, no. 684).

Central Asian craftsmanship obviously went through a critical phase when Timur in the late fourteenth century deported hundreds of artisans from the conquered lands and settled them at Samarkand. The huge vessel for drinking-water Timur commissioned for the shrine of Ahmad Yasawi at Yasi north of Tashkent together with the candlesticks donated to the mausoleum are of Iranian craftsmanship. At Samarkand the community of conscripted artisans was particularly large and when they were released six years after Timur's death, the majority presumably chose to stay.

It is possible that Samarkand was the place of production of the spouted ewer with rounded body and pointed top and a handle with an opening to fill the vessel (ill. 225). This type is known in several examples only from the Safawid period and includes one acquired by Rickmers in Bukhara (IB 3268; Westphal-Hellbusch 1974, no. 95). The cast relief design is interspersed with silver inlay. The flattened sides are particularly richly inlaid with ornamental lettering in the centre surrounded by weave-pattern medallions reminiscent of manuscript designs.

Under Timur's nephew Ulugh Beg (1417-49) cast and inlaid metalwork experienced a revival. The jade vessels he

217
Handle with head of a large feline. Cast bronze.
11 x 5 cm
Transoxiana, Budrakh, 10th/11th century
Khamza Institute of Fine Arts, Tashkent

218
Skewer rests. Cast bronze.
W: 22.0 and 11.5 cm
Transoxiana, Budrakh, 11th century
Khamza Institute of Fine Arts, Tashkent

219
Bucket. Bronze, copper inlay.
H: 17.5 cm, D: 17.4 cm (top)
Transoxiana, Merv, 12th century
Registan Museum, Samarkand

220
Basin. Bronze with silver inlay. The handles shaped in the form of human figures (cf. ill.
217). The elaborate epigraphic bands with silver inlay bestow blessings on the owner.
H: 9.0 cm, D: 33.5 cm
Afghanistan or Transoxiana, about 1200

commissioned are well-known. In 1424-5 two huge blocks of jade were transported to Samarkand from Karshi south of the city. One was designed for Timur's mausoleum in the Gur-e Mir, the other – which has survived – was fashioned into vessels, a jug and two cups with dedications to Ulugh Beg.

Local coppersmiths began to produce jugs of the same shape and also with dragon handles. An inlaid jug made at Samarkand in the workshop of Shir `Ali Dimashqi and dated 1467, is held by the Türk ve Islam Eserleri Müzesi in Istanbul (ills. 227-8). The *nisbat* (cognomen) 'Dimashqi', which also appears on a vessel of 1474-5 by the same master, obviously refers to a quarter of Samarkand, Timur having named the suburbs of his residence after famous Islamic cities (Komaroff 1992, 104). The decoration consists of inscriptions, which also indicate the function of the vessel as a wine jug, large lotus blossoms, small quatrefoil rosettes and spacious forked-leaf scrolls interspersed with trefoils, such as also appear on particularly precious examples of other locally produced items of the minor arts.

The appreciation of wine jugs at the Timurid courts is attested by one in the British Museum which bears the name of the last Timurid ruler of Herat, Sultan Husain (1470-1506). Around this time plant motifs become much simplified. A jug dated 1505 in the Museum für Islamische Kunst is covered with dense scroll-work and several inscribed cartouches (ills. 221, 222). It was made by Ala'uddin Shamsuddin Muhammad al-Birjandi, according to his cognomen a native of the provincial town of Birjand in Khuzistan, which can be ruled out as the place of manufacture (Berlin 1985, no. 339).

The inlay of the jug simply consists of thin silver wire set at the centre of its fine arabesque decoration. A copper basin acquired by Rickmers in Bukhara and presumably meant for everyday use, is devoid of all inlay so that the relatively monotonous scrollwork depends for its appeal solely on the delicate chisel-work (ill. 226). This vessel, cast and finished on the lathe, presumably dates from after the capture of Samarkand by the Uzbek Muhammad Khan Shaibani (1500-10) and thus stands at the beginning of a tradition which can be documented by numerous metal objects acquired in Bukhara during the nineteenth century (Westphal-Hellbusch 1974, no. 114).

221-222
Vessel. Brass, silver inlay.
H: 12.7 cm
Transoxiana, dated A.H. 910 (A.D. 1505)
Museum für Islamische Kunst, Berlin

224
Mirror. The back with cast relief decoration of roundels enclosing animal figures and a male figure with a club.
D: 7 cm
Transoxiana, 12th/13th century

223
Vessel, with detail of the bottom. Bronze, silver inlay.
H: 20 cm
Transoxiana, Samarkand, early 13th century
Registan Museum, Samarkand

225
Ewer. Bronze, silver inlay.
H: 27.0 cm, D: 9.5 cm (bottom)
Transoxiana, 14th/15th century

226
Copper basin. Tin-plated, with an inscription suggesting one should banish all prosaic thoughts and memories and devote oneself to pleasure.
H: 17.8 cm, greatest diameter: 40.5 cm
Transoxiana, early 16th century
Museum für Völkerkunde, Berlin

227-228
Vessel, with detail of the bottom. Brass, with gold and silver inlay.
Transoxiana, Samarkand, dated A.H. 872 (A.D. 1467)
Türk ve Islam Eserleri Müzesi
(with kind permission of the directorate)

137

Metalwork since the Fifteenth Century

Johannes Kalter

The previous essay on early Islamic metalwork included typically sophisticated productions for the Timurid courts. For a start, we shall now again treat of Timurid work, since it laid the foundations for the ornamental repertoire characteristic of the metallwork produced from the eighteenth to the early twentieth century.

The Timurid period continued to produce heavy cast-bronze objects with engraved or inlaid decoration, but also saw the beginnings of forged or chased brasswork with engraved designs.

Among the cast objects we find, for example, a circular mirror, the front decorated with a magic square of suras and religious invocations and the back with five fishes in lively motion (ill. 229). Strong Chinese influence is noticeable on a door plaque showing in relief the fight between a lion and a snake-dragon, the background decorated with chrysanthemum blossoms (ill. 231). A bronze ewer, the body originally blackened, with the spout and handle terminating in dragon heads, seems more inspired by Muslim India (ill. 233). The only decoration on this simple yet highly elegant object is an engraved band of lappets around the shoulder.

Classic Islamic traditions are represented among cast metalwork by a shield boss or a door plaque with an openwork design of plant motifs and stylised trefoils (ill. 230). The only indication of its Central Asian provenance are the roundels filled with engraved Greek crosses and motifs resembling compass roses.

Herat was the main centre for the manufacture of precious vessels with gold inlay designed for the court and of bronze objects with silver inlay for less exalted customers. A wine ewer with overhead handle and flattened body is a good example (ill. 225). The roundels on the sides are filled with inlaid silver pseudo-epigraphy, while another roundel beneath the spout shows an inlaid rosette. The weave-pattern along the handle and the plant motifs suggest a fifteenth-century date. Of the same date is a bowl from Herat with low foot and lightly ribbed body, its only decoration a silver inlay inscription running along the rim (ill. 232). The most unusual Timurid object in the Linden-Museum was also produced in Herat. The designs on the silver bowl with melon-shaped chased body and an omphalos at the base are all inlaid with copper. They consist of an epigraphic frieze interspersed with very elaborate rosettes within roundels on the rim border. The ribs are covered with fine dense scrollwork terminating in an inlaid copper crescent at the upper end. This bowl may be the only piece of Islamic silverwork of silver with copper inlay (ill. 206).

Pouring vessels with a long beak-like spout were known in Central Asia and northern Afghanistan since the Bronze Age. The Linden-Museum has two examples. The body of the earlier vessel made at Herat in about 1500 is

229
Mirror. Cast bronze, the back showing a circle around the handle and a broad band with five fishes in lively movement.
D: 7.9 cm
Central Asia, 14th/15th century

230
Door fitting or buckle of a shield (?). Cast bronze, openwork, engraved, the buckle lightly ribbed and surrounded with engraved circles, the openwork of plant motifs, heavily worn roundels enclosing engraved Greek crosses and compass roses.
H: 3.0 cm, D: 18.9 cm Herat (?), 14th/15th century

231
Fragment of a door fitting. Cast bronze, engraved, the cast relief decoration showing a battle between a snake dragon and a lion against a background of chrysanthemums.
H: 10 cm, W: 21 cm Eastern Iran or Central Asia, 14th century

completely covered with an engraved design consisting of
two bands of inscriptions in naskhi and interlaced oval
medallions filled with plant motifs (ills. 629-30). With
astonishing skill a spiralling scroll with sagittate leaves has
been made to accompany the tapering spout. The later vessel
is much more elegantly shaped and was acquired by
Rickmers in Bukhara in the late nineteenth century (ills.
631-2). The body is decorated with horizontal bands with
alternating designs of eight-pointed stars and lozenges filled
with a plant with three blossoms. A flowering scroll at the
broad end of the spout develops into a very delicately
executed spiral scroll with sagittate leaves. The outer side of
the spout and the base bear a date (A.H. 1208/A.D. 1793)
and a name (Khan or Khaqan/Husain?). A comparison of
these two ewers definitely refutes the widespread view of a
decline in eighteenth-century Bukharan craftsmanship. At
least the artist who produced the 1793 vessel showed himself
a consummate master of his craft.

232
Bowl. Cast bronze, silver inlay, blackened, engraved, the body with low ribs, along the rim
a naskhi inscription with silver inlay against a scrolling background.
H: 8.8 cm, D: 16.9 cm (top)
Eastern Khorasan or Afghanistan, late 14th/early 15th century

233
Ewer. Cast bronze, the handle and spout terminating in dragon heads, along the shoulder
an engraved frieze with niche patterns; lid missing.
H: 25.5 cm
Central Asia, 15th century
Private collection, Sindelfingen

139

Ceramics from the Ninth to the Twelfth Century

Johannes Kalter

A distinctive Islamic ceramic art first developed under the influence of the Abbasid caliphs. The earliest examples come from Samarra, the short-lived residence (836–c. 886) of the caliphs near Baghdad, which began life as a garrison of an elite Turkish regiment. With its softly rounded shapes, so-called 'Samarra ware' follows Chinese models. The main design element is a decoratively arranged inscription or epigraphic design, usually in cobalt blue over a white or buff slip.

The earliest examples of Samanid pottery made at Nishapur and Afrasiab are almost contemporary. The Samanids were famous for their sophisticated lifestyle, and at their residence at Bukhara and the governmental seat at Nishapur they presumably used many Chinese wares. For the outer circle of the court another highly refined and very distinctive ware was produced. Where the design consists of inscriptions, it is often hard to decide whether they were made at Afrasiab or Nishapur. Afrasiab in addition developed a number of independent decorative types. What follows is a description, by no means exhaustive, of the major types.

The earliest Afrasiab ware is characterised by green underglaze painting over a white slip with geometric designs or stylised plant designs with epigraphic ornamentation (ills. 253-4). Beginning in the ninth century, this style continued well into the eleventh century. Ceramics known only from Samarkand show a red slip with underglaze painting executed in ocre shading into yellow, white and manganese brown (ills. 242-3). A common motif are stylised animals inside roundels, but we also find vessels with bold manganese-brown inscriptions on a red slip. Bowls and plates with green, yellow and manganese brown running glazes and sgrafitto designs derive from Chinese Tang-dynasty prototypes (ill. 257). This ware was produced both at Nishapur and Afrasiab, tenth-century Afrasiab ware being distinguished by a much finer sgrafitto, which often gives a web-like impression. Both centres also produced bowls and vessels with inscriptions in manganese brown and more rarely in red over a white or buff slip, and here the provenance is most difficult to distinguish. Objects definitely from Transoxiana or indeed Afrasiab often have inscriptions larger and bolder than those from Nishapur. Black or dark brown wares with light green inscriptions are as yet only known from Afrasiab. Where bowls show an 'endless knot' in the well (an auspicious Buddhist symbol), they can securely be assigned to Transoxiana.

Unglazed wares with relief decoration

The majority of objects mentioned above come from the Bactrian lowlands of northern Afghanistan some forty kilometres west of Balkh near the Amu Darya. Results from several thermoluminiscence tests suggest that the earliest

pieces date from the eighth century, the latest from the eleventh century. Common to them all is that they were produced from moulds. The body of jugs with narrow necks and of ewer- and vase-shaped vessels was constructed from two parts, while the neck and handle was individually formed. The area where the two parts join, is only superficially polished. The ewers usually have a sieve inserted at the spout. Some of the objects show a complex design scheme, while others simply show geometric or epigraphic decoration.

A remarkable piece is the ewer with a freely modelled animal head (bull or ram?) forming the spout and an epigraphic band and a lotus border along the shoulder (ills. 234-7). The upper half of the body shows a band of roundels occasionally separated by 'endless knots', with trefoils and feline motifs in the spandrels. The lower part is decorated with a frieze of birds of prey turning left, and below a second frieze with rams turning right. Ewers with comparable animal heads incorporated into the spout and a similar profile were produced in the region until the twelfth/thirteenth century both in metalwork and glazed ceramics. Our ewer probably dates from the ninth century.

A frieze of ibexes, highly stylised and resembling cave paintings, also appears on a ewer with narrow neck and flaring rim recalling metalwork (ills. 244-5). The upper part of a rounded ewer with handle shows a pattern somewhat similar to the cross bonds of contemporary architecture (ills. 244, 246). The lower part is decorated with highly stylised fishes alternating with rosettes of a type known from Achaemenid and Sasanian times. Another borrowing from architectural ornaments seems to be the lozenge pattern of a ewer with waisted neck as well as the sequence of hexagons on a flat bowl with bosses recalling metalwork. A squat ewer has a vertical weave-pattern along the body which is likewise reminiscent of engraved metalwork (ill. 250).

Epigraphic designs may consist of monumental foliated kufic suggesting stencilling or of naskhi with wedge-shaped endings (*hastae*) against a scrolling background. Human figures appear only rarely on unglazed pottery. A fragment from Nishapur is decorated with the figure of a man inside a multi-lobed panel and a falcon in the spandrel above, the decoration itself being probably carved (ill. 270). The figure is carefully executed and clearly shows the drapery of the garment – presumably of silk – as well as such details as locks, beard and belt. A twelfth-century jug with handle has a moulded decoration of human couples holding hands alternating with globular medallions with an epigraphic border and filled with scrolls and addorsed geese (ill. 261). The lower part shows epigraphic designs. Comparable ewers of this type were found in Termez, Merv and elsewhere.

The potters' work methods can be illustrated with the help of moulds found in the above-mentioned area. One of the bowl-shaped moulds shows a design of cartouches with scroll pattern and a dotted ground (ill. 264). The clay, pressed into the mould, would shrink after drying and could then be removed to serve as a blank. Two moulds are cupola-shaped with carved friezes of birds of prey (ill. 263). Here the clay would be stuck to the outside of the mould and removed after drying. From the same site comes a stamp depicting a feline within a roundel, a motif found on one of the ewers in the museum's collection (ill. 265).

Freely modelled animal figures were meant as toys or as auspicious New Year presents; the site included horses, sometimes saddled, a creature combining elements of a cockerel and a ram, and a dove as a symbol of *baraka*, spiritual power or blessing (ill. 266).

Painted ceramics

Hand-moulded ceramics with manganese-brown designs over a white and occasionally red slip are documented for the region since pre-historic times. Objects in the Museum with plant motifs, wave-like scrolls and other curvilinear patterns as well as occasional shaped additions were dated by thermoluminiscence tests to the ninth to eleventh century, the Samanid period. Especially remarkable are the fragments of jugs showing an applied human face at the spout (ill. 274) and an applied snake in strong relief encircling the body (ill. 267 centre). Such objects were presumably produced by peasant women to supplement the family income. If we search for their influence on urban Samanid ceramics, the nearest thing may be the design on a shoulder pot with cover from Nishapur, its original glaze lost by soil action (ill. 269).

234-237
Ewer. Unglazed pottery, made in five sections, moulded design, incised design at the spout. The freely modelled and dysfunctional spout is in the shape of an animal head (bull?). Along the shoulder an epigraphic band and another with lotus-leaf pattern, with roundels enclosing figures of cats and separated by trefoils below (ill. 235). Along the lower part friezes with birds of prey (ill. 236) and with rams (ill. 237).
H: c. 26.5 cm
Northern Afghanistan or Central Asia, 9th century

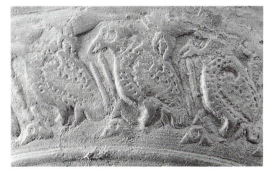

141

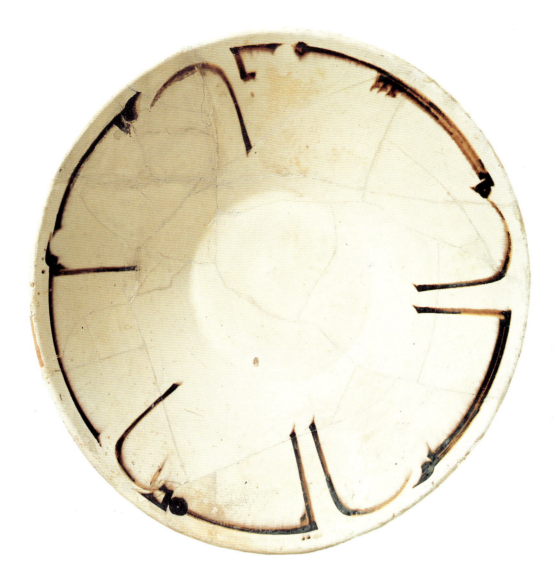

238
Bowl. Glazed earthenware, white slip, brown painting under a colourless transparent glaze.
Large bowl with flat well and everted sides on a circular foot. The only decoration consists of
a large and striking inscription in decorative kufic, the hastae boldly elongated almost to the
well: "The free man is [always] free, even if he meets with a loss. Good luck!" (read by
`Abdallah Ghouchani). The aphorism is attributed to `Ali, the son-in-law of the Prophet
and founder of the Shi`a. It is known from several bowls. Inscriptions with good wishes for
the owner, with blessings, proverbs, poems or quotations from the famous were a popular
decorative device for vessels during the Samanid period.
H: 11 cm, D: 36 cm
Uzbekistan (Afrasiab) or Iran (Nishapur), 10th century
Museum für Islamische Kunst, Berlin

239 (left)
Bowls. Glazed earthenware, white slip, epigraphic design in flowering kufic and pseudo-
epigraphic design in manganese-brown underglaze painting.
H: 8.0-9.5 cm, D: 21.5-26.0 cm
Nishapur or Afrasiab, 10th/11th century

240 (right)
Bowls. Glazed earthenware, red, manganese-brown and yellow underglaze painting showing
palmettes, pseudo-epigraphy and scattered flowers (left) and palmettes and keyfret (right).
Nishapur or Afrasiab, 10th century
The bowl in front with pseudo-epigraphy and keyfret.
H: 7.4-8.5 cm, D: 17.5-26.5 cm
Afrasiab, 11th century

241
Dish. Glazed earthenware, white slip, underglaze painting in red, green and dark brown under a transparent glaze. Around the rim a pattern of highly stylised trefoils and an 'endless knot' at the centre. H: 7.0 cm, D: 35.5 cm
Afrasiab ware found at Tashkent, 11th century Museum of Fine Arts, Tashkent

242
Bowl. Glazed earthenware, red slip, colourless transparent glaze, underglaze painting showing three stylised birds in roundels with pearl borders. H: 2.5 cm, D: 27.0 cm
Afrasiab, late 10th/early 11th century Registan Museum, Samarkand

243
(Left) Glazed earthenware vase with a repeated "good fortune" in kufic. H: 13 cm
Near Samarkand, first half 11th century
(Right) Albarello (drug jar) with a repeated "prosperity" in 'foliated' kufic. H: 18.3 cm
Afrasiab, 10th century Registan Museum, Samarkand

143

244-246
Two ewers and a shoulder pot. Unglazed earthenware, moulded relief decoration. Ill. 245 shows a detail of the left vessel with a depiction of ibexes reminiscent of rock paintings. Ill. 246 shows a detail from the central vessel with loop patterns also known from contemporaneous architectural decoration and a design of fishes alternating with rosettes below.
H: 16.5-19.0 cm
Northern Afghanistan or Central Asia, 9th-11th century

247-248
Ewers. Unglazed earthenware with moulded designs and freely modelled opening with flowering scrollwork; for the left vessel, cf. ills. 180-184. Ill. 248 shows the honeycomb-shaped decoration of the central vessel, which is paralleled by contemporaneous architectural ornamentation. The shape of the right-hand vessel is reminiscent of contemporaneous metalware.
H: 19-21 cm
Northern Afghanistan or Central Asia, 9th-11th century

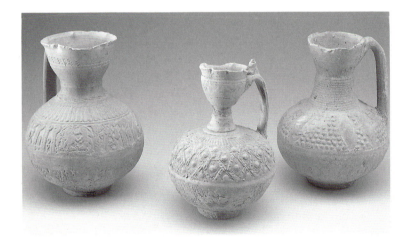

249
Ewers (partly damaged). Unglazed earthenware with moulded decoration. The main design element are inscriptions set against a scrolling background, with strong 'foliated' kufic on the left and naskhi script on the right.
H: 15 and 10 cm
Northern Afghanistan or Central Asia, 10th/11th century

144

250

(From left to right) Ewer, earthenware, incised decoration, bold horizontal plaitwork.
Northern Afghanistan or Central Asia, 9th/10th century. H: 9 cm
Footed bowl, unglazed earthenware, turned, incised decoration. Spiralling flower design
growing from a central rosette. Northern Afghanistan or Central Asia, 12th/13th century.
D: 7.8 cm.
Small vase, unglazed earthenware, moulded and stamped designs of hatching, rosettes and
circular elements. Northern Afghanistan or Central Asia, 9th century. H: 7.2 cm.

251

(Left) Bottle. Earthenware, with carved and incised decoration. The shoulder with a wave
border, the body with wave borders and ribs, the neck cut down. The shape imitates a type
of metalware ewer common in eastern Khorasan during the 8th/9th century.
(Right) Vessel with narrow neck. Unglazed earthenware, moulded design, epigraphic band
in naskhi around the shoulder. The lower part shows rosettes and star-shaped elements.
H: 25.5 and 18.5 cm
Northern Afghanistan or Central Asia, 9th-11th century.

252

Ewer. Unglazed earthenware, inset sieve, moulded designs, around the neck incised wave
pattern.
H: 28 cm
Northern Afghanistan or Central Asia, 11th/12th century.

253
Bowls. Glazed earthenware, green underglaze painting on a white slip, the designs of geometrical or highly stylised plant motifs. This type of ware seems to have been produced only at Afrasiab.
(Left) H: 10.0 cm, D: 34.5 cm; (right) H: 11.0 cm, D: 34.5 cm
Afrasiab, 10th century
Museum of Fine Arts, Tashkent

255 (opposite page)
Bowl. Glazed earthenware, underglaze painting in green, manganese-brown and yellow under a transparent glaze, sgrafitto decoration, the well with pseudo-epigraphic kufic design. Both the colour scheme and the running glaze show the influence of Chinese pottery of the Tang period on Afrasiab pottery.
H: 10 cm, D: 41 cm
Afrasiab, 10th century
Registan Museum, Samarkand

254
Bowl. Glazed earthenware, green underglaze decoration with manganese-brown contours on a white slip with geometrical, highly geometricised plant and pseudo-epigraphic designs.
H: 8.5 cm, D: 27.0 cm
Afrasiab ware, 10th century
Museum of Fine Arts, Tashkent

256
Bowl. Glazed earthenware with overglaze painting on a copper oxide slip.
The well shows a highly abstract animal figure (a bird or composite creature),
the inside a bold epigraphic frieze in 'foliated' kufic.
H: 6.5 cm, D: 20.5 cm
Afrasiab, 10th century

257
Low bowl. Glazed earthenware, red underglaze painting on white slip. The decoration
consists simply of a flattened kufic inscription running across the field.
H: 3.5 cm, D: 12.0 cm Afrasiab, 12th century Registan Museum, Samarkand

258-259
Low bowl imitating metal shapes. Unglazed earthenware, moulded decoration, the outside with globular knobs and honeycomb pattern reminiscent of architectural ornaments, the bottom decorated with concentric circles enclosing rosettes and interlocking ovals.
H: 4.8 cm, D: 15.0 cm
Northern Afghanistan or Central Asia, 10th/11th century

260
Pilgrim flask. Unglazed earthenware, carved and moulded decoration. The central medallion with a geometricised rosette is surrounded by three bands with dentiform or wheat-ear motifs. The pilgrim flask as a type is documented in the region since Parthian times.
H: 29.0 cm, D: 22.5 cm
Northern Afghanistan or Central Asia, 9th century or earlier

261
Detail from a ewer with moulded decoration. The droplet-shaped medallion encloses addorsed geese and is framed by a pseudo-epigraphic frieze.
Northern Afghanistan or Central Asia, 12th century

262
Mould. Unglazed earthenware with carved design of interlacing stars.
D: 7 cm
Iran, Timurid, 15th century

263
Moulds. Carved designs of bird friezes, the left in addition with a stamped band of roundels.
Both moulds have holds on the inside. The clay would be pressed over the mould.
H: c. 6 cm, D: 15 and 16 cm
Northern Afghanistan or Central Asia, 9th-11th century

264
Mould. Earthenware with carved designs of four cartouches with leavy scrolls against a dotted background, a pearl border around the well. The clay would be pressed into the mould.
H: 9.8 cm, D: 20.0 cm
Northern Afghanistan or Central Asia, 9th-11th century

265
Stamp. Unglazed earthenware, carved to show a lion.
D: 5.7 cm
Iran or Central Asia, 12th-14th century

266
Votive offerings or toys in animal shape. Earthenware, freely modelled. From left to right a large feline (?), H: 12 cm; a composite creature, part rooster and part ram, H: 17 cm; and a dove, H: 11 cm.
Northern Afghanistan or Central Asia, 9th-11th century

267
Freely modelled earthenware pottery. Manganese painting on a slip. (Left) Storage vessel with chequer pattern and geometric and curvilinear designs; H. 53.5 cm. (Centre) Jug, partly broken, with an apllied snake in high relief; H: 30.0 cm. (Right) Jug with narrow neck and geometric and curvilinear designs; H: 38.5 cm.
Northern Afghanistan or Central Asia, 9th-11th century

268
Double-handled jars and ewer (partly broken). Earthenware, manganese painting on a slip. H (left to right): c. 45.0 cm, 34.5 cm, 45.0 cm
Northern Afghanistan or Central Asia, 9th-11th century

269
Shoulder jar with lid. Glazed earthenware, underglaze painting in manganese-brown and red on a white slip. Due to soil action the glaze has almost completely degraded. The designs on the upper part of the body of large oval medallions, curvilinear motifs and lightly indicated leaves and birds' heads are very closely related to the objects in ills. 267 and 268. H: c. 38 cm (without lid)
Nishapur, 10th/11th century

270
Shard. Unglazed earthenware with carved decoration of a male figure within a bracket-lobed cartouche, the squinches with falcons against a scrolling background. H: 9 cm
Nishapur, 10th century

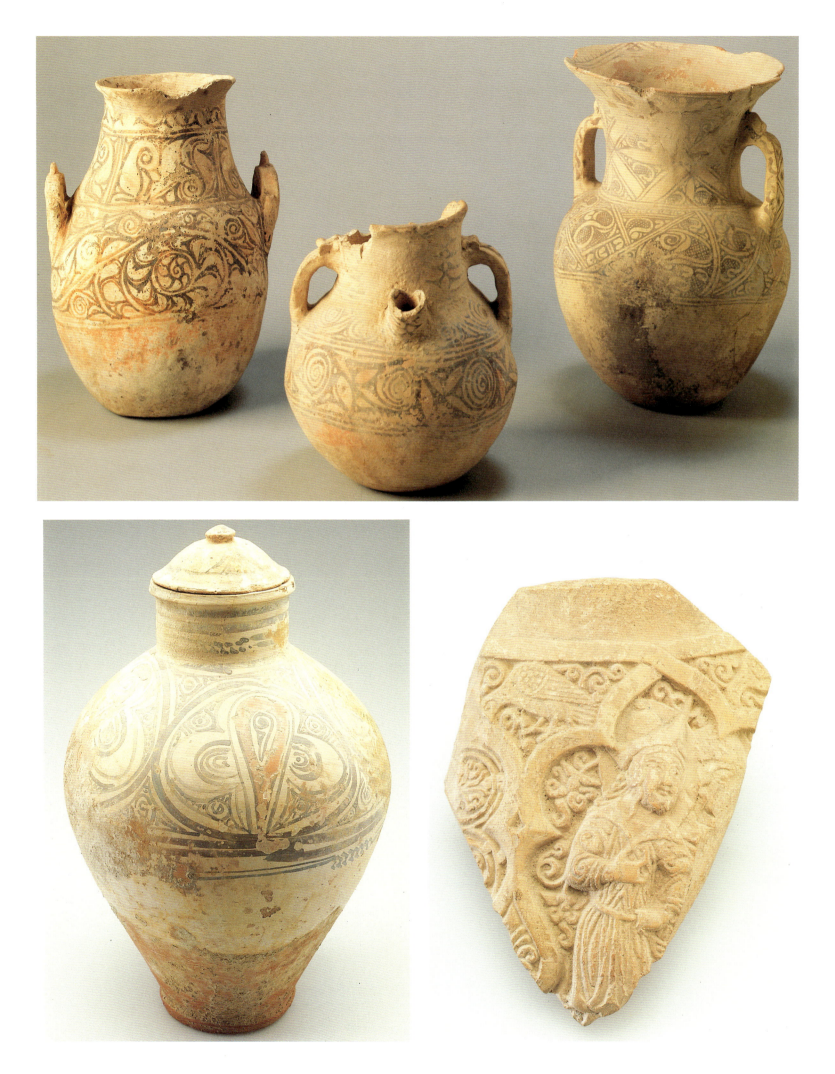

271
*Two jugs and a ewer (centre). The left jug is remarkable for the arrangement of the
ornamentation in horizontal bands, and the right jug for its plaited handle.
H (left to right): 20 cm, 23 cm, 19 cm
Northern Afghanistan or Central Asia, 9th-11th century*

272
*Bowl, earthenware with manganese painting on a slip. The unusual division into three
compartments and the pierced lug for handling suggest that the bowl was designed for offering
condiments. Glass stones are applied on the inside and atop the partitions.
H: 13.5 cm, D 20.0 cm
Northern Afghanistan or Central Asia, 9th-11th century*

273
Shoulder jar. Earthenware, freely modelled, manganese painting on a white slip. Light indentations along the rim were probably made with fingers. The bold scrolling design can also be found on 11th-century architectural decoration of the Ghaznavids in Afghanistan. The shape is reminiscent of urban censers.
H: 15 cm
Northern Afghanistan or Central Asia, 9th-11th century

274
Fragment of a jug. Freely modelled earthenware, manganese painting on a slip; handle missing. On account of heavy deterioration, the design scheme cannot be reconstructed. The applied human face is unusual.
H: c. 15 cm
Northern Afghanistan or Central Asia, 9th-11th century

277
Ewer with long neck, small spout and high five-lobed spout. Grey-white stoneware, creamy-white glaze. The shape and white glaze imitate ewers of chased metal, usually silver.
H: 27.5 cm, D: 13.2 cm
China, probably Liaoning province, Liao dynasty (907-1125), 10th century

278
Mongol horse-woman. Stone-paste, black underglaze painting and turquoise-coloured glaze. The figure is depicted holding the reins with one hand, a characteristic of all nomad horsemen; the shield on the back is a notable feature.
H: 21 cm
Iran, Kashan, mid-13th century

Like Porcelain: Ceramics of the Fourteenth to Sixteenth Century from Uzbekistan

Gisela Helmecke

When Timur ascended the throne at Samarkand in 1370, he decided to turn his new residence into a city worthy of a world conqueror. To realise this programme, he carried off the best artists and craftsmen from all the cities he conquered in Iran, the Near East and India to his capital; they often were the only ones spared when the rest of the population was massacred. Marvelling at the splendour of the new Samarkand, the Spanish ambassador Ruy Gonzales de Clavijo, who spent the years 1403 to 1406 at Timur's court, mentioned among others "the craftsmen [deported from Damascus] in glass and porcelain, who are known to be the best in all the world".[1] What he called 'porcelain', was the delicate fritware of Damascus decorated in blue on a white ground. At the time the manufacture of true porcelain was still an art only known in China and a tantalizing mystery everywhere else.

Clavijo also admired the many splendid buildings of Samarkand, especially pointing out their gold and blue tilework. This probably refers both to the so-called *lajvardina* tiles which can still be found on some of the buildings, and to *cuerda seca* tiles (which were painted with different coloured glazes kept in place by waxed outlines); they both tend to be embellished with much gold. The *lajvardina* technique (pottery painted in colours and gold over deep blue or turquoise glazes) was also used for the production of vessels, although apparently not in Central Asia (ill. 295 right).[2] This also applies to the so-called *minai* vessels (where the pottery is decorated by applying colours over the fired glaze and re-firing) with polychrome figurative decoration inspired by illustrated manuscripts, which are occasionally found in Central Asia, although the only centre of production so far known was Kashan in Iran. Presumably these wares arrived in the region mainly by way of trade, since locally the techniques were used exclusively for architectural ornamentation.

A much more important role was played by Chinese porcelains introduced to Central Asia predominantly as commercial goods traded along the Silk Route, but also by way of booty, for instance from the Tughlug Palace after the sack of Delhi in 1398, and as offical gifts presented by Chinese embassies. Porcelain was said to have various medicinal and hygienic properties, the polymath Nasir al-Din Tusi (1207-74) even claiming that it could detect poison by turning moist on contact. Such an assertion presumably contributed to the popularity of Chinese porcelain at the Timurid court.[3] Clavijo describes the huge plates from which meat was served at Timur's banquets. Some were of gold and of silver, "while others were of vitrified earthenware, or else of what is known as porcelain, and these last are much esteemed and of very high price".[4] Timur's

nephew Ulugh Beg had a Çini kösk built in a Samarkand garden, a pavilion acting as the storehouse for precious porcelains, some of which he had specifically bought for display. In 1449 the kiosk was destroyed when the Uzbeks captured the city, but it is not known if the objects themselves perished or whether they were seized and taken to the Uzbek court.

The Chinese porcelain of the Yuan and early Ming dynasties, which concerns us here, was either pure white or painted blue on a white ground. The latter type in particular, was a model and inspiration, and the royal workshops produced fine pottery imitations which were designed by the *naqqash-khane*, a kind of central studio employing the best painters and calligraphers. Motifs included peony and lotus scrolls, chrysanthemums, scenes of lotus ponds with fishes and ducks, flying cranes and other aquatic birds, auspicious Buddhist symbols like the 'endless' knot and the pearl as well as mythical animals associated with the emperor such as dragons, phoenixes and *qilins* (a hoofed creature with fiery wings). Decorations with such Chinese motifs became a typical feature of Timurid ceramics not only in Central Asia, and brought about a radical general refashioning of the repertoire of forms and patterns. Their influence was felt as far away as Mamluk Egypt. Examples of the new blue-and-white style are known from Bukhara, Shahr-i Sabz, Nisa, Urgench, Shahrukhiya, Shash (Tashkent), Merv and in particular from Samarkand. Andizhan also became a production centre when Babur succeeded his father as ruler of Fergana in 1494 and attracted artists and craftsmen to his court.[5]

Among Central Asian blue-and-white ceramics two main types can be distinguished. One is made of common clay and is covered with a thick slip, thus producing a passable likeness to true porcelain. The other consists of a silicate-rich substance (*kashin*) which could fire at higher temperatures, resulting in a ware which was lighter and more delicate. The painting was then applied directly on the very light body or over a slip also containing silicate. For both types the painters copied the Chinese models very closely. A beautiful example is a bowl from the Ulugh Beg madrasa now in the Tashkent museum, decorated with two peony blossoms surrounded by floral scrolls (ill. 281).[6] An example where the Chinese model inspired the artists to original interpretations is the bowl from Bukhara with a large, freely stylised lotus blossom in the well and plant motifs along the sides which have little in common with Chinese styles (ill. 283).[7] We also find blue-and-white vessels with designs adopted from Persian models, showing linear decoration, arabesques and Arabic inscriptions, while others again combine Chinese, Persian and local elements for a new type of imagery. Besides colourless glazes blue and turquoise glazes were applied to vessels with black underglaze painting. Since the cobalt-based blue pigment had to be imported, such ceramics remained expensive. The painters therefore more often reverted to pigments found locally, producing designs in black (usually slightly transparent) or a blackish brown as well as turquoise green and turquoise blue. Such wares mostly are of coarser clay and have thick walls, making firing less exacting. The sinicised repertoire of motifs is less apparent than on blue-and-white wares but still discernible. Thus a bowl from Bukhara comes decorated with a simple spiralloid rosette in the well and along the wall an undulating foliate scroll with four simple oval blossoms or fruit.[8] This type of ceramics was less expensive and was widely distributed, examples being known from Samarkand and many other places in Uzbekistan. It is occasionally suggested that the type evolved only during the late sixteenth century, since examples of that time have also been found, and that the blue-and-white ceramics represent an earlier stage. An explanation based on relative wealth, however, seems more likely. Not only was the expensive blue-and-white ware still being produced in the sixteenth century, but we have also to remember that besides the big urban centres there existed smaller local kiln-sites manufacturing a provincial ware.

The Museum für Islamische Kunst in Berlin holds a small collection of fragments from bowls of the fifteenth and sixteenth century presumably produced at Samarkand. They arrived at the museum together with a large amount of diverse sherds from Afrasiab (Old Samarkand). The body usually shows a reddish colour (light brick-red) and occasionally a more yellowish tint. They are all covered with white slip. The painting consists of black to brown patterns filled in with designs usually of a transparent blue, turquoise blue or turquoise green colour; some designs are executed in two colours, blue and turquoise blue or turquoise blue and light green. Brushwork is loosely and often generously applied. Chinese influence is noticeable in rosettes deriving from chrysanthemum blossoms (ill. 292)[9] or low plants with a central fruit in the well (ill. 291 bottom).[10] On some bowls the inside decoration simply consists of a patterned band recalling the Chinese rock-and-waves motif.[11] The division of the inside into petal-shaped panels may also be of Chinese inspiration.[12] The Persian tradition, especially the so-called Sultanabad ware, is represented by designs of radial panels around a central ring, the panels filled with alternating geometric patterns (e.g., cross-hatching) and arabesques (ill. 294).[13] Other designs include spiralloid floral scrolls and peacock-feather patterns (ill. 293 centre).[14]

While a host of new decorative techniques was introduced under the Timurids, some techniques had been known in Central Asia much earlier. These included the above-mentioned blue and turquoise blue glazes associated with Iran and Syria (ill. 284),[15] which are documented in Central Asia already in the thirteenth to fourteenth century. White ceramics with painting in black and light and dark blue reminiscent of Sultanabad ware date from the same time. The fragments at the Museum für Islamische Kunst mentioned earlier are proof of production continuing into the fifteenth century.

Once stablished after their conquests in the early sixteenth century, the Uzbek Shaibanid rulers showed the same preference for beautiful tableware as their predecessors, commissioning objects decorated after the fashion of the time. Particularly under `Abdullah II (1583-98), science, the arts and the minor arts experienced a revival. In 1599 Bukhara fell into the hands of the Janids from Astrakhan.

Only Khorezm remained under Shaibanid rule until 1804, Khiva becoming the capital in 1640. Bukhara saw a new cultural flowering under the early Janids, in particular under Imam Quli Khan (1608-40), and a last brilliant period under `Abdul `Aziz Khan (1647-80) and Subhan Quli (1680-1702), before the Land beyond the River was swept up by wars for a considerable time.

Only during the last few years have the ceramics of this period attracted serious scholarly interest. We already mentioned that production of blue-and-white ceramics and of coarser ware painted in black or brown and turquoise blue continued in the sixteenth century. During the seventeenth century other types of decoration seem to have become popular. From seventeenth-century Tashkent, fragments of bowls have survived decorated with regularly arranged simple patterns of lines, circles, crosses and zick-zacks.[16] Bukharan ceramics from the second half of the seventeenth century are very similar.[17] A peculiar new motif of small circles made up of small dots is found on Central Asian ceramics still in the twentieth century. Of the motifs prevalent in the seventeenth century only a few retain something of previous styles of decoration, for instance the rosettes in the well in the form of spirals, whirls and blossoms. While previously the whole surface tended to be covered with decoration, now the motifs are more sparingly used and much remains undecorated. Variously arranged circular patterns predominate. The body is usually reddish or occasionally of a yellowish tinge as before, and is covered with white slip. The palette consists only of turquoise blue and dark brown. Besides colourless glazes we sometimes also find green, yellow and brownish yellow glazes. These new developments continue into the eighteenth century and to a lesser degree until the nineteenth century.
(This is a slightly shortened version of the original German text.)

1   Clavijo 1928:288.
2   Linden-Museum, Stuttgart, inv. no. A 39 339 L.
3   3 Los Angeles 1989:228.
4   4 Clavijo 1928:224.
5   5 "Raskopki v srednevekovom Shakhristane g. Andizhana" (Excavation at the mediaeval *shahristan* of the city of Andizhan), in *Archeologicheskie raboty na novostroykakh Uzbekistana*, Tashkent, 1990.
6   6 Museum of Culture and Art of the Peoples of Uzbekistan, Tashkent, inv. no. A-151-2; cf. Moscow 1991, vol. 2, no. 754.
7   7 Archaeological Institute of the Uzbekistan Academy of Sciences, Samarkand; cf. Moscow 1991, vol. 2, no. 755.
8   8 Ibid., no. 757.
9   9 Museum für Islamische Kunst, Berlin, inv. nos. I. 8076, I. 8080.
10   10 Ibid., inv. no. I. 8083.
11   11 Ibid., inv. no. I. 8071.
12   12 Ibid., inv. nos. I. 8070, I. 8072.
13   13 Ibid., inv. nos. I. 8068, I. 8069.
14   14 Ibid., inv. no. I. 8081.
15   15 Linden-Museum, Stuttgart, on loan.
16   16 "Glazurovannaja keramika Tashkenta XVII v." (Glazed ceramics from 17th-century Tashkent), in *Archeologicheskie raboty na novostoykakh Uzbekistana*, Tashkent, 1990.
17   17 Mirzaachmedov 1990.

279
Fragment of a bowl or dish. Stone-paste, cobalt-blue painting in two shades under a colourless transparent glaze. The design of a phoenix flying across a landscape with scrollwork is derived from Chinese porcelain of the Yuan dynasty (1271-1368). Chinese blue-and-white porcelain was a popular and much sought-after luxury tableware throughout the Islamic world and·was imitated at numerous places. These imitations covered the whole spectrum from very close copies like this one, to highly individual creations. From Central Asia likewise, ceramics imitating Chinese models are known.
D: c. 23.5 cm
Iran, Bojnurd, 14th/15th century

280
Large low bowl with bracket-lobed rim. Floral decoration, blue-and-white ware. The sides are slightly lobed into twelve segments corresponding to the twelve bracket-lobes of the rim. Designs of flower sprays and flowering scrolls cover both the inside and outside surfaces; lotus, chrysanthemum, peony, camellia and morning glory can be identified.
D: 38 cm
China, Yongle period (1403-24) of the Ming dynasty (1368-1644)

281
Bowl. Earthenware, white slip, cobalt-blue painting under a transparent glaze. The well shows two large peony blossoms within a circular scroll; for Chinese models, see ill. 280.
H: c. 7.4 cm, D: 41.4 cm
Samarkand, Ulugh Beg madrasa, 15th century
Registan Museum, Samarkand

282
Pear-shaped bottle. Porcelain with blue-and-white floral decoration. The wine bottle is decorated with a sparse design of stylised flower scrolls in underglaze cobalt-blue. It represents an early example of Chinese blue-and-white porcelain, most of which was manufactured in huge amounts at Jingdezhen, Jiangxi province, at least since the Southern Song period (1127-1279) not only for the domestic market but also for export.
H: 26.6 cm
China, Yuan dynasty (1271-1368)

283
Bowl. Earthenware, white slip, painting in cobalt-blue and turquoise under a transparent glaze. The well shows an individualistic stylisation of a lotus blossom, and the sides are decorated with plant motifs.
H: 8 cm, D: 20 cm
Bukhara, 15th/16th century
Museum in the Ark, Bukhara

284-285
Bowl. Earthenware, decorated with fishes in green-black underglaze painting under a turquoise-coloured glaze. The inside shows leftward-turning fishes directed towards the well and a serrated border, the outside single boldly executed plant motifs. Fishes are a symbol of fertility and good fortune.
H: 9.4 cm, D: 19.4 cm
Iran, Sultaniya or Kashan, 13th century

286
Bowls. Light grey stoneware, the left with engraved lotus-leaf design and olive-yellow celadon glaze, the right with lotus-leaf design in carved relief and blue-green celadon glaze.
D: 16.6 cm (left), 17.5 cm (right)
China, Longquan ware, Southern Song (1127-1279)/Yuan (1271-1368), 13th century

287
Round lidded box. Carved design in relief of peonies and leafy scrolls, medium grey stoneware with dark olive-grey glaze.
H: 5.6 cm, D: 11.9 cm
China, Yue ware, about 950-980
Private collection

288
Dish with bracket-lobed rim. Applied relief decoration, light grey stoneware with bluish-green celadon glaze. The unglazed fruiting sprays, applied before firing, have auspicious connotations, symbolising wishes for long life (peach), numerous offspring (pomegranate) and good fortune (melon). Both the shape and relief decoration of the dish follow metal prototypes, usually of silver.
D: 16 cm
China, Longquan ware, Yuan dynasty (1271-1368)

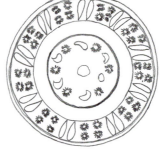

289
Six-lobed silver dish. The shape of such simple and undecorated dishes was imitated during the Song and especially the Yuan period in various ceramic wares like green-glazed celadon stoneware and white and blue-and-white porcelain.
D: 15.9 cm
China, Southern Song dynasty (1127-1279)

290
Drawings of motifs found on ceramics from Tashkent and Bukhara from the 17th century onwards, consisting of simple patterns like strokes, circles and crosses. Notable is the appearance of a motif consisting of small dots in a ray-like arrangement, which is found on Central Asian wares right up to this century. Only a few patterns in the well (rosettes arranged in spirals and whirls, and flowery rosettes) hark back to the decorative repertoire of the previous era.

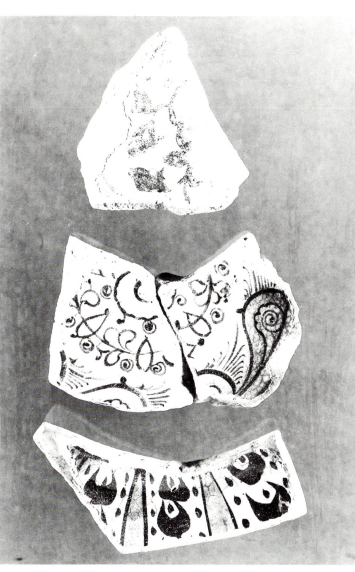

291-294
Bowl shards. Earthenware, white slip, blue and turquoise painting under a transparent glaze. The designs are painted freely and show plants (ill. 291) and rosettes (ill. 292) inspired by Chinese models and leafy scrolls and peacock's feathers (ill. 293) reminiscent of 'Sultanabad ware' as well as arabesques and geometric patterns (ill. 294).
Presumably Samarkand, 15th/16th century
Museum für Islamische Kunst, Berlin

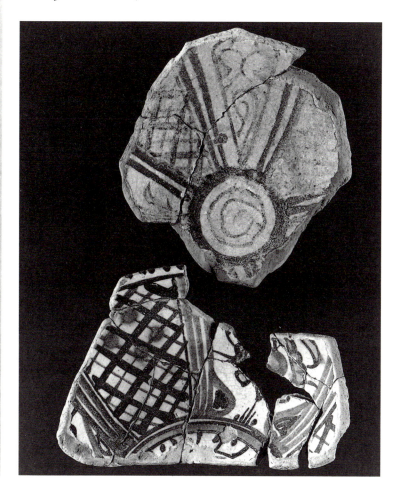

295
Bowls.
(Left) Earthenware, blue-black painting under a turquoise-coloured glaze. The inside decoration is divided into eight petal-shaped fields, of which the four opposing ones are inscribed in naskhi. H: 9.4 cm, D: 19.2 cm. Iran, Bojnurd, 15th century.
(Right) Earthenware, cobalt-blue glaze, overglaze painting in minium-red, white and gold. The interior is divided by a Greek cross decorated with stylised stalks. The four fields show pointed medallions enclosing blossoms and surrounded by spiralling scrolls. Lajvardina ware. H: 9.2 cm, D: 19.6 cm. Iran, 14th century (?).
(Front) Earthenware, white slip, black and cobalt-blue painting under a colourless glaze. The well shows a multi-petalled rosette, and the sides are decorated with niches alternating with trapezoid fields filled with a plant motif. H: 10.8 cm, D: 19.5 cm.
Iran, Bojnurd, 14th century.

296
Bowls.

(Left) Earthenware, white slip, painted in black and turquoise under a transparent glaze. The interior shows a large leafy spray, and along the rim stylised branches alternating with cloud motifs of Chinese inspiration. The loosely painted decoration is typical of the many Timurid ceramics with Chinese-inspired designs. H: 9.5 cm, D: 25.0 cm. Iran, Bojnurd, 15th century.
(Right) Earthenware, white slip, black and turquoise-coloured painting under a transparent glaze. The well with a floral rosette and the sides with pomegranate sprays. Very similar ceramics have been found in Central Asia. H: 10 cm, D: 21 cm. Iran, Bojnurd, 15th century.
(Front) Earthenware, white slip, black and turquoise-coloured painting under a transparent glaze. The well decorated with an eight-petalled rosette with highly stylised flower motifs between the rays. H: 9.1 cm, D: 20.7 cm. Iran, Bojnurd, 15th century.

297

Bowl. Earthenware, white slip, underglaze painting in dark brown, brownish yellow and green, some sgrafitto, colourless transparent glaze. The inside is decorated with four flowers, their stems forming a cross connected to a circular design in the well. The blossoms are emphasised by incised spirals. Around the rim a double line of dots, the lip painted green. In terms of drawing style and colour scheme this bowl belongs to the large group of Chinese-inspired sgrafitto vessels found throughout the Orient in many versions and variations. Stylistically the bowl can be related to Timurid vessels. Its Bojnurd provenance would suggest a rather modest local school. The structure of the design is still found on ceramics of the 19th century (cf. ill. 680).
H: 10 cm, D: 29 cm
Iran, Bojnurd, 15th century

298
[Map of Turkestan, late 18th century] Private collection, Sindelfingen

Turkestan under the Uzbek Khanates

Sixteeth to Twentieth Century

The Khanates of Bukhara, Khiva and Kokand

Margareta Pavaloi

When Europe began to become interested in Turkestan in the nineteenth century, the Silk Roads had long passed into legend, and traffic along the ancient highways was a mere trickle. Part of the route of the long-haul trade caravans led through the rival khanates of Bukhara, Khiva and Kokand in Turkestan, by now a backwater in history and mainly concerned with its own regional affairs.

Turkestan's isolation had begun in the sixteenth century. Although the Shaibanids had managed to keep intact their territories predominantly inhabited by Usbeks, they failed in establishing a durable foundation. Rivalries and power struggles within the ruling dynasty as well as perennial warfare with nomad tribes finally put an end to Shaibanid rule.

The succeeding Janid dynasty made Bukhara its capital. Under `Abd al-`Aziz Khan (1647-80) the city experienced its last cultural flowering. After his death internecine strife brought about the break-up of the empire, and the khan of Bukhara found himself ruling over a much diminished territory. After 1740 a new dynasty, the Mangits, resided at Bukhara. The *atalyq* (house-steward to the khan) Muhammad Rahim proclaimed himself Khan, his successors styling themselves emirs. Nasr Allah (1827-60) was able to enlarge his territory, although his capture of Kokand in 1842 proved short-lived. His successor Muzaffaruddin (1860-85) lost part of his territory, including Samarkand, to the Russians, but in 1873 conquered parts of the Khiva khanate.

Under the Shaibanids the royal residence in Khorezm had been moved to Urgench. During the second half of the reign of `Arab Muhammad (1603-1623) the left branch of the Amu Darya had dried up and the capital was moved back to Khiva and Khorezm became the Khanate of Khiva. The khanate consisted of a loose network of domains whose lords accepted the suzerainty of the khan of Khiva, so that the unity of the khanate depended mainly on the personal ability and authority of the incumbent khan (a title changed in the late 17th century to 'shah'). The Uzbek dynasty was succeeded by one of Genghid descent which ruled in Khiva until 1804, real power lying in the hands of the *inaq* (tribal leader) of the Qungrat tribe. During the eighteenth century decay set in. Between 1740 and 1770 Khiva was increasingly harassed by the Yomud Turkmens. In 1770 the *inaq* Muhammad Amin repelled the Turkmens and started to rebuild Khiva. Under the *inaq* Iltüzer the Khiva khanate reached its greatest extent in modern times. His successor, Muhammad Rahim Khan, was the most powerful khan of the nineteenth century. He directed several successful raids into Kazakh territory, subdued the Karakalpaks and went on looting sprees in Khorasan.

Kokand was the capital of an Uzbek khanate founded in the eighteenth century, its first ruler being Shah Rukh. After the destruction of the Kalmuck empire, China in 1758 extended its dominions to include the Fergana Valley. Nar Buta Beg (1774-89) was an ally of the Chinese and an enemy of Bukhara. His two sons `Alim and `Umar were the actual founders of the khanate. Their style of rulership was rather different. `Alim wanted to break the power of the great Uzbek families and the dervish orders and was murdered, whereas his brother devoted himself to literature and the construction of the Friday mosque at Kokand and an irrigation canal. `Umar's son Madali considerably extended the territory of Kokand. The reigns of Shir `Ali (1842-45) and his sons Khudayar (1845-58, 1865-75) and Malla (1858-62) were characterised by much unrest and bitter fighting mainly between Uzbeks and 'Sarts', a sedentary population speaking an Iranian language. In 1864 Tashkent, part of the Kokand khanate, was able to repel a Russian attack; however, the khans of Bukhara and Kokand lost their advantage by continuing to battle each other, even while the Russians were consolidating their position. In 1875 the Russians occupied the whole territory and dissolved the khanate of Kokand.

So much for the historical background leading up to the moment when the European colonial powers turned their eyes towards Turkestan - covetous in the case of czarist Russia, watchful and wary in the case of Great Britain. When the ancient Silk Road cities fell into Russian hands one after the other, the British became seriously alarmed. And as the area of neutral ground between the two great adversaries shrank, interest in Turkestan grew accordingly. Turkestan became a hotbed of undercover activities, pursued in the main by professionals, by officers of the Anglo-Indian army and secret agents of all types and allegiances. There were other individuals, travellers and eccentrics, no less daring and capable, who joined the fray, which the British called the 'Great Game' and a Russian civil servant once characterised as a "battle of shadows". Modern opinion varies, some commentators suggesting that the Game never happened, while others believe that it is still going on.

What about the khans? Their participation in the Game was partly active, partly passive. In the long run they were bound to loose. Because of their isolation, they lacked a yard-stick by which to measure the seriousness of what was to engulf them. They were as unable to assess the military and commercial potential of the European colonial powers as to fathom the Russian and British strategic interests. When they eventually began to realise what was happening, it was too late to turn the tide. The Russians had long ago decided on a military solution, and agreed with the British to end the Game (Anglo-Russian Convention of 1907).

A fortunate by-product of the Great Game for us today is a wealth of information about nineteenth-century Turkestan. Among other things it provided an impetus to assemble the first ethnographic collections, allowing us a glimpse at the material culture of the time. The great variety of personalities on the spot and their special interests is reflected in the variety of the records and collections they have left us.

On one feature all eyewitnesses tend to agree, namely the discrepancy between the enormous political changes taking place and the seeming immutability of cultural traditions and ways of life. Timurid traditions still regulated courtly life and ceremonials and defined the self-image of the rulers. Robert Shaw, one of the first Europeans to visit the almost inaccessible cities of Kashgar and Yarkand in 1868, has left us an account of his reception at the court of Yaqub Beg which in certain details is reminiscent of Timurid custom. On arrival he was led through a succession of large courtyards, passing rows of guards and members of the court dressed in brilliant colourful costumes and placed according to rank. When he finally reached the audience hall he found Yaqub Beg, the descendant of Timur and conqueror of Chinese Turkestan, sitting all alone on a carpet. The khan presented him with a robe now kept at the Ashmolean Museum in Oxford (ills. 29, 494).

The rivalries among the khans caused much disruption without, however, fundamentally changing the patterns of all livelihood and exploitation of natural resources. Yet one new development could be noticed: The diminishing area for pasture and absence of alternatives reduced the mobility of the nomads and acerberated their conflicts with the sedentary population. The nomads were increasingly forced to a more stationary life, although they continued to live in yurts.

Russian pacification of Turkestan, the advent of railways and telegraphs and the beginnings of industrialisation - Europeans looked upon these with approval as signs of progress and modernisation, as we can gather from the accounts of Henri Moser (1844-1923), the Swiss adventurer, travel writer and collector of Orientalia from Schaffhausen. At the time he was travelling around Turkestan, the region was a profitable hunting-ground for soldiers of fortune and anyone interested in furthering his commercial, military and social careers. Moser received gifts from the emir of Bukhara, became an officer in the Russian Cossack forces at Tashkent, where he also owned a bakery and a Turkish bath, traded in Turkmen stallions and Turkestan silkworm eggs and avidly collected the weapons and arts and crafts products which are now kept at the Historisches Museum in Bern.

As the changes wrought by modernisation became ever more obvious, foreigners suddenly discovered the 'old Turkestan', its picturesqueness, its history, its customs and traditions, and the more romantically inclined visitors began to fear that it might disappear forever. As Russian plans for development began to take shape, as new settlements were built which had little in common with the ancient oasis towns and the pasture grounds of the nomads were turned into cotton fields, people started to realise that this time 'dynastic' change would involve fundamental changes in the traditional ways of life. This was the impression conveyed by H. Krafft in his *A Travers le Turkestan russe* of 1902, written in the hope that his descriptions and photographs would help to record for posterity the "Muslim soul of Turkestan". His writings, and in particular his photographs, have indeed become prime documentation about a Turkestan long since vanished, just like those taken by von Schwarz and others.

Other Central Asian enthusiasts, sharing Krafft's concerns, were busy collecting material evidence of the "Muslim soul of Turkestan" with the express purpose of putting it into the safe-keeping of museums. One of them was Willi Gustav Rickmer Rickmers. Scion of a ship-owning family, he had no financial worries and was able to combine his enthusiasm for mountaineering with his geological interests. These brought him to Central Asia in 1895/96, where he managed to form a large collection of Turkestan craftsmanship. He got in touch with the Museum für Völkerkunde in Berlin, presenting it in 1896/97 with the first batch of his collection and continuing to acquire objects until 1902 for the museum, which as a result now possesses a Central Asian collection of the first rank. However, when Rickmers revisited Bukhara in 1928 to obtain objects of museum quality, he was disappointed: "The beautifully chased copper and brass vessels have disappeared, and silk is no longer what it used to be. Inexpensive utilitarian objects of good quality such as household wares and the like are all imported from Europe. Even the simplest gaudy utensils of the old days have now almost become rare art objects ... As to valuable items and everything of superior quality, the bazaars of the Orient have been moved to Liberty's in London, while our old paraffin lamps are now found among the sweet scents of Araby. The world is suffused with a strange metabolism."

Henri Moser

300
*Caparison. Full silk embroidery on a cotton ground with boteh patterns, blossoms and
stylised trees of life, the border with a leafy flowering scroll in the style of Shahr-i Sabz.
L: 164 cm, W: 135 cm
Late 19th century
Museum für Völkerkunde, Berlin, Rickmers Collection*

Aspects of an Equestrian Culture

Johannes Kalter

If you have two days more to live, take a wife and a horse.
If you have one day left, take a horse.

Still at the beginning of the present century, this well-known Turkmen saying would have been the credo of every man in Turkestan. Riding was the only acceptable means of locomotion for men, a necessity for survival for nomads and a status symbol for urban males. Nomads on horseback shaped the fate of Central Asia for more than two thousand years and made decisive forays into Europe as well. So before I discuss riders and riding in nineteenth-century Turkestan, I would like to give a short overview of the history of riding and the evolution of an equestrian nomad culture.

As far as we know, the horse was domesticated in the fourth millennium B.C. in the region of the modern Ukraine. Since the first half of the second millennium horses were used to pull fast fighting chariots on light spoked wheels. "The earliest evidence for riding on horseback is a scratched drawing on a 33mm-high piece of bone from the Elamite capital at Susa in the ancient Near East dated to 2800 B.C." (Otte 1994). According to other studies, however, it appears likely that people rode horses in the Ukraine already around 4000 B.C. The examination of the teeth of a horse from the Dereivka produced evidence that it was used for riding. "The stallion must have worn a bridle, which was held from the back either by a rider or a charioteer. But as it was only half a millennium later that the wheel appeared in this region, the stallion can only have been meant for riding. Thus it is the very first riding horse known to us" (Anthony 1992). We may assume that during the third and early second millennium horse-riding was known to the inhabitants of the Near and Middle East, but was only practised occasionally and without much consequence. The first documented deployment of cavalry dates from the battle of Kadesh in 1299 B.C. by auxiliaries of the Hittite forces.

The evolution of the highly specialised cultural system of equestrian nomads is generally dated to about 900 B.C. The first equestrian nomadic peoples known by name are the Scythians, who originally came from the Volga basin and in about 900 B.C. drove the Cimmerians from their homelands in the southern Russian steppes. They are already mentioned in the seventh century B.C. as allies of the Assyrians against the Cimmerians. In 674 B.C. a Scythian king married an Assyrian princess (Tripett 1978).

Nomadic horse-based cultures spread very rapidly from the nineth century onwards. As early as the eighth/seventh century, the Sakas established a nomadic empire in northern Central Asia which stretched from eastern Turkestan across the Aral Sea to the Caspian. Another nomad people, the Massagetae, were living to the west of Lake Balkhash. These two warlike nomadic peoples put up the fiercest resistance during Alexander the Great's conquest of Turkestan. As a result of the rapid spread of nomad horsemen, for some 2700 years the history of Central Asia was determined by a succession of dominant nomadic tribes and dynasties from the Sakas and Massagetae to the Kushans, Huns, Turks and Mongols.

Scythian tombs have brought to light types of male attire rather similar to that still worn in the nineteenth century. The horsemen wore high-heeled boots, a pair of trousers just covering the knee and very voluminous in the upper part - a fashion still frequently met with all over the Orient - and a wide coat. The most important pieces of weaponry were the reflex bow and a short sword, displaced after the fifth/sixth century A.D. by the scimitar, which remained the classic weapon for riders well until modern times. The high-pommelled saddle still common in Iran and Central Asia had already been fully developed during the Mongol era, as we know from miniatures. Where and when stirrups were first used is still a matter of debate. In any case, by the fifth century A.D. they are found throughout Central Asia. Moser and von Schwarz both mention that in their time the Kirghiz were occasionally using straps made of rope instead of stirrups, and wooden stirrups were also known. No archaeological remains of the latter two types have been found, presumably because the material has decayed. It seems highly likely that stirrups of some sort were already used long before the earliest surviving metal stirrups.

Even in the late nineteenth century only three percent of the area of Turkestan was arable. The endless steppes and deserts could only support a nomadic population. Only some of the equestrian nomads made full use of their horses. The Mongols, for instance, also slaughtered horses and drank mare's milk either fresh or fermented, which gives the intoxicating kumiss. Equestrian nomads usually kept domestic cattle, most often sheep but also goats. The poor quality of the pasture necessitated the employment of horses to keep together the herds and to obtain additional fodder. Much more important for the nomadic economy was the fact that horses were swift and strong enough to undertake lightning raids on villages and towns; and by forming larger parties, the superiority of the nomads over an urban settled population in terms of military strength was guaranteed. Without mounted escorts the transcontinental trade along the Silk Road would have been impossible, and rule over such an extended empire as that of Genghis Khan or Timur would have been much more precarious without the communication network supplied by couriers on horseback. Mongol riders were able to cover a distance of up to four hundred kilometres within twenty-four hours, and von Schwarz mentions a case when a hundred Kirghiz horsemen with two horses each accompanying a Russian officer over mountainous and stony terrain covered 320 kilometres in twenty-four hours.

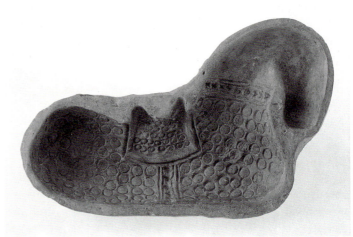

301
Horse sculptures. Earthenware, the one on the right with painted decoration. The figures were toys or presents offered during New Year celebrations. The left figure shows very clearly the bridle and the saddle of a type still in use today.
H: 10 and 15 cm
Northern Afghanistan or Central Asia, about 1000

302
Mould for the figure of a horse. Earthenware. The clearly defined caparison is of a type still in use today.
L: c. 21 cm
Bukhara region, 11th/12th century
Museum in the Ark, Bukhara

305
Bridle with snaffle and decorative neck cover. Leather, iron, fire-gilt silver, turquoise inlay. The leather straps are covered with velvet, and the tassels are of silk. A horse's trappings were the most important indicator of the rider's social position. Such elaborate trappings as these would have belonged to persons associated with the royal court.
L: 41 cm (bridle), W: 92 cm (neck cover)
Bukhara, late 18th/early 19th century

Harness and other furnishings

In Turkestan today one still meets with the small, shaggy type of Mongolian horse not much higher than a pony. But the characteristic breeds of the region from the 'blood-sweating' horses of Fergana in the east to the Achal-Tekkin and Yomud horses in the west, is a gracefully limbed (von Schwarz compares them to greyhounds) dry type of horse with a long but thin tail and a sparse mane, which is usually trimmed except for a forelock so as not to interfere with the rider doing battle. Common to them all is great speed and astonishing endurance.

The Western saddles have a deep gullet and are carved from a single piece of wood (ills. 303, 304). The panels only cover the sides, leaving the spinal column exposed. The high pommel terminates in a saddle-horn. The seat has a pronounced slope, while attached to the sides of the saddle are brass or metal rings for securing baggage, bedding or clothes during longer journeys (Schwarz 1900:110). More expensive saddles are covered with lacquer. Both the border and the rectangular openings for the stirrup band show ivory inlay. Von Schwarz gives an explanation for the high saddle-horn: "Since the steppes are bare of trees or other objects to tie a horse, the Kirghiz after dismounting make sure that their horse remains where it is simply by throwing the reigns around the horn; the horse's head is pulled back so strongly that it is unable to move and so patiently remains on the spot for hours." The saddle-horn also enables the rider to fight

with both hands: He simply puts down the reins behind the horn, and since the animal is used to riding with slack reins, the rider now handles it simply by moving his weight accordingly.

The underside of the saddle is covered with birch bark or a mixture of a kind of resin and plant fibres to absorb sweat and prevent it from warping due to moisture. The saddle is secured by a surcingle which runs across the seat. The stirrups are usually of iron or brass and have a small plate which can be of silver or gold in expensive versions. While nomads sit directly on the saddle, riders with a sedentary background usually make use of bolsters, rugs or blankets.

The bridle commonly includes a decorative element covering the neck with attached bands, a browband connected to the noseband and a soft snaggle with a jointed mouthpiece fastened to rings (ill. 305). The reins are usually made of leather, although in the case of our bridle from Khiva they consist of a broad woven band of silk velvet terminating in a knot, a custom found wherever people tend to ride singlehanded (ill. 307). The neck ornaments, decorative bands as well as browbands and nosebands are either of silver with turquoise inlay or fire-gilt with cornelians and turquoises. A head-piece in the Linden-Museum is partly made of green so-called shagreen leather from the skin of horses or donkeys and dyed with iron vitriol green (ill. 306). The peculiar grainy surface of this type of leather is the result of the following treatment: "After

303
Saddle. Wood with lacquer painting and bone inlay, border with medallions and lozenges, the secondary border with blossoms. The seat decorated with heart-shaped leaves arranged as a quatrefoil, the saddle-horn covered with leather of a later date decoratively fastened with upholstery nails.
L: 47 cm
Bukhara or Samarkand, late 19th century

304
Saddle. Wood with lacquer painting and bone inlay, border painted with plant motifs and serrated rim, the seat decorated with a double lozenge.
L: 47 cm
Bukhara, 1890s
Museum für Völkerkunde, Berlin, Rickmers Collection

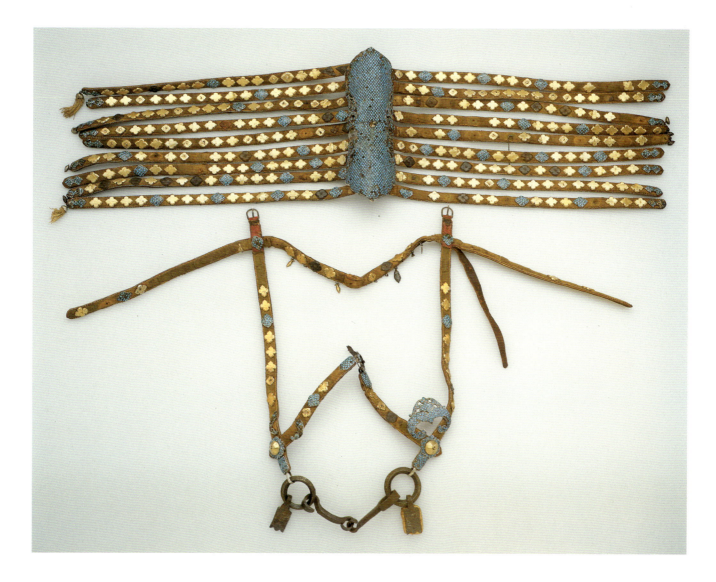

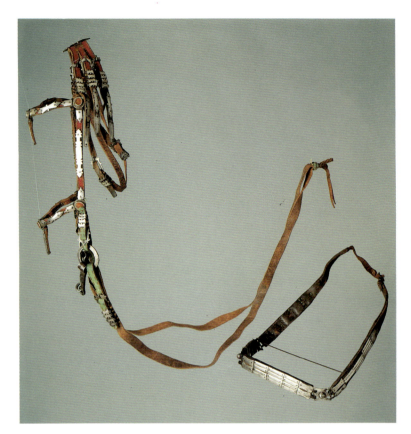

306
Bridle and breast collar. Iron, silver-plated, cornelians on green shagreen.
L: 47 cm (breast collar, closed), 45 cm (bridle)
Central Asia, late 17th/early 18th century

307
Bridle and collar ornament. Leather, iron, fire-gilt silver, cornelians and turquoises, reins of velvet straps, the collar ornament with a tassel of yak's hair.
L: 77 cm (collar ornament), 56 cm (bridle)
Khiva, late 19th century

308
Breast collar. Leather, fire-gilt and nielloed silver.
W: 160 cm
Bukhara, late 19th century
Museum in the Summer Residence, Bukhara

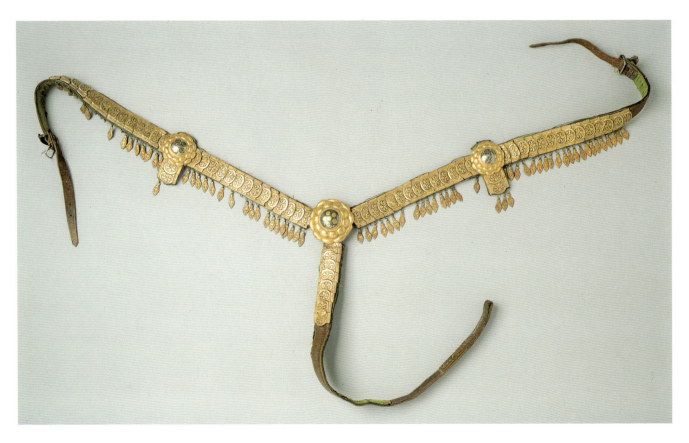

172

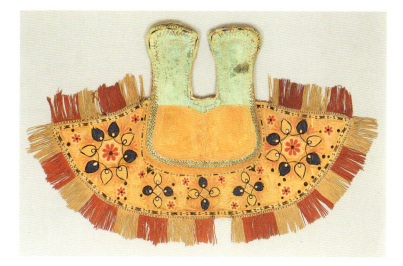

309
Skirt. Leather, horsehair, cotton, silk embroidery and silk fringe. This is one of the finest known examples of its kind on account of the exceptionally fine embroidery, the geometricised rosettes with central blossom and scattered blossoms and the woven border.
L: 70 cm, W: 113 cm
Turkestan, Bukhara (?), late 19th century
Private collection, Zurich

310
Saddle bolster. Green shagreen, horsehair, cotton, filling silk embroidery, silk fringe.
Bukhara, 1890s
Museum für Völkerkunde, Berlin

311
Saddle blanket. Top centre opening for the saddle-horn. Silk embroidery on cotton, the motifs probably associated with astral symbolism. The borders shows a scroll with stylised tulips.
64 x 62 cm
Northern Afghanistan or Surkhan Darya, Laqai Uzbeks (?), second half 19th century
Private collection, Zurich

312
Saddle blanket. Knotted wool.
66 x 66 cm
Northern Afghanistan, Uzbek work, late 19th/early 20th century

the skins have been soaked in water for several days they are sprinkled with millet, and the grains pounded with a hammer into the leather. Once the skins are completely dry, the surface is smoothed with special scrapers. During the subsequent dying process the areas compressed by the millet grains swell up to produce the typical nodular appearance of shagreen. Finally the leather is rubbed with sheep fat" (Schwarz 1900:392). Our example certainly dates from the eighteenth century and shows the leather partly embroidered with silk. The neck-piece, buckles and metal parts are of iron with silver attachments. Bridles from Bukhara are typically adorned with turquoise ornaments. But both in Bukhara and Khiva a type of bridle was also used which we associate with the Turkmens, decorated with cornelians on partly gilt silver.

Saddle-skirts

Saddle-skirts are rather seldom found in collections. They are U-shaped and made of leather bolsters usually of shagreen with attached textiles. While the sides of the 'U' are placed under the panels, its bottom curve rests under the rear part of the saddle. The semicircular drapery covers the area of the horse's kidneys. The leather bolsters are stuffed with horsehair or cotton.

Saddle-blankets

Like saddle-skirts, saddle-blankets covering the seat seldom found their way into collections. Some are knitted like our example from northern Afghanistan, which fits the shape of the saddle very well (ill. 312). Others are almost square and are embroidered in silk like our example showing whirl-like motifs and made for rural Uzbeks from northern Afghanistan or the Termez region. Both kinds of blankets have an opening for the saddle-horn.

Caparisons

On caparisons, von Schwarz has this to say: "Unlike the Kirghiz, the urban inhabitants cover their saddles with soft blankets or bolsters and for festive occasions get out splendid caparisons with gold embroidery or gold knitting which covers the horse completely to below the knee. Rich people have caparisons of gold brocade or red or green velvet or cloth, in the latter case covered all over with the most beautiful gold and silver embroidery. These gold embroidered caparisons are among the most splendid I ever saw. Especially under the brilliant light of the Turkestan sun such an array of fully decked-out horses is an overwhelming sight. In terms of eye-catching arrangements of colours and precious textiles, the people of Central Asia have a great advantage over European artists working under a leaden sky" (Schwarz 1900:372).

No part of the trappings of Turkestan horses show the love of ostentanious decoration better than the almost trapezoid caparisons (ills. 313-9). They cover the horse from the upper neck or withers to the croup, their length thus measuring between 1.75 and almost two metres and the width at the front between 1.30 and 1.40 metres. They are stuffed with a thin layer of cotton and are usually of woollen cloth, or sometimes of silk velvet or leather. Their decoration can be of brocade, of silver or gold relief embroidery or silk embroidery. The motifs include *boteh* (paisley) patterns, vases, floral scrolls or blossoms arranged within a grid pattern as on our example with a yellow ground from the Samarkand region. The back and sides of caparisons nearly always have silk tassels, sometimes decoratively plaited. The caparisons are placed either under the saddle or fall across the seat, in which case they have a slit to accomodate the saddle-horn. The area covered either by the saddle or the rider's bottom is usually left undecorated.

When the riding pace was fast, the rear part of the caparison would sometimes be folded over to reveal the underside. This explains the fact that the underside is also often lined with very precious and decorative textiles, for example with silk ikat and brocade embroidery as on our caparison, or with cotton cloth hand-stamped with designs of blossoms among floral scrolls.

The fact that care was taken to match the appearance of horse and rider, is illustrated by a caparison from Bukhara of red silk velvet with gold relief embroidery and corresponding riding breeches with identical leaf-scroll border.

Von Schwarz and Moser both mention that it was quite common to put several caparisons on top of each other. Moser illustrates ein Yomud horse covered with the same kind of saddle-cloth found among the Uzbekistan nomads. He writes: "[A Yomud horseman] keeps his horse saddled day and night. In the morning he takes off the saddle and with the sleeve of his khalat [gown] wipes across its back to smoothen the hair; then he places three or four soft felt blankets across its withers whose scars and sores the rider completely ignores. Then he puts the high saddle back in place and spreads over it two, three or even four more felt blankets which cover the horse from the ears to the tail; this is not to prevent the animal from catching cold in the winter, for during the summer it is covered with even more blankets ...

"The Turkmens hold that the heavy blankets prevent the horse from growing fat and from sweating when riding at a galopp. And indeed all these fast horses are dry; they are just skin and bones and muscles without a grain of fat. If the horse is meant to go fast, the rider removes the felt blankets from the croup to the saddle and turns those covering the neck back to the withers; as soon as the horse rests, the blankets are put back." (Moser 1888:273) The same explanation for covering a horse with blankets is found among other equestrian peoples. Another reason may be that this covering prevents the colour of the skin from fading. At the same time one has to keep in mind that the number of blankets or caparisons obviously acts as a status symbol. Just as a person of distinction wears several khalats on top of each other in winter and summer, so he will cover his horse with as many sumptuously ornamented blankets as he can afford.

The horse blanket of heavy black felt with blue and red cotton appliqué work in the Linden-Museum is extremely rare and represents the most elaborate covering to prevent sweating (ills. 321a-b). The blanket covers the horse from

313

*Caparison. Silk embroidery on wool. The main decorative field with parti-coloured
composite flowers framed by leaf and scroll motifs, the border with highly stylised trees of life.*
L: 133 cm, W: 156 cm
Turkestan, urban provenance, second half 19th century
Private collection, Zurich

314

Caparison. Brocade embroidery on silk velvet; made for a court-connected clientele.
L: 190 cm, W: 132 (top)
Bukhara, late 19th century
Private collection, Zurich

315

*Caparison. Silk embroidery and appliqué on wool. Both the upper termination and the
definition of decorative fields by distictive borders is unusual.*
L: 115 cm, W: 162 cm
Private collection, Karlsruhe

316

Caparison to be laid across the saddle. Seat of silk velvet, otherwise silk embroidery on cotton. The provenance is suggested by the boteh pattern, rosettes and insect-like motifs.
L: 123 cm, W: 149 cm
Northern Afghanistan or Surkhan Darya, Laqai Uzbeks (?), second half 19th century.

317

Caparison. Silk embroidery on cotton with highly elaborate flowering scroll border and composite flowers on the main decorative field arranged in a grid reminiscent of architectural decoration.
L: 140 cm, W: 196 cm
Samarkand (?), second half 19th century
Private collection, Zurich

318

Caparison. Brocade embroidery on leather, silk fringe. Stylistically the petalled border and the trees of life within cartouches are reminiscent of Ottoman designs.
L: 135 cm, W: 210 cm
Bukhara, acquired by Rickmers in 1897
Museum für Völkerkunde, Berlin, Rickmers Collection

319

Caparison. Silk embroidery on cotton. The very lively colours and the ornamentation suggest the same provenance as ill. 316.
L: 180 cm, W: 132 cm (top)
Northern Afghanistan or Surkhan Darya, second half 19th century
Private collection, Zurich

320

Head-dress for a horse. Silk embroidery on cotton, fully embroidered in the style of Shahr-i Sabz.
L: 39 cm, W: 43 cm, late 19th century
Private collection, Zurich

the top of the neck to beyond the croup. Openings for the stirrups and saddle-horn indicate that it was laid over the saddle. In addition to the various functions mentioned above, such felt blankets could also have served as a light armour, especially if several were used. The fact that the blanket also covered the croup and tail was perhaps also meant as a protective measure. There was a custom among Mongols and Turkmens to cut off the tail of the enemy's horse during battle and to use it as a symbol of victory and to decorate battle standards.

A final item of textile decoration for horses was an embroidered head-dress like our example from Shahr-i Sabz (ill. 320).

Riding dress and paraphernalia

As late as the 1900s the Russian governor-generalship of Turkestan kept far more horses than men. According to von Schwarz, on market days the roads in and around cities would be jammed with hundreds of thousands of horses. Boys were put on horses at the age of three or four and a man would continue to ride as long as he was at all able to move outside the house. This accounts for the absence of a destinctive riding dress. The dress usually consisted of the above-mentioned wide pair of trousers, a voluminous shirt worn outside the trousers, one or more gowns of silk ikat, cashmere or brocade according to status, a turban wound round a knitted cap, leather boots with relief embroidery or leather applications and leather stockings. Only the *jigits*, who served as grooms, valets and general attendants, had their own distinctive costume. Von Schwarz writes: "The *jigits* can be identified by their dress. They wear turbans or more commonly high fur caps similar to the Russian Cossacks' *papash* and silk khalats with wide yellow leather trousers covered with silk bands. Around the waist they tie a colourful belt of silk or cotton to which they attach the heavy domestically-made scimitar no jigit is ever seen without." Von Schwarz further comments on the superb horsemanship and endurance of the *jigits*: "All members of the higher Russian administration, such as military governors, district heads, chiefs of police, etc., have a certain number of *jigits* at their command, who are paid by the state and serve as bodyguards, clerks and messengers. *Jigits*

321a, 321b
Horse blanket. Thick felt with cotton appliqué, top and side views. The openings for the saddle-horn and the stirrup leather indicate that the blanket was positioned under the saddle.
L: 214 cm, max. width: 270 cm
Khiva (?), late 19th century

322
Riding breeches. Leather with silk embroidery. This type of breeches were worn by jingits (grooms) and the Bukharan troops.
Bukhara, 1890s
Museum für Völkerkunde, Berlin

323
Boots. Leather with velvet uppers and brocade embroidery, made for court-connected customers. The common footwear were boots with heel chops or low shoes with comparatively high heels and worn with leather stockings.
Bukhara, late 19th century
Museum für Völkerkunde, Berlin

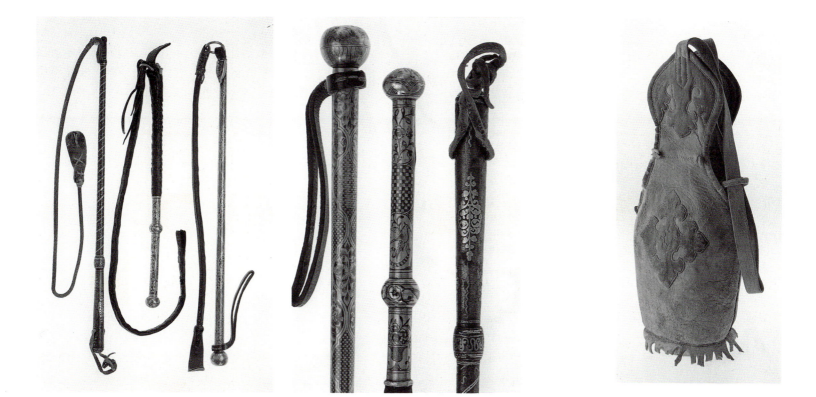

324(opposite, top)
Leather stockings with dyed leather appliqué, made for rural Uzbek customers.
L: 38 cm
Northern Afghanistan, early 20th century

325(opposite, centre)
Leather shoes and leather stockings decorated with appliqué work.
L: 44 cm
Eastern Turkestan, late 19th century

326 (opposite, bottom)
Boots. Leather with dyed leather appliqué depicting a highly stylised tree of life in a vase.
L: 43 cm
Northern Afghanistan or Uzbekistan, early 20th century

327-328
Riding crops with metal fittings.
(Left) On the left steel with silver inlay, on the right nielloed silver.
(Centre) Details of grips: on the left, nielloed silver, and on the right silver inlay. The grips in the middle with chequerboard pattern, flowers within roundels, a bird and snake, and a vase and stylised tree of life.
L: 97-114 cm
Central Asia, first half 19th century (crop with silver inlay)
Bukhara, second half 19th century (crops with silver grips)
Private collection, Zurich

329
Leather pouch. Leather appliqué in the shape of a compass rose, to be attached to the saddle-horn.
L: 43 cm
Kirghiz or Uzbek, second half 19th century
Museum für Völkerkunde, Munich

330
Leather pouch with dyed leather appliqué, wooden case for a drinking cup with coloured fittings.
L: 18 cm (pouch), D: 17 cm (case)
Kirghiz, second half 19th century
Museum für Völkerkunde, Munich

331
Travelling utensils
(Left) Leather case for a bowl. Brass wire, small gilt silver pieces, traces of a welt of dyed green ass's skin; bottom with blind tooling. Northern Afghanistan, late 19th century. L: 33.5 cm
(Centre) Tee bowl. Gardner porcelain, inscribed and dated A.H. 1328 (A.D. 1910).
(Right) Leather case for a bowl. Decorative seams and hangings, with fitted tin-plated copper bowl.
L: 40.8 cm (case)
Bukhara, late 19th century
Museum für Völkerkunde, Berlin, Rickmers Collection

179

employed by the native population do not receive proper wages but only food and lodging from themselves and their horses and occasional presents, if their master is pleased with them. If they execute an order badly or too slowly, on the other hand, they are punished by having their horses taken away and forced to ride a donkey, the greatest insult you can do to a *jigit*" (Schwarz 1900:376). The yellow trousers were also part of the uniform of the Bukharan army, which was made up exclusively of cavalry. Spurs were unknown in Turkestan. Riding crops commonly consisted of a rather short wooden handle as thick as a finger with plaited leather thongs of similar thickness, frequently with leaf-shaped terminations (ill. 327). They were secured with a leather loop at the wrist. People of distinction carried riding crops with an iron handle with silver inlay or silver fittings sometimes decorated with a nielloed design as on our example from Bukhara (ill. 328).

An indispensable part of a rider's paraphernalia were cases for drinking cups or plates of brass or porcelain (ills. 330-3). They are usually made of leather with decorative seams, of leather throngs or wire or silk, and more rarely of embroidered silk with applied silver over a body of wood or papier-mâché. Sometimes leather bags for hookahs, etc., completed the number of accessories. All such leather cases were secured with leather strips to the saddle-horn or the belt.

332
Case for a bowl. Silk embroidery on cotton, chased silver appliqué.
L: c. 50 cm
Northern Afghanistan, Laqai Uzbeks (?), first half 20th century

333
Travelling utensils.
(Left) Copper plate. Tin-plated and chased, leather case with decorative seams.
(Right) Turned metal bowl with engraved poem. Leather case with decorative seams.
D: 29 cm (case) D:20 cm (plate)
Eastern Iran or Central Asia, second half 19th century

334
Powder-flask. Silver, part gilt, chased and engraved, leather fitting.
H: 16 cm
Kirghiz (?), second half 19th century
Museum für Völkerkunde, Munich

Weapons

Thanks to exhibitions and publications of Henri Moser's collection of Oriental weapons at the Historisches Museum in Bern, weaponry is probably the most widely known and extensively researched aspect of Turkestan's material culture. We therefore shall deal only with the major types of weapons still in use in the eighteenth and nineteenth centuries.

The classical type of Central Asian scimitar can be illustrated with a example from a private collection which has a bone hilt, a damascened blade with etched decorative lettering, and niello work both on the haft and hilt (ill. 337). The upper and lower part of the sheath are mounted with with silver decorated with chased scroll designs; the upper mount is inset with turquoise, a feature indicating its Bukhara origin.

Two scimitars in the museum collection illustrate the communication network of the region and its influence on the character of the material culture. One comes with a blade of Caucasian design and nielloed silver haft shells produced at Kabul for customers in northern Afghanistan or Turkestan (ill. 338 bottom). Even more convincing evidence that it was designed for a Central Asian clientele is supplied by the relief design of the sheath, the nielloed upper and lower mounts and the horizontal fastening with leather straps, which belongs to a distinctive Central Asian tradition (ill. 338 top). The survival of Chinese influence in nineteenth-century Turkestan can be observed on a scimitar with a blade-and-hilt construction of Chinese type and a dragon engraved along the upper part of the blade.

Daggers and dagger knives by this time presumably were more of ornamental than practical use. Even in the eighteenth/nineteenth century excellent damascened blades were produced in Turkestan. The handles are usually of walrus bone, rhinoceros horn or wood; those from Bukhara are sometimes inlaid with turquoise (ill. 341 centre and bottom). The fire-gilt silver sheaths can be studded with glass beads and/or turquoise. The very meticulously executed floral designs are chased either in poussée or repoussée (ills. 339-40). After the Russian conquest the sheaths produced at Bukhara are characterised by very finely enamelled mounts in light and dark blue, green and white, a colour combination unknown in the area in pre-czarist times (ill. 345). Besides local products the Turkestani also used all kinds of weapons from booty. The Linden-Museum has a very beautiful specimen in the shape of a lightly curved dagger (ill. 343 bottom). The incised scroll design along the sides of the blade and the cartouches with birds and hares on the back as well as the etched decoration of the guard showing leafy scrolls indicate that the blade was manufactured in Iran during the time of the Zand dynasty between 1715 and 1794. The mount of the sheath consisting of partly gilt silver fittings and imitated granulation, suggests that it was made in Khorezm during the late nineteenth century. One of its last owners presumably was a wealthy Karakalpak. Another knife acquired in Turkestan has a north Indian blade with characteristic gold blossom design executed in *kuftgari* ('inlaid metal') technique (ill. 343 top).

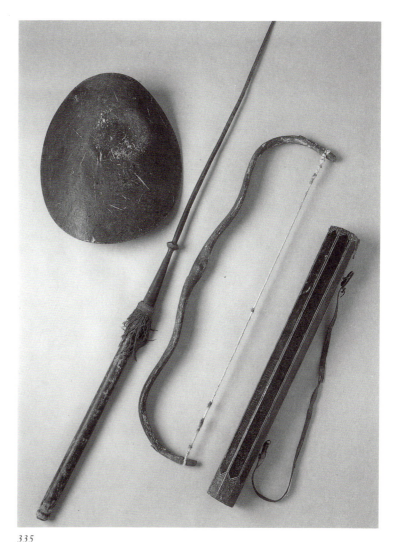

335
Arms of a Bukharan horseman, consisting of a round shield, lance, reflex bow and quiver.
Leather, wood, iron.
L: 178 cm (lance)
18th century
Museum in the Ark, Bukhara

336
Hawking drum. Chased and engraved brass, cast fittings.
D: 25 cm
Bukhara, 18th century
Museum of Fine Arts, Tashkent

181

337
Sabre. Steel with silver inlay; hilt of nielloed silver and ivory; sheath of wood covered with black shagreen, engraved silver fittings, turquoises.
The slightly curved single-edged blade has a hollow running parallel to the blunt back to the tip, with an adjoining blood groove. Its right side shows an inscribed cartouche ("I trust in God, 1265. Made at noble Bukhara."), with forked-leaf pendant in silver inlay. The left side shows a corresponding elogated inscribed cartouche with the name of the workshop ("Made by Hadji Sa`duddin Kashgari in 1265 at noble Bukhara.").
L: 86.5 cm (overall)
Bukhara, dated A.H. 1265 (A.D. 1848/9)

338
(Top) *Sabre. Damascus blade with deep blood groove and engraved dragon, wooden haft with steel fittings; sheath with wood core covered with chrome-leather, steel fittings. L: 85.5 cm (overall).*
Eastern Turkestan, 19th century.

(Bottom) *Sabre. Caucasian type, steel blade with double blood groove, pounced workshop marks, the back with a flash along the lower third. The haft shells of silver, nielloed with a floral design. The sheath covered with leather blind-stamped with boteh patterns, the fittings of nielloed silver, the straps with silver fittings.*
L: 97 cm (overall)
Northern Afghanistan, Herat (?), 19th century

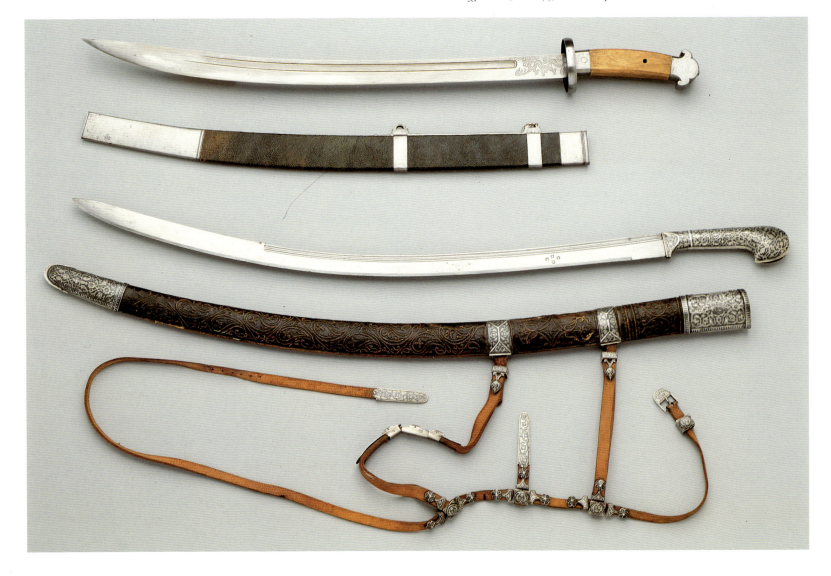

339-340

Weapons from Bukhara

(Top) Dagger. Damascus blade and wooden haft shells.

(Centre) Dagger. Damascus blade, haft shells of rhinoceros horn fitted with gilt sheet silver decorated with turqoises and glass beads underlaid with foil.

(Bottom) Dagger. A rare example of a Bukharan curved dagger of Arab type, the haft shells of whalebone fitted with silver and glass stones.

The blades all of gilt silver with floral designs chased in poussé-repoussé technique. The reinforced tip of the top dagger sheath is decorated with turquoises, the top reinforcement a later replacement.

(Detail) Chasing on the sheath of the top dagger showing scrollwork with lotus in a niche-shaped field.

L: 34.5-55.5 cm

Bukhara, 19th century

341

Knives from Bukhara.

(Top) Steel blade, haft shells of dyed green bone with design of circles. This type is still manufactured in Uzbekistan today.

(Centre) Damascus blade, haft shells with turquoise inlay.

(Bottom) Damascus blade, haft shells of whalebone, tang of nielloed silver.

L: 30.6-33.6 cm

Bukhara, second half 19th century

342

Dagger. Wooden haft shells, Damascus blade, the sheath with a wooden core covered with velvet and turquoises, silk tassels.

L: 53 cm

Bukhara, mid-19th century

183

343-344

Weapons from Turkestan.

(Top) Knife. Damascus blade, tang and top of blade with floral designs in kuftgari technique. The haft shells of nielloed silver, the sheath covered with velvet over a wooden core and with silver fittings. The blade was imported from northern India, while the haft shells and sheath fittings were probably made at Herat in the 19th century. L: 47 cm (knife)

(Bottom) Dagger. Damascus blade with engraved plant design, haft shells of whalebone. The animals motifs within cartouches on the back of the blade and the flowering scroll along the tang indicate that the knife was made in Iran in the mid-18th century. The silver fittings with fluted and fire-gilt designs of the sheath were manufactured in Khorezm in the second half of the 19th century. L: 37 cm (knife), 30.5 cm (sheath)

345

Knives from Bukhara. Haft shells of rhinoceros horn, tang and hilt of silver with nielloed design. The enamel colours of the silver fittings of the sheath show Russian influence. L: 34 cm. Bukhara, late 19th century

Belt pouch: Leather with gilt silver appliqué and glass beads. L (with tassels): c. 54 cm. Turkestan, 19th century

346
Buzkashi was a popular sport in northern Afghanistan and Turkestan. The riders would try with every means available to seize a dead sheep or calf from the opponents. The first to carry the carcass past the post was greatly admired and received presents including magnificently caparisoned horses and gowns of honour. The photograph was taken in about 1900 among the hills of Afrasiab (Old Samarkand).

347
A buzkashi player, Samarkand, about 1900.

The nielloed haft shells and engraved silver fittings of the sheath recall the typical Herat style of the late nineteenth century. In Uzbekistan less expensive knives often have bone handles dyed green with copper vitriol and decorated with ring patterns (ill. 341). Two specimens in the Linden-Museum were acquired by von Rickmers in the 1890s. The same type of knives is still produced today.

Notes on horses, carts and horsemanship

The horses of the nomads only know two paces, the walk and the gallop, according to Henri Moser (Moser 1888:273). Von Schwarz writes: "Riding speed is very strictly bound up with the social position of the rider. One never sees a dignitary riding at a trott, not to speak of a full gallop; only *jigits* and plebeians are allowed such speeds. On journeys etiquette demands that the length of the daily stages is in inverse proportion to the rank of the traveller. Thus the emir of Bukhara … on his annual tour to Samarkand and Shahr-i Sabz seldom covered more than a *tash* (roughly eight kilometres) per day. Distinguished persons on a ride usually have one or two runners next to them leading the animal by the reins" (Schwarz 1900:287). A meeting of two riders also involved strict rituals, the one of lower rank having to dismount.

The Central Asian riding style has nothing in common with the Western sport. Because of the many blankets the rider is perched above the horse with spread legs. When galloping the rider stands upright in the reins.

The typical Central Asian two-wheeled cart, the single-axel *arba*, is driven by one man. Von Schwarz describes the vehicle: "Only horses are used to pull the *arba*. A distinctive type of collar consisting of a thick leather pad stuffed with straw or reed is placed across the neck and fastened as tightly as possible to the two shafts. A second broad strap attached to the shafts lies across the horse's back, so that the load rests not on the neck but on the back. So the traction animals are saddled the same way as riding horses with the rear strap running across the saddle. The driver's place is not in the cart but atop the horse, and he drives the animal just like a riding horse and with the same type of reins. His feet do not rest in the stirrups, however, but on the shafts to increase their weight and thus the traction-power of the horse" (Schwarz 1900:333). Until the early years of our century the *arba* was the common vehicle to transport agricultural goods in the oasis regions, and was also much more common for inter-urban commercial traffic than the camel caravan.

The value and importance of horses in Central Asia is also indicated by the fact that they formed part of the tribute collected by the khan. Von Schwarz has this to say on the subject: "In Turkestan the payment of tribute by the begs to the khan is of a peculiar nature. Tribute is not paid in money but in the form of gifts. In Bukhara, for example, this is arranged in the following way. Twice a year, in spring and autumn, all begs have to present themselves in ranking order at the emir's court to deliver gifts ... The gifts consist of: a) eighty-six horses with blankets of silk, velvet and gold an silver embroidery and with harnesses with silver fittings studded with turquoises and other semi-precious stones" (Schwarz 1900:182). The begs and court officials in turn were presented with horses during the emir's New Year's reception. Horses together with sumptuous gowns were also the most important gifts to guests. During his travels in Turkestan Henri Moser was presented with a total of thirty-three splendidly decked-out and harnessed horses.

Polo, a popular sport throughout the Near and Middle East since the Middle Ages, seems to have disappeared in Turkestan by the nineteenth century. It is also surprising that among the nineteenth-century travel writers only Moser mentions *buzkashi* at all (ills. 346-7). This is a very rough game on horseback where the skin of a calf or sheep is thrown among two teams, who have to get it across the finishing line. The riders jostle ferociously, hit each other with their crops and try to throw their opponents off the saddle. Until the 1970s the sport was as popular in northern Afghanistan as football is in our part of the world.

The importance of horses is also reflected in the custom to present one's friends with small horse sculptures during the New Year celebrations. That person must have been a great horse-lover who in the sixteenth century commissioned a door decorated with horses carved in relief (ill. 355). It is the only instance known to me of carved animal figures in the arts of Muslim Central Asia.

348
Pack-saddle. Wood with carved decoration and brass rings.
H: 50 cm, L: 47 cm
Khiva, 19th century
Museum in the Ark, Khiva

349
Part of the harness connecting shaft and yoke. Wood with carved decoration, fittings and hangings of iron.
L: 114 cm
Khiva, 19th century
Museum in the Ark, Khiva

350
*Cart (arba) on a narrow mountain road, about 1900. The arba, a cart with outsized
wheels, remained in use in rural areas until the mid-20th century. Supplied with a cover, it
was also used to transport people and goods between the urban centres in Turkestan.*

351
Urban reception room, Turkestan, about 1900. Its sparse furnishings are typical of Central Asia. People sat on quilted blankets stuffed with cotton. The niches were mainly used for display.

Houses and Their Furnishings

Johannes Kalter

In this chapter I shall discuss a number of selected objects together, which elsewhere in the present publication are treated separately, and place them within a larger context.

The traditional house was a one-storey mud building with a flat roof which in summer served as a living and, more importantly, as a sleeping area. If there was a second storey, it was used solely for storage. "All houses conform to the same style. The only differences between the houses of the poor and the rich is that the latter have more spacious courtyards and gardens, higher walls, a greater number of rooms, more elaborate furnishings and are built with better materials. The main feature of Central Asian houses is the high wall which encloses the house together with the garden and all secondary buildings, effectively sealing it off from the outside world. The external wall is provided with a single entrance portal opening onto the street, while a second inside wall running parallel to the entrace blocks the view from the street into the courtyard, the whole arrangement appearing somewhat like a fortress preventing anyone unauthorized from entering the private realm ... The area enclosed by the main wall is divided into two parts which are strictly separated by a wall, the only connection being a low and narrow garden gate. The larger part adjacent to the street, is the male preserve, the living quarters of the head of the household, his grown-up sons and perhaps other male relatives and servants, as well as the office and the reception area for visitors and strangers. The other part is exclusively reserved for the female members of the household and the children and the only male permitted entry is the family head. Both parts are again subdivided into two or three smaller partitions, the actual living quarters, the courtyard and the garden, the latter usually only found in the houses of the wealthy. In more arid regions and in densely built-up settlements the gardens would normally lie beyond the town walls. Gardens within the housing compound are generally again enclosed by a wall" (Schwarz 1900:228).

Ceilings were constructed with wooden beams and with reed or brushwood to fill the gaps in between. While in houses of the poor the only opening admitting light would be the door, the wealthy had windows of paper instead of glass. Generally the mud walls were not whitewashed, although more substantial houses might be decorated with cut stucco. The low doors generally had two wings, each so narrow that to enter both had to be opened. Only the very wealthy had doors with carved designs. Examples in the Linden-Museum from the thirteenth to the nineteenth century include carved doors with coffered decoration and floral designs within oval medallions as well as a single-leaf door with ornaments reminiscent of felt designs and figures of horses (ills. 354-7).

Interior furnishings in the Western sense of static furniture were almost completely absent. For sitting and

352
This view of the Old Town of Bukhara in about 1900 shows single-storey houses with inner courtyards and narrow unpaved streets.

353
Traditional reception in a courtyard garden of a wealthy townsman, about 1900.

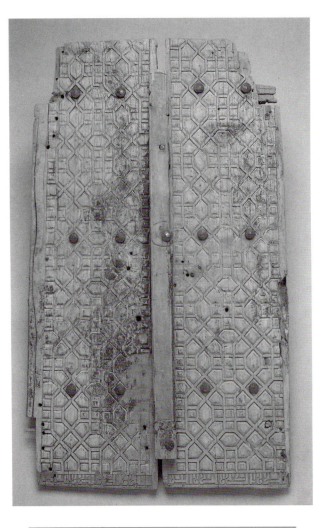

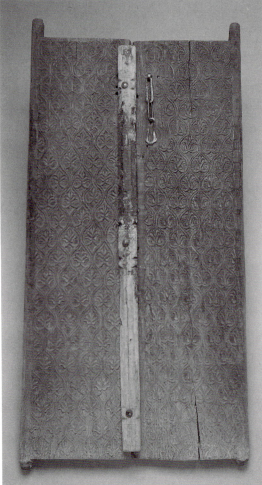

358
Hookah. The bottle-gourd vase with brass fittings, ceramic head.
H: 64 cm (without mouthpiece)
Bukhara, second half 19th century
Museum für Völkerkunde, Munich

359
Tea drinkers, about 1900. The pots and bowls are Gardner porcelain produced in Russia for the Turkestan market.

360
Men by a brazier, about 1900. The main form of heating in Turkestan houses were braziers placed under a low table covered with a blanket, under which one would put one's hands and feet for warming-up.

361
Shop selling cradles in the bazaar of a Turkestan town, about 1900. The same type of cradles are still produced in Uzbekistan today.

354-357
(Top left) Wooden door. Carved decoration, hand-forged iron nails, in the threshold area kufic inscription. H: 138 cm, W: 85 cm. Northern Afghanistan, late 13th century
(Top right) Single-leaf wooden door. Iron fittings, leather fastenings, carvings, cartouches with leaf borders and delicately serrated rosettes, the lower half with figures of four horses. H: 120 cm, W: 72 cm. Northern Afghanistan, 16th/17th century
(Bottom left) Wooden door. Carved decoration, iron fittings. The design of palmettes within oval medallions suggests Indian influence. H: 149 cm, W: 81 cm. Northern Afghanistan or Central Asia, 17th century
(Bottom right) Wooden door. Carved decoration, iron fittings, square and rectangular coffers with flower designs within quatrefoils. H: 164 cm, W: 80 cm. Northern Afghanistan, late 19th/early 20th century

sleeping purposes blankets stuffed with cotton and with a cover of printed cotton cloth, ikat cloth or brocade were used and sausage-shaped cushions covered with ikat cloth or cashmere (ills. 366-67). Food was served in bowls on a brass tray or directly on a 'table-cloth' spread out on the floor. Beds only featured in the houses of the very rich and were constructed with a simple wooden frame laced with bands of horsehair in a net-like pattern. The only piece of furniture was a cradle of a type common among all Turkish and Mongol peoples from eastern Turkey to China. Built-in niches served as cupboards especially in urban houses, those in the living room frequently left open for the display of rosewater bottles, candlesticks, pieces of fine tableware, hookahs and the like (ill. 351). Niches for storing clothes and linen were hung with curtains, embroidered *suzanis* or ikat cloth. The walls of the reception area were hung with horizontal *suzanis* or gold relief embroideries in the Ottoman taste. In urban houses the floor was covered with knotted carpets with typical Uzbek designs on a red ground like roses (*gül*) and blue, yellow and white patterns, for instance of octagonal stars within octagonal fields. Among all levels of society felt floor covers were popular, decorated with impressed or applied ornaments such as the powerful rams' horns of the Linden-Museum's example (ill. 392). Kilims with red or white ground and composed of several narrow strips with bold colourful cotton embroidery were popular among peasants and nomads. From the Surkhan Darya region felt carpets are known with cotton or silk embroidery and triangular or lozenge-shaped fields (ill. 391).

I am unaware of prayer rugs of distinctive Uzbek design. Prayer cloths and prayer blankets were also often found at home. Examples in the Museum collection include a thick woollen cloth with the stylised design of a mosque in white silk embroidery (ill. 375), a gold brocade with a *boteh* pattern on a blue ground in the niche (ill. 373) and a *suzani*-type embroidered cloth with a prayer niche made at Tashkurgan in the mid-twentieth century (ill. 374).

362
Plate. Slate, an Uzbek poem inscribed on the rim.
D: 36.5 cm
Fergana Valley, 19th century

364
Traditional Uzbek knot wool carpet.
Typical features are the pale red ground and a
predeliction for eight-pointed star designs.
233 x 286 cm
Fergana Valley, 19th century

365
A silk ikat cloth used as a curtain for a niche.
197 x 154 cm
Fergana Valley, about 1870

363
Women in the harem courtyard of a Bukharan mansion, about 1900.

366-367
High-quality cushions.
(Top) Cushion. Cover of cashmere and velvet with brocade embroidery. Museum für Völkerkunde, Berlin
(Bottom) Cushion. Silk ikat cover. L: c. 80 cm. Bukhara, late 19th century

368
Small cloth used to cover a brazier. Silk embroidery on velvet.
D: c. 82 cm
Bukhara, late 19th century

369
Wall hanging for an urban reception room. Fully embroidered with a suzani-like designs. The niche-shaped sections indicate individual seating-spaces for guests.
H: 59.5 cm, W: 294 cm
Tashkent, late 19th century
Museum für Völkerkunde, Berlin

370
Wall hanging for the reception room of a member of the urban upper class. Brocade embroidery on woollen ground with designs of Ottoman inspiration; the central medallion is surrounded by four lions.
135 x 256 cm
Bukhara, late 19th century

371
Woodblock-printed cotton cloth, originally used as a quilt.
240 x 172 cm
Samarkand or Bukhara, first half 20th century

372
Quilt. Upside of gold brocade on a red ground showing boteh patterns on the inner field and various floral motifs along the border, downside of whitish-green silk ikat.
219 x 145 cm
Bukhara, about 1900

373-375
Prayer mats. Almost anything mat-like could be used on which to perform one's prayers, e.g., plaited mats, carpets or pieces of cloth. Prayer mats often formed part of the dowry.
(Top left) Gold brocade with boteh pattern in the niche framed by boteh-shaped flower sprays. 54 x 90 cm. Bukhara, second half 19th century
(Top right) Silk embroidery on woollen felt, silk tassels. Here again the strong Ottoman influence on 19th-century Bukharan designs is noticeable. 101 x 156 cm. Bukhara, 19th century
(Left) Silk embroidery on cotton with colourful designs popular among the rural Uzbeks of northern Afghanistan; vases with flower arrangements are particularly in demand. 143 x 107 cm. Northern Afghanistan, 20th century. Private collection, Heidelberg

195

376-377
*Ceremonial tent of a nobleman from Bukhara. People
usually spent only the coldest time of the year in solid
houses. Whoever could afford it, would erect a tent for
receptions in his courtyard. The outer cover tended to be of
inconspicuous green-dyed sackcloth, while the inside was
decorated with ikats with appliqué decoration. The row of
niches relates to the wall hangings used in urban houses.
The tent presumably dates from the 1870s and was
acquired by Rickmers in Bukhara.*
*The illustrations show the pyramidal ceiling and a view of
the interior of the tent.*
H: c. 400 cm, floor space: c. 370 x 370 cm

378
Reception in front of an urban tent, about 1900.

379
Wall hanging. Full silk embroidery in the style of Shahr-i Sabz, about 1900.
90 x 95 cm

380
Dignitaries from Bukhara inside a tent, about 1900.

197

381
(Left) Hookah vase. H: 29.5 cm
(Right) Teapot. Chinese export porcelain for the Central Asian market. H: 38 cm
China, 19th century
Museum in the Summer Residence, Bukhara

382
Pen-case. Lacquer painting on wood, ornamental writing on the top and sides of the cover.
Tashkent, 19th century
Museum für Völkerkunde, Berlin

383 *Porcelain tableware.*
(Left) Russian copy of a Chinese prototype. D: 26.5 cm. 19th century
(Right) Chinese export-ware dish. D: 37.4 cm. 19th century
Both acquired in Uzbek settlements in northern Afghanistan.

The most striking difference between the furnishings of urban houses and the dwellings of peasants and nomads was the use of textiles for decoration. A relationship between peasant and nomad households manifested itself frequently through similar or related forms. While they travelled, for instance, the nomads used five-cornered tent-bags to protect the ends of the yurt's roof-beams (ill. 404). They were either of knotwork or flat-weave or sewn together from strips of sturdy woollen felt and had a fringe of tassels made of wool or silk or sometimes of horsehair. This item metamorphosed into a flat decorative textile wall-hanging found in rural Uzbek areas of northern Afghanistan and the Surkhan Darya region (ills. 399-401, 403). In the art market they are usually known as Laqai embroidery, although their distribution in fact extends far beyond the homeland of this Uzbek sub-tribe.

During the day blankets were deposited on top of chests, and to decorate this bundle both peasants and nomads used edge-shaped pieces of cloth or bands which frequently were trimmed with tassels (ills. 393-6). They were either embroidered throughout in silk or decorated with silk embroidery on a red and sometimes black ground. Like on decorated wall hangings, the most common types of embroidery were cross-stitch, petit point or tent stitch, and chain-stitch. Patterns and motifs included suns, bands of lozenges and triangles, stylised rams' heads, yurts and eagles, rosettes and *boteh* patterns as well as numerous elements we are no longer able to identify. But there is no doubt that they are of pre-Islamic inspiration, which is not so surprising if one remembers that many nomad tribes were converted to Islam only in the sixteenth/seventeenth century and even then only superficially.

Among the nomads' most cherished objects were mirrors, which were kept in special cases and additionally protected by mirror bags (ills. 397, 398). Many of the square or rectangular textile wall hangings with very finely worked ornamentation presumably derive from such mirror bags. They come in two distinctive types. There is patchwork combining cotton cloth, ikats, velvets and occasionally brocades and usually designed with lozenge or triangular patterns; the most sophisticated examples also have an embroidered border. The second type of wall hangings consists of silk embroidery on a red and sometimes black woollen ground. Motifs include stylised suns, rosettes, low plants, occasionally shapes recalling butterflies or other insects, and rams' horns. Exclusive to nomadic culture are large bags (*tshoval*) either of knotted or woven cloth, and narrow rectangular ones (*torba*) which may likewise be knotted but also occur with patches of embroidery on the outside.

384

Wares imported for the Bukharan upper class.
(Left) Lidded container from Kütahya, Turkey. H: 24.5 cm
(Right) Vase from Qajar Iran (1794-1925). H: 21.5 cm
Both items were acquired by Rickmers in Bukhara in the 1890s.

385

Russian export ware for the Turkestan market.
The teapot, cup and saucer and the blue bowl with flower sprays were produced in czarist Russia, while the white tea bowl with flower sprays was made after 1920. Russian export ware was highly regarded throughout Central Asia, and was bought by wealthy peasants as well as by the Bukharan court.
H: 12 cm (teapot), 5.5 and c. 10.5 cm (bowls)
Acquired in northern Afghanistan

386

Food bowls.
(Left) Earthenware, running glaze in green, brown and yellow under a transparent glaze. The popularity of this colour scheme, perhaps originally inspired by Chinese Tang-dynasty 'three-colour' glazes, remained popular in the region from the 9th to the 20th century.
(Right) Rice bowl, Gardner porcelain.
D: 26 and 18.5 cm
Tashkurgan, early 20th century

387

Wooden bowls.
The bowl on the left was turned on the lathe and decorated with lacquer painting. Russian export ware for the Central Asian market, about 1900. The bowl on the right and the plate, both of walnut, were turned on the lathe and manufactured at Tashkurgan during the first half of the 20th century.
D: 23.4-34.0 cm
Acquired in northern Afghanistan

388
A village street in Turkestan, about 1900.

389
Kilim. Wool with cotton embroidery, fashioned from twelve separate horizontal textile bands. The interior design of the octagonal güls (tulips) are related to Turkmen motifs. The border decoration of stylised rams' heads, yurts and camels is reminiscent of Uzbek rural embroideries.
410 x 129 cm
Northern Afghanistan, Laqai Uzbeks, late 19th century

390
Kilim (detail). Wool with cotton embroidery, fashioned from separate textile bands. The highly unorthodox alternation of patterns showing star motifs, insect-like shapes, lozenges, rams' horns and sun discs again is reminiscent of Uzbek rural embroideries. The ascription of these and other textiles to the Laqai Uzbeks must remain tentative for the time being.
283 x 136 cm
Northern Afghanistan, mid-19th century

391
Felt floor cover. Woven border, embroidery and appliqué in cotton.
327 x 127 cm
Uzbekistan, probably Surkhan Darya, early 20th century

392
Felt floor cover. Appliqué, fringes along one side, tripartite central field, borders with geometric patterns, rams' horn motifs.
224 x 107 cm
Northern Afghanistan, Laqai Uzbeks, first half 20th century

393
Decoration on a blanket for covering the bedding stored in yurts on chests during the day, embroidered with flowery rosettes.
192 x 184 cm
Uzbekistan, early 20th century

394-396
Decorative bands for covering blankets.
Such ornamental bands can be fully embroidered with a suzani-type pattern (ill. 394 top

left), show bold individual motifs on a red and sometimes a black ground (ills. 394 centre and bottom) or have highly geometricised motifs worked in petit point (half cross stitch). Until the late 1970s, such bands could be bought at the Kabul bazaar and were made both by Uzbeks living in northern Afghanistan and in Uzbekistan itself. Regional identifications are next to impossible, and it is equally difficult to interpret the motifs. The example on the bottom left has shapes reminiscent of astral symbolism, while that at the centre of the illustration on the top right very likely shows a highly stylised eagle, and the one below stylised yurts. The example at the centre of the lower right illustration is decorated with rams' horns. All these border ornaments should have fringes; where they are missing, this is due to 'commercial cosmetics'.
W: 85-110 cm (diagonal of cover blanket), 7-14 cm (corner ornaments)
Northern Afghanistan or Turkestan, late 19th to mid-20th century

397-398

Mirror pouches. Nomads have a genius for packaging. Mirrors being among their most highly treasured belongings, much thought and art was devoted to make them safe for travel. The results are elaborately decorated pockets like the one above with a design of flowers and butterfly-like shapes, or the one below with patchwork and embroidery on an ikat ground; both types were used concurrently in Northern Afghanistan It seems impossible to assign them to specific Uzbek sub-tribes.
52 x 55 cm; 60 x 60 cm
Northern Afghanistan, late 19th/early 20th century

399-401

Decorative wall hangings inspired by travelling bags.
The majority of Uzbek nomads became settled during the last century. The manufacture of travelling pouches or bags (see ills. 397-398) therefore became obsolete. The decorative fronts, however, remained attractive and were refashioned to serve a similar function as the suzanis among the urban population, namely as wall hangings. One can often discover traces of clay or mud on the back, indicating that they were put up before the walls had dried completely.
60 x 60 - 74 x 78 cm
Northern Afghanistan and Uzbekistan, late 19th/early 20th century

402-403
Bag and bag-like wall hanging.
(Left) 60 x 60 cm, (right) 48 x 40 cm
Northern Afghanistan, early 20th century

405
Bags of the same type but used only for decorative purposes.
H: 45 cm Northern Afghanistan, late 19th/early 20th century

404
(Left) Felt bag. Embroidery and horsehair tassels. H: 69 cm
(Right) Knotted bag. H: 57 cm
Bags like these were used to cover the ends of yurt beams during migrations.
Northern Afghanistan, early 20th century

407
Bag fronts. Two exceptionally fine examples, one with more geometric, the other with curvilinear designs.
H: 43 cm (left), 63 cm (right) Northern Afghanistan or Uzbekistan, early 20th century

406
Adapting this pair of bag fronts for purely decorative use, the size was reduced while the embroidery was executed with great refinement and sophistication.
Northern Afghanistan or Uzbekistan, early 20th century

408
Knotted tent-bag for home and transport (mafrash).
C. 86 x 40 cm
Northern Afghanistan, early 20th century

409
Tent-bag for home and transport (mafrash). Embroidered front.
C. 86 x 40 cm
Northern Afghanistan, early 20th century

410
Large saddle-bag used in pairs on camels (tshoval).
87 x 104 cm
Northern Afghanistan, made by Uzbeks, late 19th century

411
(Left) Container for chewing-tobacco. Gourd with silver mount. H: 18 cm. Made by Uzbeks in northern Afghanistan, first half 20th century
(Right) Flask for ointments. Carved jade. H: 7 cm. Acquired by Rickmers in Bukhara in the 1890s.

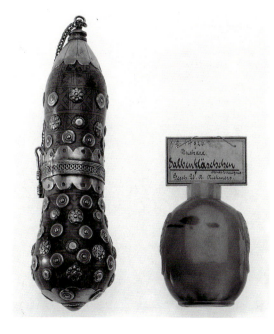

Among townspeople, *suzanis* were part of the dowry. The nomads also had special textiles for the bridal procession. The bride's camel was furnished with openwork patchwork cloth attached with feathers or more rarely with human hair, and wore a head ornament of embroidered or knotted bands (ills. 416, 415). The dowry was wrapped in kilims of thin flatweave with triangular embroidery in two opposite corners (ill. 417). The popularity of red colours for peasant and nomad textiles is probably partly due to its association with life and fertility.

The nomads were masters in the art of packaging. The main materials were wool (used, for instance, for the above-mentioned bags) and leather. Leather was used for the construction of cylindrical containers for food and clothes on journeys but also in the yurt as a protection against vermin and insects (ill. 421). Leather travel cases with decorative seams and applications were used by both townspeople and nomads.

For other household goods, differences were based less on lifestyle (sedentary vs. nomad) than on wealth. Among the bowls in use were turned bowls of walnut wood, imported bowls from Russia with lacquer painting and ceramics, either domestically produced or also imported from Russia ('Gardner porcelain') and China, preferably in famille rose (ills. 383-7). In the late nineteenth century, locally made teapots of copper or brass became increasingly sidelined by imported Gardner ware. The custom for Chinese teapots produced in shapes adapted to the Central Asian market and of hookah vases of Chinese porcelain was presumably restricted to court circles. The illustrated examples come from the summer residence of the emirs of Bukhara (ill. 381).

Wealthy people were in the habit of spending the summer months in a tent in their garden. The tent had a square plan and a pyramidal roof. The outside was lined with plain sackcloth normally dyed green, while the interior was decorated with ikats and applied textiles, like the tent in the Museum's collection, possibly the only such tent in a public collection in central Europe (ills. 376-7).

Peasants usually spent the summer in yurts. In northern Afghanistan even in the 1970s one very frequently came upon a yurt erected inside the walled enclosure of a farm. The yurt, a kind of collapsible circular hut with a wooden frame and felt covering, represents the traditional living quarters of all equestrian nomads in Central Asia.

The history of the yurt is known only in broad outlines. In Herodotus' day the Scythians still seem to have journeyed across the steppe in heavy waggons. In the thirteenth century, the Franciscan friar William of Rubruck noticed the transport of entire round huts on the top of ox carts in Central Asia. From the same century dates the earliest mention, by John of Plano Carpini, of the type of yurt with a lattice frame that has survived to the present: "A yurt consists of the following main elements: 1. The wooden structure: Lattice frame, rafters, roof crown, door frames with or without wings; 2. Felt covering; 3. Woven bands and straps of wool and cotton [with an abundance of wool, the use of cotton was probably a recent innovation – J.K.] to secure the wooden frame and fasten the felt covers" (Johannsen 1975).

413
Nomad family in front of a yurt, about 1900.

414
Bell for the last animal of a camel caravan. Iron with bone clapper.
L: 75 cm
Northern Afghanistan, early 20th century

415
Head ornament for the bridal camel. Wool. The cowry shells, blue glass beads and the mirror were regarded as amulets.
Acquired by Rickmers at Bukhara in the 1890s
Museum für Völkerkunde, Berlin, Rickmers Collection

412
Nomads resting during their migration to new pastures, about 1900. The camels are loaded with lattice frames and roof hoops.

416
Flank cover for the bridal camel. Patchwork of cotton cloth, brocades and ikats; the applied chicken feathers were regarded as amulets.
L:170 cm, W: 150 cm
Northern Afghanistan, early 20th century (acquired at Akcha in 1978)

417
Wrap for the bridewealth of a nomad bride. Flatweave, wool with cotton embroidery, six narrow strips combined. The tasselled bands are for tying up the parcel.
H: 163 cm, L: 158 cm
Uzbekistan, Surkhan Darya (?), early 20th century

418
Kazakh yurt.

419
Travelling case. This is a typical example of a type used by nomads and townspeople. Wood, mortised, leather cover, striped cotton lining, forged iron handles and lock, decorative seams and appliqué. The centre decorated with a teapot symbolising hospitality.
W: 68.5 cm
Turkestan, mid-19th century

420
Cosmetic box. It presumably belonged to a wealthy nomad lady and comes with built-in mirror, lacquer painting and painting on wood. Urban manufacture for nomad customers.
H: 24.0 cm, W: 31.5 cm, D: 37.5 cm
Turkestan, mid-19th century

421
Storage and travelling containers for food and clothes. Leather with appliqué.
(Left) H: 21 cm, D: 15 cm; (right) H: 30 cm, D: 23 cm
Kirghiz, second half 19th century
Museum für Völkerkunde, Munich

422
Ornamental gear for a fighting ram. Leather with cast brass fittings and brass bell, iron chain with peg and lock. Rams' fights were among the most popular forms of entertainment in 19th-century Turkestan, and high sums were betted.
H: c. 41 cm
Turkestan, second half 19th century
Museum für Völkerkunde, Munich

423
Peasant wall decoration. Silk embroidery on cotton.
D: c. 23 cm
Northern Afghanistan, early 20th century

424
Niche curtain. Silk ikat with boteh and amulet patterns.
L: 190 cm, W: 104 cm
Bukhara, about 1880

The Textile Arts of Uzbekistan

Maria Zerrnickel

Travelling through Uzbekistan, the general impression is of desolate countryside covered with saksaule, of steppe with grazing flocks of sheep, and of endless cotton fields with a network of irrigation channels along which mulberry trees grow. The mainly sedentary Tajik population of the oases practises intensive agriculture, with cotton and silkworm cultivation being major occupations since pre-Islamic times. The towns along the ancient Silk Road in Turkestan produced sophisticated arts and crafts, some of which have continued to the present day, for instance ceramics, ikat, printed cloth and embroidery. Beyond the oases, the countryside is still inhabited by cattle breeders. There is a lively trade and exchange of goods between the three main occupational groups of farmers, cattle breeders and artisans.

The raw materials
Wool (*yung, zun, pashm*)

The means of subsistence of the Uzbek nomads was cattle, mainly sheep. The word for wool, *yung*, in the ninth century also meant cotton and fluff (Barthold 1963). The fact that in Old Turkish *yung* meant both wool and cotton indicates that during the Middle Ages the cultivation of cotton was unknown among the Turkic Uzbeks. In modern Uzbekistan sheep farming remains a major economic activity. The country produces two-thirds of the Karakul sheep in the CIS and one-third of its Karakul hides. A large part of wool processing is performed by the women at home: cleaning, carding, spinning, weaving, felting and sometimes knotting. Spinning and weaving is done with simple old-fashioned spindles (*urchuk*) and horizontal looms (*urmak, kuzak*) easy to set up and dismantle (Sukhareva 1981; Zerrnickel in Kalter 1992).

The women make sacks (*kop*), coarse cloth for men's coats (*chakman*) and flat-weave with ornamental stripes (*gilam, gilem*). The Arab women produce flat-weaves of good quality with small designs, blankets for the charcoal brazier, the *sandal* (*sandalipuch*), special cloth (*buqchoma*) for wrapping clean laundry and dowries and for covering the piled-up bedding during the day, and also table-cloth (*dastarkhon*) of grey wool with blue and orange or black and brown borders. They also make good felt carpets for their own homes.

Cotton (*pakhta*)

According to Chinese chronicles, cotton was cultivated in India by 2500 B.C. Excavations in Sind (in modern Pakistan) have brought to light the earliest known cotton textiles dated to the third millennium B.C. (Zukovskij 1964). When the cotton plant was first introduced to China from India in antiquity, the Chinese silk manufacturers objected to its commercial exploitation and would only allow its cultivation

as a decorative shrub. Cotton has been grown commercially in China only since the eleventh to thirteenth century and was called *mian*, a term originally reserved for silk; during the Han dynasty (2nd century B.C.-3rd century A.D.) *mian* meant floss silk (Lyubo-Lesnizhenko 1961). Herodotus (5th century B.C.) recounts that in India wool grew on trees. According to the chronicle of the Liang dynasty (6th century), Turfan "has many herbs, the fruits of which are like cocoons. In the cocoons are fine fibres like silk. Many people of that country take the material and weave it into cloth, which is soft and white. It is used for trade at the market" (Needham 1988:58).

In the sixth century B.C. cotton reached Persia from India. The Indian variety, the perennial tree-like cotton plant (Gossypium arboreum), proved unsuitable for the continental climate with its hot summers and harsh winters. In the sixth century B.C. the grass-like annual (Gossypium herbaceum) was introduced from Persia to Turkestan, into the region of the modern Central Asian republics.

After colonising western Turkestan in the nineteenth century, Russia further encouraged silk production and the cultivation of cotton. This policy continued under the Soviet regime from the 1920s onwards, so that now more than fifty per cent of the irrigated area in Uzbekistan is planted with cotton and mulberry. In certain regions like the Fergana Valley cotton is a monoculture, and the Valley is the largest production area in Uzbekistan for cotton and silk. Soviet experts have produced a wide range of cotton plant varieties, and for the time being Uzbekistan only grows its own medium- and long-fibre types.

Huge amounts of fertilizer, pesticides and defoliation chemicals together with the intensive irrigation have increased the salidity of the soil and seriously affect the health of the population. Yet there is little the country can do about the situation, because cotton and the rearing of silkworms remain its two most important industries.

Silk (*ipak, shoyi, gozi abreshim*)

A mutually advantageous symbiosis exists between the cotton-plants and mulberry trees. The area along the irrigation canals is carefully utilised: The biomass for silkworm-rearing is grown here and evaporation and soil erosion are forestalled, while the heavily fertilised plants provide the trees with necessary nutrients. Before the first centuries A.D., the art of rearing silkworms and cultivating the indispensable white mulberry (Bombyx mori, locally called *tut*) was unknown in western Turkestan. In China, the discovery and domestication of the silkworm moth seems to go back at least to the fifth millennium B.C. Archaeological evidence itself reaches far back into prehistory. Neolithic petrographs resembling silkworms have been found in Shaguotun in Liaoning province in northeast China, while the Neolithic site of Xiaxiang Xiyincun in Shanxi province in central China revealed a cocoon cut in two. Further south, at Wuxingxian in Zhejiang province, today a centre of Chinese silk production, excavations produced a 4700-year-old bamboo casket which contained a piece of woven silk.

425
Needles with hand-shaped terminations. Carved ivory.
L: 7-13 cm
Dal'verzintepa, 1st/2nd century
Khamza Institute of Fine Arts, Tashkent

426
Hand-shaped instrument for reeling silk threads. Carved ivory, iron.
Scale 1:1
Khalchayan, castle, 1st/2nd century
Khamza Institute of Fine Arts, Tashkent

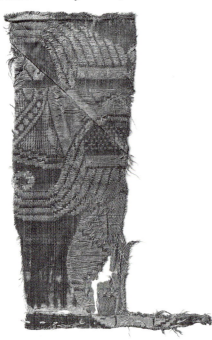

This is the earliest example of textile silk (Whitfield and Farrer 1990). Already by the middle of the second millennium B.C., Chinese silks had found their way into the region later known as Bactria, as we know from the tomb of a lady at Sapalle-tepe (Akhbarov 1973). Numerous examples of Han date have been found in Central Asia and further west (Bühler 1972).

For millennia, China had a monopoly on silk production. In other parts of Asia more or less accidental use was made of the floss silk of wild silkworms. Chinese silks were of excellent quality and very much in demand abroad. With the export of raw silk (silk yarn) by way of the Silk Road – a very lucrative trade for Chinese merchants – silk weaving started to establish itself as an industry in countries further west. Silk stuffs were exported from China to Japan and the West. Although this export started much earlier, it reached a high point during the Han dynasty, one of the most brilliant periods in Chinese history. Silk was China's most important merchandise and the main reason for her efforts to safeguard the trading routes to Central Asia. And Central Asia was the first region outside China to weave the real silk imported from China.

In Persia, Syria, Mesopotamia, Egypt, Greece, Rome and Byzantium the first silk used for weaving was Chinese raw silk or the threads produced after unravelling Chinese textiles, which then were often mixed with wool or linen. The rearing of silk worms outside China was first practised at Khotan in the Tarim basin, probably as early as the late second century B.C. By this time a new Silk Route had been established, running from China via Khotan to Bactria and onwards via Persia to Syria and Byzantium.

In Central Asia and western Turkestan the weavers soon realised that for their purposes the unravelled silk fibres were more suitable than wool, cotton or linen, which all needed to be spun beforehand. Excavations in 1984 at the tomb towers of Kampyr-tepe, thirty kilometres west of Termez, brought to light the small figure of a female deity, which was dated on the strength of an accompanying coin from the reign of the Kushan king Huvischka to the second century A.D. Under the shoulders of the pottery figure traces of a silk fabric were discovered which according to an expert from the Heritage was possibly woven in Bactria (Jerusalimskaya 1972). The thread of this linen cloth shows a slight Z-twist. The weft is much thicker and stronger than the Chinese export cloth. A characteristic of Chinese silks of this period is that weft and warp are of identical strength, and we know that before the early Middle Ages Chinese silks were never twisted. Excavations of the royal residence at Khalchayan in 1964 at levels of the first and second century brought to light a carved ivory hand with a broken metal shaft (ill. 426). Fingers and thumb are shaped to form a circle. Examination shows traces of fine grooves along the fingers and palm caused by threading yarn. This delicate tool

427
Textile fragment with griffin. Silk. The technique is similar to weavings from Zandane (?).
H: 20 cm, W: 13 cm
Khocho, Temple, 8th/9th century
Museum für Indische Kunst, Berlin

428
Silk brocade, star-shaped interlacing pattern with rosettes. This and the following item reflect the far-flung textile trade conducted along the Silk Road.
H: 20 cm, L: 66 cm
Iran, 12th century (discovered in a Buddhist monastery in Tibet)

429
Silk brocade. Addorsed griffins within roundels.
H: 33.7 cm, L: 98.5 cm
Iran, 12th century

was used to reel silk threads from the cocoons boiled in hot steam or water (Pugachenkova 1966). Both these discoveries published by Russian scholars would suggest that both the cultivation of silkworms and silk production were known in western Turkestan already in the second century A.D., two hundred years earlier than was generally assumed before the 1960s.

Across the centuries, silk production was often threatened by natural catastrophes, wars or diseases of the mulberry trees or the silkworms. In Bactria, Sogdiana and Khorezm, the techniques of silk production have been passed on from one generation to the next down until the present. In modern Uzbekistan the cultivation of silkworms and mulberry trees is managed on a broad basis by the state. In breeding factories the eggs of the butterflies from the best cocoons are collected and kept at a constant temperature of 4°C for about ten months until the breeding period in February–March, when the mulberry trees show their first shoots and the leaves start to uncurl.

Then the eggs are hatched in incubators under controlled conditions and distributed to selected households with the necessary equipment and experience for silkworm-rearing. Rearing the tiny caterpillars until they start spinning the cocoon needs great care, cleanliness and regular feeding. After some fifty-five days the cocoons start to grow. They are collected and examined, the best ones going to the breeding factory and the rest delivered by weight to the reeling factories, where the thread is reeled off in a steam-bath, debasted, twilled, dyed or left plain, beamed and finally woven into cloth.

430
Ikat gown with feather pattern (detail; see ill. 489).

Woven stuffs were in demand not only in Turkestan, but also in Russia, the Arab countries and in Turkey. Over time, two major branches of weaving developed, one producing simple, rather inexpensive and widely distributed cotton cloth, the other exquisite and expensive silks. While cotton weaving was traditionally almost exclusively the domain of women, the production of silks was a male occupation except for the rearing of silkworms. In villages and towns it was common to find many houses and workshops equipped with one or more shaft-looms or pit-looms for weaving the various cloths of cotton, cotton and silk or pure silk.

From among the many Uzbek cotton textiles we shall concentrate on two of the most popular. *Karbas (baz, buz)*, a traditional, durable, strong and warm cloth of linen binding, was produced in large quantities for personal, domestic and foreign consumption. It was sold either in monochrome or printed with stamps (*kalib*) in two colours (black and red) or more, and was the common material for dresses and for shirts (*küylak*, *kurtay*) and trousers (*ishton, ezor, shalwor*). Polychrome baz was turned into quilts (*kürpa*), seat cushions (*östik, bolish*), table-cloths (*dastarkhon, dasturkhon*) and small bags (*khalta*). According to sixteenth-century sources, *baz*

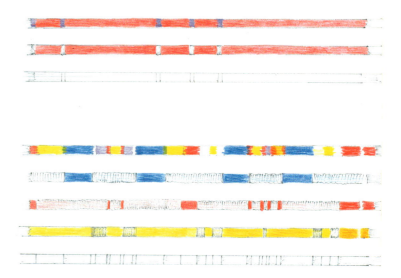

Much expertise is needed for the various aspects of textile production from handling the tools for spinning, reeling, twilling and weaving and the working of different types of looms (upright warp-weighted loom, horizontal loom, shaft loom, pit loom, hybrid loom, drawloom, Jacquard loom and the modern semi- and fully automatic industrial looms) to knowledge about dyes, drawing techniques, tie-dying, printing and dressing (Zerrnickel in Kalter 1992).

Several towns have been known for centuries for their excellent arts and crafts and in particular for their cotton and silk weaving (*karbas* or *baz* or *buz*, *alacha*, *zandanechi*, *bekasab*, as well as various types of ikat like *shoyi*, *atlas*, *khan atlas*, *adras* and *bakhmal*): Fergana, Margilan, Kokand, Tashkent, Samarkand, Shahr-i Sabz, Urgut, Bukhara, Zandane, Wardane, Kitab and Karshi.

Until the 1920s textile production as a cottage industry with a long tradition was a highly developed craft in Uzbekistan based on division of labour. There were many specialist occupations: cotton weavers (*alachabof*), cloth printers (*chitkar*), dyers (*büökchi*), silk reelers (*pillakash*), the specialist (*charhochi*) for turning the wheel (*charh*), the person who wound up the silk (*naychawar*) and who twilled it (*charhtob*), the ikat designer (*chizmachi*), the tie-dying master (*abrbandchi*) and the silk weaver (*shoyibof*).

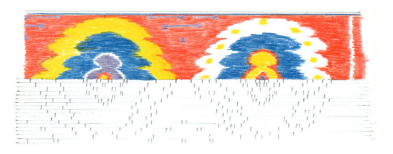

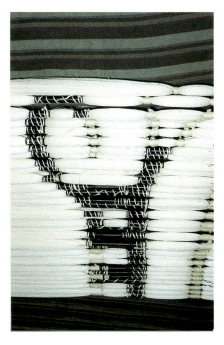

432
Processing silk cocoons at an ikat weaving mill, Margilan.

433
Tied warp threads.

434
Dyeing the warp threads.

435
Ikat weaving mill with looms, Margilan.

431 (opposite page)
Ikat. The illustration shows the dyeing process and is based on the women's gown in ill.
497. For the repeat pattern seventeen bundles of forty threads, each with a length of c. 280
cm, have to be dressed on the loom and dyed.
(Bottom) Dressed warp bundles. The upper section shows the pattern after dyeing and
unbinding, the lower section the pattern marked with lamp-black before the threads are tied
together.
(Centre; read from bottom to top) First binding of the marked pattern; first dye (yellow);
second binding and second dye (red); third binding and third dye (blue). The top bar shows
the end-result of all the dyeing dips - the pattern of this skein matches the central section of
the design below.
(Top) The binding and dyeing of the border skein, i.e. the upper termination of the design
below.

215

that had been colour-printed at the printing workshop (*chitkar-khana*) was called *chit*. Originally *chit* was sold by length but at the end of the nineteenth century was only offered fully finished as blankets, curtains or table-cloths, the competition from Persian and Russian factory-made printed stuffs having proved too strong for the *chitkar* with their traditional ware to compete with. During the first half of the nineteenth century the centre for printed cloths was Bukhara, with smaller amounts being produced at Samarkand, Urgut, Kattakurgan, Shahr-i Sabz, Fergana and Tashkent. A sixteenth-century Uzbek text has survived which gives a detailed description of cloth-printing (Mukminova 1976).

The second interesting cloth is *alacha* ('colourful', 'brilliant'), a high-quality, strong and durable cotton textile with vertical stripes of dark or very light and brilliant colours and a dark, usually blue weft in linen binding. The finest traditional *alacha* came from Samarkand, an age-old centre for cotton textiles. A sixteenth-century document tells us that at Samarkand there was a bazaar exclusively for *alacha*. The cloth was produced in great quantities at smaller places like Urgut and Nurata, but also in towns belonging to the Bukhara khanate, at Shahr-i Sabz, Karshi, Kitab and at Namangan in the Fergana Valley. At Karshi, Kitab, Zandane near Bukhara and at Bukhara itself *alacha* with silk warp and cotton weft were produced in reps and sometimes in satin weave. In the late nineteenth century these were called *bekasab*. Cotton and cotton-silk *alacha* are both decorated with vertical repeating bands, but differ in type: While the patterns of cotton *alacha* are narrow, colourful and shiny, those of the *bekasab* are broad and often ornamented with small and narrow ikat designs. Khorezm produced an exceptional cotton *alacha* which was dressed to a very high sheen and thus resembled finest silk satin. For four centuries both types of fabric were known under the same name, *alacha*. In the twentieth century it became customary to use the term *alacha* exclusively for the cotton cloth with narrow and highly colourful stripes which continued to be produced in the villages until the 1960s. This is the most common material for winter and summer khalats. Cotton-silk mixed weave with broad stripes and lacking ikat patterns are nowadays called *bekasab* or *bekasam*.

This is the most popular cloth sold by length for the festive national dress, the khalat. *Banoras* is another type of *bekasab* and comes with light, unobtrusive and very narrow patterned stripes; it is only used for the *paranja*, the cloak women wear outside the house and which completely veils them. Mediaeval sources mention a *zandanechi*, a cloth of great renown since the seventh century, its name deriving from the Sogdian settlement of Zandane near Bukhara, which was famous for its silk-weaving during the seventh/eighth century (Mukminova 1976). *Zandanechi* were produced in silk and in cotton. As it became ever more popular, weavers elsewhere (e.g. at Bukhara) also started to call their cloth *zandanechi*. In the tenth century, silk *zandanechi* was renamed. The close similarity of Sogdian silk stuffs with those of Sasanian and Byzantine origin caused much confusion. In 1959 two American scholars, the textile historian D. Shepherd and the Iranianist B. Henning, succeeded in deciphering a Sogdian ink inscription on a piece of cloth kept at the cathedral in Jui (Belgium), which turned out to be a *zandanechi* from Sogd (Shepherd and Henning 1959). After this discovery and further analyses of weaves, designs and colours, more examples of ancient textiles in various museums all over the world have been identified as *zandanechi*. Thirteen years after the discovery the textile researcher A. Jerusalimskaya, basing herself on Shepherd and Henning's publication, was able to identify a whole group consisting of some two thousand textile fragments from tombs in the northern Caucasus as silks of Sogdian origin (Jerusalimskaya 1967, 1972). Her detailed and wide-ranging study presents a clear exposition of the origins and development of silk-weaving in Sogd.

Ikat: *abrbandi* ('banded cloud', 'cloud-band')

The Malay-Indonesian term 'ikat' for cloth patterned by tie-dying, has been adopted by Western languages. In Turkestan and modern Uzbekistan the technique is called *abrbandi*, the craftsman *abrbandchi*, and any textile thus patterned, *abr* cloth. Tie-dyed cloths had and sometimes still have many applications: coats, dresses, trousers, waist-bands, blankets, table-cloths, bath towels, loin cloths, covers for cushions and matresses, saddle cloths, *suzani*, women's head-scarves, patchwork products, small pouches, tent hangings and back-pieces for the distinctive veil (*kiyimishek*) worn by Karakalpak women.

The silks (*shoyi*, satin, *khan* satin) and mixed silks (*adras*, *bakhmal*) are traditional textiles widely used for clothes and in the household. Except for a number of catalogues accompanying ikat exhibitions in Europe and the United States (see bibliography) with some good illustrations and short descriptions, the literature on this technique of tie-dyeing consists of scattered remarks in connection with general historical discussions of textiles. Some authors from Uzbekistan and the CIS countries drew attention to this unusual technique within the framework of their ethnographical textile researches. In 1963, S. Machkamova published a short book about *abr* cloths from Uzbekistan, analysing and describing the contemporary situation of the ikat industry. In her various contributions O. Sukhareva repeatedly discusses resist-dyeing techniques and *abr* textiles (Sukhareva 1953, 1962, 1981). The art historian D. Fakhretdinova has published a large volume on the decorative applied arts of Uzbekistan (Fakhetdinova 1972), which includes a discussion of the historical development of textile manufacture with frequent mentions of *abr* wares. The exhibition catalogue by Kalter, Pavaloi and Zerrnickel (Kalter 1992) presents examples of warp ikat techniques from Aleppo and Hama which once had been very widespread, but now are largely lost and forgotten. The short contribution by A. Janata (1978) is about an ikat collection in Vienna and gives illustrations and some rarely archival photographs. A main concern of the essay was to draw attention to the three-volume publication by A. Bühler (1992). Thanks to Alfred Bühler's scientifically sound

436
Niche curtain. Ikat, silk.
L: 526 cm, W: 136 cm
Fergana, late 18th/early 19th century
Private collection, Esslingen

437
Niche curtain. Ikat reps, mixed weave of silk and cotton, design of strips with alternating trefoil sprays and boteh patterns.
L: 210 cm, W: 129 cm
Fergana, first half 19th century

438
Blanket. Ikat reps, mixed weave of silk and cotton, light padding, designs of cypress patterns and cartouches with blossoms, the back block-printed cotton.
L: 198 cm, W: 116 cm
Fergana, second half 19th century

research, we have a relatively clear picture of ikat techniques, their emergence, evolution, spread and alteration as well as their decline and disappearance. As his comprehensive bibliography shows, interest in the cultural and technical aspects of textiles is documented by a few scattered items of the late eighteenth century and arose again only from the second half of the nineteenth century onwards. Bühler surveyed and evaluated the literature on textiles from the eighteenth century to the 1970s and also studied the ikats accessible to him as well as providing his own conclusions. Among other things he tried to trace the origin of reserve decoration and especially of patterning on the yarn, and arrived at the following result: The original centre of tie-dyeing was presumably India or possibly southern China. From there the technique spread to western and central Asia as well as to western Turkestan. First the fabrics and then the technical know-how reached western Turkestan (Bactria, Sogdiana) in the wake of Buddhism. The spread of Buddhism with its great influence on all aspects of the arts and crafts from India to central Asia and western Turkestan was especially strong during the Gupta period (4th–6th century A.D.). Very early centres of ikat manufacture are found in India and South China. Their influence spread as far as Yemen, as can be documented by similarities in motifs and styles. In India and East Asia very important types of ikat (weft ikat and double ikat) occur which are either unknown or as yet undocumented for western and central Asia. Western Turkestan only produces warp ikat with fully tie-dyed warp threads and patterns which completely cover the woven area. Ikats with only the warp tie-dyed are called warp ikats.

The ikateurs of Uzbekistan produce two types of warp ikat: full ikat where the warp is completely tie-dyed, and strip ikat with the warp arranged in stripes of tie-dyed and monochrome thread.

Over time two main types of tie-dyeing and patterning have evolved which apply to every kind of ikat, whether it is warp ikat, weft ikat or double ikat.

For the first type the pattern is produced by skeins of tie-dyed yarn arranged to match their occurence in the cloth. For warp ikat the warp threads are positioned on the beam where they would be during weaving, with the crossing of the threads fixed at the same time. This arrangement permits a variety of patterns. Tie-dyeing of the threads can be much simplified by combining them into thick skeins.

The second resist-dyeing method uses separate skeins without prior consideration of their eventual position in the cloth. The pattern is determined by positioning the tie-dyed threads while arranging them on the beam; a simple way of patterning is to stretch or shift single threads or skeins. The evolution of this method became possible with the introduction of the weaving comb and especially of shafts and treadles. This made for much longer warps, which were then arranged on the beam only after having been tie-dyed. The method allows the production of a large number of patterns.

It seems that in Turkestan the older first method was used for quite a long time before the simple weaving methods were modernised by introducing more sophisticated treadle-operated shaft- and pit-looms. Throughout Asia these looms are used to produce ikat cloths; for ikating the warp threads, the second method is used.

Presumably the two methods of ikat patterning derived from the same prototype. In some respects, ikat is a precursor of other methods of patterning (brocade, damask). More advanced looms such as the drawloom, made possible the production of highly complicated patterns by manipulating the weft. While tie-dyeing declined in countries where drawlooms appeared early (China, western Asia), it remained important in regions with more primitive weaving technology.

Tie-dyeing (abrbandi) was and still is used primarily for patterning silks. According to the type of raw material and weaving technique, there are different names for the various kinds of cloths in Uzbekistan. Silks in rep, satin or plain weave and the rarer twill weave, formerly known as shoyi or shokhi, as today called called atlas or khan atlas, mixed silks (silk warp and cotton weft) are known as adras or yakruya, and velvet of silk or mixed silk as bakhmal. It has been suggested – and we agree – that the technique of dyeing yarn and tying it prior to weaving (ikat) developed from the tie-dying of woven cloth (plangi) called bandan (Machkamova 1963). The latter method was known in Bukhara, Samarkand and the Fergana Valley already in late antiquity.

The plangi method is simpler but allows only a limited number of patterns, mainly circles, lozenges, squares and dots. The variety of possible ornaments is much greater for ikats, even though it is limited to the manipulation of warp and weft. They offer the artist greater creative freedom in his choice of shapes and colours. The long-established and highly developed cultivation of silk and the widespread masterly handling of ikat techniques in the Fergana Valley (Margilan, Andizhan, Kokand, etc.) would suggest that tie-dyeing has been practised here for a long time and that the concept of ikat patterns for full warp ikat made of silk or silk and cotton, arose in the Fergana Valley or more broadly in eastern Turkestan. Archaeological evidence supports this view. Unlike the full warp ikats made of silk, Egyptian ikats, for example, are striped ikats of linen, sometimes with

439
Blanket. Ikat reps, mixed weave of silk and cotton, designs of lozenges and zigzag bands.
L: 197 cm, W: 154 cm
Fergana, mid-19th century
Private collection, Sindelfingen

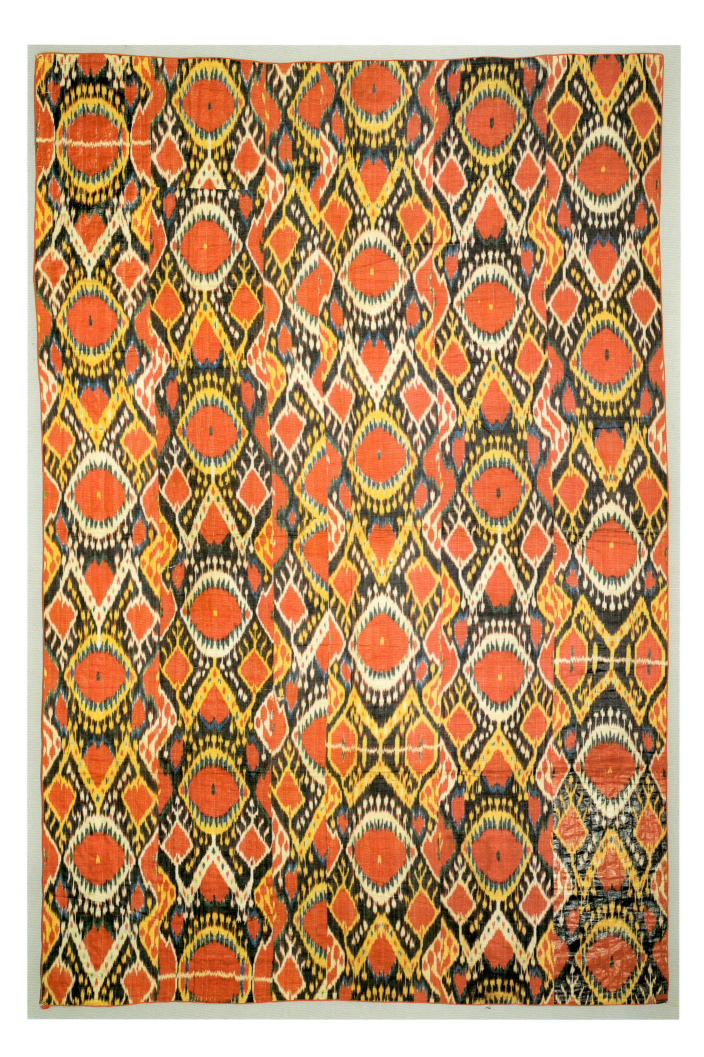

monochrome silk areas; the striped ikats from Yemen are of cotton, while those from Syria consist of alternating stripes of cotton and silk. The same situation exists today. Although silk and mixed silk (silk for the warp, cotton for the weft) are very common and cotton is only rarely used, both raw materials can be found wherever ikats are produced (India, Arabia, western Asia, Persia, Turkestan). Bühler's comments on the early appearance of ikat are worth quoting: "For early ikat both the archaeological and the literary evidence give matching dates. The textiles surviving in Japan are dated to the Asuka (552-644) and Nara (646-781) periods; the wall-paintings at Ajanta in India with depictions of ikats date mainly from the seventh/eighth century; from the same time date the earliest Yemeni ikats. The earliest examples of Yemeni and Syrian ikats discovered in Egypt are slightly later (2nd half of 9th/10th century). Depictions of ikat on silk banners from Gansu province (West China) are dated to the eleventh century. From this we may conclude that the ikat technique was possibly known by the early seventh century in an area comprising India, East, Central and West Asia, Arabia and Egypt" (Bühler 1972). The famous and outstanding *abrbandchi* from Margilan, Abdusamat Achmedov, questioned about the origins of *abrbandi*, replied with a smile: "Although there is a legend about a time when silk cocoons were unknown, there is none about a time without *abrbandi*." Central Asian sources of the tenth/eleventh century mention the widespread use not only of monochrome but also of polychrome decorated cloth. Designs were produced with a stamp (*kalib*) or by using dyed warp threads for striped cloth (*yolak*, *alacha*) or ikats.

The word *esri* is of great interest; Mahmud Kashgari provides the glosses 'speckled, colourful' or 'coloured thread' (*esri-yishig*). 'Coloured thread' may refer to a two-colour twisted thread or a colourfully speckled one. Explanations of the verb *esrila*, 'applying patterns that look like a tiger's spots', suggest that ikating was known by the eleventh century (Kononov 1970; Klyashtornyi 1970, 1972). Bühler suggested that tie-dyeing was known in the above-mentioned regions already in pre-Islamic times. Should it refer indirectly to tie-dyeing, the following quotation is of interest: "The Han dynasty collapsed in 220 A.D., and throughout the succeeding periods of the Three Kingdoms (220-65) and the two Jin (265-420) the textile industry of Sichuan province emerged to lead the country in silk production. The introduction of the 'horse-bit' loom made possible a variety of new designs, and for the first time gold

440
Blanket. Ikat reps, mixed weave of silk and cotton, five strips combined, the design showing trees of life with pomegranates.
L: 194 cm, W: 146 cm
Bukhara, second half 19th century
Private collection, Sindelfingen

441
Niche curtain. Ikat reps, mixed weave of silk and cotton, vertical bands with flower sprays.
L: 210 cm, W: 129 cm
Bukhara, about 1900

was added to brocade cloths. The silks of Sichuan were transported right across China to the north and east.

"During the period of the Northern and Southern dynasties (420-589) a most important technical development occurred. Han dynasty silks and the later products from Sichuan, however fine, were always patterned in the warp, but during the fifth century, weft-patterned silks appeared for the first time. Patterning the weft allows far more complex designs and a wider cloth than is possible in a warp-patterned fabric. The technique had been used for wool-weaving amongst the northwestern border peoples since the Eastern Han dynasty, but the central Chinese tradition had remained firmly warp-patterned for a further two centuries" (Whitfield and Farrer 1990:110).

Sukhareva suggests that the textiles preserved at Nara (Japan) were produced in Central Asia (Turkestan), possibly an ancient centre of ikat production; the argument is supported by Tajiks in Bukhara, Urgut, Margilan and Namangan, who regard ikat cloth and especially mixed-silk types (*adrasse*) as part of their own traditional culture. Sukhareva refers in particular to the simple ikat techniques used at Nurata, Karshi and Andizhan, which may be indicative of a tradition of great antiquity. She also emphasises that textiles with narrow ikat strips and with stepped and lozenge designs between unpatterend stripes belong to a type different from that associated with Bukhara. Bukhara ikats are very narrow woven strips and of various weaves with bold repeating designs not always calculated for a certain length. At regular intervals they show a horizontal 'parting' or 'weft markers', part of the tie-dyed pattern but differing in colour from the background. We would suggest that these distinctive wefts were meant to simplify measuring and cutting the piece of cloth at the point of sale with the least damage to the overall ornamentation. If the piece of fabric was to be made into blankets or curtains, then these markers indicated the full length of such conventional items. The textiles are of silk or silk warp with cotton for the weft and for the warp of the selvedge. Whether the cloth is full ikat or strip ikat, the designs are almost without exception colourful, striking and full of different shapes in almost endless variations.

Ikat cloth occurs with every type of weave. Warp ikat, however, appears at its best with a weave were the warp is more appealing than the weft either on one side or on both, which can be achieved most easily and successfully with warp rep.

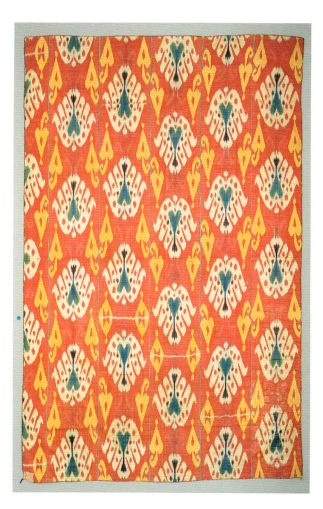

442
Niche curtain. Ikat, silk, oval elements within zigzag bands decorated with boteh motifs.
L: 220 cm, W: 150 cm
Samarkand, second half 19th century

443
Blanket. Ikat reps, mixed weave of silk and cotton, light padding, design of palmettes and boteh patterns.
L: 225 cm, W: 147 cm
Bukhara, late 19th century

The most important centre of the Central Asian silk industry was and still is Uzbekistan, principally the Fergana Valley, which had a thriving textile production already in late antiquity. To this day Kokand, Margilan and Namangan, among others, are famous for their silks. Some, like Margilan, manage to remain competitive producers of the very popular ikat fabrics. Already in the late nineteenth century and later under Soviet rule, the *abrbandchi* with their homespun fabrics had found themselves unable to compete with factory-produced wares.

The apprentice ikateur usually receives his education within the family. At first he only does chores like reserving the warp yarn by following the master's drawings, assisting with the dyeing, arranging of patterns, beaming of the tie-dyed assymmetrical warp threads, and so on. Depending on talent and application, the period of apprenticeship lasts from three to six years.

In autumn 1994, we visited the Margilan silk factory, which had been formed in the 1960s through the merger of numerous languishing small artisanal workshops. The *abrbandchi* were concerned about the future of their traditional skills. For the smaller workshops, opportunities for training apprentices for such a complex craft were very limited. Financial considerations as well as the mistaken belief of various Soviet agencies that these traditional methods were not economically viable, were the reasons why tie-dyeing had not been given any support for a long time.

We were allowed to inspect and photograph every stage of the ikat production process, from cocoons and debasting, spinning, twisting and preparing the skeins, sketching the designs, tying the skeins, tie-dyeing the pattern relating to the vertical axial symmetry of the beaming down to the weaving process itself, cutting and sewing of the clothes and wadding and quilting mattresses and blankets. We also watched young women knotting colourful carpets (*chulkhirs*) from floss silk (the rough outside of the cocoon). It was interesting to note that reeling and weaving was almost exclusively performed by women, because until the 1930s this had been men's work. We also noticed that despite a certain degree of automation, the workers were frequently able to put their traditional techniques and experience to good use.

Aniline dyes, however, prove detrimental to the appearance of the textiles; they tend to fade and to discolour rapidly, and the colours themselves are garish and often clash. Still the *abrbandchi* often succeed in coaxing these aniline colours into joyful, brilliant harmony. The most important figure in the production of ikat textiles, which involves a variety of specialists, is the master designer (*chizmachi*). He decides on the raw material, the width and density, the type of weave, the length of the repeat pattern and the overall design and colour scheme.

444
Length of ikat, silk velvet. Such lengths were used to make coats for (mainly male) members of the upper class.
W: 34 cm
Bukhara, late 19th century

The first step is to soak the silk cocoons in hot water to kill the larvae and dissolve the bast (glue). After removing the floss silk, three to ten cocoons are reeled, producing between three hundred and eight hundred metres of grège (raw silk). At Margilan, some reeling is done in the traditional manner with a small stick, but most of it with mechanical reeling machinery. The carefully prepared warp threads, some two to three hundred metres long, are divided into small sets of about forty to sixty threads, each arranged on a special construction.

The number of threads per set is determined by the width and density of the piece of cloth. Sets are paired by twisting and wound around two horizontal beams of the frame. The beams are usually between 140 and 225 centimetres apart, but occasionally even wider, depending on the length of the repeat pattern. Once the warp sets have been fastened to the beams with special loops, the *abrbandchi* ties up the whole length of the threads for the required pattern. After dyeing, the horizontal 'parting' appears as a fine jagged line, indicating the beginning of the repeat pattern. The 'weft markers', on the other hand, are produced by warp sets not attached to loops. The designer draws short contour lines for half of the intended pattern alinged along a vertical axis onto the stretched-out threads with a small stick and lamp-black (a mixture of soot and water). Master designers have an extensive repertoire of traditional ornaments and patterns at their fingertips and do without preliminary sketches or stencils. We know of some forty to fifty main motifs and patterns which form the basis for countless variations. The master designer can fully give free rein to his creative imagination. The designer's art of patterning and colouration is usually transmitted within the family from one generation to the next.

When drawing a pattern, the designer is careful to make different colours come together no closer than five centimetres. Such a gap is necessary to ensure that the colour reproduces evenly along the entire warp set. Once the pattern is drawn, the *abrbandchi* ties up the appropriate warp sets with thick coarse cotton string and sends them to the dyer.

For polychrome patterns a strict sequence of tying and dyeing the individual sets has to be followed. If, for example, white, pink, yellow, red and blue are to be used along one thread, it has to be tied and dyed three times in succession. Usually the ikateur ties the lighter colours (white and pink) first and then dyes the cloth yellow; next, all parts are reserved except for those to be dyed red. Red tends to run into the yellow, and so acquires a warm yellowish glow. Then the red areas are reserved and those sets to be dyed blue untied. The third immersion produces a mix of yellow and blue resulting in a slightly greenish tinge. If true blue is

445
Length of ikat, silk velvet.
B: 35 cm
Bukhara, c. 1880

223

required, those areas have to be reserved before the threads are dyed yellow. Finally the blue areas are reserved and the threads dyed pink. If very little pink is required, instead of totally immersing the threads, the sections are simply dipped very quickly in a basin (*kosa-buëk*) with a boiling dye emulsion.

Then follows the fixing of the colours, reeling of the warp threads, removal of the tying string and drying of the sets. The craftsmen carefully disentangle the sets by spreading them across street fences, inspect and order the threads, mend torn bits and wind the threads around a stick into bundles. The patterning of the tie-dyed warp is done by two artisans, the designer (*chizmachi*) and the warp shearer. They separate the skeins and arrange them symmetrically along the vertical axis; then the warp skeins are beamed and readied for weaving. This is invariably done on a shaft loom with treadles (pedals) and a dobby mechanism. The loom can have up to twelve shafts. For satin-weave textiles twelve shafts are used, whereas for simple ikat satin four shafts suffice. The famous and much sought-after *khan* satin is woven on looms with eight or twelve shafts (*sakkiz-tepkilik, ünikki-tepkilik*). The more shafts are available, the clearer the ikat pattern appears on the *khan* satin. At the Margilan factory we were told that the first *khan* satins were woven at Margilan in about 1856 by order of the Kokand ruler. To provide an extra sheen they are finished with a special egg-white emulsion. This emulsion is applied to one end of the length of material, which is then rolled up, after which the finishing master pounces the moist emulsion evenly into the cloth with a wooden hammer (*kudung*). At the Margilan factory there was one craftsman who worked a specially constructed finishing-machine. Besides ikat of standard lengths, in the late nineteenth century and particularly in Samarkand the weavers started to produce again large silk ikat blankets and curtains with large-scale patterns somewhat similar to print designs, with bold central ornaments, niches, birds (peacocks), rosettes and medallions.

Already in the seventh/eighth century Sogdian artisans wove cloth not only by length, but also curtains and blankets with broad stripes and multiple niches of colourful and multi-shaped design. These cloths were called *zandanechi* and served the weavers of Uzbekistan as models over many generations.

Ikat designs: *abrnakshi* ('ikat colour play')

Patterns, styles, motifs and colouration of ikat ware are largely independent of the raw material. Colour was always an important element in Uzbekistan ikats. People there love strong colours. In the various regions of the republic traditional colour combinations partly survive, preserving the tonalities characteristic of abr textiles. In Khojent red colours are especially popular, in Kokand shades of blue, in Bukhara claret, yellow and pink, while in Fergana and Margilan the imaginative designs make use of up to seven colours, a golden yellow as the main colour, claret, green or blue, black, pink and purple together with white as the background colour. To achieve a harmonious combination, a

446
Ikat coat (detail of ill. 481). The design shows strong Chinese influence. Samarkand (?), mid-19th century

strict sequence of dyeing has to be observed: claret and green follow on yellow, resulting in a reddish-yellow or greenish-yellow shimmer; black or blue follows on claret and results in a reddish-brown or purple shade. An additional factor in harmonisation is supplied by the coloured weft, which usually appears in claret and yellow and more rarely in white; a claret-coloured weft produces a pink shimmer and a yellow weft a silvery shine. A white double weft of thick twisted cotton is used only for mixed silk cloth.

Women wore certain colours according to age, with young females and those of marriageable age wearing light colours and various shades of red, while the older women dressed in more subdued darkish colours. The generation a woman belonged to could be easily recognised by the colour of her dress. Both colour and ornament were originally imbued with magic and mystic-religious significance, of which today only villagers, in particular women, are still aware.

For all their variety, ikat patterns are broadly based on a few types. A major type for fully tie-dyed ikats is the web pattern, which comes in different versions: sometimes it emphasises the rows of small single ornaments with clear, precise outlines, while on others the vertical and horizontal stripes themselves provide a web pattern. The ornaments often show geometrically stylised floral motifs. These patterns are typical of Bukhara ikats and to a smaller extent also of Margilan ikats. A second major type consists of large and small ornaments arranged in vertical strips often separated by undyed warp lines. Here one notices the designers' extraordinary feeling for proportion. This type as well exists in many variations, where the strips are filled with repeats of one or more motifs, and the strips themselves can be of different width and juxtaposed in many ways. The decoration is usually of geometricised floral and occasionally of naturalistic character. Fergana ikats frequently consisted of bands with small and highly detailed designs, sometimes showing geometricised plant motifs.

A third type of patterning consists of large ornaments interspersed with smaller ones, the design filling the whole surface from top to bottom. This group comprises full ikats with ornaments which are often difficult to identify and include geometric elements, plant and animal shapes as well as anthropomorphic forms and images of objects. Among the geometric elements we find circles with enclosures, double circles, hooks, spirals, flame symbols and spiky lozenges. Floral ornaments consist of heart-shaped leaves, palmettes, trees of life, rosettes, pomegranates, blossoms, almonds, cypresses, flower bouquets, etc. Objects like vases with flowers, oil lamps, candlesticks, combs, drums and jugs are used for both the central motif and to fill the space between decorative fields. The strangest type of ornamentation consists of shapes, either in full or pars pro toto, reminiscent of peacocks and peacock tails, of scorpions, snakes and rams' horns and also of human eyes and hands.

This seems to us to be the most complex group of a highly dynamic and unique style. It is particularly well represented in Uzbekistan. Despite its singular appearance it probably incorporates various influences besides the local

447
Ikat coat (detail). Medallion with feather motif.
Fergana Valley, mid-19th century

225

nomad Turkish style, in particular those from Sasanian and Sino-Mongolian prototypes. One example are the Sogdian *zandanechi* with their central design of Byzantine inspiration presenting the decorative elements (birds, animals, etc.) as symmetrical mirror-images, which also appears in a modified and highly stylised version on Uzbek full ikats. Another example of Sogdian influence are the well-known, widely distributed nineteenth-century ikats with vertical patterns of circles with enclosures, double circles and central rosettes.

In Uzbek and Tajik usage, the patterns are identified according to the predominant colour or the type of weave, e.g., *nilobi* (blue design), *kora atlas* (black atlas), *ok arkok* (white weft) or *beskhörma* (of five parts). Sometimes they refer to the place or people where the pattern originated, e.g., *fergona nuskha* (Fergana design), *buchoro nuskha* (Bukhara design), *jakhundij nuskha* (Jewish design) or *züjut küli* (Jewish flower).

Small linear elements and secondary designs played an important part in the overall ornamentation, e.g. *tarok* (combs), *kosa gul* (flowers in a bowl), *shokila* (pendants), *shokh* (horns), *bodomcha* (small almonds), *ilon izi* (snake trails), *sim-sima* (openwork) and *tumorcha* (small amulets). Multi-coloured (seven colours) patterns, which produce a feeling of gaiety and happiness, are called *tijri kamon* (rainbow) or *bakhor* (spring). Some terms from *suzani* embroidery are also used for ikats, e.g., *kora palak* and *ok palak* (black and white sky). Objects are sometimes represented with clear outlines despite the common tendency towards pronounced stylization, e.g., *tarok* (combs), *nogora* (drums), *oftoba* or *kumgon* (jugs) and *tsharog* (candlesticks, oil lamps). Among floral and plant ornaments we find *darakht* (trees), *tuvakda gul* (flowers in a vase), *shokh(a)* (twigs), *bodom* (almonds), *nok* (pears) and *anor* (pomegranates). Animal and human figures appear in highly stylised or much modified shapes with indistinct and almost unrecognisable contours. Anthropomorphic motifs usually show figures linked by arms and legs to form scroll designs; they take on a mysterious presence in the ikat cloths and are still said to have magic powers. Although barely recognisable, the magic resonance of these ornaments can be inferred from their names, e.g., *kütshkor shokhi* (rams' horns), *yülbars dumi* (tiger tails), *tuyu paypok* (camel trails), *kapalak* (butterflies), *tshaön* (scorpions) and *sapsar korga* (purple ravens). The majority of ikat patterns were meant to protect against evil spirits and the 'evil eye'. They were believed to promote fertility and express hope for a happy life. Until the 1930s large-scale repeat and web patterns were widely distributed. The designs were very similar to those of hand-printed textiles with their rich ornamental repertoire. After the Second World War narrow stripes became popular once more. The designs varied in quality, and one could also find cheap ikat cloth with printed designs. Since the 1960s the situation of traditional ikat production has improved, for which the above-mentioned Margilan products can serve as an example.

Something of a speciality are velvets (*bakhmal* or *makhmal*) including the brilliant, unique ikat velvet. Velvet textiles have two warps, one for the ground and the other for the pole warp which also connects with the ground weft but protrudes between the werfts on one side as a tuft or loop. The latter after cutting produce a short velvet pile or a long plush pile. If all pole warps are tie-dyed, the result is ikat velvet or ikat plush. Velvet ikats are sold by the metre and used for khalats/coats, belts, female caps and in the household. They are the most interesting, charming and valuable textiles. In Turkestan narrow and fully patterned velvet ikats (width 35-45 cm) are very popular. The selvedges are smooth and plain. There are also broad striped velvet ikats with a clear three-part division, a central band with large motifs and the borders with smaller patterns. Some of these textiles with borders along the warp line served as curtains or as prayer rugs with niche designs. There is documentary evidence that narrow velvets were produced both in Bukhara and Samarkand. In the nineteenth century, Bukhara produced colourful and fully tie-dyed velvets both in silk and mixed-silk, the latter either with cotton warp or with both warp and weft of cotton and only the pole warp of silk. Samarkand, on the other hand, was famous from the Middle Ages until the late nineteenth century for its claret velvets, which were not tie-dyed. In Timurid and Shaibanid times one of the most prestigious textiles worn by the aristocracy on festive occasions was the purple velvet from Samarkand, *keremezi*. It was also famous abroad and was exported to western Europe, Russia and the Near East (Mukminova 1976).

The patterns of ikat velvets are similar to those found on fully tie-dyed silk ikats. The broad striped ikat velvets are decorated along the central band with niches with birds (peacocks), hills, cypresses, rosettes, etc. It seems likely that these designs were taken from knotted carpets, particularly since the manufacturing process for both textiles is largely similar.

448-449 (opposite page)
Ikat coats (details of ills. 507, 512).

450
Wall hanging. Brocade, warp: gold thread and silk, weft: cotton decorated with flower sprays and rosettes.
L: 242 cm, W: 105 cm
Bukhara, late 19th century

451
Niche curtain or wall hanging. Brocade, warp: silver thread and silk, weft: cotton with palmette design.
L: 231 cm, W: 105 cm
Bukhara, about 1900

452
Wedding-dress. Ikat reps, mixed weave of silk and cotton, the trimmings in tambour
embroidery of silk on cotton.
L: 126.0 cm, W: 197.5 cm
Samarkand (?), about 1900

Some other textile techniques

Further to our discussion of the indigenous traditional textiles of Uzbekistan we shall now take a closer look at the sewing of khalats, brocade embroidery and the manufacture of caps and decorative borders.

The sewing of khalats

All the major urban centres in Uzbekistan produced khalats, and some still do today. Various textiles were used, e.g., cotton, silk and mixed silk, the latter two often tie-dyed, as well as velvet with brocade embroidery. Male khalats from Bukhara and Samarkand came in brilliant colours (ikat, velvet), while in Tashkent and the Fergana Valley black and green predominated, and in Khorezm red cloth with narrow stripes. Variations in the cut of this outer garment followed the same regional divisions. Female khalats (*mursak, kamsul, nimcha*) were made from local and imported cloth. Until the late nineteenth century, a light ikat khalat for women (*munisak-kaltacha*) was wide-spread; today it appears only as part of the dowry and is used during mourning periods and at the owner's burial.

The first sewing machines appeared in Uzbekistan early in the twentieth century. The male seamstresses, formerly called *tukuwchi*, now became *mashinachi*. The khalat would be cut on the spot at the shop in the bazaar. In the 1930s there were still more than a thousand *mashinachi* producing khalats in Tashkent. At the bazaar one would have a choice of several shops selling khalats of different material, e.g., silk, velvet, ikat cloth and *alacha* (made with Russian yarn). The basic equipment of the seamstresses consisted of sewing needles, thimbles, a flatiron and ironing-board. Normally the proprietor of the workshop would be his own cutter, although one could employ professional cutters (*bichikchi*) who worked on a piece-rate basis. On average the daily output of a cutter was fifteen silk khalats or thirty regular ones and that of a *mashinachi* three or four khalats. Quilting and tacking was done by special tailoresses (*düsanda*), who also prepared the cotton for padding. From start to finish the production of a khalat usually took a day. Decorative borders were added either by the tailoress herself or by specialists called *guldon zhiyakchi*; machine-made borders were seldom used. The wages per khalat amounted to twenty-five to thirty kopecks for the *mashinachi*, two to four kopecks for the cutter and ten to twenty kopecks for the *düsanda*. Khiva was one of the centres of khalat manufacture in Central Asia, producing high-quality ware which sold very well.

Khalats were also used as gifts of honour. The ruler and court officials would present them for meritorious service, distribute them during the New Year's reception and give them to guests of honour and foreign emissaries. It was a special mark of recognition if the ruler took off his own khalat and placed it around the shoulders of his guest. This custom still survives in Uzbekistan, where khalats are presented as gifts to foreign heads of state and during marriage and circumcision ceremonies. From nineteenth-century travellers' accounts we know that the dress-code was

strictly defined by rank. The ruler and the highest court officials would dress in silk velvet khalats with gold embroidery, the next rank would be permitted to wear khalats made of valuable cloth imported from Kashmir, wealthy merchants and scholars dressed in silk ikat, while the khalats worn by peasants and nomads were of rather coarse wool.

The custom of offering light silk khalats as gifts resulted in their distribution across the length and breadth of Turkestan, so that these ikat gowns found their way to the remotest desert and mountain regions. Ikat textiles form an integral part of the culture of the Tajiks, Uzbeks, Karakalpaks, Turkmens and Uighurs and to a lesser extent of the Kirghiz, Kazakhs and other peoples, irrespective of whether they pursue an urban or a nomad lifestyle.

453
Men's coat. Cotton, with suitable cap.
L: 149 cm, W: 210 cm
Samarkand, about 1920

229

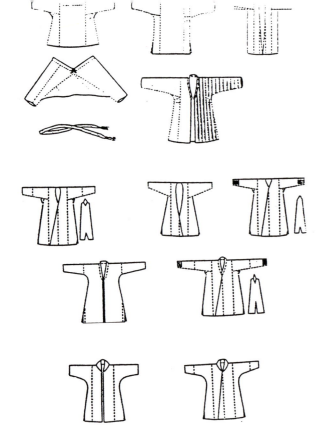

456
Shop in the bazaar selling coats, about 1900.

454
Paper patterns.
(Top) Men's shirts, trousers with hidden belt, traditional men's coat.
(Centre) Some earlier coat shapes (from left to right): Uzbek and Karakalpak, Uzbek (Tashkent, Fergana), Turkmen (Merv, middle Amu Darya), and below Tajik (left) and Turkmen and Kazakh.
(Bottom) Collared version, Uzbek (Tashkent, Fergana).

457
Old Tajik from Bukhara dressed in a silk ikat coat, about 1900.

455
Paper patterns.
(Left) Cut. (Centre) Complete view and two men's coats (Tajik, Uzbek). (Bottom) Men's padded coats, Tajik (Fergana Valley).

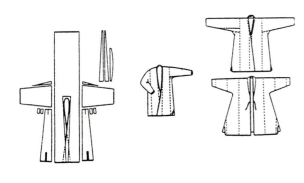

458
Men's coat. Ikat, silk velvet, lining of printed cotton, trimmings of silk ikat, polychrome woven borders. The trimmings of the sleeves are embroidered in the style of the Erzari Turkmens.
L: 125 cm, W: 190 cm
Ikat from Bukhara, tailored presumably in Khorezm, late 19th century

Embroidery

From the late nineteenth century to the early twentieth century, embroidery played an important role in the daily life of Uzbekistan's population. A considerable amount of *suzanis*, embroidered clothes, coats, caps and saddle-cloths were exported to Europe, while Western travellers to the region also brought back a great variety of objects, a splendid example being the collection of *suzanis* at the Museum für Völkerkunde in Berlin, acquired by Rickmer Rickmers in the 1890s.

Since embroidering large pieces of cloth, for instance *suzanis*, required much labour and dedication, Sukhareva has suggested that at least in Bukhara ikat textiles have partly replaced the use of embroidered wall hangings and other decorative furnishings. (The main types of embroidered textiles like wall hangings, niche curtains, prayer mats, marriage sheets and wrappings for the bridewealth are discussed in another part of this book.) From the mid-nineteenth century, embroidered textiles began to lose their original function and came to be used exclusively for decorative purposes, e.g., to beautify the home particularly for festive occasions like weddings. It was customary to leave part of the embroidery unfinished, so that "the weddings would never end" and "the daughter would live and happiness at home be ever-lasting".

Handmade embroidery is still a living tradition, although the manufacture no longer takes place at home but in cooperatives of craftsmen and embroiderers. The art of embroidery is now performed at large state-owned enterprises. Unfortunately, this change has frequently been accompanied by a noticeable loss of individuality in design and execution. During a visit to Urgut in autumn 1994 we were allowed to watch several female embroiderers at work and also see the famous eldery designer of *suzanis*, Tschizmakasch-Rassoma.

Brocade embroidery

Brocade embroidery is documented in Sogdiana as early as the seventh century. It reached a high point in the region of present-day Uzbekistan during the nineteenth century. It was mainly used for the clothes of the nobility and for certain household goods of the rich upper class. Many of the master embroiderers (*zarduz*) were employed by the Bukhara court while others worked in private workshops. A length of cotton cloth would be tied to a specially constructed wooden stretcher (*kochüb*). Once the embroiderer had received the cut cloth and the complete design he would attach the various sections to the cotton ground. The embroidery itself was frequently executed by several master craftsmen. Notes on the great variety of embroidery stitches can be found in Gontcharova 1986 and Sidorenko and Radzabov 1981.

The ground for brocade embroidery was supplied by domestic or imported velvets in red, purple, green and blue, by silk atlas, woollen cloth, fine cotton cloth and leather. Red velvet was particularly popular for women's and

459
Pouches. Embroidered, from various regions in Turkestan. Eastern costume usually comes without pockets, so both men and women used small pockets or pouches worn on the belt.
Late 19th century
Museum für Völkerkunde, Berlin

460-461
Borders with brocade embroidery on velvet, and a headscarf with a similar border.
L: 68 cm, W: 128 cm (scarf)
Bukhara, about 1900

childrens' clothes. Velvet was preferred for female headbands and plait caps, the top layer of childrens' and men's boots, galoshes for boots, men's trousers, cushions and caps for men, women and children, and more recently for vests, small pouches and belts. Deep red or deep green velvets from Bukhara were most frequently used for caparisons.

Silk and atlas silk was often used to make female dresses and headbands as well as sashes for men and children. Uniforms for high-ranking officers were made from woollen cloth. A fine cotton weave (*doka*) was used exclusively for the manufacture of the finest turban cloth used by the upper class.

The embroidery process consists of first arranging the metal threads in parallel rows on the ground material and then couching them with silk or cotton thread (Gontcharova 1986; Zerrnickel 1991). During the nineteenth century a technique called *zardüzi zamindüzi* was quite common, where the ground material was fully covered with embroidery. Here the gold thread made the thin threads laid out along the ground completely invisible.

A technique called *zardüzi guldüzi* evolved during the twentieth century, whereby the design elements cut from thick paper, cardboard or more rarely leather, would be placed on the ground, secured and then embroidered with gold thread. For this the master craftsman (*tarkash*) would draw the design elements on a piece of paper, prick the contours with a needle, place the paper on cardboard, copy the pricking marks with powdered soot and finally cut out the copied shapes from the cardboard with a special pair of scissors. Then the cardboard pieces would be attached to the piece of cloth stretched on a frame and given to the embroiderer.

The ornaments were edged in a technique called *takhrir* ('to outline') or with a thin cord of gold thread or *kabuli* (threads made of linked loops, a speciality of Kabul). Then the plain ground was covered with spirals and scrolls. Ornamentation was rarely geometric (circles, lozenges) and mainly floral, consisting of stylised plants and fruit, e.g., almonds (*bodom*), bitter oranges (*turunsh*), pomegranates (*anor*) and tulips (*lola*), as well as of palmettes and vases with flowers. During the Soviet period brocades found some new uses, for instance as stage curtains designed by state-educated artists. Today brocaded caps, women's vests, belts, small pouches, slippers, cushions and tapestries are also widely available; the embroidery thread is usually of Lurex.

Caps: *kulakh, arakchin-tokya, düppi, chyubeteika, kultapushak*

A large number of curious Central Asian headgear can be found in museums in Uzbekistan and Europe and in private collections. To mention just a few: the *kulakh* worn under the turban sash (*sallya*), the *duppi* and *tus-tuppi* from *Chust* and *gilam-düppi* from Shahr-i Sabz, the small okpar ('white feathers') from Kokand with mirror images of almonds (*bodomi*) on the four sections of the crown, the brocaded male cap from Bukhara (*kallyapush*), women's caps (*tuppi-taksimigi*), plait caps (*kultapushak*), the *tuppi-tos kandakori* worn by Jewish girls in Bukhara, and fur caps (*telpok*).

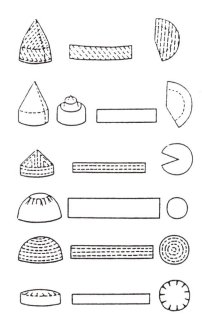

463
High conical and domed caps.
Rows 1-2: hard, ribbed, padded, cut.
Row 3: low conical shape, hard, ribbed, cut.
Row 4: low domed shape, soft, with high border and small top, cut.
Row 5: low domed shape, soft, with high border and large top, cut.
Row 6: most recent type, soft, with low border and flat top.

464
Men's caps from Khorezm.
Row 1: (left) padded, quilted, ribbed, cut; (right) medium height, top in two sections, cut.
Row 2: (left) low dome, low border, ribbed, padded, circular top; (right) high dome, padded, with fur border, cut.
Bottom: fur hats and their cut.

  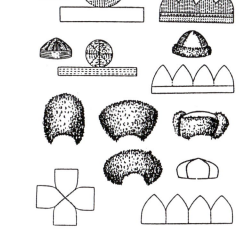

462
Half-finished cap.
D: 18.5 cm
Shahr-i Sabz, 1994

233

The most common headgear was and still is of the type called *düppi*. There are many regional variations as well as special shapes according to the gender and age of the wearer. *Düppi* can be pointed or conical, flat or domed, round or square, with a broad or narrow rim and trimmed with woven borders. They are made of several layers of stuff which is reinforced and quilted and normally embroidered with silk or cotton or metal (gold, silver) thread. At Chust men's caps are made of black satin, and women's caps of coloured silk or brocade. Plait caps from Bukhara are also occasionally embroidered. The cap worn under the turban sash originally was conical with a high rim, which made it particularly suitable for wrapping. A second cap (*arakchin*) of plain cotton acted as a sweat band.

During the Soviet period the shape of caps underwent considerable change, the crown tending to be simply circular or square and the rim rather narrow. In Tashkent and the Fergana Valley a Chust-type cap (*chyubeteika*) is regarded as part of the regional costume, and is also worn with Western-style clothes by those who feel strongly about their Uzbek identity. The distinctive design consists of a single motif – a highly stylised pepper pod regarded as a charm, or an almond leaf said to increase fertility – repeated on the four sections of the crown and along the rim. These delicately executed ornaments are laid on very thin strips of white paper and worked with white silk thread – or more rarely cotton – on the ground in imitation of brocade. The only difference between caps from Chust and the modern ones worn in Margilan is the curiously thin and elongated shape of the pepper pod motif. The designs on the highly original and famous caps from Shahr-i Sabz cover the entire ground and show colourful patterns of flowering bushes or branches giving the impression of a meadow full of flowers.

In and around Samarkand, Baysun and the Surkhan Darya area the caps are vertically ribbed, the ribs being shaped by inserted rolls of paper or cotton. The crown is decorated with a central star-like embroidered rosette with rays extending to the rim. The Surkhan Darya area in southern-most Uzbekistan borders on Tajikistan and Turkmenistan, two regions with strong influence on Uzbek culture. In Tashkent and the Fergana Valley we also find parti-coloured female caps entirely embroidered in *iroqi* stitch.

These caps bear designs of bushes covered with blossoms and blue or green birds on branches. Blue birds are a symbol of good fortune, and in Margilan the design is called 'nightingale pattern' (*bulbul nusha*). The typical decoration of Tashkent caps shows rose branches of deep red or pink silk on a white ground. Sometimes female names or short phrases are added, e.g., *Fargona tong otguncha* ('Fergana's rose-coloured dawn'). Square women's caps (*düppi*) are sometimes of light silver or gold brocade, the crown divided into four sections by black lines, and each segment embroidered with blossoming bushes. Besides embroidered headgear there are also caps of patterned cloth or velvet, and they look very splendid indeed.

465
Quilted cap. Silk ikat, calico, cotton and silk thread.
H: 11 cm, W: 54 cm
Presumably made in Khorezm, acquired in Bukhara in 1891
Museum für Völkerkunde, Berlin

466
Caps from Bukhara.
(Left) Quilted, gold brocade, atlas ikat, silk and cotton thread. H: 11 cm, W: 56 cm. Bukhara, 1902
(Right) Quilted, silk, calico, wool, cotton. H: 12.5 cm, W: 59.0 cm. Bukhara, 1903
Museum für Völkerkunde, Berlin, Rickmers Collection

467
Headdress from Bukhara.
(Left) Cap. Knotted, wool, cotton, fur. H: 14 cm, W: 66 cm. Bukhara, 1903
(Right) Felt hat. Cotton, calico. H: 24 cm, W: 117 cm. Bukhara, 1902
Museum für Völkerkunde, Berlin, Rickmers Collection

468
(Left) Men's cap. Embroidered, silk, cotton, wool. H: 10.5 cm, W: 55.0 cm. Bukhara, 1902
(Right) Women's cap. Embroidered, cotton, silk. H: 7.5-8 cm, W: 56 cm. Bukhara, 1902
Museum für Völkerkunde, Berlin, Rickmers Collection

470
Turban cloth of cashmere. Fabrics from Kashmir were especially sought-after by upper-class customers.
W: 62 cm
Acquired by Rickmers in the 1890s
Museum für Völkerkunde, Berlin, Rickmers Collection

469
Turban. Cotton.
L: 500 cm, W: 88 cm.
Bukhara, 1891
Museum für Völkerkunde, Berlin

471
Uzbek from Khojent with his child, about 1900

235

472
Wool imitating cashmere from Yazd.
W: 130 cm
Acquired by Rickmers in Bukhara in the 1890s
Museum für Völkerkunde, Berlin, Rickmers Collection

Borders and decorative bands: *dziyak, zikhak, zekh, sheroza*

Colourful borders decorating items of clothing as well as large and small textiles are generally called *dziyak* and are known in Bukhara, Samarkand and Urgut also as *zekh* and in the Surkhan Darya region as *sheroza*. The manufacture and use of such borders has a long history. They are used to decorate traditional items of clothing like khalats, dresses, trousers and caps as well as large decorative embroidery (e.g. *suzanis*) and smaller types for domestic use (shawls, caparisons, saddle blankets, mirror pouches, belts, belt pockets, etc. For centuries this has been an independent craft, with specialists producing decorative trimmings, borders, piping, braids, tassels and silk pendants for plaits and ears. Simple finger-plaited 'ur-borders' were made long before the development of mechanical weaving.

Woven decorative borders with open slits (kilim technique) first appear among the Chinese silks of the Tang dynasty. There they come as narrow strips of up to two centimetres in width, which were called *kesi*, and were used among others things also for decorative borders (Whitfield and Farrer 1990:112). Four types of *dziyak* can be distinguished according to the methods of production:
a) simple *dziyak* plaited with the fingers;

b) complicated *dziyak*, where the weft thread is applied to the background with a needle;
c) borders woven on a special device; and
d) narrow strips of cloth embroidered with cross stitch or broad chain stitch executed with a hooked neddle (*iroqi* or *yürma*).

The simplest method of producing a border is to plait it with one's fingers. The thread is wound several times around the big toe and the left thumb, and then the loops on the thumb are transferred to all fingers of both hands. The loops transferred from the fingers of one hand to the fingers of the other hand interlace, and the resulting skeins are tied together with a thread acting as the weft. Several such skeins produce a colourful pattern.

For method b) two women work together. Once the required number of threads of a certain colour has been assembled, one end of the threads is sewn on the background. The next step resembles the one described above: One woman provides the shed during plaiting, and the other inserts the weft with a needle and sews the resulting section of the border on the textile background.

In the Fergana Valley a special device (*zikhak dukon*) is used for the manufacture of borders. It consists of a square frame with an additional horizontal slat at the bottom to improve stability. Up to seventeen round poles are inserted vertically with grooves about ten centimeters long on the left side. These grooves take the black warp threads running the length of the eventual *dziyak* in a calculated sequence. A comb (*shona*) is used to make the shed required for the weft thread (Sadykova 1986). The finished weave borders are then colourfully ornamented with fine cross stitch and sewn on the background, be it the rim of a cap or a piece of clothing. The yarn may be silk, artificial silk, good-quality cotton or increasingly Lurex. A similar kind of frame is still used in Chust for the manufacture of borders for caps.

Another device (*dukoni kokma*) for weaving borders consists of a square piece of cardboard, leather or plastic with a corner hole for the warp thread. Turning the flat sheet gives both a shed and the required pattern, while the weft is inserted with a shuttle. The end-product is a patterned band (Zerrnickel 1991:208). For method d) a narrow strip of cloth is stretched on a tambour and entirely covered with cross stitch (*iroqi*) or broad chain stitch executed with a hooked needle (*yürma*). Such borders are produced mainly at Bukhara and Urgut.

Borders for men's and women's khalats and for large pieces of embroidery are woven several metres long, while those for caps are only thirty-five to forty centimetres long. For women's trousers, matching borders of black cotton or silk yarn are used fringed with tufts at the end. Traditional female costume especially at Bukhara has decorative borders (*zekhi kurta, pesh kurta*) along the collar (110–120 cm) and the neckline slit.

The predominant motifs for borders, which have evolved over the centuries, are of geometric shape and include circles, triangles, lozenges, squares, hooks, spirals, S-shaped figures and various linear patterns. There are also floral motifs of different degrees of stylisation (blossoms, scrolling foliage, short branches, both single and combined) as well as depictions of inanimate objects and zoomorphic and more rarely anthropomorphic figures. One feature is common to all borders, however strongly they may differ in other respects – they all show a narrow and conspiciously coloured edging along the selvedges of indigo or light blue, grey or mottled colours; these are variously called *suv* (water), *kovurga* (rib), *mizza* (eyelash) or *terna* (crane). The central band of the edging is much broader and decorated with colourful repeat patterns.

The border strips, acting as a boundary for the individual piece of fabric, are said to protect against evil spirits. In most localities, certain border motifs predominate, e.g., in Bukhara *bodom* (almonds), in Urgut *moripechin* (winding snakes), *bulbul küzi* (nightingale eyes) and *marzoncha* (small corals), in Samarkand *mushek küz* (cats' eyes), *shabaka* (openwork bracelets), in Baysun *muguz* (horns), *sirga* (earrings) and *zahzira* (decorative necklaces). Decorative borders, especially for caps and women's trousers, are still an indispensable part of popular dress, and can be found at the bazaar in the main cities and in villages all over the country.

The traditional costume of Uzbekistan

The shape and style of the costume of Uzbekistan has been determined by family and tribal traditions, custom and usage and climatic conditions. Despite various influences and changes in fashion, until the early years of this century people by and large dressed the same way they had done for centuries, in clothes which were long and wide, cut straight from a length of cloth and designed to hide the body contour as much as possible. Differences existed between clothes for everday use, for festive occasions and for mourning. Summer and winter clothes were made of the same material. Men, women and children wore clothes very similar in shape and cut.

Male costume

Men usually wore long cotton shirts (*kuylak*) of straight cut beneath a coat (*khalat, tun, chakman*). Summer coats were of light material and winter coats padded and quilted. Coats always had slits on both sides, which was more convenient for walking, riding and sitting on the floor. For travel and during very cold weather a fur coat would be worn. For belts the common people would wear sashes (*uramal, belbag*). Coats were an important part of courtly and festive dress, and so were belts (*kamar*). They could be of brocaded velvet, brocades and ikat fabrics, of cotton or leather decorated with silk embroidery and of leather covered with velvet with fastenings and fittings of silver (see chapter on jewellery). Members of the upper class usually had attachments on their belts for knives and a pouch containing money, tobacco and the like, while the common people kept these things tucked into their sashes.

Men's trousers (*ishton, balak*) were very wide and cut straight, with a gusset and tapering legs. The headgear consisted of a smaller cap to soak up sweat and an

473-474
Men's coat. Brocade, silk velvet, silk ikat lining, polychrome woven border with ornaments strongly influenced by Chinese designs. The detail shows a medallion with a central star and scrollwork.
L: 147 cm, W: 210 cm
Samarkand, about 1890
Private collection, Karlsruhe

237

embroidered one on top, around which the turban sash would be wrapped. These sashes were usually plain or striped, those worn at court brocaded with gold or silver thread. Occasionally fur caps were worn. For footgear people wore leather boots and soft leather stockings.

476
Trousers for great ceremonies. Silk, brocade embroidery, sable trimmings. Presumably owned by a Bukharan emir or high court official.
H: 62 cm, W: 113 cm
Bukhara, second half 19th century
Museum in the Summer Residence, Bukhara

475
Dignitary from Samarkand in official festive dress, about 1900

477
Leather stockings with silk embroidery.
Bukhara, late 19th century
Museum für Völkerkunde, Berlin, Rickmers Collection

238

478
Coat of an emir or high official. Gold brocade embroidery on silk velvet, silk ikat lining, woven and embroidered border. The bold and distinctive scrollwork is reminiscent of late Ottoman brocade embroidery. The Bukharan court was in close contact with the Ottoman court.
L: 136 cm, W: 203 cm
Bukhara, about 1880

479
Men's coat. Gold brocade on silk, silk ikat lining, woven border.
L: 128 cm, W: 189 cm
Bukhara, about 1900

480
Men's coat. Imported cashmere, silk lining. The sumptuary laws being very strict, only persons connected to the court were permitted to wear coats of silk velvet with brocade embroidery or of cashmere.
Bukhara, late 19th century
Museum für Völkerkunde, Berlin, Rickmers Collection

481
Coat Silk ikat, Chinese-inspired designs, monochrome woven border.
Silk coats were worn by members of the upper class and by officials of middle rank. They as well as brocade and cashmere coats, would be bestowed by the emir as a mark of honour during official occasions. The measure of the emir's favour could be ascertained from the quality of the coats.
L: 129.5 cm, W: 142.0 cm
Samarkand, about 1870

482
Men's garment of rough cotton worn by members of the urban lower class and by peasants.
L: 115 cm, W: 200 cm
Turkestan, late 19th century

483
Men's coat. Flatweave, camel's hair. Garments of this type were worn by nomads.
L: 122 cm, W: 186 cm
Khorezm (?), second half 19th century

484
Women's coat. Quilted and padded ikat reps, mixed weave of silk and cotton, lining and trimmings of printed cotton, monochrome woven border. Coats with narrow quilted bands are typical of Khorezm costume.
L: 122.5 cm, W: 140.0 cm
Khorezm, about 1900

485
Women's coat. Padded and quilted ikat reps, mixed fabric of silk and cotton, trimmings of ikat reps, lining of printed cotton with designs of stylised cypresses and amulets. The colour scheme and design of very narrow strips indicate a rather early date. The relative shortness of the coats may reflect the fact that both men and women also wore them on horseback; riding was common among both sexes.
L: 124.5 cm, W: 129.0 cm
Khorezm, mid-19th century

486
Men's coat. Ikat reps, mixed weave of silk and cotton, silk lining, polychrome woven border. The severe geometrical design is typical of Samarkand ikats of the 1920s and early 1930s.
L: 146 cm, W: 200 cm
Samarkand, about 1900. Acquired in Mazar-i-Sharif (north Afghanistan) in 1978

487
Men's coat. Silk embroidery on cotton. The style and technique of the dense embroidery
suggests a Shahr-i Sabz provenance.
Acquired by Rickmers in Bukhara between 1894 and 1898
Museum für Völkerkunde, Berlin, Rickmers Collection

242

488
Men's coat. Silk embroidery on cotton, polychrome woven border. Such large-sized motifs of
stylised flower sprays, palmettes and boteh patterns are exceptional even for the imaginative
repertoire of Shahr-i Sabz embroidery.
L: 130 cm, W: 173 cm
Shahr-i Sabz, late 19th century

489
*Men's summer coat. Unlined ikat reps, mixed weave of silk and cotton, with feather motifs
and 'comb' patterns in yellow.
L: 132 cm, W: 197 cm
Fergana, late 19th century*

490
Women's coat. Ikat reps, mixed weave of silk and cotton, printed cotton lining, below the
sleeves needlepoint with green cotton thread; for a front view, see ill. 510.
L: 114 cm, W: 133 cm
Fergana, about 1890
Private collection, Karlsruhe

491
Women's coat. Ikat reps, mixed weave of silk and cotton, polychrome woven border, design of
stylised cypresses.
L: 127 cm, W: 146 cm
Samarkand region, about 1900

492
Men's coat with collar. Padded ikat, cotton. The items acquired by Robert Shaw between
1868 and 1869 on his journey to Yarkand and Kashgar are among the few securely dated
objects and therefore provide important references for the study of Central Asian ikats. The
cut is of standard eastern Turkestan style, while the design is similar to ikats from the
Fergana Valley.
L: 121.9 cm, W: 184.0 cm
Acquired by Shaw in 1868-9
Ashmolean Museum, Oxford, Department of Eastern Art, X 3987

493
Men's coat. Silk ikat with collar and Chinese-inspired design. The waisted cut, unusual width of the lower third and the cut of the sleeves are similar to coats also worn by dancing boys, as we know from historical photographs.
L: 121.9 cm, W: 152.4 cm
Acquired by Shaw in 1868/9
Ashmolean Museum, Oxford, Department of Eastern Art, X 3985

494
Men's coat. Chinese silk brocade. This coat was presented to Shaw as a gift of honour by Ya`qub Beg, the khan of Kashgar; see also ill. 29.
L: 147, W: 222 cm
Ashmolean Museum, Oxford, Department of Eastern Art, X 3975

495
Men's coat. Padded ikat reps, mixed weave of silk and cotton.
L: 121.9 cm, W: 213.4 cm
Ashmolean Museum, Oxford, Department of Eastern Art, X 3977

496
Coat. Lightly padded silk ikat, designs of pomegranates, trees of life and 'combs'.
L: 123 cm, W: 180 cm

497
Women's summer coat. Unlined ikat reps, mixed weave of silk and cotton, lower end partly cut off. The elaborate tie-dyeing technique suggests a rather early date; for the patterning procedure, see ill. 431
L: 115 cm, W: 176 cm
Fergana (?), mid-19th century

498
Children's coat. Lightly padded ikat reps, mixed weave of silk and cotton, lining of striped cotton. The breast pocket and cut of the lapels suggest that the coat was copied from a European men's jacket.
L: 122.5 cm, W: 140.0 cm
Bukhara, about 1920

499
Boys' coat. Brocade embroidery on silk velvet, ikat reps lining, polychrome woven border.
L: 90 cm, W: 133 cm
Bukhara, about 1920
Private collection, Zurich

Female costume

Female costume consisted of a coat, a dress and a pair of trousers, all cut straight and wide, both coat and dress without collar. When moving outside the house, a woman would cover herself from head to toe with a wide ankle-length *paranja* with mock sleeves on the back and a horsehair veil. Female headgear consisted of three major items, the combination and style of wear differing regionally: a plaid cap (*kultapushak*) for women, a small cap (*düppi*) for girls, and a kerchief. Women and young girls wore trousers under their dresses, cut the same way as male trousers but with a decorative border at the bottom. Female footgear again was basically similar to that of men.

Children were dressed the same as adults, and even babies wore tiny caps.

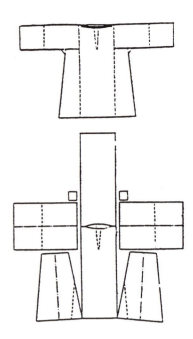

501
Paper pattern for a padded men's shirt.

500
Paper patterns of women's costume.
(Top) Coats and caps, one with plait cover.
(Centre) Standard cuts of women's dresses and trousers.
(Bottom right) System of folding the scarf worn over the head-dress.

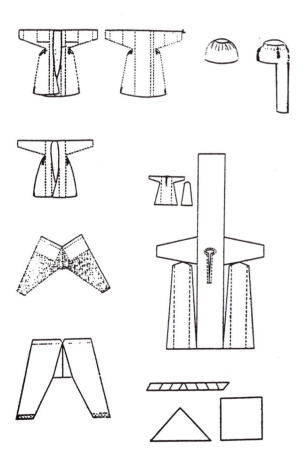

502
Wedding-dress. Silk atlas, brocade embroidery, polychrome woven border. The trimmings of the long opening at the neck are decorated with amulet motifs, the sleeves embroidered with calligraphy.
L: 120 cm, W: 192 cm
Bukhara, late 18th/early 19th century

503
Tajik women's dress. Silk embroidery on cotton.
L: 120 cm, W: 192 cm
Northern Afghanistan or Uzbekistan, early 20th century
Private collection, Zurich

504
Women's coat. Lightly padded silk ikat, lining of printed cotton, polychrome woven border.
L: 129 cm, W: 188 cm
Samarkand, second half 19th century

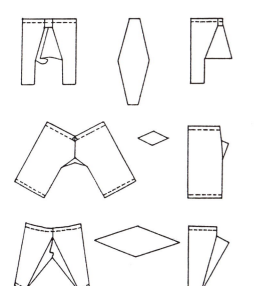

505
Paper patterns for men's trousers of a cut worn throughout Central Asia in the 19th/20th century.

506
Women's trousers. Plain cotton, the legs of ikat reps, mixed weave of silk and cotton, the gusset of striped cotton.
L: 92 cm, W: 64 cm
Bukhara, early 20th century

507
Women's coat. Lightly padded silk ikat, lining of printed cotton, the flap with ikat reps,
polychrome woven border.
L: 129.5 cm, W: 171.0 cm
Bukhara, about 1880

508
*Women's coat. Silk ikat, polychrome woven border. The reddish-purple sheen is the result of
the weft threads, which are normally white, having been dyed red.*
L: 130 cm, W: 168 cm
Samarkand, about 1880

509
Coat. Brocade embroidery on silk velvet, ikat reps lining with large boteh patterns; the shape of the collar and cut suggest Uighur manufacture.
Acquired in Bukhara, about 1900
Museun für Völkerkunde, Berlin

510
Coat (front view of ill. 490).
L: 114 cm, W: 133 cm
Fergana, about 1890
Private collection, Karlsruhe

511
Women's coat. Silk ikat, polychrome woven border. The design of trees of life growing from amulets is unusual.
L: 130 cm, W: 133 cm
Bukhara, about 1900

512
Women's coat. Lightly padded silk ikat, polychrome woven border. Some of the toothed wedges forming the overall pattern are decorated with boteh patterns and human figures (adamlyk).
L: 133 cm, W: 186 cm
Samarkand region, late 19th centuty

513
Women's coat. Padded ikat reps, mixed weave of silk and cotton, polychrome woven border.
The design shows feathered lozenges and palmettes alternating with amulet motifs.
L: 120 cm, W: 170 cm
Bukhara (?), about 1900

514
Women's coat. Lightly padded ikat reps, mixed weave of silk and cotton, needlepoint under
the sleeves. The design consists of oval medallions and delicately executed pomegranates.
L: 115.5 cm, W: 137.5 cm
Probably Fergana, second half 19th century

516
Women's trousers. Silk brocade, imported Russian fabric (with factory label), design of
alternating stars and flowery palmettes, the top of printed cotton.
L: 94 cm, W: 80 cm
Bukhara, about 1920-30

515
Women's coat. Quilted and padded ikat reps, mixed weave of silk and cotton, lining of
printed cotton, the flap with striped cotton.
L: 128.0 cm, W: 128.5 cm
Khorezm, about 1900

518
Young woman from Bukhara in her wedding-dress, about 1900.

517
Women's coat. Ikat reps, mixed weave of silk and cotton, around the neck cotton embroidery in the style of Erzari Turkmens, polychrome woven border.
L: 127.0 cm, W: 136.5 cm
Ikat from Bukhara, about 1920; probably tailored and embroidered in Khorezm

519
Women's caps with plait cover. Brocade embroidery on silk velvet, from Bukhara; on the left a rural version from the Surkhan Darya region.
L: 54 cm, W: 13-7 cm
Bukhara and Surkhan Darya, about 1900

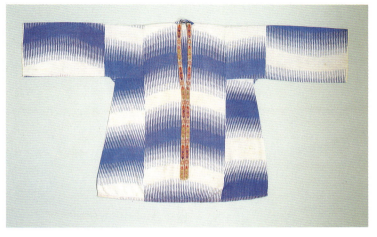

520
Women's dress. Silk ikat, cotton embroidery, piping along the borders, attached cotton turnbacks with cotton embroidery. The turnbacks reflect the earlier custom of wearing several layers of clothes on top of each other for festive occasions.
L: 126 cm, W: 229 cm
Bukhara, about 1900; turnbacks about 1960-70

521
Wedding-dress. Ikat reps, mixed weave of silk and cotton, polychrome cotton embroidery along the borders, the hem with wave patterns in machine embroidery.
L: 126 cm, W: 225 cm
Bukhara, about 1920

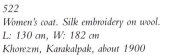

522
Women's coat. Silk embroidery on wool.
L: 130 cm, W: 182 cm
Khorezm, Karakalpak, about 1900

523
Women's coat. Silk embroidery on indigo-dyed homespun cotton.
L: 126 cm, W: 152 cm
Khorezm, Karakalpak, late 19th century

524-525
Women in typical urban veiling apparel (paranja), veiled (left) and unveiled (right).
Turkestan, about 1900

526
Veiling garment (paranja). Cotton embroidery, homespun cotton with blue stripes,
polychrome woven border. A typical feature of Turkestan paranjas are the false sleeves on the
back joined with a short ribbon.
L: 160.5 cm, W: 192.0 cm (bottom)
Tajik, 1920

527
Veiling garment (paranja). Silk embroidery on silk reps, lining of ikat reps.
L: 160.5 cm, W: 192.0 cm (bottom)
Probably Bukhara, Tajik, about 1900 or earlier

Wedding costume and the bride's dowry

The five major events of a Muslim's life are birth, circumcision, marriage, the pilgrimage to Mecca, and death.

Soon after the birth of a child, the parents start to save money for the celebration of circumcision and marriage, and to prepare the gifts and dowry of the bride. Preparations for the dowry are especially elaborate. All female relatives lend a hand at embroidering caps, *suzanis*, waist sashes, etc. Some of the embroidery may be bought at the bazaar or ordered from a professional embroiderer. The dowry includes numerous dresses, fabrics by the metre, coats of various cuts, brocades, jewellery, tableware, blankets and cushions and much more.

Wedding celebrations usually go on for three or four days or even longer. Around Samarkand and Bukhara the bride on her wedding day wears two dresses together, while in Khorezm and the Surkhan Darya region she wears them one after the other. One dress is usually white or light pink, the other of red silk. The white dress has very long sleeves with a broad (20-30 cm) embroidered band at the hem. In the Surkhan Darya region the white dress is exchanged on the second or third day for a red one, symbolising the bride's new status and alluding to female fertility.

From the early twentieth century brides increasingly wore a 'modern' ikat dress with a collar and of Western cut, a red brocaded pair of trousers, embroidered shoes, a white veil with highly colourful ornamental borders, and a khalat (Zerrnickel 1985). The wedding headdress covered the head completely. The jewellery worn across the forehead terminated in colourful birds' feathers. In her left the bride would carry a piece of cloth folded into a triangle and embroidered with a tree of life and billing birds, symbols of fertility and mutual happiness. The bride held this cloth at chest height to be able to cover her face against intrusive glances.

The bridegroom wore a white shirt with red armpit gussets or embroidery. His ceremonial khalat was belted with a red silk sash, his cap embroidered by the bride. The red gussets and sash were meant to heighten his virility.

Nowadays Uzbek women usually wear ikat dresses, ikat trousers and a parti-coloured embroidered cap. This very conspicuous and colourful costume is partly a way to dissociate themselves from the fashions of Russia and China, long regarded as oppressors, and thus an expression of the national identity of the new Uzbekistan.

528
Bridal pair in traditional urban wedding-dress.
Bukhara, 1989

529
Men's wedding sash. Silk with patterns in reserve and silk embroidery.
L: 232 cm, W: 54 cm
Bukhara, early 19th century

530
Elderly woman in traditional costume, Urgench.

531
Woman wearing a fashionable ikat dress on the Margilan bazaar.

532
Women selling caps on the bazaar in Bukhara.

533
This street scene from Bukhara shows the diversity of dress styles worn today.

533a
Detail of the back of the coat in ill. 488.

534
Suzani. The use of kanda khayal stitch suggests Shahr-i Sabz as the place of origin.
Ground: homespun cotton; embroidery thread: silk, cotton; technique: areas filled in basma,
kanda khayal and chain stitch, lines in chain stitch, stem stitch and open chain stitch.
L: 230 cm, W: 158 cm

262

Suzanis: Embroideries from Central Asia

Gisela Dombrowski

One of the most beautiful products of traditional Turkestan culture are the large silk embroideries known collectively as *suzanis* or as 'Bukhara embroidery', because the name of that city, famous as an entrepot for the much esteemed Turkmen carpets, was familiar to many and indicated a certain geographical region, however vague. Since embroidering was a technique of decoration within everybody's reach, it was both popular and common in Central Asia (as it was elsewhere) at least until the introduction of cheaper printed fabrics imported from abroad. Practised among both the sedentary and nomad population, it sometimes reached the heights of artistic perfection.

The large embroideries we shall discuss here were meant to decorate the interior of houses and are thus only found in settled communities. Their area of distribution corresponds to that of modern Uzbekistan (excluding the Khiva region) and northern Tajikistan.

Suzanis (Pers. *suzan*, needle) formed an important part of a bride's dowry. After the birth of a girl, the mother would start to embroider; later the daughter would join her and as the day of the wedding approached, female relatives and neighbours would be asked to lend a hand. At Nurata, for example, the dowry of a bride from a well-off family was expected to include ten suzanis of different size and function.

The largest embroideries, the suzani proper, measured on average 160 to 220 by 220 to 270 centimetres, and were used as wall hangings, as were the smaller blankets called *nimsuzani* (half-sized suzanis). Large pieces of cloth embroidered along the long sides and along one short side and called *ruijo*, were used as spreads for the bridal bed. Smaller pieces about the size of a *nimsuzani* and known in Nurata as *takyapush*, in Bukhara and Samarkand as *bolinpush* and in Shahr-i Sabz and Tashkent as *yastikpush*, would first be spread over the bridal cushion and then used to cover the bedding stored in niches during the day. If the room was big enough, one might hang up long and narrow textiles (*sardewar*) as a kind of frieze immediately below the ceiling (ill. 369). *Sandalipush* are small square pieces of cloth (about 90 x 90 cm) to cover the low table (*sandal*) above the charcoal brazier, which was the only source of heating during the winter; here the family would gather, slipping their arms and feet under the blanket and enjoying the modest warmth. Other relatively small embroidered textiles, called *joinamaz,* served as prayer mats. Besides these most common types of embroideries there were others particular to a region, for instance the Tashkent *dorpech*, similar to the narrow *sardewar* used to cover the clothes hung from a beam, or the small square cloth typically used to wrap bread and other things (ill. 551). All these embroideries formed part of the dowry and were highly treasured, and after the wedding ceremony would be taken out again only for special occasions.

The background material for suzanis was usually a quite coarse cotton cloth (average width 26-40 cm) produced by cottage industry, normally undyed but occasionally given a light brown tint by immersion in a bath of tea leaves or onion peel. Since about 1880 imported cotton from Russia, machine woven and sometimes dyed, was also used. At the same time coloured silks are said to have first appeared as stitching ground.

The embroidery yarn was loosely spun domestic silk, dyed with natural dyestuffs by mostly Jewish specialists. They seem to have been unable to produce an intense light red colour, which was very popular, for we know that between 1850 and 1880 large amounts of an expensive cinnabar-coloured wool was imported from India. Luckily it was used only sparsely, probably on account of its price, since it turned out to be quite unstable. A similar loss occured with black silk thread where the dye could be made either from pomegranate peel with an iron oxide mordant, from pistachio gall nuts or from mallow blossoms; it remains unclear which of the three agents caused the deterioration.

The most dominant colour by far is red in various shades. It used to be made from madder root or cochineal imported from Russia; yellow was extracted from a yellow variety of larkspur (Delphinium sulphureum; *isparak*) or the flowers of the Japanese pagoda tree (Sophora japonica; *tuchmak*); blue was based on indigo imported from India, and green from the purplish-red fuchsine imported from Russia since the 1880s. Slightly later other aniline colours appeared, which were rather unstable at first. It was only the introduction of fast Indanthrene dyes in the early twentieth century what finally spelled the end for natural dyestuffs.

Suzanis were manufactured exclusively by women. The first step was to cut the lengths of cloth according to the required shape and stitch them loosely together. On this backing the designs would be drawn, either by a member of the family or a professional draughtswoman (*kalamkash*, from *kalam*, nib). After deciding on the general pattern, she would sketch the designs in black ink mainly free-handed, using a bowl or some other circular object only to do the circles. Such drawing skills were usually handed down in the family.

Next the stitches were undone except in the case of very small items, where two lengths were sometimes sewn together before ornamentation. Then the lenghts were embroidered separately. This would allow several women to work the suzani simultaneously if need arose. To attain the required tautness, the women, who sat cross-legged on the ground, would fasten the top end to their dress, arrange the fabric across their angled left leg, hold down the bottom with the left foot and with the left hand pull the fabric tight (Taube 1994:11). Once finished, the strips would be sewn together. This procedure explains the frequent irregularities along the seams as well as disparities in the colours of the different strips. In some cases these irregularities are masked by additional stitching.

The types of embroidery stitches used on suzanis is limited. Most typical is *basma* (or *bosma*) stitch, where a long thread is laid across the motif and then – working in the opposite direction – secured by short couching stitches,

535
Nimsuzani. The designs perhaps show flower sprays with the blossoms degenerated into circles, a feature typical of the end-phase of Nurata embroidery (Tschepelewezkaja 1991:25).

Ground: factory-made cotton; embroidery thread: silk, cotton; technique: chain stitch.
L: 170 cm, W: 124 cm
Nurata, about 1900 (?)
Museum für Völkerkunde, Berlin

536
Suzani. The style of decoration is rather late, as the multi-structured plants or trees depicted in a restricted colour scheme would indicate.
Ground: factory-made cotton; embroidery thread: silk, cotton; technique: areas in basma stitch, contours and lines in chain stitch.
L: 275 cm, W: 205 cm
Samarkand, about 1900
Museum für Völkerkunde, Berlin

537
An elderly female expert sketching a design for a suzani, Urgut.

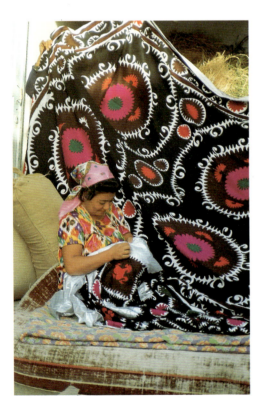

538
Tajik woman embroidering a suzani, Urgut.

variations of the angle and spacing of the latter producing varied effects. The wrong side of the fabric shows only parts of the returning couching stitch but nothing of the laid thread.

A variant of *basma* stitch particular to Shahr-i Sabz and near-by Kitab, is called *kanda khayal* (or *khayol*, sometimes misspelled *khayöl*). This consists of long and rather loose couching stitches almost parallel to the laid thread, giving the appearance of a somewhat loosely twisted rope; the wrong side shows very short stitches. Both *basma* and *kanda khayol* are similar to Romanian or Renaissance stitch and in English are sometimes called 'Bukhara couching'.

Another common filling stitch is broad chain stitch (*yurma*). It can be worked with a normal embroidery needle, but usually the embroiderers seem to have used a special one similar to a fine crocheting hook. In the case of this tamboured chain stitch, the thread is pulled unevenly so that the 'chain' shows on one side a continuous line or 'ridge', and only on the other the typical chain stitch loop (Tschepelewezkaja 1991:22). This produces a relief-like effect, which is enhanced by shimmering light effects resulting from the practice of stitching neighbouring rows in opposite directions. In about 1900 machines were introduced which produced chain stitch embroidery mechanically. While chain stitch is used for contours throughout the suzani-producing area, as a filling stitch it is used mainly in Bukhara and to a lesser extend in Shahr-i Sabz. The antiquity of chain stitch is documented, for instance, by a fragment of Chinese embroidery discovered at Pazyryk (6th/5th century B.C.).

Half cross stitch (*iroqi*, *iraqi*) is also used as a filling stitch. Here the laid thread is secured with very short, regular and closely set couching stitches at an angle of forty-five degrees. It usually covers the entire surface so that the ground is completely hidden from view. Its use for large embroideries is known only from Shahr-i Sabz and examples are rare. It has been suggested that *iroqi* stitch was restricted to embroidering ceremonial robes and the like commissioned by the court (ills. 487-8).

For contours and straight lines both simple chain stitch and very closely worked open chain stitch are used. Whereas chain stitch shows a straight threading line on the back, open chain stitch produces a row of parallel stitches whose angle and density can vary. Presumably *ilmak* (or *ilmok*) stitch, often mentioned and variously defined, is identical with open chain stitch. On Shahr-i Sabz embroidery one occasionally finds stem stitch. A laid thread couched with a thread of different colour or a row of detached chain stitches which produce a dotted line, can also be used to emphasise the outlines of a motif. It is worth mentioning that contours were almost invariably used for leaves and stems, but only rarely for blossoms.

It has been suggested that on average a suzani took two to two and a half years to complete, and longer if the embroidery was particularly dense (Tschepelewezkaja 1991:19). This calculation is probably based on the assumption of a single person working the entire piece; at a rate of two hours per day this would average forty to fifty

266

square centimetres of embroidery per hour. In such a situation the advantage of working the suzani section by section becomes obvious: Not only does it ease handling, but it is also psychologically more satisfying in that the embroideress is then able to appreciate the progress she is making sooner than if she was working the whole huge piece of fabric.

The designs consisted chiefly of flowers and leaves or of shapes that may be interpreted as floral. This interpretation finds support in the appearance of suzanis from Nurata which look like a well-ordered flowering garden landscape reminiscent of the 'garden carpets' of Persia. The subject was naturally attractive to oasis dwellers surrounded by deserts and steppes and may have been given further encouragement by the Muslim predilection for floral ornamentation. Scholars have suggested that some design elements found on suzanis are of pre-Islamic origin and were only later 'translated' into a floral language. This seems particularly the case with suzanis produced in the northeastern area of suzani ditribution around Tashkent, where the whole surface is covered with circular motifs said to derive from ancient cosmological symbols. A more obvious example are the suzanis from Pskent with their brilliant suns and stars (ill. 560) and the Tashkent embroideries explicitly called *yulduz palak* and *ai palak*, 'starry sky' and 'lunar sky' (ill. 561). The very widespread rosette design may originally also have referred to celestial bodies.

In a strictly Islamic region the rarity of designs with animal motifs – not to mention human figures – comes as no surprise. An exception are the depictions of birds and fishes, the latter often hard to make out. Like a picture puzzle, a careful reading of a leaf or an almond-shaped motif may suddenly discover it turning into a fish or birds with blossoms in their tails and crests. The same is true of inanimate objects, the predominant being the ewer (*aftabah*). Like the birds, it is usually quite easy to recognise, although it may sometimes be almost totally hidden within a scrollwork of leaves and flowers.

The ewer can be read as an allusion to the Islamic requirement of ritual purity, but it can be a symbol of water in general and its life-giving qualities as well (Taube 1993:54). The natural affinity of fish and water would suggest that where a fish appears at the foot of a flowering bush, it is meant to symbolize the water of life and not female fertility, with which it is also often associated. The depiction of birds and bird-like creatures usually identified as roosters, peacocks and the like, has been interpreted in many ways, of which we only mention the association of birds with images of the soul and their role as mediators between different spheres. The flowering bushes and plants can be understood as late descendants of the ubiquitous tree of life.

A certain bold and slightly curved leaf-shaped motif has been interpreted as the common Central Asian knife (*kord-i osh*) invested with the same protective and apotropaic properties ascribed to all things sharp and cutting (Sucharewa 1991:78). Some Turkestan ceramics are decorated with realistically depicted knives (ill. 675). The decoration of suzanis with explicit apotropaic motifs is documented by

539
Half of a suzani decorated with delicate scrollwork.
Ground: homespun cotton; embroidery thread: silk, some wool; technique: chain stitch.
L: 232 cm, W: 82 cm
Museum für Völkerkunde, Berlin, Rickmers Collection 1902

540
Fully embroidered suzani. The circular motifs suggesting fruits or blossoms derive from pre-Islamic astral imagery.

Ground: homespun cotton; embroidery thread: silk, some wool; technique: areas in basma stitch, contours mainly in simple chain stitch with some very fine open chain stitch.

L: 254 cm, W: 169 cm
Tashkent
Museum für Völkerkunde, Berlin, Rickmers Collection 1902

541
Embroidered blanket (bedspread). An early example of Shahr-i Sabz work.
Ground: homespun cotton; embroidery thread: silk; technique: areas in kanda khayal stitch,

lines and contours in open chain stitch.
L: 290 cm, W: 223 cm

269

examples from Dzhizak showing the well-known triangular female amulets (*tumar*) at the corners (ills. 543, 547). Also of pre-Islamic origin is the motif called *chahar cheragh* (four lamps), constructed from a central rosette with four attached pointed blossoms and interpreted as an oil lamp with four openings for the wicks, the points symbolising flames (ills. 547-8). Small motifs reminiscent of flames are sometimes found scattered across a suzani, where they may be taken as a vague echo of ancient Indo-Persian fire-worship or at least as a reference to the life-sustaining energies of fire. The Central Asian belief in fire (or light) as a protective agent still finds expression in the custom of keeping a light constantly burning in the room of newly-weds, of women in labour and of new-born infants.

Final mention should be made of a motif which on account of its vegetal character was not in need of modification or disguise, namely the pomegranate. Because of its numerous seeds many cultures used it as a symbol of fecundity and it therefore was especially prominent in connection with wedding rituals; in Bukhara, for example, it was customary to throw pomegranates into the bride's lap (Sucharewa 1991:84).

A completely different approach to discover the symbolic message on suzanis focuses on the identification of individual flowers and plants. It is based on the assumption that the embroiderers, being women and therefore knowledgeable about the medicinal properties of plants, would have chosen to represent plants of practical use. Among the easily recognisable plants, for instance, the iris (Iris germanica) is well-known for its various medicinal properties. The argument becomes more difficult to follow in the case of the most frequently depicted floral shape, the rosette, said to represent the poppy flower and so to suggest the curative powers of opium, or in the case of the second most frequent motif, the palmette, interpreted as the blossom of the pomegranate and thus as partaking of the latter's benign effects (Cadoux 1990). – It should be mentioned in passing that similar representations of the iris appear on high-quality Persian fabrics of the seventeenth century, which may have been the original inspiration for its use on Turkestan embroidery.

Despite their wide distribution, suzanis show some common features which allow us to identify them as embroideries from Turkestan. Although difficult to pinpoint, their characteristics depend on a distinct combination of material, colour, embroidery techniques and stylistic factors apparent both in the overall composition and in the execution of details. In spite of these common features it is possible to distinguish a certain number of local styles. Thanks to the research of Russian scholars like Chepelevetskaya and Sukhareva, who were able to interview embroideresses and draughtswomen with a practical knowledge of the situation in the late nineteenth century, when suzani production was still flourishing, we are in a position to know at least the characteristics of the main local styles (Sucharewa 1991:77). This allows us to identify some of the suzanis in public and private collections, most of which arrived there without a provenance. The majority of

543
Embroidery (ruidjo?).
Ground: homespun cotton; embroidery thread: silk; technique: areas in basma, lines and contours in open chain stitch, partly couched.
L: 219 cm, W: 134 cm
Dzhizak
Museum für Völkerkunde, Berlin, Rickmers Collection 1902

544
Bridal bedspread (ruidjo).
Ground: homespun cotton; border trimmings ikat; embroidery thread: silk; technique: areas in basma, contours and lines in open chain stitch.
L: 244 cm, W: 138 cm
Kostakos (Tajik region of the Fergana Valley)
Museum für Völkerkunde, Berlin, Rickmers Collection 1902

542
Bridal bedspread (ruidjo).
Grund: part silk (warp reps); embroidery thread: silk; technique: chain stitch, border in open chain stitch.
L: 256 cm, W: 165 cm
Bukhara or Shahr-i Sabz

545 (following page, top left)
Suzani. A curious imbalance is produced by the naive but inspired ornamentation and the refined execution of the chain stitch work.
Ground: homespun cotton; embroidery thread: silk, wool; technique: chain stitch.
L: 228 cm, W: 164 cm
Bukhara (?)
Private collection, Karlsruhe

547 (following page, bottom left)
Suzani. Monochrome rosettes surrounded by semicircular wreaths and alternating with 'four lamps' motifs, the corners with women's amulets enclosing animal figures which also appear scattered across the entire decorative field.
Ground: cotton; embroidery thread: silk; technique: areas in basma stitch, contours in open chain stitch, partly couched.
L: 240 cm, W: 215 cm
Dzhizak
Museum für Völkerkunde, Berlin, Rickmers Collection 1902

546 (following page, top right)
Suzani.
Ground: homespun cotton; embroidery thread: silk, some wool; technique: areas in basma stitch, contours in chain stitch, couching, border lines in open chain stitch.
L: 238 cm, W: 182 cm
Ura-Tyube (Tajikistan)
Museum für Völkerkunde, Berlin, Rickmers Collection 1902

548 (following page, bottom right)
Suzani. The composition and techniques are typical of Shahr-i Sabz work. At the centre and along the borders are chahar cheragh motifs ('four lamps').
Ground: homespun cotton; border trimmings ikat; embroidery thread: silk; technique: areas in kanda khayal stitch, lines and contours in chain stitch.
L: 258 cm, W: 210 cm
Shahr-i Sabz
Museum für Islamische Kunst, Berlin

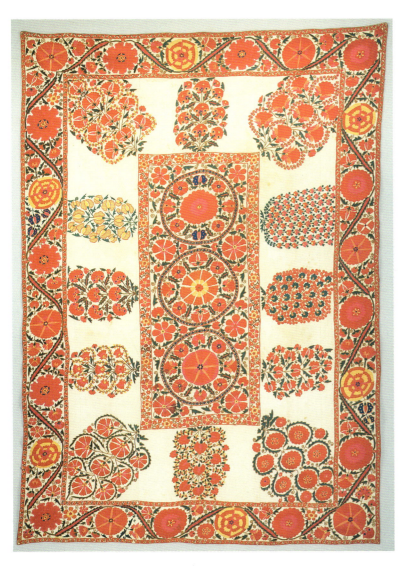

549 (top left)
Suzani. The centre bush on the right shows green blossoms and red scrolls, a design known from Nurata embroidery whose meaning is still unclear.
Ground: homespun cotton; border trimmings ikat; embroidery thread: silk; technique: areas in basma stitch, lines and contours in chain stitch and open chain stitch.
L: 232 cm, W: 171 cm
Nurata
Museum für Völkerkunde, Berlin, Rickmers Collection 1902

550 (top right)
'Flower blanket' (gulkurpa).
Ground: homespun (?) cotton; embroidery thread: silk, some wool; technique: areas in basma stitch, lines and contours in chain stitch.
L: 231 cm, W: 186 cm
Tashkent
Museum für Völkerkunde, Berlin

551
Wrapping cloth. Few such small embroideries survive; they were presumably used as long as possible before being discarded.
Ground: factory-made cotton; embroidery thread: silk.
L: 67 cm, W: 65 cm
Nurata

pieces, however, share characteristics from more than one locality or from styles not yet identified, and in that case ascriptions have to be based largely on experience and intuition, a procedure which may result in the postulation of intermediate or transitional styles and a geographical localisation somewhere between more securely defined centres of production. Where the present publication follows common practice and gives a provenance for a suzani, it should be kept in mind that in no case can this be stated with absolute certainty and that the given designation should be understood rather as a stylistic 'school' of embroidery.

It is even more difficult to date a suzani than to suggest a place of origin. A few broad bench-marks exist, e.g., the introduction of aniline colours to Central Asia in about 1880 which, however, did not immediately replace natural dyestuffs; or the use of cinnabar-red wool mentioned above roughly between 1850 and 1880, but here scholars disagree about the exact time-span. Industrially-produced white, coloured or patterned cotton from Russia for background fabric and lining seems to have come into use around 1880 as well, and it has been argued that domestically-produced coloured silks for the ground also first appeared about this time.

The condition of suzanis should not be taken as an indication of their age, since they were exposed to different situations of wear and tear and were frequently carefully stored like treasure. Heavy wear may have set in considerably later, e.g., after the item was sold to Europeans. It is generally agreed that the majority of surviving suzanis date from the second half of the nineteenth century. Recent opinion holds that even some eighteenth-century suzanis have survived. The view that suzanis are a purely nineteenth-century phenomenon is anyhow hardly convincing, since such an artistic achievement surely can only be the result of a long period of growth and development.

So far only three dated suzanis are known, one in a Tashkent private collection (Taube 1994:11), one dated A.H. 1146 (A.D. 1733/4; see Hali 78 [1994/95], p. 131) and one in the Berlin Museum für Völkerkunde (ill. 555). The latter bears a Persian/Tajik inscription at the lower right (ill. 557): "It was the era of Sayyid the Chosen, 1224 [A.D. 1809]".[1] Emir Sayyid (Haydar) of Bukhara ruled from 1800 to 1826. If we take the date as referring to the year of manufacture (possibly for the court) – and no other explanation would make much sense – then this piece represents a very early suzani from Bukhara. Furthermore it refutes the claim that coloured silk ground only came into use at the end of the century. Additional features suggesting a Bukhara provenance are the very fine chain stitch, the diversity of ornamental patterns and the variety of harmonious colours.

A roll-call of major centres of suzani production from west to east starts with Bukhara. The city produced a great variety of embroideries (making ascription more difficult), probably because it was the emir's residence, was situated at the junction of major trade routes, contained a very mixed population and was exposed to many influences. Among the main characteristics of Bukhara suzanis are the delicately worked chain stitch and a rich and sensitive use of colour.

Rosettes and palmettes are strongly articulated (ill. 555) and stems and scrolls remarkably delicate (ill. 539). The main border is usually quite wide and tends to give the decorated surface a rather broad format. Delicately-worked prayer mats (ill. 552) and mihrab-shaped arches even on bridal bedspreads (ill. 542) are regarded as typical examples of Bukhara suzanis.

Nurata embroidery typically shows colourful bushes with flowers of almost naturalistic appearance. They are arranged around a central star (ill. 551) or a rectangle (ill. 549) or may be scattered across the whole surface. Dividing the main panel by flower-studded trelliswork is typical of Nurata and also of Bukhara and Shahr-i Sabz. The relationship of such features to Persian and Mughal designs comes out more clearly in products from these three cities than from other centres of suzani manufacture. The bushes are loosely arranged across the whole decorated field, leaving empty much of the usually white background, and the colours are light and warm. The magnificent variety and thick scattering of blossoms on bushes diminishes at the end of the nineteenth century until only a few monotonous circles remain (ill. 535). Most Nurata suzanis are rather narrow with a narrow border, and are worked mainly in *basma* stitch.

Like Bukhara, Shahr-i Sabz is renowned for the high quality of its embroideries and riches of ornamental designs. Suzanis are usually worked in *kanda khayal* stitch, although *basma*, broad chain stitch (*yurma*) and half cross stitch (*iroqi*) are also used. Typical Shahr-i Sabz suzanis appear heavier than the examples discussed above, show stronger colours and have a wide border often decorated with asymmetrically arranged rosettes. The 'four lamp' motif (*chahar cheragh*) is quite common (ill. 548).

552 (opposite page, top)
Prayer mat (joinamaz), embroidery on ikat.
Ground: silk ikat; embroidery thread: silk; technique: chain stitch, border in broad open chain stitch.
L: 137 cm, W: 105 cm
Bukhara, late 19th century
Museum für Völkerkunde, Berlin

553 (opposite page, bottom)
Suzani. Embroidery on ikat showing two birds in the central field. A special feature is the use of red wool for the contours.
Ground: silk ikat, border edging ikat; embroidery thread: silk, some wool; technique: chain stitch.
L: 230 cm, W: 167 cm
Bukhara, late 19th century

554 (top) Suzani.
Ground: silk, border trimmings of cotton; embroidery thread: silk, wool; technique: areas in basma stitch, contours and lines in chain stitch.
L: 226 cm, W: 178 cm
Fergana, late 19th century

555 (bottom)
Suzani (detail). An inscription in the bottom right corner (see ill. 557).
Ground: silk, border trimmings in ikat; embroidery thread: silk; technique: chain stitch, narrow applied border in open chain stitch.
L: 204 cm, W: 186 cm
Bukhara, dated 1809
Museum für Völkerkunde, Berlin, Rickmers Collection 1902

Samarkand embroidery has a character mediating between the southwesterly and northeasterly areas of suzani distribution. The traditional design consists of large symmetrically arranged rosettes surrounded by a heavy crown of leaves, similar to that known from Shahr-i Sabz suzanis. Over time the features grew coarser and the colour spectrum more restricted until around the turn of the century a pattern became popular which showed a debased crown of leaves depicted as a spirally 'vine of the melon' in only three colours (red and black embroidery on a white ground; ill. 559). At the same time a completely new pattern was introduced of identical highly articulated bushes in alternating colours (ill. 536). Samarkand suzanis have very narrow borders and are usually worked in *basma* stitch.

Suzanis from Dzhizak, a small town between Samarkand and Tashkent, have a dominant pattern of monochrome rose-coloured rosettes formed by several concentric circles separated by a narrow space exposing the ground. The rosettes are surrounded by a crown of leaves open on two sides and slightly bent outwards; the corners show a triangular femal amulet (*tumar*) with pendants. The border is very narrow and extremely simple, since all that remains of the original wavy scroll motif are leaves pointing right and left in alternation (ills. 543, 547). The filling stitch is *basma*, while the contours are worked in open chain stitch and emphasised by the use of a thick black thread, a feature found throughout the northeastern part of the suzani area.

Typical Tashkent suzanis are almost entirely covered with predominantly red embroidery and show roundels inside the main panel and along the borders, remains of old cosmological symbols. During the nineteenth century the circle became ever larger until finally almost the entire surface was filled by a huge concentric pattern known as *ai palak*, 'lunar sky' (ill. 561). It is remarkable that despite the increasing density of the embroidery, quality has not deteriorated. Tashkent suzanis are almost square. Narrower *gulkurpa* (flower plaid) were meant to be hung on both sides of the ai palak in the wedding chamber (ill. 550). *Gulkurpa* are suzanis decorated with floral motifs and on first sight resemble Nurata embroidery, but differ in being less colourful, showing the *ai palak* motif and having much abbreviated flowering bushes. The filling stitch for Tashkent suzanis is *basma*, and contours are worked in open chain stitch for which a thicker thread is sometimes used, or in simple chain stitch. Closely related to the later version of Tashkent *ai palak* suzanis are those reputedly produced at Pskent further southeast which show large star motifs surrounded by geometric figures and are called *palak*, 'sky' (ill. 560). They are almost square and worked entirely in *basma*, with red and yellow predominating.

We know least about the suzanis from the Fergana Valley. The items said to come from there are a very motley lot and can seldom be attributed to an exact location, a rare exception being an embroidery from Kostakos, a Tajik settlement (ill. 544). Since the valley is inhabited by various peoples (Uzbeks, Tajiks, Kirghiz, etc.) and has been exposed since ancient times to the most varied influences, it seems likely that the numerous types of embroidery derive from different local and ethnic traditions, and need further research before one can say anything more precise. Features common to most suzanis from this area seem to be a somewhat loose *basma* stitch often on a coloured ground, and the use of a tightly spun or twisted thread. There are stylistic affinities to the northeastern types of suzanis (from Samarkand to Tashkent), although the embroidery is much less dense than on Tashkent and Pskent suzanis.

1   I am grateful to Siawosh U. Azardi and Dr. Johannes Taube for reading the inscription.

556 Suzani. Ground: silk, border in cotton; embroidery thread: silk, cotton; technique: areas in basma stitch, contours and border-line in chain stitch.
L: 165 cm, W: 145
Fergana or Kirghiz work (?), late 19th century

557 Detail from ill. 555. The inscription reads: "It was the era of Sayyid the Chosen, 1224 [A.D. 1809]."

558 (opposite page, top left)
Suzani. This standard design shows a regular arrangement of circular leaf scrolls surrounded by rosettes. Ground: factory-made cotton; embroidery thread: cotton; technique: basma stitch.
L: 262 cm, W: 215 cm Samarkand, late 19th/early 20th century

559 Suzani.
A typical feature of late Samarkand work is the restricted colour scheme and the transformation of the leafy scrolls around the rosettes into so-called 'scrolls of the melon plant'. Ground: factory-made cotton; embroidery thread: cotton, silk; technique: the areas in basma stitch, contours in chain stitch, border-line in kanda khayal stitch.
L: 316 cm, W: 250 cm, Samarkand, about 1900

560 (bottom)
Wall hanging called 'sky' (palak).
Ground: homespun cotton; embroidery thread: silk, wool, some cotton; technique: areas in basma stitch, contours and lines in open chain stitch.
L: 268 cm, W: 233 cm Pskent, about 1900 Museum für Völkerkunde, Berlin

561
Typical 'moon sky' (ai palak) embroidery. Ground: factory-made cotton; embroidery thread: silk; technique: areas in loose basma stitch, contours in chain stitch.
L: 223 cm, W: 211 cm Tashkent, about 1900 Museum für Völkerkunde, Berlin

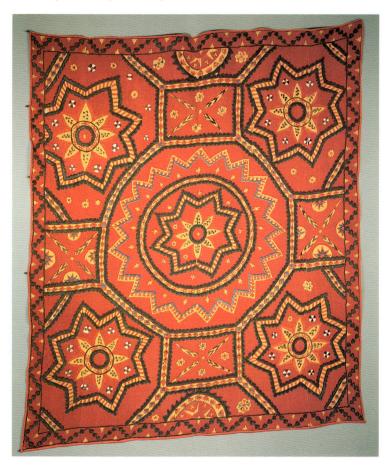

562
Large medallion suzani.
L: 262.0 cm, W: 168.5 cm
Uzbekistan, 19th century
Museum für Islamische Kunst, Berlin

Large Medallion Suzanis: An Essay in Interpretation

Gisela Helmecke

Among the large Central Asian embroideries known as suzanis there is one type which is particularly impressive and mysterious, the 'large medallion suzani'.

It takes its name from the eye-catching main design, a very large central medallion with an inscribed rosette and ray-like patterned stripes entirely covering the ground. On our example the medallion is in the shape of a hexagonal lozenge (182 x 122 cm; ill. 562) with four decorative bars. The corners are decorated with roundels encircled by curved elements. Small floral designs are scattered across the ground. A border (width 3-4 cm) with horn-shaped twin leaves provides the frame.

The embroidery gives a powerful impression. The strong colours, dominant central pattern and balanced composition are fascinating. One is immediately struck by its underlying harmony despite its many obvious irregularities and the absence of straight lines. Nothing is identical but everything is related and derives from an inner order which becomes intelligible on closer reading.

The composition is oriented on a central and a diagonal axis. The diagonally opposed motifs are matched: the corner rosettes, the rays of the main medallion, the corresponding bars. The composition ignores the arrangement to which almost all suzanis adhere, namely a large central area surrounded by a wide border.

A closer look also shows that the floral motifs usually dominating suzani designs here play a minor part. Instead both the composition and patterning rely mainly on abstract geometric shapes whose impact is slightly diminished by the abundance of ornamental filling and small subordinate motifs, but still clearly discernible and effective.

If we consider the structural features – the radial structure of the large medallion originating from the central rosette, the repetition of the interior motifs outside the medallion, the radial-axial symmetry suggestive of movement, and the border emphasising the unity of the overall composition – we cannot but realise the actuality of a grand underlying theme, a depiction of a world in motion, forever changing yet always remaining the same, and of a real and a mythic universe ruled over by the sun and the moon. We shall try to substantiate this concept by analysing certain patterns and structural aspects.

To begin with the composition of the large medallion: It is built up from clearly defined components which in our specimen, however, are not always easy to make out (ill. 563). From the rosette, formed by several rings with an outer circle of a double spiral, four straight lines and four diagonals emanate. These rays consist of a patterned central strip and two matching outside bands. Beneath the eight rays lies a round field, partly indicated by a zigzag line, partly by orange-red, slightly jagged oblique stripes following the curvature. On other large medallion suzanis this field is

uninterrupted and gives the impression of a glittering sun disc; it usually underlies the whole medallion, whereas in our example it is only partially visible. This second roundel sends out narrow rays with adjoining broad stripes which fan out towards the rim. Above the merlon border of the medallion a row of indigo horn-shaped double leaves provides a second edging. A wave-like pattern of double spirals acts as a frame for the overall central composition.

At first sight the filling designs appear to be geometric – straight and oblique bands, merlons, zigzags, lozenges, squares and triangles. But one soon discovers plant and animal motifs, blossoms and buds, leaves, leafy scrolls, paisley (ill. 565) and rams' horn motifs (see below). Along the strips terminating at the lozenge points one can recognize jugs and small birds. Since the rays are quite narrow, the more complicated and detailed motifs appear on the broader fanning stripes.

The basic structure of the central rosette with eight rays and the partially visible disc appears to symbolise the sun. A repeat of the rosette appears in two diagonally opposed corners with a border of whorls instead of double spirals. The latter edging, however, appears on the other paired corner rosettes representing a star design. The motif of the whirling, i.e. moving sun again appears as a small pattern. Remnants of ancient sun-worshipping cults have survived to this day in popular Central Asian beliefs where, for instance, images of the sun are said to protect against evil and all kinds of contamination (Snessarew 1976:158), and the sun is depicted as a circle or a whorl (Tschepelewezkaja 1991:86). In Tajik embroidery the sun provides something of a leitmotif, represented as a disc formed of several rings (as on our suzani) with a whorl border especially on embroideries from Ura Tepe on the northern approaches of the Turkestan mountains (Isaeva-Yunusova 1979:47, ills. 1, 3, 6). A floral version typical of Tajik suzanis shows the sun (oftob) as a single blossom or a rosette surrounded by other floral designs and known as yak lola (yak means tulip) (Isaeva-Yunusova 1979:47). This motif also appears on Uzbek embroidery. At a village near Bukhara a certain combination of flower and rosette was called oftob nuskha. In Samarkand the rosettes are called 'tulips', suggesting a shift of associations (on tulips see Tschepelewezkaja 1991:86).

Rosettes are not always interpreted as sun symbols. In Tashkent, for example, large rosettes are called 'moon' (oy), and the Tajiks identify a large ornament inscribed by a circle also with the moon (Belinskaya 1965: fig. 9/22). Thus the two corner medallions of rings might also be understood as representing the moon. In ancient cults the moon was associated with the cyclical renewal of the earth's and man's fecundity, with the female element in general and in particular with the calendrical speculations based on the motion of fixed stars and of great importance for agriculture.

A third complex of interpretations of the whorls, the rosette and the large central medallion itself focuses on the imagery of the wheel. This motif connects with notions of eternal return and perennial change and of the world as a disc with four heavenly corners represented by the image of a wheel with four spokes (Taube in Vok 1993:118-28).

563
Structural diagram of the large medallion.

Rudiments of all these archaic cosmological interpretations survived in Central Asia into modern times. We know that by the end of the last century, however, the embroideresses became less aware of the old associations or tended to supply new 'modern' explanations. To the Tajiks the rosette is also simply 'a flower' (Belinskaya 1965: fig. 9/9).

It would be wrong to consider every rosette or flower design a refashioning of astral or mythical symbolism. A case in point is the blue iris on our large-medallion suzani. Irises are among the easily recognisable plants and the embroideresses always identify them correctly (Tschepelewezkaja 1991:54). Another flower, sixfoil and as yet unidentified, appears on our suzani in two variants and indeed is found on all seven comparable suzanis (see below). The *boteh* (paisley) pattern is an interesting motif associated with fertility and creative powers in general. On account of its shape it is usually known in Central Asia as *bodom* (almond), while a more slender version is called *kalamfur* or *kalampir* (chilli), the terminology often varying from village to village. The significance and origin of this very widespread motif also found in Europe, have been much speculated about, but we still lack a definitve study. In Central Asia it is invested with apotropaic powers, and children of all ages as well as women in critical circumstances, e.g. during pregnancy, are given amulets of or with almonds and chillies. The alleged protective properties are presumably based on the heat of the plant and its bitterness, which taken in large quantities can verge on the poisonous (Tschepelewezkaja 1991:81).

The three-part merlon border is a very old and widespread Near Eastern framing pattern found also in Central Asian architecture, and on carpets from Asia Minor of the fifteenth and sixteenth centuries, the so-called 'Holbein' carpets. Various interpretations have been offered – for instance as symbolising Old Iranian deities (Herrmann 1990:138) – but they largely remain speculative. The motif often appears with leaf-like shapes or formed like a chalice, e.g. in Ottoman art.

Another prominent pattern is the rams' or wethers' horn motif. It appears in the shape of rows of double spirals along the border or in leaf-like shapes of two varieties along an applied border; as a minor pattern it can consist of single spirals or double leaves. The motif is likewise very old and is found from Siberia to Asia Minor, especially among Turkic peoples. The neighbouring Kirghiz and Kazakhs know it both as a major and minor element, while on suzanis – as on ours – it only appears along frames and borders. The motif and its variants are known under various names, all referring to 'horn' in one way or another. Vegetal variations are also known, for instance the Kazakh 'forked horn' reminiscent of the leaf-like variant on our suzani (Mukanov 1979: fig. 12m).

The motif is meant to represent the horns of a ram or wether and is supposed to protect against calamities and sickness. "The ram (*kuchkor*) was regarded as having magic powers. In families where the male offspring tended to die early, the new-born infant would be called '*kuchkor*' to protect him against evil spirits and ensure his survival. The Uzbeks of Khorezm used to keep a ram in their courtyard for protection against evil influences: They believed that the evil eye would be attracted to the animal's horns and thereby lose its potency" (Tschepelewezkaja 1991:84). For the same reason rams' skulls would be displayed at the gate, the entrance to the house or in the garden. They were also frequently used for ritual slaughter. It was a belief that could be accomodated with Islamic practice, where sheep and especially rams were among the most frequently sacrificed animals. This connection perhaps explains why in Central Asia the ram is also known as *rachmoni* (Tschepelewezkaja 1991:843) after Arabic *ar-Rahman*, 'the Compassionate', one of the Prophet's epithets.

There is a second line of interpretation about the rams' horn motif which argues that especially its spiral version is derived from the ancient cosmological symbol of the spiral and that it thus signifies the universe. The spiral is also a symbol of infinity which the Kazakhs interpret as perennial motion (Dzhanibekov 1982:25, ill. 28).

A small bird appears in each corner beyond the roundel. Although differently ornamented and patterned, they all show the slender, slightly curved shape typical of Central Asian embroidery. Three hold a leaf in their beak and have forked tails. Two in diagonally opposed positions wear a three-part head ornament depicting three feathers or a crown. One of the birds has a slight protuberance on its back, while another one with curved tail and feathery crest sits on one of the large medallion's points.

Like the sun and the ram's horn, the bird is a traditional and widespread Central Asian motif. In Old Turkish religion it was a symbol of the soul. As a soul-bird it acted as a messenger or mediator between men and gods. As such it was also regarded as bringing the water of life, just as it was associated with the tree of life. A mythical bird takes the gods' potion to the Chosen One, the ruler, a concept often met with in Indian mythology; the symbol of rulership might also be a diadem, a band of pearls or a crown. A bird with a string of pearls frequently appears in Old Iranian and Sogdian art. A bird with a leaf in its beak may well refer to this ancient imagery or to the tree of life; in any case its function is that of a messenger. Generally speaking, the bird is an auspicious symbol.

It is difficult to be more precise about what kind of bird it is. Sometimes a cockerel may have been intended. Among the Tajiks a motif resembling the shape of forked birds' tails is known as a cockerel's tails (Belinskaya 1965: fig. 8/42). A certain floral design on suzanis from Dzhizak is known as 'cockscomb' (*Tajik toyi khurus*). The plant allegedly had curative powers and used to be grown close to the house (Tschepelewezkaja 1991:83). In Islam, too, the cockerel – preferably a white one – is regarded as a good omen: he is the muezzin among the animals.

Jugs (*oftoba*, *aftaba*, *obtoba*) only appear in the main decorative field and play a minor role. They have the slender shape typical of such vessels from Central Asia and Persia, where they were used for washing one's hands. They are a symbol of water, and of the water of life in particular. We find jugs already in Old Iranian depictions, where they hold the tree of life, an image that was to pass into Islamic art and can also be found on prayer rugs from Asia Minor.

The last feature we shall attempt to elucidate are the several elongated shapes, sometimes called bars, with their interior ornamentation. The smaller ones also appear on standard suzanis and are called 'kitchen knives' (*kord-i osh*). Many cultures including Central Asian ones express a traditional belief in sharp and pointed objects as invested with the power to protect against calamities and evil spirits (cf. Tschepelewezkaja 1991:79-80). Objects made of metal and especially of iron are thought to be particularly efficacious. At the same time they are symbols of vitality. The interior decoration of these kitchen knives consists of oblique lines, zigzags and lozenges, while the border shows horn-shaped leaves or in the case of parallel bars, a row of pomegranates. The long bars on our suzani and others are very similar but their shape is as straight as a sword. Furthermore they are decorated at both ends with a 'pommel' in the shape of a pomegranate. These pommels can also be seen on the kitchen knives decorating other large medallion suzanis, although they are missing from our example. The framing border of our suzani also derives from the knife motif associated with vitality and protective properties, and thus 'protects' the whole design. What we have called the 'rays' of the large medallion basically have the same shape as the knives. This is no coincidence, since such lanceolate shapes inscribed within rosettes are called *tig* (blade, edge, head) on suzanis from Samarkand, Tashkent, Pskent and Shahr-i Sabz (Tschepelewezkaja 1991:79). The 'blades' sometimes have a filling decoration comparable to that on our suzani, including the small jugs which appear in two of the rays on our piece. All the interior elements of the 'sharp' motifs have been associated with water. The frequent use of blue colour seems therefore particularly appropriate. The oblique lines or 'teeth' of the central ribs of the rings accompanying the large rosettes found on Samarkand suzanis were known as *abr-i bakhor*, 'spring clouds' (Tschepelewezkaja 1991:86). Perhaps the expression implies a connection with rain and thus with fertility and at the same time with the ancient symbol for water, the snake (Taube in Vok 1994:53-54).

Water as a symbol of life and vitality fits in well with the conceptual field of the 'knife'. Also symbolising vitality and fertility is the pomegranate (*anor*). The tree of life is sometimes depicted as a pomegranate tree or branch. In pre-Islamic times it was an attribute of the goddess Anahita, and traces of this very ancient cult of the mother goddess, the river and fertility could be found in Central Asia, for instance in Khorezm, until modern times (Snessarew 1976).

Finally we draw attention to a very special ornament resembling a centipede, which is worked in light yellow silk and found among the leaves on one of the long sides (ill. 564). Its meaning – perhaps a magic symbol or the mark or signature of the embroideress – remains a mystery.

One of the difficulties of interpreting the underlying symbolism and significance of suzani designs is due to the fact that they were produced in the female sphere. Although male offspring were part of it from an early age and continued to move freely within the family compound so that they were familiar with much of it, certain concepts and talents were only passed on to daughters. In many cultures the female sphere acted as a keeper of traditions, which in the world beyond had lost much of their significance or changed their meaning. It was an area completely closed to males not belonging to the family. Now the first Western scholars to show an interest in the ethnography of Central Asia were invariably men, so that much of what were probably still living traditions known to women naturally escaped them. While many ancient patterns are even today preserved in the minds and work of the women of Central Asia, their older meaning has often been lost. Many ornaments have acquired new and more 'modern' interpretations, and at the same time entirely new motifs have evolved. This process has presumably always been at work, as for example the documented 'floralisation' of many motifs would suggest. The twentieth century, however, brought with it fundamental changes and disruptions to Central Asian societies, which also affected the spiritual life and the creative imagination of women. Large medallion suzanis must have had a special function about which we know nothing, as we are also totally ignorant about their origins. In technique and ornamentation they have affinities especially with embroideries from Bukhara, Shahr-i Sabz and Samarkand.

It seems that Russian and Soviet scholars never discussed this type of suzani. Even the most comprehensive work to date on suzanis (Chepelevetskaya 1960) fails to mention a single large medallion suzani (the identification of ill. 55 as a detail from a large medallion suzani remains tentative). In is only due to the existence of individual pieces in European and American collections and the fact that some of them reached the art market, that interest in this special type was aroused. We owe the first publication on these embroideries to two British art dealers who also coined the term under which they continue to be known (Franses and Pinner 1978).

It was clear already from this early article that although the group is rather small, several different varieties can be distinguished and also transitional examples connecting the group with other types of suzanis. By 1991 twenty-three large medallion suzanis had been recorded (*Hali* 57/1991:167). Only a few of them closely match our own specimen; they all show a large elongated hexagon at the centre with two bars at each end as well as four corner rosettes and a narrow border. Altogether eight companion pieces are known to the author:

1. Wher collection (Switzerland), 183 x 282 cm (185 x 280 cm) from a private collection in Münster (Germany); see *Hali* 1, no. 2 (1978):128, fig. 3; *Hali* 3, no. 4 (1981):314, ill. 1.

2. Munich, private collection; see *Hali* 5, no. 2 (1982):205.

3. Berlin, Museum für Islamische Kunst, on loan from the Johannes R. Becher-Archiv (Berlin), 168.5 x 262 cm, acquired in Central Asia; see Helmecke 1983:122, ill. 5.

4. Ex art market (Herrmann, Munich), 183 x 281 cm; see Herrmann 1990: no. 67.

5. Ex art market (Boswell, Wiesbaden); see *Hali* 60 (1991):60.

6. Ex art market (Nagel, Stuttgart), 163 x 260 cm; see *Hali* 61 (1992):37.

7. Ex art market (Loveless, London), 173 x 290 cm; see *Hali* 65 (1992):21.

8. Vok collection, Munich, 187 x 288 cm; see Vok 1994: no. 47.

Technical data
Measurements: c. 262 x 168.5 cm
Ground: plain cotton, 14/151 Z/Z, of differing strength and unevenly twisted (homespun), home-woven, six lengths of 26 cm each, one length of 127 cm, sewn together with cotton yarn, the two central strips with red silk thread.
Lining: lost (light blue silk threads on the back might have served to attach the lining).
Trimming: industrially produced white cotton band, edging the border on one long side, otherwise only on the back to take in the overlap.
Embroidery: domestic silk, slightly twisted, almost flat, but some parts strongly twisted; plain cotton, thick thread for one corner rosette; industrially produced twisted silk presumably indicating later restitching.
Technique: traces of preparatory drawing.
Filling: *basma* and chainstitch, some buttonhole stitch (probably later addition, only on one corner rosette).
Lines: chain stitch; stem stitch and split stitch for the mark on the border.
Remarks:
- nine weft threads of white cotton at regular intervals close to one vertical border on the back;
- the two centre strips were probably embroidered by one person, while the right and left strips of the large medallion were done by two different artists, one working mainly with red, blue, black and brown thread, the other using a variety of yellow tints.

565
Boteh pattern with coloured lozenge design.

564
Stitched mark, possibly relating to the embroideress.

566
'Bridal crown', diadem for hanging on the bonnet. Gilt silver set with glass stones and
baroque pearls, filigreed and engraved. The basic shape follows the line of the eyebrows. The
middle level decorated with a cock and teapot on both sides, probably symbols of hospitality
and fertility.
W: 16.6 cm
Bukhara, late 19th century
Private collection, Zurich

567
'Bridal crown', diadem for hanging on the bonnet. Filigreed and engraved gilt silver,
turquoises, glass stones on foil, baroque pearls, red and purple velvet.
W: 22.8 cm
Samarkand, late 19th century

Urban jewellery from Uzbekistan and Karakalpak jewellery
from Khorezm province are sparsely represented in museums
outside the former Soviet Union; private collectors have
likewise neglected this particular branch of craftwork. Only
two publications in Western languages contain a significant
number of pieces (Hasson 1987; Kalter 1983). A very
thorough survey was published in Russian, however, which
opens with an examination of prehistoric jewellery from the
first millennium B.C., analyses the jewellery depicted on the
Afrasiab wall paintings, gives examples of jewellery from the
Samanids to the Timurids and discusses the jewellery from
various Uzbekistan production centres according to the way
it was worn (Fakhretdinova 1988). I have organised this
chapter in the same way since it is almost impossible to
ascribe jewellery to specific regions, the exception being
Khorezm with jewellery from urban Khiva and the
Karakalpaks.

568 (top to bottom)
Segmented diadem of rectangular plaques, chased and gilt silver, corals and glass stones. W:
c. 39 cm. Samarkand or Bukhara, late 19th century. Private collection, Zurich
Segmented diadem, fire-gilt silver, turquoises, corals, sewn-on appliqué, openwork segments
in the shape of highly stylised human figures topped by double-headed eagles. W: 47 cm.
Khiva (Khorezm), late 19th century
Frontal jewellery, silk embroidery on cotton, sewn-on appliqué of silver elements chased in
matrices, gilded and in the shape of a rose-water bottle, glass beads and corals. W: 57 cm.
Northern Afghanistan, first half 20th century
Segmented diadem of kopecks (with dates between 1861 and 1911) joined by chains,
gilded, with pendent corals and globular silver elements. W: 56 cm. Bukhara or Samarkand,
about 1920

284

Silver jewellery was mainly produced by Tajiks and by Indians or Persians, the latter two also making rare gold jewellery. Jewellery was made at Bukhara, Khiva, Kokand, Samarkand, Shahr-i Sabz, Karshi, Tashkent, Margilan, Namangan, Andizhan, Urgench, Nurata and elsewhere – that is to say, at nearly every market town in modern Uzbekistan. Besides workshops situated in bazaars, there seem to have been whole settlements specialising in the craft like Zargarlik near Dzhizak and Gishduwan near Bukhara. More significant than a listing of the places of manufacture is probably the number of workshops at a given place. In Khiva in 1860 there were twelve workshops, while in Tashkent there were twenty in 1866 and fifty only a year later (probably due to a rise in demand by the city's Russian population), while by 1903 the number had sunk to forty. In 1870 there were twenty-three workshops in Samarkand and twenty by 1893, while Bukhara is said to have boasted perhaps as many as four hundred workshops in the early twentieth century (Fakhretdinova 1988:72-73).

Unfortunately, little is known about the source of the materials. In the case of silver, we are totally in the dark. It seems reasonable therefore to assume that as in most parts of the Islamic world, in Uzbekisan worn silver jewellery also was melted down and refashioned as were local coins and roubles of czarist times, both of high silver content. Gold was imported from the mountainous regions of Badakhshan in Afghanistan (Fakhretdinova 1988) or extracted in small amounts from the silt of the Zeruashan and the Amu Darya and its tributaries (Schwarz 1900). Turquoise is said to have been imported from Nishapur (Fakhretdinova 1988:57), although a German traveller mentioned indigenous deposits: "Turquoise is found in Turkestan in large amounts, although it is mostly of small size, pale blue or green and of inferior quality. Large stones of deep blue are relatively rare and thus quite expensive. Turquoise is quarried at many places, for instance in the Nuratau, the Bukan mountains and near the Jus-Kuduk well" (Schwarz 1900:404). Popular baroque pearls

569
Textile back ornaments, cover or sheath for the plait. On the left item, the most remarkable motif are the water jugs symbolising ritual purity and depicted in the upper third and at the bottom. The other two items are stylistically related to 18th-century Ottoman embroidery.
L (left to right): 156 cm, 133 cm, 142 cm
Turkestan, second half 19th/early 20th century

570
Plait jewellery, silk-covered cotton cord, silk tassels, silver fittings, glass beads.
L: 61 cm
Uzbekistan or north Afghanistan, late 19th century
Private collection, Zurich

571
Plait jewellery, silk cords and tassels, part-gilt silver fittings.
Eastern Turkestan, second half 19th century
Museum für Völkerkunde, Munich

572
Plait jewellery.
(Left to right) Cotton cord, enamelled silver, silk tassels. W: c. 55 cm. Bukhara emirate, about 1900
Cotton and silk cords fitted inside tubes of gilt silver, corals and turquoises. W: 38 cm. Bukhara, second half 19th century. Private collection, Zurich
Pair of temple or plait jewellery. Broché silk cords, chased gilt silver elements, corals, turquoises, the top in the shape of an 'endless knot'. L: 28 and 38 cm. Khiva (Khorezm), late 19th century

came from the Ottoman empire, emeralds from Egypt and rubies from Yemen. Coral was much used and although there is no documentation, it seems likely that it was imported from India. "The native silversmiths make much use of coloured stones but they are seldom genuine. Of genuine stones about the only ones used are turquoises, the favourite gem of Central Asia. Cornelian and agate mainly decorate silver-decked horse harnesses. All other coloured stones are either of Bohemian glass or simply consist of clear glass underlaid with a piece of coloured paper" (Schwarz 1900:399).

It has to be kept in mind that jewellery is not regarded as an item chosen purely for individual aesthetic reasons, but forms a group of types whose shape, material and design follow local and regional traditions, sometimes also indicating ethnic identity. Single items are not meant to be appreciated individually but as part of an ensemble. Ensembles are made up of frontal jewellery, temple jewellery, ear jewellery, plait jewellery, the occasional nose ring, necklaces, amulets or amulet containers either pendent or sewn onto clothing and matching pairs of armlets and finger rings; anklets are not usually worn. Among the neighbouring Turkmens the jewellery has a marked emphasis on the head, completely framing the face of the wearer.

573-576
Head-dress jewellery. Typical of this type of jewellery are the thin sheets of silver attached to a paste-like substance. The standard elements are gilt silver, glass stones over foil, on the top left item with cornelians, and invariably corals. The designs are filigreed and occasionally engraved. All late 19th century
(Top) Jewellery worn on top of the bonnet, c. 10.5 x 10.5 cm. Private collection, Zurich
(Bottom) Jewellery for the bonnet top of rare hexagonal shape. D: 13.5 cm
(Right, above) Jewellery for fastening to the bonnet, on the left in the shape of a highly stylised double-headed eagle (H: c. 18 cm), on the right of boteh shape (H: 15 cm).
(Right, below) Jewellery for a headband or to fasten to the bonnet in the shape of three combined botehs above a crescent. Khorezm, Karakalpak

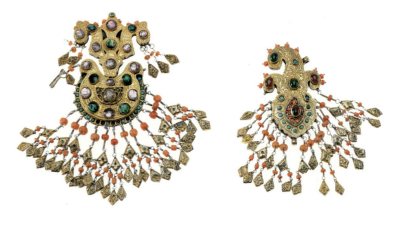

Khorezm jewellery

In terms of material, Khorezm jewellery presents a very uniform style. The basic material is extremely thin sheet silver, usually lightly fire-gilt. Corals and turquoises feature invariably. Coloured glass or glass on coloured paper might be substituted by cornelians. The surface is sometimes engraved but usually covered with exeedingly fine filigree work. Open-work filigree is applied to a background of sheet foil with a coloured mount (usually in red) or of silver-plated copper foil. Khorezm jewellery always comes with pendants on wires with corals and articulated lozenge-shaped leaves for the outer ring and pentagonal leaves set with turquoises for the inner ring. The most varied part of the ensemble are the items worn on the head. There are square and hexagonal headgears with *boteh* (paisley) motifs within a crescent, combined jewellery sewn onto the bonnet, double eagle heads or oval discs applied to the bonnet, curved amulets sometimes either including or surmounted by a triangular amulet (ills. 573-7). Both the shapes and combinations of the material suggest influences from northern India or Nepal. We know that trade relations between Khiva, the old Khorezm capital, and India still existed during the nineteenth century. The relevant literature is silent about any definite stylistic connections between the types of jewellery prevalent in Khiva and those in India or Nepal.

One of the strangest types of Khiva jewellery is an ensemble consisting of earrings, a tripartite necklace and temple hangings, which exemplifies the continous decorative line from head to chest typical of the region (ill. 582). Another unusual item in terms of material and workmanship is a back jewellery consisting of an upper section of filigree surmounted by double eagle heads and several rows of chains with unusually large and well-cut corals (ill. 579). The key-shaped pendent terminations have provoked Soviet scholars to speculate that these keys were both functional and symbolical and a reference to the control the housewife exerted over the chests and cupboards of the home. The shape of the keys, however, appears totally dysfunctional. Furthermore it would seem highly impractical if opening the chests necessitated taking off one's back jewellery. A more likely explanation for the keys would draw on their documented interpretation in neighbouring Iran and Afghanistan and regard them as symbols of the keys to paradise. It may be that Soviet scholars were discouraged from such an interpretation by the proclaimed atheism of their regime.

All these types of jewellery from Khorezm show a grotesque discrepancy between the work expended on them and the modest value of the materials involved. The only solid jewellery from Khorezm are heavy silver and fire-gilt armlets, cast and reforged and set with turquoises or glass (ill. 610).

Like the Uzbeks and Karakalpaks, the Turkmens constitute a important part of the population of Khorezm. Their jewellery has been the subject of several Western-language books published over the last twenty years; it was

therefore decided not to include it in the present discussion. We would like to mention a curious piece probably from Khiva, however, of an urban type and showing Turkmen influence. It is small heart-shaped plate like those worn by Turkmens on their back, with a typically urban decoration of interlacing nielloed scrolls and a central quatrefoil medallion ornamented with a design similar to a Greek cross, which symbolises the four points of the compass and the four elements (ill. 584). Turkmen amulet containers are often confused with those worn by Karakalpaks (ill. 600). The latter are shaped like a tube to hold texts from the Koran or prayers for protection, with projections and pendants. The floral motifs are chased – a technique never found on Turkmen jewellery – and/or lightly fire-gilt, and their simplicity and monumentality is more reminiscent of felt than of metal ornamentation.

577

Jewellery for fastening to the bonnet. Fire-gilt silver, glass beads, corals, on the left also a cornelian and mother-of-pearl disc (H: 13.5 cm), on the right filigree over foil (H: 14 cm). Khorezm, Karakalpak, late 19th century

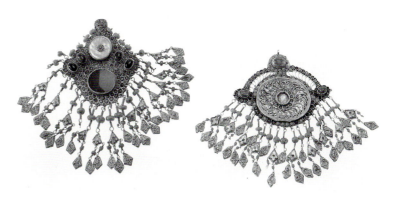

578

Amulets for attaching to the bonnet.
On the left a semicircular arrangement with two opposed triangles and a cylindrical knob reminiscent of an amulet container (H: c. 20 cm), and on the right an amulet (H: c. 12 cm).
Khiva (Khorezm), late 19th century

579
Pendant. Filigreed silver, chased and gilded, corals, glass beads. The top shows two versions of the double-headed eagle. The pendent keys were regarded as amulets symbolising the 'keys to paradise'.
L: c. 40 cm
Khiva (Khorezm), late 19th century

580
Necklace. Silver, appliqué of glass stones, some facetted, turquoise-coloured glass beads on bridges of cord wire and filigree, the linking chains with alternating rows of mother-of-pearl beads and corals. For this type of necklace the quality of the silver and craftsmanship is exceptional.
L: c. 43 cm
Samarkand, late 19th century
Private collection, Zurich

581
Jewellery set. Silver, partly fire-gilt, corals, glass stones, glass beads (pressed into a wax-like substance), mother-of-pearl. The frontal ornament, necklace and amulet container made in open filigree.
L: c. 22 cm (frontal ornament), c. 60 cm (necklace); W: 11 and 10 cm (amulet containers)
Bukhara, late 19th/early 20th century

582
Jewellery set consisting of earrings, temple hangings and a triple necklace. Silver, filigreed and fire-gilded, corals, turquoises, cornelians and glass stones; the plait hangings of silver globes in open filigree and triangular amulets at the end. The unusual type of jewellery includes ornamental elements occasionally found among the Tajiks of north Afghanistan, where they are completely of silver and of much inferior craftsmanship.
L: c. 42 cm
Khiva (Khorezm), late 19th century

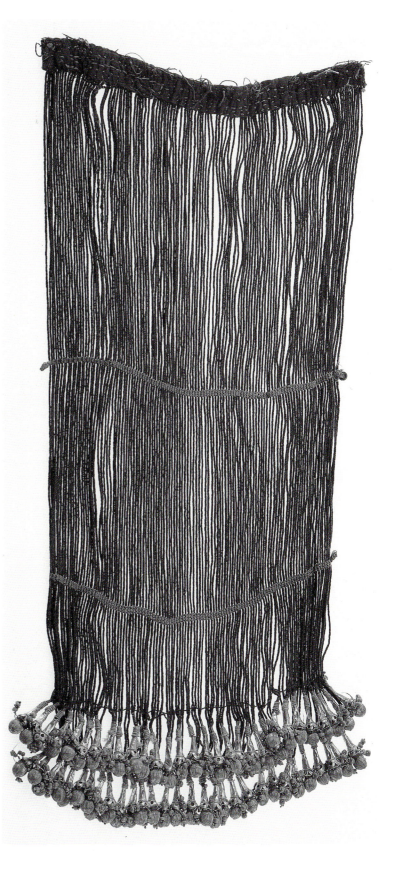

583
Necklace. Gilt silver, turquoises, corals, domed elements engraved and punched and set with turquoises.
L: c. 30 cm
Khorezm, late 19th century

584
Pendant (dorsal jewellery?). Nielloed and engraved silver, heavily worn border with pearl-and-reel pattern. The centre with a typical Central Asian quatrefoil motif. Such heart-shaped pendants are only known from Turkmen jewellery where nielloed silverwork, however, hardly exists at all and then only in partly gilded examples.
H: 7.5 cm
Khiva, Turkmen work, about 1880
Private collection, Sindelfingen

585
Veil. Cotton, silver, corals, silver-covered silk strings.
L: c. 54 cm
Khorezm, 19th century

586
Necklace with heart-shaped centre-piece, triangular terminations and rectangular plaques.
Enamelled silver, glass stones, baroque pearls, corals. Although this type of necklace is not
unknown, the present example is distinguished by the quality of its silver and exceptional
craftsmanship.
L: 46 cm
Bukhara, late 19th century

587
Necklace. Gilt silver, chased and filigreed, glass stones on coloured foil in a dog-toothed setting, blue glass beads. All linking chains with alternating rows of corals and mother-of-pearl beads.
L: c. 40 cm
Bukhara, about 1920

588
Necklace. Silver, corals, large glass beads, cast openwork silver pearls, flat circular silver pieces with imitation granules and corals.
L: 48 cm
Northern Afghanistan or Central Asia, Tajik, first half 20th century

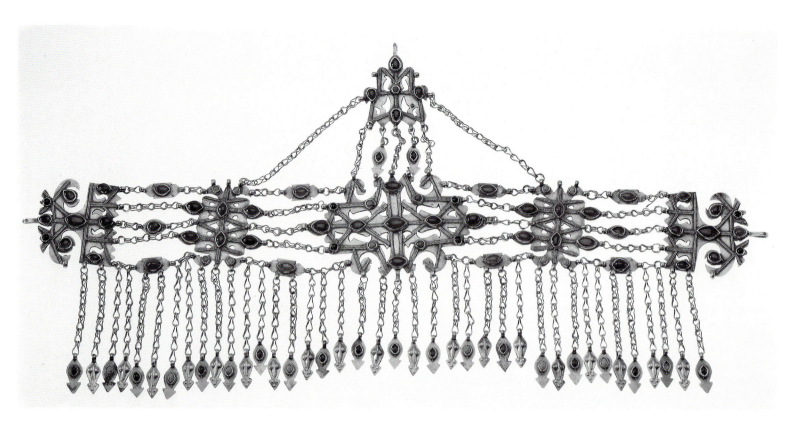

589
'Bridal crown', segmented diadem. Segments in openwork with wire bridges in appliqué, glass stones on foil, chains with fish-shaped pendants, three hooks for fastening to a bonnet.
W: 56 cm
Northern Afghanistan, made for rural Uzbeks, late 19th century
Private collection, Zurich

590
Diadem. Silver, imitation granules, glass stones, chain with lozenge-shaped pendants.
W: 22 cm (excluding neck chain)
Northern Afghanistan, made for rural Uzbeks, late 19th century

Frontal jewellery

From Bukhara, Khiva and Tashkent we know bridal crowns, their basic shape following the lines of the eyebrows, and worn attached to the bonnet (ills. 566-7). They are made of gilt silver and have mounts of vegetal shapes combined with circular or lanceolate medallions and a liberal sprinkling of turquoises and glass. The pendants are composed of chains interspersed with baroque pearls and terminating in almond-shaped chased elements. My earlier hypothesis that this type of jewellery was modelled on diadems from czarist Russia has to be abandoned. Meanwhile I have had the opportunity to examine early examples of this type, which lack mounts and simply consist of a curved band repeating the lines of the eyebrows even more emphatically than the illustrated items. This shape has no known prototype among Western diadems. More common than one-piece diadems are those with mutiple units (ill. 568 top). In Khiva they often show highly stylised human figures comparable to the Turkmen *adamlyks*, mounted double eagle heads and typical Khorezm pendants of pentagonal and lozenge leaves with coral (ill. 568 upper centre). From the Surkhan Darya and from rural Uzbeks living in northern Afghanistan we know cut and gilt silver ornaments chased on matrices in the shape of stylised rose-water bottles sewn onto a cotton band with silk embroidery (ill. 568 lower centre). The most basic diadems consist of gilt kopecks linked by chains and with Khorezm pendants (ill. 568 bottom).

Among the north Afghanistan Uzbeks are also found jointed diadems set with cornelians and turquoise-coloured glass stones obviously modelled on the bridal headwear of the Ersar or Yomud Turkmens, but also very simple types consisting of two rectangular elements surrounding a disc with openwork filigree and decorated with fake granules and applied glass (ills. 589-90). All the various types of linked diadems have something in common: They are either attached to the bonnet with a hook or sewn onto the clothing and have pendants in the shape of almond leaves, lozenges or fishes.

Plait jewellery usually consists of black or colourful silk tassels which in Bukhara are threaded through tubes of silver enamel or gilt silver and elsewhere of silver or gilt elements with alternating corals or pearls. Our pair of matching plait jewellery shows at the top a design in the shape of an 'endless knot', a Buddhist emblem of good fortune (ill. 572 right). This feature might be another indication of a relationship between Khorezm and Nepalese jewellery.

Temple and ear jewellery

A characteristic of traditional urban Tajik costume is temple jewellery with a crescent-shaped base and a merlon-like silver superstructure decorated with glass or cornelians and hanging chains with glass stones (ill. 611). A special design made for Bukhara's wealthy Jews consisted of rectangular temple ornaments of chased gold to be sewn onto the bonnet, with pendants of baroque pearls and decorative stones such as malachite, jadeite and topaz (ill. 597 left). In the Fergana Valley circular temple ornaments were produced,

591 Pendant. Silver, gilded, chased and engraved, turquoises, corals, iron. The key-shaped pendants symbolise the 'keys to paradise'.
L. ca. 30 cm Khorezm, late 19th century

592 Pendant. Engraved and granulated silver, glass stones. The exceptionally fine chain hangings terminate in chased globes. One of the chains terminates in a nail-cleaner.
L: c. 20 cm Bukhara, late 19th century

decorated with granulated beads and a medallion showing a dove to symbolise *baraka*, spiritual power and heavenly blessing; these were attached to the bonnet with hooks on long chains (ill. 613). The same location produced earrings with thin clips and three globes, presumably representing stylised fruit, either of openwork or chased and gilt (ill. 614 bottom). Throughout Uzbekistan and neighbouring Kirghiztan and Tajikistan one finds earrings of coarse openwork and hangings with coral (ill. 614 top left). From the city of Bukhara come earrings of various shapes with a turquoise-studded shaft terminating in a polyhedron set with turquoises, and from the emirate of Bukhara earrings in the shape of little baskets and with blue enamel inlay (ills. 612, 614). In all major cities in Uzbekistan one can find earrings in the shape of small baskets with crescent-shaped nielloed silver decoration and coral hangings terminating in bell-shaped ornaments (ill. 613 top). Earrings from Khorezm are easily identifiable by their glass stones surrounded by turquoises and hangings with alternating corals and pentagonal lozenge-shaped leaves.

Nose rings, invariably of gold, are much the same among the various peoples of Turkestan (ill. 596). Their lower part is set with baroque pearls and ornamental stones sometimes with a granulated gilt rosette at the centre.

593
Necklace. Gilt silver, glass stones, corals, wire fastening covered with silk cord. The necklace
was owned by the last emir of Bukhara.
W: 37 cm
Treasury of the Museum in the Ark, Bukhara

594
Earrings. Gold, malachites, topazes, baroque pearls, amethysts.
L: c. 8 cm
Museum für Völkerkunde, Berlin

595
Earring. Gold, filigree, granulate, gems. From the property of the last emir of Bukhara.
L: 11 cm
Bukhara, late 19th century. Treasury of the Museum in the Ark, Bukhara

596
Nose-rings. Gold, baroque pearls, gems.
D: 3.0-4.5 cm
Turkestan or north Afghanistan, late 19th/early 20th century

597
(Left) Pair of temple hangings. Gold, topazes, jades, baroque pearls. Made for Bukharan Jews. L: c. 13 cm (with hangings). Bukhara, about 1880
(Top right) Frontal jewellery. Filigreed gold, glass stones, pearls. L: c. 6 cm. Bukhara, late 19th century.
(Bottom right) Nose-ring. Gold, topazes, aventurines (?), baroque pearls, interspersed with granulated elements. L: 4 cm. Bukhara, second half 19th century.
Private collection, Zurich (the two objects on the right)

Amulets and amulet containers

In Bukhara, Tashkent and Samarkand the most common type are cylindrical amulet cases with openwork filigree and glass stone hangings and a triangular tab which is sewn onto the clothing (ills. 581). They are nearly always worn in pairs. Khorezm amulet containers with their triangular mounts are basically similar to those of the neighbouring Turkmens, but can be identified as from the region by their gilding, filigree, set stones and coral hangings (ill. 600).

Bukhara produced the greatest variety of amulet cases. Here we find polygon containers stylistically reminiscent of amulets from Herat with Koran inscriptions (ill. 598 top left). Their Bukhara origin, however, is indicated by the applied turquoises and traces of niello. The same applies to a rectangular container with nielloed rosettes and an interlacing scrollwork border. Among Tajik jewellery one also occasionally finds rectangular amulet cases with engraved and filigree design and fire-gilt inscriptions.

Only men wore octagonal containers on the upper arm which were designed to hold a miniature Koran and are sometimes combined with cylindrical cases (ill. 598). They can be chased, engraved or enamelled. Rather similar is the rectangular container to be worn on the upper arm which shows on the back an exceptionally fine enamelled floral decoration reminiscent of Indian prototypes (ills. 598 top left, 599). The back has a dark red glass stone with engraved Koran inscriptions; the only indication of its Bukhara origin are the inlaid turquoises in the stone's setting.

Necklaces and pendants

Since the late nineteenth century, necklaces in Uzbekistan have been of a fairly uniform type. Five to seven chains with corals, red glass stones and baroque pearls are linked by gem-studded silver plaques (ill. 581). The terminations are dome-shaped or almost triangular, while the plaques are square or rectangular. The central decorative element is sometimes heart-shaped or quatrefoil with attachments. In Bukhara the silver parts usually have blue enamel, while in all other urban centres they are richly decorated with glass stones and/or pearls and filigree (ill. 586). It seems that multi-string coral necklaces with silver globes embellished with fake granulate and silver beads alternating with glass beads were exclusively produced for Tajik customers (ill. 588). From Bukhara and Khiva cup-shaped pendants with hangings typical of the region are known (ills. 591-2).

598-599
Amulets worn on the upper arm.
(Top left) Enamelled silver, the main panel with flower sprays, the sides decorated with flowering plants, heart-shaped clasps in openwork. The back of deep red glass with engraved Koran quotations and invocations (cf. ill. 599). Setting with turquoises. W: 5 cm. Bukhara, 1880 or earlier
(Bottom left) Chased and enamelled silver. W: 5 cm. Bukhara, late 19th century
(Right) Combined amulet cases. Chased and engraved silver. W: c. 10 cm. Herat (Afghanistan), Tajik, about 1900

600
Karakalpak amulet containers. Pounced silver, with wire bridges or loop-in-loop chains, cornelians in plain setting on the rectangular containers.
W: 22.5 cm (object on the left)
Khorezm, second half 19th/early 20th century
Private collection, Zurich (bottom right only)

601
Amulets.
(Top left) Rectangular amulet container. Nielloed silver, central roundel with epigraphic design and surrounded by scrolling spirals, border with interlacing scrollwork. W: 12.9 cm. Bukhara, late 19th century
(Bottom left) Three-part amulet worn on the upper arm. Nielloed silver, main design a quatrefoil medallion, the sides with leafy sprays. W: 12.5 cm. Bukhara, about 1880
(Right) Rectangular amulet container. Engraved and filigreed silver, fire-gilt inscription. Hanging with chased gilt pendants and mother-of-pearl beads. W: 11 cm. Turkestan or northern Afghanistan, made for Tajiks, second half 19th century

602
Triangular amulet containers. Gild and engraved silver, corals, turquoises and glass stones, the filigree over coloured silvery foil.
W: 9-13 cm, L: c. 43 cm (amulet with chain)
Khorezm, late 19th century
Private collection, Zurich (top right only)

603
Young Uzbek woman wearing a pair of cylindrical amulet containers, about 1900.

Bracelets and finger-rings

The most sophisticated examples invariably come from
Bukhara. These were pairs of bracelets with hinge and
cotter. They are of partly gilt openwork and have square or
rectangular enamelled clasps. The most common decorative
design consists of interlacing leafy scrolls, although items of
superior quality may also show enamelled roundels or
quatrefoils. The cotter pin is secured with a short chain with
corals. Finger-rings are very rare in our collections. This was
probably because they were the first to be replaced by gold
rings. The bezels are normally set with red and blue glass
stones or with alternating cornelians and turquoises or
sometimes with a single cornelian (ill. 606).

604
*Amulet container with triangular wire hanger. Silver, open filigree, appliqué of small silver
discs chased in matrices and gilded; hangings with corals, glass beads and press glass.*
W: 11 cm Bukhara, about 1900 Private collection, Zurich

605
*Amulet container. Cast silver, openwork, punched and engraved, turqoise inlay. The design
of the hexagonal case shows alternating bands with inscriptions and geometric motifs.*
W: 8.6 cm Bukhara, mid-19th century

606
*Tajik finger rings. Silver appliqué with glass stones, turquoises, corals and cornelians; the
design variously filigreed, granulated, engraved and pounced.*
D: 2.0-2.2 cm
Northern Afghanistan or southern Uzbekistan, late 19th/early 20th century
Private collection, Zurich

607
Jewellery for sale at a silversmith's in the bazaar. Bukhara, about 1900.

608
Bracelets.
(Left to right) Silver, partly fire-gilt, openwork. Silver, V-shaped design between astragals, enamelled clasp. Enamelled and openwork silver.
W: 2.8-4.5 cm, D: 6.0-6.6 cm
Bukhara, 1880s

609
Bracelets from the property of the last emir of Bukhara. Silver, fire-gilt, enamelled, openwork. Clasp with cotter pin similar to those in ill. 608; here the pin is secured by a chain with corals.
W: 3.5 cm, D: 7.0 cm (left); W: 3.5 cm, D: 6.0 cm (right)
Treasury of the Museum in the Ark, Bukhara

610
Bracelets. Cast silver, additional forging, fire-gilt, turquoise inlay.
W: 2.0 cm, D: 7.5 cm
Khiva (Khorezm), 19th century

611
Temple hangings. Chased silver, loop-in-loop wire chains, glass stones and corals. The shape combines a pannier and merlon.
L: 16 cm
Northern Afghanistan or Central Asia, Tajik, late 19th/early 20th century

612
Jewellery from the Bukhara emirate.
(Left to right) Pair of earrings; silver, enamelled, cut and engraved. L: 11 cm. Pendant; silver, engraved and pounced, traces of enamelling. The design is related to the Turkmen motif of small human figures (adamlyk). L: 7.6 and 9.3 cm
Late 19th century

614
Earrings.
(Top left) Silver, filigreed and granulated, corals and coral pendants. During the first half of the 20th century, this type could be found throughout Uzbekistan. L: 8.2 cm
(Top right) Silver, granulated and engraved, turquoises. H: c. 6 cm. Bukhara, second half 19th century
(Bottom left): Cast silver, openwork, granulated, glass stones. The globular elements may represent pomegranates. L: 7.8 cm. Northern Afghanistan or Herat, late 19th century
(Bottom right) Gilt silver, chased and engraved, traces of a red-coloured setting, glass stones. L: c. 5.5 cm. Fergana Valley, late 19th century

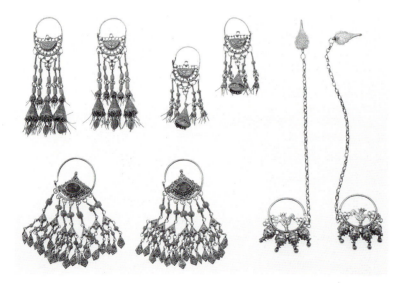

613
(Top) Two pairs of earrings. Silver, nielloed, chased and filigreed, corals, bell-shaped pendants with glass stones as clapper. L: 12 and 9 cm. Bukhara, about 1900
(Bottom left) Earrings. Gilt silver, turquoises, corals, faceted glass stones over foil. Decorated on both sides. L: c. 12 cm. Khiva (Khorezm), late 19th century
(Bottom right) Earrings. Cast silver, openwork, engraved, with a chain for attaching them to the bonnet, design of a bird inside the ring. L: 27.5 cm (with chain). Herat (Afghanistan), Tajik, early 20th century

615
The young woman wears the complete ornate wedding jewellery typical of wealthy city dwellers.
Bukhara or Samarkand, late 19th century

616-617
*Belt and clasp (detail). Leather covered with velvet and gold brocade embroidery in the
Ottoman style. Fittings: fire-gilt silver, enamelled and nielloed. Sewn-on pouch with design
of a flowering tree in a vase. This is among the most excellent 19th-century examples of
Bukharan silverwork.*
Belt, L: 63 cm (closed); buckle, L: 19 cm, H: 11 cm
Last third 19th century
Museum in the Summer Residence, Bukhara

618

Men's belts from Bukhara.

(Top) Silk embroidery on cotton, buckle and rosette-shaped fittings of fire-gilt silver, chased, engraved and enamelled. L: 51 cm (closed), W: 10 cm. Private collection, Zurich

(Centre) Silk velvet on leather, buckle with cotter pin, nielloed and enamelled silver, fittings of nielloed silver. L: 45 cm (closed). Private collection, Zurich

(Bottom) Originally silk velvet, now worn down to the ground layer, buckle and fittings of nielloed and enamelled silver. L: 38 cm (closed)

Bukhara, 1860-80

619

Belt buckles from Bukhara.

(Top) Openwork silver, engraved, enamelled and nielloed, partly fire-gilt. L: 17.0 cm, H: 9.5 cm. Bukhara, about 1880. Private collection, Zurich

(Left): Openwork silver, engraved and nielloed, oval clasp with lacquer inlay. L: 16 cm, H: 9 cm. Bukhara, about 1860

(Right) Openwork silver, engraved and nielloed. The colour scheme of the enamels suggests Russian influence. H: 10 cm. Bukhara, early 20th century

Belts

Instead of belts, the common people wore sashes of the same cut as turban wraps. Broad leather belts, usually covered with silk velvet and studded with heavy silver ornaments, were restricted to men of high standing. Illustrations in nineteenth-century travel books frequently show such belts worn by noblemen, high court officials and officers (ill. 621). Belt fasteners and fittings were therefore both in terms of weight and craftsmanship much superior to other silver jewellery of the region and show what the workers were capable of producing for their high-ranking clients. The wide fasteners usually had a lacquered border sometimes done in openwork and were enamelled and/or nielloed with occasional fire-gilt. The most common design consisted of fine scrollwork often interspersed with blossoms. A belt fastener made in czarist times and embellished with enamel in rare white, green, light blue and red shows in addition a design of flower sprays (ill. 619 bottom right). The fittings include discs sometimes in openwork and with a flower border, as well as quatrefoil shapes and S-shaped hooks. Only in Bukhara were turquoises sometimes used to decorate the discs or line the fasteners (ill. 624). From the Uzbeks of northern Afghanistan comes a belt with a fastener with gold overlay and pockets decorated with sumptuous silver openwork (ill. 620 top). Gilt and nielloed silver belts with rectangular members and chunky buckle fasteners are known from Khorezm; they show stylistic and technical affinities with belts from the Caucasus (ill. 620 bottom).

The most magnificent example comes from the treasury of the last emir of Bukhara (ills. 616-7). The red velvet belt is embroidered with tulips. The embroidery suggests Ottoman influence and is of a kind occasionally found on objects formerly owned by persons connected to the Bukhara court. The execution of the scrollwork, especially on the fastener, is equal to the best Timurid productions.

A belt clasp with baroque scrolling and relief decoration with colourful underlay probably was made at Herat in about 1900 for Tajik customers (ill. 622).

Jigits (grooms or pages attached to a noble household) wore colourful belts entirely covered with silk embroidery and silver appliqué, to which knife-pockets and embroidered pouches were often attached (ill. 623). Similar belts, only differing in size from those of the *jigits*, were worn by women. From northern Afghanistan come embroidered belts with fasteners in very fine openwork and often with epigraphic decoration (ill. 626 bottom). The basic plate is made of iron frequently covered with sheet silver coated in red, and the openwork cover of brass.

To Western eyes, jewellery seems to have been the area of Turkestan's material culture most difficult to appreciate, and it was the last to catch the interest of scholars and collectors outside the former Soviet Union. After some acquaintance with the material one realises, however, that in the use of colour, delicate modelling of details and choice of designs it is a direct reflection of urban culture. Once acknowledged to form an integral part of ethnic life and culture of the region and its peoples, Turkestan jewellery will have to be accorded its rightful place in all future research.

620

(Top) Leather belt with a narrow and a broad pocket on each side decorated with openwork cast silver appliqué. The fastener with cotter pin and gold inlay. L: 42.5 cm (closed). Herat or Bukhara, Tajik, first half 19th century. Private collection, Zurich

(Bottom) Articulated silver belt, nielloed and gilded, the segments attached to a leather ground, semicircular buckle with petalled rim. L: 42 cm (closed). Khorezm, late 19th century. Private collection, Zurich

621
Reception of Russian officers at the Bukhara court. The emir and high court officials all wear broad belts with silver fittings. Only members of the urban upper class were allowed to wear such belts.

622
Belt buckle. Silver, cast relief decoration over foil and riveted to the ground, engraved border.
W: 6.7 cm
Herat, made for Tajiks, about 1900
Private collection, Zurich

623
*Belt worn by jigits (grooms or attendants). Silk embroidery on cotton
with little bags and sheaths, the buckle of chased silver with turquoises.
Belt, L: 51.0 cm (closed); buckle, H: 8.5 cm
Turkestan, late 19th century*

624
*Belts and buckles.
(Top) Two-part buckle, thin gilt silver-foil, chased and attached to paste ground,
turquoises on the copper ground. W: 17.4 cm. Bukhara, 1880-90
(Left) Nielloed silver, partly fire-gilt, engraved and pounced.
W: 7 cm. Bukhara, 1880-90
(Right) Enamelled silver, partly gilt, engraved, turquoise inlay.
W: 9 cm. Bukhara, about 1880*

625
Men's belt with sheaths. Silk embroidery on cotton, the small pocket of leather
with a silk-embroidered front on cotton.
Belt, L: 81 cm, W: 10 cm; pocket, H: 14 cm, W: 19 cm.
Northern Afghanistan, made for Uzbeks, early 20th century

626
(Top) Belt of silk embroidery on cotton with silver appliqué. L: 54 cm (closed).
Northern Afghanistan, late 19th/early 20th century
(Bottom) Leather belt with cotton covering and silk embroidery.
Buckle of openwork brass with epigraphic design over foil.
L: 42 cm (closed). Herat, late 19th/early 20th century

627
Belts. Silk embroidery on cotton, some silver appliqué.
L: 69-100 cm, W: 7-10 cm.
Northern Afghanistan or Turkestan, late 19th/early 20th century

628
Coppersmith in the bazaar at Bukhara, about 1900. With the Islamic conquest, Bukhara became the centre for metalwork in Turkestan.

Turkestan Metalwork of the Seventeenth to Nineteenth Century

Johannes Kalter

During the period under discussion, tin-plated copper was by far the most common material in both Safawid Iran and Ottoman Turkey. In Central Asia just the opposite was the case, tin-plated copper being the exception, and brass the standard material, although cast bronze was also occasionally used. The earliest examples in our collection are a bowl with animal figures, Buddhist 'endless knots' and bold floral motifs (ills. 188-90) and an exceptionally tall (49 cm) vessel obviously used for cooking (ills. 633-4). The design is arranged in horizontal bands. Such roundels with star flowers along the neck and the quatrefoils on the shoulder are known from seventeenth-century local architectural decoration.

The most frequent type of vessels made of tin-plated copper are vase-shaped containers with a narrow shoulder and slightly everted neck, the design often consisting of vegetal motifs covering the whole body except for the base, although ornamentation may be restricted to the neck area. Some examples are inscribed in elegant *taliq*. It is noticeable that on tin-plated pieces of the eighteenth/nineteenth century the surface decoration shows a marked tendency towards the baroque. Earlier examples are either only partly decorated or where the decoration covers the entire surface, the designs are very boldly displayed. A bucket from the eighteenth century is completely covered with leafy flower scrolls, and only the severely geometrical trefoil border around the neck gives a hint of earlier decorative styles of Central Asian metalwork (ill. 652). The same applies to one of the rare examples of copper teapots (ill. 640). The design is heavily influenced by Kashmiri wares and seems more appropriate for carpets than for metalwork. The neck is decorated with bands of plants and cartouches and of scrollwork; further down diagonal bands are filled with flower scrolls. The body shows a broad band of flower sprays and the lower part a dense pattern of single blossoms. Such overall floral ornamentation is typical of nineteenth-century Kokand products. A masterpiece of the same provenance is the samovar with heavily emphasised ribs filled with bold blossoms among vine scrolls (ill. 651 right). A faint echo of a metal design dating from the Middle Ages can be noticed on a flat cup (kept in a leather case) acquired by Rickmers in Bukhara in the late nineteenth century (ills. 645-6). The base is decorated on the inside with a riding scene framed by an abbreviated interlacing scroll, and on the outside with the figure of a demon riding an elephant.

629-630
Pouring vessel. Tin-plated copper, chased and engraved, on the top and bottom rim a frieze of epigraphic cartouches in naskhi, on the body interlacing medallions with scrollwork. The spout with interlacing bands of foliate scrollwork and merlon-shaped elements on the underside. H: 12.5 cm, L: 33.5 cm (with spout) Herat (?), 15th century

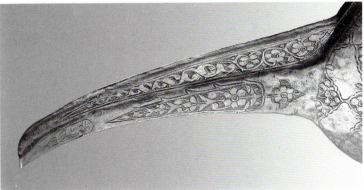

631-632
Pouring vessel. Tin-plated copper, chased and engraved. The spout decorated with a flowering scroll. The main decoration is arranged in horizontal bands showing in alternation lozenges and eight-pointed stars with trefoil flower sprays. On the bottom a much-worn stamp of the workshop and/or owner dated A.H. 1208 (A.D. 1793). The same date together with a name ('Khan' or 'Khaqan Husain') within a cartouche is engraved on the underside of the spout. H: 11.8 cm, L: 31 cm (with spout) Bukhara, dated corresponding to 1793

633-634
Shoulder pot. Tin-plated copper, engraved. Assembled from two sections, reinforced lip.
Design arranged in horizontal bands. The lip with leafy flower scroll, the neck with roundels
enclosing star-shaped blossoms between two bands with flowering scrollwork. The shoulder
decorated with bracket-shaped quatrefoils enclosing blossoms and alternating with cartouches
filled with plant motifs. The decorated surface terminates in trilobed pendants. The lower
half blackened by fire, so the vessel was presumably used as a cooking-pot. The leafy
flowering scrollwork and trilobed pendants (see detail) continue Timurid traditions. The
rosettes within roundels along the neck also appear on contemporaneous architecture.
H: 49 cm
Turkestan, 17th century

635-636

Teapot. Chased brass, cast handle and knob on lid. The beaded bottom of copper. The sides decorated with an almond-shaped medallion in repoussé work surrounded by unusually fine engraved interlacing scrollwork. The front with a trilobed pendant (see detail).
H: 27.5 cm
Bukhara, 17th/early 18th century

637
Bowls. Tin-plated and engraved copper. The type of bowl on the right is discussed in "Is there a distinctive Central Asian type of Islamic art?".
(Left) H: 11.0 cm. Turkestan, 17th/18th century
(Right) H: 13.5 cm. Bukhara (?), late 16th/early 17th century

638
Vase-shaped sherbet containers. Tin-plated copper, chased and engraved, floral designs.
(Left) Epigraphic frieze in naskhi around the neck interspersed with clematis blossoms. Turkestan, 17th/18th century
(Centre) Turkestan, late 18th century
(Right) Exceptionally sparse decoration, owner's inscription within a cartouche. Turkestan, 17th century
H: 12-13 cm

639
Bowl. Copper with traces of tin-plate, black lacquer inlay, chased, turned and engraved. The rim with highly stylised flower motifs. Between medallions with floral designs a cartouche with the owner's name ('Khan'?).
H: 15 cm
Bukhara, 17th/18th century

640
Teapot. Tin-plated copper, chased and engraved, the handle cast brass. The dense floral design was presumably inspired by Kashmir metalwork. The lid is probably a replacement.
H: 23.2 cm
Northern Afghanistan or Bukhara, mid-19th century

641
Covered vessel. Tin-plated copper, brass, asphalt.
H: 16 cm
Bukhara, late 19th century
Museum für Völkerkunde, Berlin, Rickmers Collection

642
Casket. Tin-plated and engraved copper, brass, asphalt.
H: 10.5 cm, W: 17.0 cm
Bukhara, late 19th century
Museum für Völkerkunde, Berlin, Rickmers Collection

643 Cover of a food bowl. Engraved brass, the knob terminating in a large rooster. Turquoise appliqué.
D: 21.5 cm Bukhara, early 19th century Museum in the Ark, Bukhara

644 Dish-cover. Copper with traces of tin-plate, engraved.
D: 33 cm Bukhara, 18th/19th century Museum in the Ark, Bukhara

645-646 Drinking cup. Copper with traces of tin-plate, engraved. The well with the figure of a horseman, the bottom showing a demon riding an elephant.
H: 4 cm, D: 14 cm Bukhara, 1890s Museum für Völkerkunde, Berlin, Rickmers Collection

647-648

Teapot. Cast brass, engraved and with openwork lid. Glass stone on both sides, riveted medallions in dog-tooth setting. The geometrical network of floral scrolls along the neck, the interlacing scrollwork on the sides, the trilobed terminations of the body and the spiral scrolls around the foot (see detail) all echo the best of Timurid traditions. This is the largest and most carefully executed teapot known to us.

H: 46.5 cm

Bukhara, late 18th/early 19th century

Hookah. Brass, chased and turned, turquoise appliqué. Mouthpiece and connecting section of wood turned on the lathe.
H: 78 cm
Bukhara, 18th century

Hookah vase. Bottle-gourd with brass mount, engraved, turquoise appliqué.
H: 39 cm
Bukhara, late 19th century
Museum für Völkerkunde, Berlin, Rickmers Collection

651
Samovars. Tin-plated copper, openwork and engraved, the handle of cast brass. The exceptionally fine lotus decoration on the ribs of the vessel on the right as well as the bold flourish of the ornate handle with stylised dragon heads suggest Bukharan work of the second half of the 19th century. This samovar in particular suggests that the lamentations of many visitors at the time about the deterioration of Bukharan metalwork were exaggerated. The support is an ill-fitting replacement.
H: 28 cm (left), 30 cm (right)
(Left) Northern Afghanistan, late 19th/early 20th century
(Right) Bukhara, second half 19th century

653-654
'Magic bowls'. Cast brass, engraved. Such bowls were used for invocations benefitting the sick "with God's help", as the inscriptions phrase it, a custom of long standing in Islamic medicine.
14th century (top), 18th century (bottom); acquired by Rickmers in Bukhara
Museum für Völkerkunde, Berlin, Rickmers Collection

652
Bucket. Bronze, copper, traces of tin-plate, chased, turned, engraved, cast handle. The trilobed scroll along the neck and the epigraphic frieze interspersed with bracket-lobed quatrefoils suggest the bucket was made in Turkestan in the late 18th/early 19th century.
H: 19 cm

655
Teapots.
(Left) Copper with traces of tin-plate, chased and engraved. Handle and finial of cast brass. H: 32.5 cm. Bukhara (?), early 19th century
(Centre) Copper, brass, glass beads, cast, chased and engraved. H: 31.0 cm. Bukhara (?), mid-19th century
(Right) Cast brass, copper bottom, silver appliqué, engraved, pounced and filed. H: 31.5 cm. Bukhara, early 19th century.

656-657
(Left) Ewer. Cast and engraved brass. The shape and style of floral ornamentation suggest western Uzbekistan or neighbouring Iran as the place of origin. Acquired in Bukhara. H: 35.0 cm. Second half 19th century
(Centre) Ewer. Cast and engraved brass, the handle with the signature of the craftsman, "'amal Hadji Ruzi"(?). H: 35.5 cm. Bukhara, late 19th century
(Right) Teapot. Brass, chased, engraved and openwork. The flattened sides, almond-shaped medallions with lotus blossoms and leafy scrolls and the bold lotus scroll along the foot (see detail) are typical of ewers from Kokand.
H: 36.0 cm
Kokand, first half 19th century

658
Teapot. Brass, cast, chased and engraved. The floral design around the neck and the trilobed terminations along the strongly ribbed bulbous body are related to the ewer in ills. 647-48. With date and maker's signature.
H: 34.2 cm Bukhara, 18th century

321

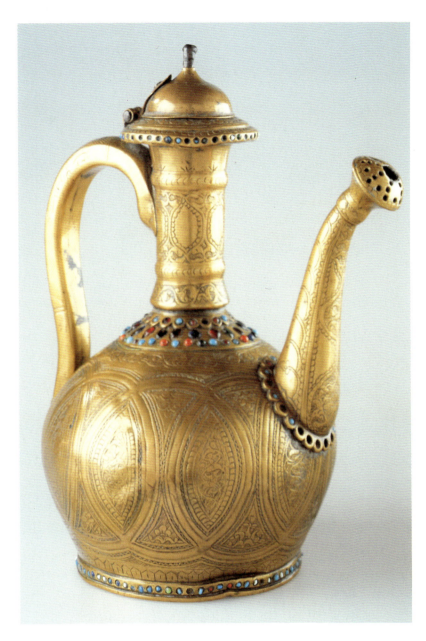

659-660
Ewer. Brass, chased and engraved, glass inlay, the spout decorated with a tree of life (see detail).
H: 23 cm
Karshi (Bukhara emirate), dated A.H. 1284 (A.D. 1867)

Typical examples of eighteenth/nineteenth-century metalwork

Nineteenth-century travellers have very little to say about the workshops and work methods of coppersmiths. A description of the Bukhara bazaar, for instance, contains only cursory information: "The carpet bazaar is one one the strangest sights and not to be missed. Here one will find every variety of this versatile article from the modest felts of the nomads to the most luxurious specimens. Not far away lies the noisiest bazaar of all, that of the boilermakers, where the various items of their trade are produced accompanied by a most terrifying din" (Moser 1888:165). Von Schwarz, who is usually a very careful observer, provides only slightly more detail. He mentions that coppersmiths are nearly as numerous as blacksmiths, and lists their products: "The native coppersmiths use both brass and copper to make *kungans* (teapots), wash-basins, circular trays, oil lamps,

hookahs, bowls, camel bells, etc." (Schwarz 1900:397f.). His remark that they did not make new samovars but only repaired old Russian ones, is not quite true, as examples from our collection show. After discussing the tinning of copper vessels and the popularity of engraved decoration, von Schwarz writes in conclusion: "The coppersmiths, who are always very well represented in the bazaars and make a tremendous noise with their incessant hammering and beating, usually work alone or at most with an apprentice. Therefore their stock is very limited and only a few pieces tend to be on offer right inside the workshop. Here again the artisan as a rule specialises in one particular type of ware" (von Schwarz 1900:398). The statement about the modest supply is a bit astonishing, because photographs of shops made in the 1880s and '90s quite often show a rich and varied stock of metalware. Von Schwarz also fails to mention that the metal workers specialised in separate stages of the

production process. The rather meagre amount of information given by Moser and von Schwarz is representative of nineteenth-century travel literature in general, the reason presumably being that the coppersmiths's craft was so much taken for granted by contemporary observers that it did not seem to require extended discussion.

As for the division of labour, it seems that some craftsmen specialised in producing basic forms in copper and brass and tinning them, while others cast attachments like handles, finials for covers, spouts and terminations, hinges, etc., and others again did the embossing and engraving (Westphal-Hellbusch 1974, quoting Abdullayev 1970).

661
Wash-set consisting of a ewer and wash-basin with removable sieve. Cast brass, chased and engraved, turquoises, the ewer turned. The almond-shaped medallions with floral designs and the decoration along the basin's shoulder were originally covered with sheet silver. The ill-fitting sieve is of later date. Ewers for wash-sets from Khiva and neighbouring regions in north Afghanistan had no handle but instead a solid reinforced rim with thumb plate, as on this example.
H: 31.5 cm (ewer), 11.5 cm (basin), D: 25.5 cm (basin top)
Khiva, 18th century

662
Teapot. Cast brass, chased and engraved. The unusually bold spiralling scrollwork along the neck and the wavy scrolls on the ribbed body suggest Samarkand as the place of origin.
H: 31.5 cm
Samarkand, early 19th century

Having examined examples from regions where traditional practices were still alive (e.g., Afghanistan during the 1970s) or were being revived (e.g., Isfahan), we can be more specific about the division of labour. The production of a chased vessel with a cast handle and surface decoration would have required the following specialists: a coppersmith to shape the individual parts; a foundryman to cast handles, finials, etc.; and a specialist to assemble the separate items. The body of ewers are usually made of two or more parts which need to be fitted and soldered. The base has to be flanged, while the handle is attached to the body with rivets and handle and cover connected by a hinge. Another specialist would produce the engraved or chased decoration, and if the vessel was of copper a tinsmith would be needed. Besides the artisans engaged in various phases of the production process, there are others who specialise in different types of objects such as teapots, hookahs, water jugs, wash-basins and the like.

A very comprehensive collection of accounts by early travellers concerning the production of metalware can be found in the introduction to Westphal–Hellbusch 1974. It is an attempt to find out the date at which traditional metalwork ceased to be produced in Central Asia with the help of travelogues and later Russian documentation. The evidence is highly contradictory. As early as 1874 Kuhn reported from Bukhara that "every caravanserai and stall is literally packed with manufactured goods from Russia". This is echoed by von Le Coq, who wrote about his last journey to Turkestan in 1913: "Among other changes I sadly noticed that articles of Persian–Turkish craftsmanship which could still occasionally be found in 1906 – knotted carpets and embroideries, chased and engraved tea services and cooking utensils of tin-plated copper and brass and other such things – have become even rarer or rather have been swept away completely by trash from Europe" (Westphal–Hellbusch 1974:16-17). This is contradicted by Sukhareya and Abdullayev who suggest that native handicrafts slowly vanished only some time after the Russian Revolution of 1917 (Abdullayev 1986).

Recent attempts to revive the metalworking crafts do not look very promising. Workshops have been established at the major sites so that tourists can watch the craftsmen at work; but the only objects produced are small plates or trays with bland and unspecific decoration. One cannot help concluding that the thousand-year-old tradition of Islamic metalwork has disappeared in Uzbekistan. It is time for a comprehensive stock-taking so that the wares of the eighteenth and nineteenth century become better known and appreciated by scholars and the general public. An important beginning has been made by Westphal–Hellbusch, based on the relatively few pieces in the Rickmers collection. A more recent study presents objects from the eighteenth and nineteenth century within the context of pre-Islamic and early Islamic metalwork and jewellery (Abdullayev 1986). But again the material is too limited to give more than a glimpse at the great variety of well-made objects produced in Uzbekistan at a time when traditional workmanship in Iran and the Ottoman empire had already declined much further. The following discussion of metal objects will include a fair amount of photographic detail in order to show that the artisans were continuing the best traditions of Islamic crafts, especially those from Timurid times onwards.

Teapots

On account both of their shapes and the quality of their decoration, teapots are certainly the most unusual examples of late metalwork from the region. Westphal-Hellbusch has identified three basic types:

a) *Filta*, teapots with rounded ribs. The body has a melon-like shape reminiscend of Timurid domes and documented in metalwork of the region since the Timurids.

b) *Satrandsh*, teapots with a flattened oval body. Flat pots of this type are especially associated with Kokand; but there are also teapots only partly flat, the rest having ribs similar to the *filta*.

c) *Isfhona*, globular teapots. Examples of this type show the greatest variety of decorative bodywork.

All these types share a high, slightly tapering foot, a curved cast handle connected to the cover and often decorated with dragons' heads at both ends, and a spout which remains quite close to the body over its entire length and terminates only slightly above the neck or begins very high up and stays completely attached to the body. This type was produced by every metalworking centre in Uzbekistan since the eighteenth century and depicted on ceramic plates and on leather appliqué for wooden travelling chests. What is surprising is that no trace earlier than the eighteenth century has yet been found of this ubiquitous item, when it appears fully formed in both technical and artistic terms.

The most perfect example in our collection is also one of the smallest (height 27.5 cm) and probably dates from the early eighteenth century (ills. 635-6). Its great beauty lies in the perfectly balanced proportions, sparing use of ornament and excellent design and execution of the decoration. The sides are decorated with an almond-shaped medallion chased in relief with a border of interlacing cusped leaves and above a medallion and half-medallion filled with scrolls. On the front, the merlon motif with scrolls is very delicately executed and in no way inferior to the spout of the above-mentioned Timurid vessel.

The most unusual piece in our teapot collection is also the largest (height 46.5 cm; ills. 647-8). Compared against dated examples in Russian publications, the vessel must still be of the eighteenth century. The designer obviously tried to include the complete range of contemporary metal ornamentation on what presumably was a commissioned work. The foot area shows spiral scrolls, wavy scrolling and a band with niche-shaped motifs. Both back and front are divided by ribs which at the bottom end show merlon motifs filled with scrolling. The central ornament of the flat area is an almond-shaped medallion with a blue glass stone probably serving as an amulet. The border consists of interlacing spiral scrollwork up to the neck ring decorated with palmettes. The neck is covered with a delicate repeat pattern of

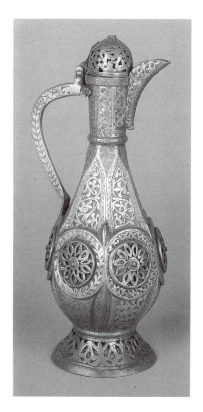

663
Teapot. Brass, copper, tin, asphalt. The openwork rosettes of the body suggest Kokand as the place of origin.
H: 29 cm
Acquired by Rickmers in Bukhara in the late 19th century
Museum für Völkerkunde, Berlin, Rickmers Collection

664
Teapot. Cast brass, engraved, inlaid glass stones, copper bottom. The shape follows Russian prototypes.
H: 23 cm
Bukhara, early 20th century

325

665

Ewer. Cast and engraved brass. The shape, sumptuous vegetal decoration and cartouches with poetic inscriptions indicate Safawid Iran as the place of manufacture. Rickmers acquired the ewer in Bukhara in the late 19th century.
H: c. 40.4 cm
Iran, 17th century
Museum für Völkerkunde, Berlin, Rickmers Collection

666

Wash-set consisting of ewer, removable sieve and basin. Chased silver, made at St. Petersburg and presented to the Bukhara court presumably in the late 19th century.
H: 25.6 cm (ewer), D: 27.0 cm (basin)
St. Petersburg

667
Ewers made at Uzbek settlements in northern Afghanistan.
(Left) Chased copper, cast rim. H: 39.0 cm. Akcha, second half 19th century
(Right) Chased copper with silver appliqué. The roundel shows the cosmic snake curled
around a stylised tree of life. H: 35.5 cm. Tashkurgan, second half 19th century

blossoms and tracery. The cover of very precise openwork ends in a down-turned lotus blossom and a lotus bud as the finial. It is rare to find a jug where the shape, decoration, handle, finial and the fitting of the separate parts are all executed with the same consummate skill. The vessel is perfect both in conception and execution and must be regarded as a masterpiece of late Central Asian metalwork.

These two vessels very likely were made at Bukhara, the centre for metalwork of this late period. A melon-shaped vessel with decoration chased in relief, the cover entirely of openwork and a lotus-like ring between neck and body, can probably be ascribed to Samarkand on account of its bold scrollwork, while another vessel, again with pronounced ribs and merlon motifs and floral scrolls along the neck, was produced at Bukhara in the late eighteenth century (ills. 662, 658).

A ewer from Kokand is remarkable for its unusually slender shape and the delicate and well-balanced decoration (ill. 656 right). The lotus scroll at the foot and the S-shaped hooks along the border are striking features. The decoration and application of blue glass stones of the teapot made at Kokand in the late nineteenth century strictly follows local traditions; the shape itself, however, imitates Gardner porcelain imported from Russia (ill. 664).

668
Wash-set. Cast and chased brass, partly tin-plated, engraved, silver appliqué with turquoises and glass stones over foil. The removable sieve is fastened to the basin with a screw.
H: 38.5 cm (ewer), 14.8 cm (basin), D: 38.0 cm (basin)
Bukhara, made for court circles, late 19th century

Wash-basins and ewers

Every well-to-do household had a washing-set consisting of a basin with detachable sieve and a ewer. It was usually made of brass and sometimes of copper and would often be decorated with turquoises, semi-precious stones or glass stones backed by foil. Von Schwarz was once offered in Bukhara a set covered with sheet gold. Often the surface is partly tinned to produce a colour contrast, and one also finds examples decorated with sheet silver. Our earliest example was probably made at Khiva at the beginning of the eighteenth century (ill. 661). The neck and sieve are studded with turquoises. The background structure of the almond-shaped medallions with plant designs along the sides suggests that they were originally covered with sheet silver. Water jugs without handle and cover and with a spout fitted with a cast ring with a projection to secure one's hold are typical products of Khiva and northern Afghanistan (ill. 667).

The wash-set with soldered silver bands and silver rosettes on a very finely engraved background which even covers the handle, spout and finial, was probably made at Bukhara during the second half of the nineteenth century (ill. 668). Here the craftsmen obviously used the contrast between the tinned and untinned areas for decorative effect, creating a work which in spite of the fine workmanship appears almost too rich and baroque. More restrained is a brass wash-set with engraved design and black inlay (possibly lacquer or asphalt) at the neck of the ewer (ill. 669). The squat globular shape would point to Karshi in the Bukhara emirate as its place of origin. The inlay of small silver rosettes just below the neck is an unusual feature. Also from Karshi comes a globular ewer with a design of overlapping circles on the body (ills. 659-60). The segments are filled with plant motifs, and the rim of the cover, the base of the spout (and originally also its top) and the foot are embellished with coloured glass inlay. To decorate the entire length of the spout – from which flows life-giving water – with a tree of life was a charming idea. The handle bears a craftman's mark and the date A.H. 1284 (A.D. 1867).

669
Wash-set. Brass with silver appliqué along the ewer's shoulder, chased and engraved, the neck possibly blackened with asphalt. The basin has been turned, the sieve is a later replacement.
H: 14.5 cm (basin), 31.0 cm (ewer), D: 32.5 (basin)
Karshi (Bukhara emirate), first half 19th century

Some of the most elegant ewers come from northern Afghanistan. They have a slender shape, no handle, are made of copper and usually without decoration (ill. 667). One example in our collection has been worn to a high polish and shows a lozenge-shaped, originally silver-plated copper appliqué and on the sides sheet silver chased in matrices with a representation of the cosmic tree flanked by two birds and enclosed by the cosmic snake.

Hookahs

The simplest types of hookahs have a body or vase of glazed ceramics, a ceramic head and a wooden stem. Sometimes the body is made from a bottle-gourd, and the more expensive of these have a metal mount set with glass stones. "In rare cases the body of a hookah might be made entirely of brass; but even then the material imitates the shape of the bottle-gourd" (Schwarz 1900:243).

The only complete hookah in our collection was probably made at Bukhara in the eigteenth century (ill. 649). It is chased with additional turning. The design consists of turned grooves and rosettes with turquoise inlay on the flat sections of the body. The body of a hookah made at Kokand early in the nineteenth century shows traces of sheet silver along the foot and shoulder (ill. 670 left). The lappet design along the upper part still has the entire original silver foil. The background hatching of the almond-shaped medallion in the centre of the body suggests that this design originally was also covered with sheet silver. A most curious decoration appears on a hookah from northern Afghanistan or Uzbekistan, where cut emblems in the shape of lappets, escrutcheons with almond-shaped motifs and roundels are soldered to the body (ill. 670 right). The inner ornamentation shows lotus blossoms, leafy scrolls and geometrical motifs.

329

670-671
Hookah vases.
(Left) Brass, chased and engraved, with traces of applied sheet silver. The niches with scrollwork against a hatched background (see detail) indicate that these areas were also prepared to take sheet silver. H: 32.2 cm. Bukhara (?), early 19th century
(Centre) Chased brass with cast and decorated appliqué. H: c. 35.0 cm. Bukhara (?), early 19th century
(Right) Chased copper with engraved brass appliqué, highly polished. Some of the applications probably were taken from older vessels. H: 34.0 cm. Northern Afghanistan or Uzbekistan, early 19th century

Imported metalwork

Although the region itself was producing metalwork in large quantities during the eighteenth and nineteenth century, foreign wares continued to be imported, either as valuable gifts for the court or as commercial goods to compete with domestic produce. Thus in the 1890s Rickmers acquired in Bukhara a Safawid ewer which most probably was not produced at that city, (ill. 665). The majority of Bukhara's population were Tajiks who spoke an East Iranian dialect and were mainly craftsmen and merchants; but some of the Bukhara metalwork was certainly also produced by Iranian prisoners of war, sold as slaves on the markets in Khiva and Bukhara. In the case of this particular ewer it is more likely, however, that it was presented as a gift by an Iranian embassy to the court at Bukhara. A similar provenance certainly applies to an unusually fine chased silver wash-set with a Russian mark and probably made at St Petersburg; it must have been a gift from a Russian embassy to the Bukhara court (ill. 666).

China during the Ming period (1368-1644) produced heavy squat vessels of cast bronze with two handles for the Central Asian market (ills. 672-3). They are decorated with elongated ogival cartouches with inscriptions on both sides.

Among the Uzbeks of northern Afghanistan cast-iron ewers from Russia had replaced more expensive native products by the end of the last century (ill. 674 left). Heavy iron cooking pots cast in three segments and produced in the Badakhshan mountains are quite rare. Their rarity is confirmed by the fact that our example bears a relief inscription dated A.H. 1321 (A.D. 1903) both on the cover and the body.

We hope that this overview of Central Asian metalwork of the eighteenth and nineteenth century has shown that contrary to the negative impression received by Western travellers at the time, the standard of workmanship was still very high. The ornamental repertoire realistically reflects the cultural setting of the region. It shows the survival of Timurid influence noticeable also in other branches of the arts and crafts, as well as Indian influence partly traceable back to the tenth century, and elements derived from Iranian and Chinese shapes and forms. What needs to be emphasised is that all these various influences were not adopted wholesale so as to produce something basically alien to the spirit of Central Asian culture, but were rather adapted to create a persuasive synthesis. As a result Central Asian metalwork presents us with a language of ornament all its own, which makes it possible to credit the region with a great variety of differently shaped and decorated vessels and utensils.

672-673
Vessels with handles. Cast bronze.
H: 8.0 and 9.5 cm, D: 14.0 and 16.5 cm
China, made for the Central Asian market, 16th century
Private collection, Hamburg

674
(Left) Cast-iron teapot. The neck shows a Russian factory mark. H: 23.5 cm. Russia, made for the Central Asian market
(Right) Cast-iron lidded pot. H: 20.0 cm, D: 26.5 cm. Northern Afghanistan, dated A.H. 1340 (A.D. 1921)

331

675
Dish. Glazed earthenware, underglaze painting showing in the well a teapot flanked by
knives presumably meant as amulets. - The entire collection of late ceramics from Turkestan
at the Berlin Museum für Völkerkunde was presumably acquired by Rickmers in Bukhara
in the 1910s.
D: 49 cm
Rishtan, 18th/19th century
Museum für Völkerkunde, Berlin

Ceramics from the Eighteenth to the Twentieth Century

Johannes Kalter

Almost every ethnographic museum in Europe holds a few ceramics from the Uzbekistan region. Exact places of origin are seldom known. The largest collection I know is that of the Berlin Museum für Völkerkunde. The majority of items are said to have been acquired by Rickmer Rickmers, who also supplied the few secure ascriptions we shall rely on. On pottery in general, von Schwarz has the following to say: "Turkestan pottery is highly developed and produced in large amounts, which is not surprising since the necessary materials can be found everywhere. The native potters use a common potter's wheel to make bowls, plates, cups, short wide conduits for channelling water underneath roads ... Turkestan pottery vessels have the same shape as those discovered in buildings and prehistoric graves in Europe ... The pottery is nearly always glazed in the same colours we have at home, namely white, yellow, green, grey, dark red and azure. The most beautiful items are drinking bowls glazed green–blue or dark blue, the glaze probably being more delicate and durable than what we produce ourselves. The designs following Arabic models are also admirable ... Special care is taken in the manufacture of the small semi-circular drinking cups which form an indispensable part of the traveller's equipment – like it was in the times of the ancient Scythians – and which the natives and following their example, the Russian soldiers and Cossacks usually carry in specially made leather cases on their belts or tie to the saddle horn. The wealthy use drinking bowls not of native manufacture but imported from China and either of genuine or fake porcelain; these are quite expensive and can cost up to twenty-five marks. Such high prices go to show how much the natives value their drinking cups. A very recent development has seen cheaper porcelain cups imported from Russia slowly driving out the Chinese products" (Schwarz 1900:408-9).

The last observation is important, for it indicates why native pottery seems to have vanished almost completely by the end of the century. A revival had to wait until the Soviet era. Then large manufactories were often combined with studios for master craftsmen, e.g. at Rishtan, whose products were highly regarded by the population and were acquired by arts and crafts museums as masterpieces made by individual artists.

The ceramics produced from the eighteenth to the twentieth century can be grouped into four distinctive styles. The first would be a purely native style with local motifs, some of them of great antiquity. The second style is characterised by sinicised designs, and there exist more or less successful combinations of these two. The third style appears to me to be influenced by late Ottoman fashions and shows parallels with Kütahya ware. The fourth group includes ceramics inspired by Iranian models.

A similar attempt to produce domestic wares of the same quality as the Chinese imports were made in Safawid Iran. It manifests itself in the progressive stylisation of plant motifs to resemble Chinese models and also in the copying of Chinese marks at the bottom. A very successful example of this is a plate which reveals its Central Asian origin only through the Greek cross in the well (ill. 678). An interesting example of a stylistic mix can be seen on a drinking bowl where the delicate sinicised scrollwork is interspersed with dark blue and manganese brown blossoms (ill. 679 right). Both items probably date from the late eighteenth or early nineteenth century. Such very fine blue-and-white ware was mainly produced at Rishtan in the Fergana Valley. A plate with painting in cobalt blue, turquoise and ochre and a green rim combines Chinese and Central Asian elements (ill. 676 right). The disparate features are even more noticeable on a plate with a chequerboard pattern in the well and a border of S-shaped hooks. The rim shows chrysanthemum blossoms alternating with roundels with geometric motifs also of Chinese inspiration.

A purely Central Asian tradition is exemplified by a plate with the well inscribed with a Greek cross terminating in rosettes, and the rim decorated with hatched lozenges. Similar designs are known already from Timurid ceramics produced at Bojnurd (ill. 680). Local traditions are perhaps best illustrated on a plate decorated with a teapot flanked by scimitars (ill. 675). The teapot presumably symbolises hospitality and the scimitars stand for might and power. Its large size would suggest that it was used for banquets. It is highly likely that these two plates were made at Rishtan. A rose-water bottle and a ewer both with bold scrolling spirals along the shoulder, probably come from Samarkand (ill. 681).

Polychrome ceramics mainly in yellow, red, brown and green and with flower paintings reminiscend of European 'peasant' art, were made at Samarkand and Khiva. A ewer of white ground with dots and stripes along the neck, handle and spout and simple rosettes on the body probably was modelled on Kütahya ware and most likely produced at Bukhara (ill. 682).

A small plate decorated with delicate and lightly painted tree motifs shows Iranian influence and probably comes from Rishtan.

This short introduction to later ceramics of the region presumably raises more questions than it can possibly answer. It seemed important to show, however, that unlike all the neighbouring countries of the Islamic world, the region retained its great individuality, which was first defined in post-Timurid times and reached its brilliant maturity during the eighteenth and nineteenth centuries; and that this is true not only for metalware and the more important textile productions but also for ceramics.

676
Tea bowls and dishes. Earthenware with painting in turquoise, cobalt-blue and manganese under a transparent glaze. The dish on the left is a typical example of a local style developed in Turkestan. The dish on the right shows strong Chinese influence, and the one in the centre with its lightly painted plant motifs derives its inspiration from Iran.
D: 16.5-35.0 cmRishtan (?), 18th/19th century Museum für Völkerkunde, Berlin

677
Dish. Earthenware, white slip, blue painting under a transparent glaze. Although the design can be traced to the 15th century, the grey tinge of the underglaze painting suggests a later date for this piece.
D: 36 cm Bukhara, probably late 17th/early 18th century Museum in the Ark, Bukhara

678
Dish. Earthenware with underglaze painting. The painting style is related to Chinese blue-and-white porcelain of the Ming dynasty (1368-1644), and only the division of the well by a Greek cross indicates Turkestan as the place of origin.
D: 35 cm
Rishtan, 18th/19th century
Museum für Völkerkunde, Berlin

679
Teacup and food bowl. Earthenware, white slip, underglaze painting under a transparent glaze, the bottom with pseudo-Chinese marks. Members of the upper class preferably used Chinese porcelain. Turkestan potters produced accurate copies of Chinese export ware.
D: 19 and 29 cm Rishtan, 18th/19th century
Museum für Völkerkunde, Berlin

681
Rose-water bottles and ewer. Earthenware, turquoise, cobalt-blue and manganese-brown painting under a transparent glaze. The freely-painted floral design of the rose-water bottle on the right was inspired by Iranian models, whereas the wavy scrollwork of the other two vessels reflects local traditions.
H: 29 cm (left), 25 cm (centre), 27 cm (right)
Left probably Bukhara or Samarkand, centre and right Rishtan, 18th/19th century
Museum für Völkerkunde, Berlin

680
Dish. Earthenware, white slip, cobalt-blue and manganese-brown painting under a transparent glaze. The division of the well goes back to late Timurid ceramics (cf. ill. 297).
D: 34 cm
Samarkand (?), 18th/19th century
Museum für Völkerkunde, Berlin

683
Rose-water bottle. Earthenware, brown foundation glaze with green-coloured slip under a transparent glaze, sgrafitto and lightly incised designs.
H: 38 cm
Bukhara (?), second half 19th century
Museum für Völkerkunde, Berlin

682
Ewer. Earthenware, underglaze painting and sgrafitto designs. Both colour scheme and painting style are related to late Ottoman ceramics from Kütahya.
H: 26 cm
Samarkand, second half 19th century
Museum für Völkerkunde, Berlin

Uzbekistan

685
The next-to-last khan of Khiva with his ministers, before 1896.

From the Russian Conquest to the Declaration of Sovereignty

Reinhard Eisener

Any statement concerning the history of Uzbekistan in the nineteenth and especially in the twentieth century is fraught with problems. Due to political developments following the end of the First World War, much of Uzbekistan's recent history is wrapped in secrecy. Ideological considerations together with restrictions on information and research more or less define the current state of affairs. Such a situation necessarily leads to highly divergent modes of interpretation. Exposure to decades of confrontation between East and West and the experiences of cold and hot wars cannot be undone at a stroke even while one glosses them over or tries to ignore them for pragmatic reasons.

Uzbekistan exists only since 1924 as a territorial unit, a 'national state' or even simply as a meaningful concept. The idea of such a political entity had vaguely taken shape among the top leadership in Moscow in 1920. The present borders between the Central Asian republics of the Commonwealth of Independent States (Kirghiztan, Tajikistan, Turkmenistan and Uzbekistan) largely follow the lines proposed for the so-called 'national-territorial delimitation' of Central Asia in 1924/5 with some later corrections. The arguments for this measure were and still are controversial. Its proponents declared it an unprecedented example of the principle of the 'people's right to self-determination', liberating the population from 'czarist ethnic incarceration', while its opponents saw it as nothing more than a brutal example of divide and rule conceived by some Moscow bureaucrats or, more crassly put, by Stalin. Behind all these polemics one fact remains: Central Asia became part of a regime which was Europe-oriented, and its subsequent history was shaped accordingly. The origins of this imperialist dominion predate the creation of Uzbekistan.

Central Asia became an object of Western colonial expansion only quite late, in the mid-nineteenth century. Driven by both aggressive and defensive considerations, Russia moved into the 'power vacuum' of the Central Asian steppes and deserts. Limits to this expansion were set only by the countervailing pressure of the British colonial forces. Neither the difficult ground nor resistance by nomad tribes and the three Muslim states of Kokand, Khiva and Bukhara seriously impeded the Russian advance and conquest.

After the formal subjection of the nomads living in the so-called 'Kirghiz steppe' (in fact it was inhabited by Kazakhs) in 1847, two lines of Russian military outposts had by 1853/4 reached Kokand's sphere of interest, the 'New Siberian Line' at Verny (modern Alma-Ata) and the 'Syr Darya Line' at Perovsk (modern Kzyl-Orda). Then came a temporary halt to further southward expansion. Russian forces were tied up elsewhere by the Crimean War (1853-56) and the subjection of the Caucasus (1856-64), costly

686

Outfit of a itinerant dervish from Turkestan. Islamisation brought to Central Asia not only the religious teachings and practices advocated by legal and Koranic scholars, but also Islamic mysticism. Itinerant dervishes and members of the Sufi orders and brotherhoods spread their teachings across the Central Asian steppes. Due to their efficient organisation, some like the Naqshbandis gained political influence at an early date. Sufi masters frequently acted as highly respected advisers to the court since Timurid times, a tradition which continued under the Turkestan khans. Even after the Russian conquest of Turkestan, the brotherhoods retained their influence and authority particularly among the rural population.
Bukhara, late 19th century
Museum in the Ark, Bukhara

687

Coat of the Sufi master Amir Haidar. The robe is decorated with Koranic verses, prayers and magic squares, and together with the accessories belonged to Amir Haidar (d. 1825), a master of the Naqshbandi order. Baha'uddin Naqshband, founder of the order, which is still among the largest of Sufi orders, was born near Bukhara in the 14th century. Later he became the patron saint of the city.
Baha'uddin Naqshbandi Museum, Bukhara

688
Wandering dervishes of Turkestan, about 1900.

689
Finial from a standard. Cast brass, openwork, epigraphic design ("O `Ali! O Allah! O Mohammed!").
H: 51 cm
19th century
Baha'uddin Naqshbandi Museum, Bukhara

both in lives and material. Only in 1864 was Russia able to close the east-west gap between the two advance lines by creating the 'Kokand Line' and to move further south against Kokand. In 1865 Tashkent was taken against Alexander II's explicit order. The commanding officer, General Cherniaev, informed the czar that the order had reached him only after the conquest of the city which he respectfully put at His Majesty's disposal. Kokand fell in 1866, and 1867 saw the creation of the 'Turkestan Government-General' with Tashkent as its capital and Konstantin von Kaufmann its first governor (until his death in 1882). The historicising name 'Turkestan' (Land of the Turks) was chosen by the Russian conquerors.

Having lost much of its territory, the Kokand khanate lived on as a small vassal of Russia. The same happened shortly afterwards to Bukhara after the troops of Emir Muzaffaruddin suffered two decisive defeats. Bukhara became a Russian protectorate, but with Samarkand and territory on the upper reaches of the Zeravshan being incorporated into the czarist empire, Russia now controlled the lifeline of the Bukhara oasis.

The conquest of Central Asia went on apace. The khanate of Khiva, the last of the independent Muslim states, was defeated in 1873 after a well-planned campaign and, deprived of some of its territory, also sank to the status of a protectorate. In 1876 unrest in the Kokand khanate precipitated its final annexation. Renamed 'Province of Fergana', it was incorporated with the Turkestan government-general. In 1885 Russian expansion came to an end with the conquest of the area inhabited by the Turkmens east of the Caspian Sea and including the Merv oasis. This finalised the establishment of czarist Russia's southern borders which survive to this day and define the borders of the CIS with Iran and Afghanistan.

Russia's conquests and its rule over Central Asia was regarded by outside observers during the nineteenth century basically as part of a 'civilising mission', except perhaps in the eyes of Great Britain while it was engaged in the 'Great Game'. Central Asia generally was seen as a playground of nomads and robbers to be reined in by Russia. Near the end of his career, Konstantin von Kaufmann declared as the overall goal "to further develop Turkestan as a fundamental part of Russia along purely Russian lines and to improve it in accordance with the natives' perception of our greatness and to impress the neighbouring masses by the advantages of the Russian order we have established." (Quoted in O. Hoetzsch, *Rußland in Asien*, Stuttgart 1966:94)

Until the First World War this meant that Turkestan was governed by a civil bureaucracy modelled on Russia's, with officers filling the higher ranks. It was not subjected to direct Russification and retained both its Islamic system of jurisdiction and its local administration. The traditional order including the Islamic educational system, was left basically intact. No missionary activities were allowed during von Kaufmann's time. The Muslim population did not hold Russian citizenship and was thus exempt from military service. When it was contemplated to change this rule and enlist Muslims as auxiliaries in 1916, revolts followed.

690
Palace of the khan of Kokand, with Russian officers, about 1900.

691
Russian house with portico in Oriental style. Samarkand, about 1900.

692
General Konstantin Petrovich von Kaufmann (1818-82), the first Russian governor-general of Turkestan, about 1870.

693
Inauguration of a section of the Trans-Caspian railway, about 1890s.

The main interference in Turkestan life concerned the economy and infrastructure. Trade, industry and agricultural production were progressively attuned to Russian interests. This was the case also in Bukhara and Khiva, nominally independent protectorates. Central Asia was increasingly used as an outlet for Russian industrial products and as a supplier of raw materials to those industries. Here cotton played a major part, the large-scale cultivation of cotton making Turkestan heavily dependent on Russian wheat supplies. When these failed to arrive as a consequence of the October Revolution in 1917/18, the result was wide-spread famine.

The main factor to improve the communication system was the railway. In 1899 the Trans-Caspian line was opened, running from the Caspian Sea through the emirate of Bukhara to Samarkand and Tashkent, and in 1906 Tashkent was connected to Orenburg. The construction of railway tracks and establishment of small industries like cotton processing brought Russian workers to Turkestan. A policy of resettlement of Russian peasants was only pursued on a large scale in the Kazakh steppes; elsewhere measures remained modest. Before the First World War Russians constituted barely five per cent of the Turkestan population, and most of them lived in separate settlements along the railway lines, in garrisons and in Russian 'new towns' built on the outskirts of the native 'old towns'. The Russian presence in Turkestan was strong enough, however, for the

political upheavals of 1917 to have immediate repercussions. After the fall of the monarchy in February 1917, city governments and executive committees were set up as organs of the Provisional Government of Russia, while the opposition created councils of Workers' and Soldiers' Deputies representing the forces hell-bent on revolution.

The demise of the old order continued inexorably during the political upheavals of 1917. The most radical forces, armed with a vision of 'freedom and justice', won the day. One important factor was that their representatives and followers were mainly workers and soldiers, putting into their hands two highly effective instruments of power, namely the army and the railways. Taking over control was not particularly difficult at first. In November 1917 the vestiges of political authority almost automatically fell into the hands of the councils of workers' and soldiers' deputies. No effective political opposition existed in Turkestan. The revolutionaries fought their enemies or supposed enemies without mercy. Except for a very small group of politically ambitious reformers, the Muslim population took no part in the revolutionary events. It bore the main brunt, however, of the consequences, of arbitrary decisions, the breakdown of the economy and supply-lines, looting and general violence.

The October Revolution mainly affected the immigrants from Russia. In Turkestan in 1918/19 the power of the soviets ('councils') was concentrated in Tashkent and

694
Emir Sayyid Muzaffaruddin Bahadur (1860-85), Khan of Bukhara.

695
Seal of the emir of Bukhara. Brass, engraved, with silver setting.
H: 3.3 cm, W: 4.1 cm
Dated 1871
Museum in the Ark, Bukhara

696
Seals of two officials from Bukhara. Brass, engraved, the seal on the left with nielloed silver setting.
(Left) D: 4.4 cm. Dated A.H. 1315 (A.D. 1897)
(Right) H: 4.1 cm. Dated A.H. 1277 (A.D. 1860)

697
Printing-blocks for Bukharan banknotes.
H: 7.3-10.0 cm, W: 14.3-19.5 cm
Late 19th century
Museum in the Ark, Bukhara

698
Bukharan banknote.
H: 12.5 cm, W: 27.5 cm
Museum in the Ark, Bukhara

barely extended beyond some Russian new towns and settlements and the railway lines. Soon civil war broke out in several places. The Russian central authorities were only an indirect influence on events in the region. Their authority was mainly restricted to what reached Tashkent by way of telegraph and radio and its interpretation by local revolutionaries. So developments took a decidedly unorthodox turn. The members of the Turkestan soviets were mostly workers. The representatives of the Russian Social-Democratic Workers' Party (RSDRP, the precursor of the Communist Party) were a minority among the revolutionaries. Only in June 1918 did the most radical members of the Turkestan RSDRP form a united Party of the "Communists-Bolsheviks" which by spring 1919 had succeeded in becoming the sole authority in power. At the same time Moscow directly intervened to strengthen the influence of Muslim communists.

Railway communications had been interrupted for longer periods because of the civil war raging in Russia until September 1919. As the central authorities were mainly engaged in military campaigns they had very few forces to spare for organising activities in Turkestan. This only changed at the end of 1919, and then very much so. Moscow assumed direct control over Turkestan affairs. Although there was as yet little concentrated effort to institute a socialist order, the new policies showed besides

699
Cotton harvest in Turkestan, late 19th century.

their visionary drive a measure of professionalism. Moscow was interested in Turkestan partly as a supplier of much-needed raw materials and also as the envisioned cradle of a revolution in the East. Special attention was focused on British India. These plans achieved little more than the dissolution in 1920 of the khanate of Khiva and the emirate of Bukhara, both measures proclaimed as steps towards 'world revolution'. Ostensibly to help the staged 'revolutions', the Red Army intervened in Khiva in February 1920 and in Bukhara in September. A 'People's Republic of Khorezm' and a 'People's Republic of Bukhara' were established under Soviet control, and Turkestan became an 'Autonomous Socialist Soviet Republic'.

The main difference between the old and the new Russian regime was the latter's totalitarian ideology, which was enforced in all her conquered lands regardless of their individual character and situation. The government believed it possible to anticipate the future by putting its basic ideas and ideals into practice, and therefore set about a complete reshaping of the prevalent conditions. Time and again ideas and actualities clashed, and the newly-created realities needed to be corrected. Such corrections were guided by ideology mixed with robust self-interest. It took the new Soviet power many years to put their concepts even partially into effect and the endeavour was never fully realised.

By 1924 the top leadership in Moscow and its representatives in Tashkent, the 'Central Asian Bureau', had finally come to the conclusion that the territorial division of Central Asia had to be rearranged. The reasoning was partly based on the ideology of the 'nationalities policy' – before

the establishment of a unitary state, countries had to pass through the stage of nationhood – and on practical considerations to strengthen the command structure. The Muslim leadership was sometimes heavily split and there was a tendency to pursue an independent political course. In addition, the implementation of the modernisation of Central Asia was often hampered by militant resistance fighters, the so-called *basmachi*, who wanted to preserve the traditional order. These conflicts continued into the 1930s.

The main criterion for the territorial division of Central Asia was said to be the concept of a 'nation' (defined ethnically and linguistically), a European notion that was alien to the Muslim population's sense of identity. The result was a patchwork of four officially recognised nationalities (Kirghiz, Tajik, Turkmen and Uzbek) gathered together in separate 'republics'. This system was hastily and crudely implemented. Its deficiencies were particularly glaring in the case of the sedentary populations where over the centuries an ethnic mixture of Turkic and Iranian elements had evolved which now was divided into 'Uzbeks' and 'Tajiks'. The resulting tensions are still with us. The Tajiks, for instance, lay claim to the cities of Bukhara and Samarkand (the capital of the Uzbek Socialist Soviet Republic from 1924 to 1930) which at the time had been awarded to Uzbekistan.

The establishment of 'national' republics in Central Asia – the entire region itself continued to be treated as a single economic entity – was accompanied by the intensification of 'socialist construction', which soon was applied to every sphere of life. The Soviet Union had been founded in 1923, and in 1925 Stalin's policy of 'socialism in one country' began to take effect. From now on, events in Uzbekistan largely mirrored those in other parts of the Soviet empire.

Huge campaigns were started in the mid 1920s (and became regulated by five-year plans after 1929) to radically change the country and its people: collectivisation of agriculture (1928-37), including mechanisation and large-scale cultivation of cotton, and industrialisation with the emphasis on heavy industry, exploitation of natural resources and power generation. In the course of this economic construction and reform huge resettlement programs were undertaken to move people to wherever they were needed most in the interests of planning and development. These projects and other factors led hundreds of thousands to escape to Afghanistan. After the German invasion (1941) many industries were moved from the danger zones in the West to the East, with some hundred larger enterprises being relocated to Uzbekistan. During the war, cotton production declined, but afterwards quickly reached its former level. The 'white gold' remained the crucial factor of Uzbekistan's existence. Until very recently new areas were being put under cultivation with the help of vast irrigation projects and yields increased manifold.

In social and cultural affairs likewise great changes were taking place from the mid 1920s onwards. Atheism being among the tenets of the new Soviet ideology, a general attack on Islam was started, mosques and religious schools were closed, the courts secularised, religious foundations confiscated and the wearing of veils by women actively discouraged. At the same time mass campaigns were launched for the eradication of illiteracy, political education, improved hygienic conditions and better medical care.

In about 1930 the Arabic script was replaced by the Latin alphabet which in the early 1940s was superseded by the Cyrillic alphabet. An Uzbek language was created based mainly on the vernacular of Tashkent and Fergana. After failed efforts to make this the official language of the administration, Russian became the dominant language used in politics, public affairs and science. The principle of 'national form and socialist content' played an important part in cultural matters and also, for instance, in historiography. 'National' traditions were invented and a 'national' history going far back in time was constructed from a Marxist-Leninist viewpoint. The catch-phrase 'national form' gave some leeway for the preservation and development of regional characteristics.

In politics as in all other spheres, the CPSU was the dominating power. Although since the mid 1920s the leaders of the Uzbekistan Communist Party were drawn from the native population, their immediate subordinates, who had a European-Russian background, were the real 'power behind the throne' and ensured that Moscow's line was followed. Several political purges, culminating in Stalin's terrible persecutions of the mid to late 1930s, hit Uzbekistan with full force. The native intelligentsia including political leaders from the earliest days, was severely decimated. In the third and largest of the Moscow show trials in March 1938, the two most prominent politicians of Uzbekistan, Faizullah Khodzhaev and Akmal Ikramov, were convicted and sentenced to death.

After Stalin's death in 1953, politics in Uzbekistan were dominated by Sharaf Rashidov, who held the position of First Party Secretary from 1959 until his death in 1983. Over the years he created a power network which was completely subservient to him. He was also involved in Moscow Party affairs. During the period of *perestroika* (reform) after 1986, the public for the first time learnt much about Rashidov's activities and also about the consequences of all the above-mentioned measures taken during Soviet rule.

It is still almost impossible to define or evaluate the legacy of Soviet rule in Uzbekistan. Some idea may be gained from the public discussions and mutual recriminations of the last few years about the Soviet impact on politics and social structures. The Russian side accused the leadership and general population of Uzbekistan of corruption, protectionism, 'Oriental insufficiency', lazyness and backwardness. It claimed that Uzbekistan was a centre of organised crime in the Soviet Union through its black economy, and that its population was Russiaphobe and clung to traditional religious customs. Uzbekistan countered with the argument that it was just doing what everybody else did, and it charged Moscow with behaving like colonialists and exploiters. The 'white gold' now turned out to be a curse. The gigantic irrigation projects are bringing about an ecological catastrophe. The Aral Sea, one of the world's largest inland waters, is on the brink of drying up. Decades

of massive use of fertilisers and pesticides are causing health problems among the population. A solution to these problems is not in sight, and the cultivation of cotton as the major industrial crop continues unabated.

Like other countries of the erstwhile Soviet empire, the government of Uzbekistan issued a proclamation in June 1990 demanding certain sovereign rights from the Union such as supreme power over all natural ressources and the republic's territory and precedence of its own laws over those of the Union. Having remained uncommitted during the August putsch that lead to the break-up of the Soviet Union, Uzbekistan declared itself a fully independent state on August 31, 1991. Its historical legacy, however, effectively curtails its sovereignty. First the country will have to extricate itself from the close interrelationships and dependencies that were an intrinsic part of the old political structure in order to gain a greater measure of independence. Its situation, at least if measured against that of many other countries of the Third World, is not entirely gloomy: There are some basic industries, power supplies, a health care system and a network of educational institutions. Illiteracy has been 'liquidated'.

700
Packing cotton. Turkestan, late 19th century.

701
Foothills of the Tianshan near Urgut.

Uzbekistan: Geographical Aspects of a Post-Soviet Successor State in Central Asia

Jörg Stadelbauer

Introduction: The Soviet legacy in the Islamic Orient

Uzbekistan belongs to the medium-sized successor states of the former Soviet Union. On an area of 447 400 sq.km lives a population of about twenty-three million people, of which two-fifth live in urban centres. In terms of size, Uzbekistan takes fifth position and in terms of population third position among the successor states. The population average of 51.4 per sq.km does not give a true picture, since most of the area consists of very sparsely populated deserts and high mountain ranges, while most of the population is concentrated in oasis settlements. Broadly speaking, the topography is defined by very rugged mountain chains rising to more than 4000 metres and forming part of the Tianshan mountain system, and by the Turan depression, with the oases as the human foci of the country.

During the decline of the Soviet Union, Islam gained new importance, and old mosques were refurbished and new ones built. Like the other Central Asian and Caucasian successor states, Uzbekistan belongs to the zone exposed both to Islamic and oriental influences and to Eastern European and Slav ones, the latter apparently less deeply rooted, although they were mainly responsible for the modernisation of the region. In geopolitical terms the country is part of the Central Asian area where Russia in the nineteenth century secured its southern frontiers. This is the background for the continuing presence of Russian troops in some of the successor states.

Since Soviet times the country has been divided into twelve districts (Rus. *oblast*, Uzbek *viloyat*), with Karakalpakia constituting a special ethnic and territorial entity within Uzbekistan.

State and frontier

As a territorially independent unit Uzbekistan is of rather recent date. After the emirate of Bukhara and the khanate of Khorezm (Khiva) legally ceased to exist, an Uzbekistan Autonomous Soviet Republic was created in the 1920s, with frontiers deliberately drawn so that they did not coincide with the former border line. By 1924 the 'national delimitation' of Uzbekistan and Tajikistan had been achieved (for a detailed account of the re-drawing of the borders, see Baldauf 1991 and Baldauf 1995). Although not as politically volatile as neighbouring Tajikistan rent by civil war, Uzbekistan's domestic situation is still far from stable.

The configuration of the frontier line is especially complicated among the mountains and valleys of the Central

702
Irrigating cotton fields near Urgench.

703
Road across the Kyzylkum desert.

704
Eastern Turkestan landscape. The topography of Turkestan is characterised by the contrast between arid mountain deserts and fertile river oases.

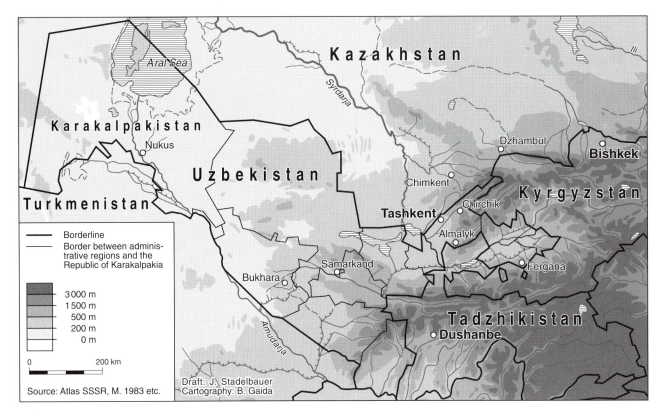

705
Uzbekistan and her neighbours.

706
Land utilisation in Uzbekistan

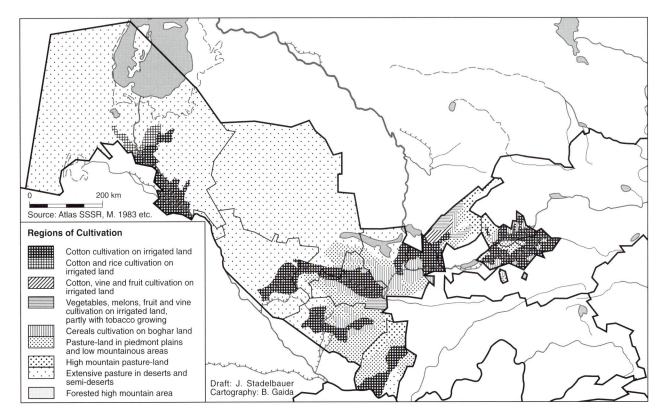

Regions of Cultivation

Cotton cultivation on irrigated land
Cotton and rice cultivation on irrigated land
Cotton, vine and fruit cultivation on irrigated land
Vegetables, melons, fruit and vine cultivation on irrigated land, partly with tobacco growing
Cereals cultivation on boghar land
Pasture-land in piedmont plains and low mountainous areas
High mountain pasture-land
Extensive pasture in deserts and semi-deserts
Forested high mountain area

348

Asian mountain ranges, where the territories of Uzbekistan, Kirghizstan and Tajikistan meet along very ragged borders. East of the Aral Sea the state frontier crosses the Kyzylkum (Red Sand) desert, divides the Chardara reservoir east of Tashkent between Uzbekistan and Kazakhstan and the riverine areas of Keles and Chirchik and runs across the Ugam range towards the Talas-Alatau mountains. Following the Pskem, Keksuj, Chatkal and Kuramin ranges, the frontier almost completely encircles the Fergana valley at a height of between 1500 and 4000 metres, making detours into several other valleys, then follows the Syr Darya and finally ascends the Kuramin again. The frontier skirts around Khojent (formerly Leninabad), cuts across the Zeravshan valley and range and passes the Hissar and Babatag chains to reach the Amu Darya. It follows the river-bank for some 140 kilometres downstream and then cuts off the Turkmenistan Sundukli desert from the main stretch of the Kyzylkum. Between Dayakhatyn and Besergen the frontier is defined by the Amu Darya, then the border line takes in the upper Amu Darya delta except for its western part, which belongs to Karakalpakia. The western border follows the steep slope of the Ustyurt plateau to the Usboy depression, turns westward straight across the Kaplankyr plateau and is defined north of the Kazalkhlyshor by the 56. degree of longitude across the Ustyurt plateau before the line turns north-eastward towards the western shores of the Aral Sea. The area of the Aral Sea is almost equally divided between Uzbekistan and Kazakhstan.

Topography: The contrast between lowlands and highlands

The main topographical feature is the contrast between the desert-like lowlands which make up four-fifth of the country's total area, and the highlands which rise towards the level of permanent glaciation. The mountain ranges to the north of the depression formed by the Fergana Valley and the Aydarkul are part of the western Tianshan, those to the south belonging to the Hissar-Alai system. The latter continues westward with heavily eroded mountains and hills, providing the Kyzylkum desert with low-lying bay-shaped areas, the largest of which are the Hungry and Karshi Steppes. While the river valleys and especially those points where rivers emerge from the mountains, have been hospitable ground for the emergence of oasis cultures for millennia, the lowland steppes have only been under irrigated cultivation for the last hundred years. We know that in historical times, however, remarkable cultures knowledgeable about irrigation techniques lived in the Kyzylkum southeast of the Aral Sea.

Geological structure and variety

The greater part of Uzbekistan is characterised by Variscan mountain formations. In the northeast the central Tianshan range represents a tectonic elevation, with the Maydantala, Pskem and Ugam ranges striking from northeast to southwest representing faults of Carboniferous limestone and

intrusive rock and the intervening valleys representing synclines or rifts. Southeast of this self-contained system which also includes the Chatkal and Kuramin ranges, the Fergana basin represents a large elliptical syncline filled with a great amount of sedimentation and showing along the rim Palaeocene strata. The central region of Uzbekistan from the central Ustyurt in the northwest via the hilly to mountainous stretches north of the Zeravshan to the Nurat-Alai system represents a horst-like fault, adjoined in the southwest by the southwestern foothills of the Hissar.

Since the early Tertiary new mountain ranges rose with subsequent erosion, the formation of broad foothills and the sedimentation of basins both between mountains and at their ends. On the upper reaches of the foothills so-called *boghar* tillage using spring water surplus is practised, while the loose sedimentation of the basins acts as a reservoir for natural gas and oil. Tertiary basins are found near Tashkent, in the Hungry Steppe, in the Fergana Valley, the Zeravshan valley and along the Kashka Darya and Surkhan Darya; the thickness of Neocene deposits alone reaches a height of six thousand metres in the Fergana basin. Earthquakes are common (e.g. at Tashkent in 1966) and show that tectonic activity is still going on.

The high mountain relief (above 3000 metres) of the Tianshan range is a result of glacial and periglacial formation after the Neocene and Quaternary elevation of the range itself. During cold periods the snowline lay three to five hundred metres below the present one. At present, however, glacial formation is very modest. Erosion of the highlands digitates with terrace formation in the valleys. Smooth reliefs indicate areas where Cretaceous and Neozoic deposits have been covered by loess. Erosion from the cold periods, deposited in huge cones around the foothills, has been broken by alternating erosion and accumulation. In limestone areas one often finds various types of karstification, such as deep karstic wells. The wide plains of the Kyzylkum and Sundukli deserts show more recent sedimentation with overlay caused by the wind. To the early stages of the formation of the Amu Darya delta belong the Khorezm delta on the western bank and the southern and eastern delta on its eastern bank above Nukus. A very serious ecological problem is the filling-up with sedimentation of the Aral Sea, a process accelerated after the dramatic drop of the water level (see most recently *The Aral Sea Basin*, 1995).

Mineral resources: a comparatively rich source of raw materials

Uzbekistan is rich in mineral resources, most of which only began to be exploited during the Soviet period and now play an important role in the country's quest for economic independence.

Among the earliest known and exploited resources were the natural gas and oil deposits of the Fergana Valley and the foothills of the mountains. Petroleum from the Fergana Valley now supports an important industry. The deposits in the Surkhan Darya are found in the anticlinal structures of Palaeocene sediments. In the south-westerly

707
Uzbek woman and Turkmen on the Khiva market.

708
Selling vegetables on the Tashkent market.

Hissar range and on the Ustyurt plateau (at Shachpakhty and Kuanysh) several gas deposits are exploited. The most important gas resources are those at Gazli, about hundred kilometres northwest of Bukhara, where the gas has a methane content of ninety-six to ninety-seven per cent. There are three important coal mining centres. The richest deposits are found in the Angren valley, but the brown coal burned at a thermal power station has a low heat value. The highest calorific value (up to 5980 kcal) is produced by the coal from Sargun associated with pre-Cambrian gneisses and schists.

Due to the complex formation of the rock, metal ores often lie on the surface and seem to have been made use of since early times. Waste heaps along the Angren indicate that a first period of activity ended in the tenth – twelfth century. The next phase started only with Russian explorations following the annexation of Tashkent (1865). Magmatic iron ore has been found in western Uzbekistan (Tebinbulak). Post-magmatic iron-ore formations occur at several locations along the Tianshan range in northern Uzbekistan. Triassic sedimentary formations, however, only show an iron content of between twenty and forty per cent, are rather flat and of little commercial interest. Although the manganese ore deposits along the foothills are not particularly thick, their manganese content of between eight and twenty-eight per cent should make them interesting in the future. Chromite ores are exploited in the Tamdytau and Sultan-Uvaysh mountains.

Among non-ferrous ores the most interesting is copper, often associated with other metal ores, e.g. molybdenum. Some nine hundred deposits are known but only three are exploited in the central Tianshan range, where they are the basis of the combined steel and iron plant at Almalyk. At Lyangar a plant has been in operation since 1929. Tin and zinc have been found in the Hissar and Tianshan, the ore being processed at Almalyk. Although more than a hundred tin deposits are known, the metal was mined only at Karnab in the 1950s. Raw materials for aluminium production are obtained from plentiful bauxite deposits, the most important site for Palaeozoic bauxite being Aktau in the Tamdytau mountains, while other deposits in the Hissar and the Kyzylkum are earmarked for future exploitation. Alunite is worked in the Kuramin, Chatkal and Hissar ranges. Among the rarer metal ores the most important is wolfram found in the central and southern stretches of the Tianshan at Lyangar and Koytash. Bismuth from the Chatkal and Kuramin is processed at Ustarasay.

Among precious metal the most important is gold found in veins or alluvial deposits particularly in the mountainous regions of the Kyzylkum (Muruntau, Kokpatash); annual production is about seventy tons. It is a very valuable resource for the young independent republic, since its reserves amount to no less than eighteen per cent of the total of the former Soviet Union.

Non-metal raw materials include salts, sulphur (in the Fergana Valley), fluorspar, feldspar, glauconite, wollastonite, graphite, asbestos and precious and semi-precious stones. Building materials are abundant, such as various types of

709
Chahar Minar madrasa, built 1807, Bukhara.

710
Monumental mosaic including an Uzbek lute player, put up during the Soviet period, Tashkent. It is a typical example of using folkloristic subjects presented in the style of 'socialist realism' for propaganda purposes.

stones in the mountains, silica sands (e.g. around Tashkent), loess clay for brick-making as well as limestone and gravel.

Climate: Hot summers, freezing winters

Uzbekistan's climate, characterised by large seasonal variations in temperature and precipitation, is basically continental and moderate and in the south continental and subtropical. Rather dry winters are followed by cool and wet springs with maximum rainfall; summers are dry and hot, and in autumn the temperature starts to fall again, with increasing cloud cover and night-frost. The length of winter rapidly increases from the south (1½ to 2 months) to the northwest (5 months on the Ustyurt plateau).

Circulation is influenced by arctic, moderate and tropical air masses. From November to April the coincidence of hot tropical air over the Iranian uplands and cold air over Kazakhstan and northern Central Asia creates high pressure resulting in precipitative cyclones. Cold air blowing from the Arctic and the occurence of high pressure areas are quite often encountered in winter which therefore tends to be harsh but seldom very wet. From May to October continental tropical air masses cause the virtual absence of cyclones.

Annual temperatures vary greatly both in seasonal and regional terms. In January, the coldest month, there is a noticeable north-south gradient. In the south only at sheltered locations does the monthly average stay above freezing point, and even in the Fergana Valley temperatures fall a few degrees below zero, but to the north of the mountains they fall to -10°C on the Ustyurt plateau. Absolute minima can reach -38°C on the Ustyurt and -30°C in the south. At the same time one might encounter January temperatures of between 15°C and 20°C. The July average is 30°C, but it can often be much warmer; in the foothills maxima of 42°C to 47°C are common. Changes in temperature during the transitional periods are less marked. During September and October the air cools down rather fast, and in late October/early November the first frost marks the end of the cotton-growing season. Spring is usually quite wet; the transition into summer takes only about ten to fifteen days in the low-lying regions (late February/early March), while in the uplands 3½ months is the average.

The longest periods of dry weather in the south can last for up to 220 days, during which the humidity never rises above thirty per cent. The high air temperature causes much evaporation, with an annual average of nine hundred millimetres on the banks of the Aral Sea and twelve hundred to fifteen hundred millimetres in the southern Kyzylkum. Such high degrees of evaporation are not at all compensated for by precipitation which in the lowlands is only one hundred to two hunded millimetres. In the shadow of the mountain ranges this rises to three hundred to four hundred millimetres, just permitting some types of agriculture, while in the mountains themselves precipitation is about eight hundred to one thousand millimetres (Tianshan). Besides seasonal variations, annual variations also have to be taken into account: In wet years the amount of precipitation can double, while in dry years it can fall by a quarter to a third.

The warm climate permits cultivation of sensitive crops like cotton, *kenaf* (or *ambari*; Hibiscus cannabinus), fruiting plants and in the far south even some sugar-cane. At the same time it necessitates large-scale irrigation systems which then again cause much evaporation.

Water supply: A scarce resource

The largest amount of surface drainage comes from the mountains, while the Amu Darya and Syr Darya are lowland rivers with sources outside the country. Of their annual discharge (79 and 38 sq.km, respectively) only ten and eight per cent respectively goes to Uzbekistan. Most of the other large rivers likewise have their main catchment areas in neighbouring countries. The amounts of water from the mountains is dependent on melting snow and glacial ice, and in the lower reaches on the spring rains. During the second March decade melting water comes from a height of two thousand metres and during the first April decade from a height of three thousand metres. In the foothills and lowlands natural drainage has been much interfered with by irrigation and damming-up.

The character of these discharges is closely related to the formation of slush caused by a sudden rise in the amount of water rushing over loose sediment. Like a landslide, the slush quickly gravitates down the steep slopes, posing a constant threat to the foothill settlements. Slushes are most likely in April and May after a rapid rise in the temperature and happen most frequently on the north side of the Fergana Valley.

The most important use of drainage water is for irrigation and power generation. The energetic potential of Uzbekistan's rivers has been calculated at 7.1 million kW, which could produce an annual output of 107 billion kW. The best locations for hydroelectric power plants are the Fergana Valley and the Zeravshan, Chirchik and Surkhan rivers.

Population: Rapid increase and employment problems

Already during the Soviet era Uzbekistan had the highest population growth rate of all republics. In the early 1990s the excess of births over deaths was 33.3 to 6.3 (per 1000), giving a natural growth rate of twenty-seven. The highest rural population density is found in the district of Andizhan in the Fergana basin (427 inhabitants per sq.km). The lack of employment opportunities has led to increasing migration to larger towns and cities, but even there demand for jobs much exceeds supply.

Employment in the primary sector still predominates. In 1987 nearly as many people were employed in agriculture (*sovkhozes*) and ancillary occupations (905.000) as in manufacturing (1.017.500). Most of the 1.041.000 members of kolkhozes must be added to this number of agricultural workers, and even then family members helping out on

private plots are not yet taken into account. Since the break-up of the Soviet Union the situation has deteriorated even further because of a considerable fall in orders for industrial goods. It is only due to the fact that privatisation has barely started that unemployment has so far not reached dramatic proportions.

Employment also has an ethnic dimension. Employment of Uzbeks was considerably higher in agriculture (76 per cent; Uzbeks make up 71.4 per cent of the total population) than in industry (53 per cent). This means that a disproportionate number of qualified jobs in industry is filled by Russians. Now, however, pressure is put on the Russians to leave the country and some have already done so. As a consequence the already scarce jobs in industry will need to be filled by less qualified personnel which will further diminish their economic value.

Ethnic composition and ethno-territorial conflicts

Like the former Soviet Caucasus, the countries of Central Asia have repeatedly been heavily impeded in their socio-economic development by ethnic conflicts. Inter-ethnic disputes about land-ownership in the Osh area in 1990 and pogroms against the Meskhetians deported in 1944 from southern Georgia to Central Asia, in particular to the Fergana Valley, illustrate the potential dangers in a markedly multi-ethnic region (Halbach 1991). It is perhaps revealing that in czarist times Central Asia including southern Kazakhstan was called 'Russian Turkestan' (the best comprehensive account is still Machatschek 1921). A major reason for dividing up this large region, which in the early years of this century was beginning to regard itself as an entity in its own right, were fears of the early Soviet regime about an emerging Pan-Turkic movement.

If we go far back in time we encounter the somewhat similar cultural diversity of Transoxiana in Hellenistic times. Since the High Middle Ages the region first saw the arrival of Turkic-speaking groups from Inner Asia and then their slow merging in terms of socio-economics, linguistics, culture and politics, too (Fragner 1989:19). While the Turkish nomads and horsemen became settled and drawn into the orbit of Iranian-influenced urban culture, most of the other peoples in turn adopted Turkic languages. The settled urban and rural population not organised on tribal lines became known as 'Sarts' or 'Tajiks', both appellations having slightly pejorative connotations. ('Tajik' was at first also used in the Iranian region as a term for a non-tribal people, and only later acquired its modern ethno-linguistic sense.)

The traditional division distinguishes between the nomads and nomadic pastoral peoples living according to customary laws (*adat*) on the one hand, and the sedentary urban (merchants, craftsmen) and rural (peasants) population on the other. People defined themselves according to religious and regional affiliations and not - as nowadays - by the languages they speak, so that simplistic polarising concepts (Iranian - Turkish, urban - nomadic, bureaucracy -

army) tended to be rough and not very meaningful (Baldauf 1995). Against the background of socio-economic and ethno-linguistic differentiations, the Pan-Turkic concern was a somewhat artificial phenomenon, as Turkestan lacked a common cultural denominator. At the time of the creation of Russian Turkestan in the late nineteenth century and of the Turkestan Autonomous Socialist Soviet Republic (1918), Khiva and Bukhara were still independent states. The creation of a separate political entity and later of a republic by the Soviets gave the Uzbeks a highly valued focus for identification. The pejorative term 'Sart' disappeared and Eastern Turkish, the language of the educated, became the basis of a distinct cultural development.

The arguments about Bukhara and Samarkand (Tajik claims) and Tajik Khojent (Uzbek claims) go to show that the historical background to the artificial creation of 'nations' remains unforgotten. History is indeed a benchmark of all the present areas of confrontation (Glezer et al. 1991):

- With varying determination Karakalpakia aims at secession from Uzbekistan and possible merger with Kazakhstan. The Karakalpaks are a people of mixed Uzbek-Kazakh origin, whose economy is mainly based on the Ustyurt plateau - the greater part of which belongs to Kazakhstan - and the chief victims of the ecological calamities resulting from the drying-up of the Aral Sea.
- Uzbekistan, regarding herself as the territorial successor state of the Khiva khanate and Bukhara emirate, lays claim to part of the Tashauz and Chardzhou districts in Turkmenistan, which formerly belonged to these states.
- The Turkmens in turn claim back from Uzbekistan the lands along the Amu Darya.
- Uzbekistan demands from Kazakhstan the southern part of Chimkent. - Tajikistan claims parts of Samarkand and Bukhara located in the Zeravshan valley, on the grounds of the high Tajik percentage of the population. For the same reason it lays claim to the section of the Surkhan Darya in southern Uzbekistan.
- Constant friction exists between the indigenous population and more recent arrivals from Slavonic countries on account of which large parts of the Russian population have left. A particularly dramatic case was the enforced resettlement of Meskhetians after pogrom-like riots in the Fergana Valley.
- The tense situation in the Fergana basin is caused equally by Uzbekistan, Kirghizstan and Tajikistan. Here the main conflict revolves around the age-old antagonisms between farmers and herdsmen.

Agriculture: The burden of cotton monoculture

In the Soviet empire, Uzbekistan was by far the largest producer of cotton (1990: 5.06 mill. tons raw cotton, i.e., 60.9 per cent of Soviet production). Because Uzbekistan's climate is not as warm as that of Tajikistan or Turkmenistan, only a third of its cotton is suitable for industrial processing. The present-day cotton crisis results from increasing soil degradation. Since the late 1920s, and on a much larger scale since the 1950s and 1960s, when agriculture was restructured, the irrigation areas for cotton were constantly enlarged, the consumption of water for irrigation rose, the percentage of other crops for rotation was cut back with fertilisers and the soil and surface became ever more saltified due to other chemicals. Large areas have already become unsuitable for cultivation, the situation being most critical in the Amu Darya delta.

Other factors have contributed to the cotton crisis: The expansion undertaken with a view of supplying the world market drove up investment costs until the capital outlay for agriculture reached one-third of total capital investment. The rising costs of labour, mechanisation and chemicals were an additional burden. In the mid-1980s it was discovered that for years statistics had been manipulated, showing much higher output to obtain more subsidies.

Since the nineteenth century there has been a disparity between cultivation and processing. Uzbekistan was increasingly placed at a structural disadvantage, since processing was mainly done at locations within Russia proper so that this added value was lost to her.

Since the 1980s attempts have been made to change the structure of cultivation, but this has proved difficult on account of the degraded soil. It has been decided that more space should be provided for the growing of cereals for bread-making to ensure a basic supply of foodstuff. During the 1980s there were relatively large variations in the yields, mostly of wheat and especially among winter crops. Today the neglect of cereal cultivation causes regional shortages of wheat and bread; even the less populated regions have to make do with ever-decreasing rations.

The agricultural situation in Central Asia makes land reform imperative. The problem is closely bound up with questions of privatisation and especially with ownership of real estate. One often encounters the argument that private ownership of land has no tradition in Central Asia; there seems therefore to be little initiative for change. For the present Uzbekistan has strictly rejected privatisation of land and only allows leasehold arrangements.

Industrial development

Uzbekistan's rich deposits of raw materials are not matched by adequate industrial exploitation. Industrialisation came with the construction of railways, with the repair workshops forming the nucleus of metal-processing industries and later of engineering industries. Modern cotton gins as well as other agro-industrial installations followed the expansion of the rail network. Under Stalin, in Central Asia as in other greater regions iron and steel works were set up even if the supply of basic raw materials was inadequate. Right from the beginning Bekabad was among the less profitable enterprises. During the Second World War the industrialisation of Central Asia was boosted by the transfer of complete plants from the western Soviet republics, which sometimes also involved resettlement of personnel. These factories are now technically outdated. Some new projects were started after

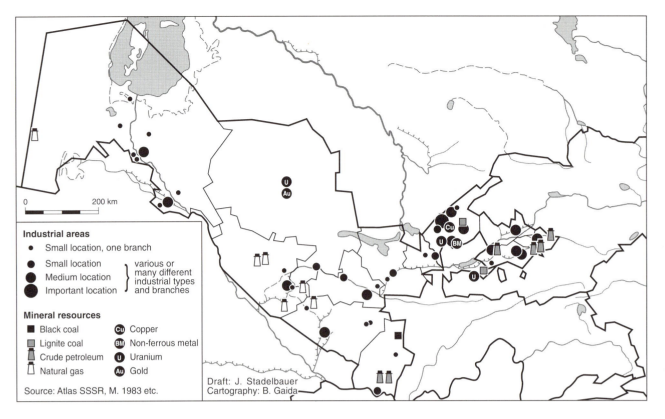

711
Industrial areas in Uzbekistan.

the War, but the very low rate of investment has hampered such efforts. More importantly, demands to absorb part of the rural labour force into industrial projects were never seriously addressed.

Tourism: An underexploited industry

Tourism started already in the 1920s and 30s, but remained relatively modest before the 1960s. It was then that a denser network of facilities and organisations was developed throughout the country but in particular in Tashkent, the Fergana Valley and the picturesque 'oriental' cities of Samarkand, Khiva and Bukhara. At the same time the number of visitors from abroad greatly increased, their main destinations being then as now the historical city sights. The mountainous regions to the south and east of Tashkent are a potentially rich area for excursions but have so far remained largely unexplored. For winter sports the Chimgan area is mainly attracting urbanites from Tashkent. Meanwhile Uzbekistan again makes efforts to attract foreign tourists which might also help to revive traditional arts and crafts.

Socio-economic transformation

'Transformation' is the general term for the recent economic policies pursued by the successor states of the former Soviet Union which aim at privatisation, the transition to a market economy and access to international markets. Although Uzbekistan has made a start in this direction, compared to other successor states it lags behind in introducing both privatisation of industries and market-oriented measures. Like other Central Asian states, Uzbekistan seems to develop a way of its own which does not follow the Western model. Some Western concepts are being adopted, but simultaneously there is a revaluation of Islamic traditions which for the time being has eschewed fundamentalist doctrines. People are wary of Western democratic concepts and seem to be averse to a multi-party system. So in regard to systemic changes as well, Uzbekistan represents a mixture of East European and Oriental features.

(In this essay place-names follow the Russian toponyms except for the Tianshan (Russ. and Uzbek: Tyan Shan), since most maps still lack Uzbek versions.)

The Aral Sea: A Regional Ecologic Disaster with Global Implications

Jörg Stadelbauer

The problem of the Aral Sea – A focal issue of the ecology and regional development of Central Asia

The fact that the water level of the Aral Sea is constantly decreasing and that the lake may eventually disappear altogether, has been known for several years, but the phenomenon could not be explained conclusively. In recent years new insights have been gained thanks to research by West and East European scholars, but so far no solution for the impending disaster has been found.

The one-sided orientation of agriculture towards cotton and rice (the latter mainly along the lower reaches of the Syr Darya) necessitated a great amount of irrigation. Rice cultivation started in the early 1960s after the Soviet Union had broken off relations with China and needed food crops, while the expansion of cotton-growing was partly to supply foreign markets. Increased irrigation greatly reduced the amount of water discharged into the Aral Sea and began to lower the water level.

Covering an area of 69,500 sq.km in 1960, the Aral Sea was the world's fourth-largest lake. Since then the water surface has been reduced by half (33,600 sq.km in 1993 according to satellite data) and the water mass by more than three quarters (from 1040 to 231 cu.km) (Dech and Ressl 1993). By far the largest amounts of discharge comes from the Syr Darya and Amu Darya which in their headwater regions on the Tianshan and Pamir ranges annually collect some 55 cu.km of water. However, of this less than ten per cent reaches the Aral Sea (average 5 cu.km). As a result the salinity has risen between 1960 and 1992 from five to thirty grammes per litre. During the same period the water level has sunk from fifty-three to 36.5 metres above mean sea-level, for the last few years at an annual rate of ninety centimetres. Since 1987 the Aral Sea is dividing up into two smaller lakes each with its separate water economy and linked only by a canal.

Causes: An unsuitable irrigation system

The chief culprit of these developments was the Soviet agrarian policy with its reliance on giant agricultural units. Before 1917 the most common unit was the small farm of two to three hectares, of which fields accounted for 0.3 to 0.8 hectares. Although much water was lost through infiltration and evaporation (up to 30 per cent), altogether utilisation was more efficient than it is today. There was less saltification of the soil and of excess irrigation water and less loss of soil fertility, eventually resulting in higher yields (Micklin 1992:270).

Since the 1920s modern irrigation techniques have changed the situation by farming much larger plots with more efficient machinery. Since the 1950s the irrigation area has been continually expanded, in the 1980s from 3.5 to 4.2 million hectares (*Narodnoye ... Uzbekskoy* 1991:255).

At the turn of the century the irrigated area fed by tributaries of the Aral Sea covered some 2.8 million hectares as against the present 7.5 million, according to official statistics. In some of the areas the soil is too saltified to produce reasonable yields. This means that only part of the total irrigated area is worked efficiently and that much water is lost above the normal rate of infiltration and evaporation.

Further losses are caused by transportation along long-distance canals such as the Karshi and Amu-Bukhara Canals. Leakage occurs at the floor and sides of the conduits because of bad insulation, while further losses are sustained through evaporation along uncovered stretches of the canals.

For an overall perspective of the problem, we need to take into account the traditional significance of water in Islamic countries of the East, where water was as important a resource as land. Therefore the problems of the Aral Sea are connected with the more general question of privatisation of land. Soviet policies had the effect of estranging the rural population from traditional methods of managing scarce resources.

Consequences: Health problems

The most dramatic consequence besides the loss of water is the damage caused to the health of the population. Chemicals used for agricultural purposes seep into the subsoil and are carried by excess irrigation water into the Aral basin. The lake's diminishing water mass has resulted in higher salinity, and because of the drop in the water level the chemical salts now lie exposed, contaminating the sand and dust blown everywhere by the wind. An estimated amount of seventy-five million tons of salt and sand in the atmosphere thus spreads across the delta region and further away. The result will be serious health damages in the vicinity of the Aral Sea, especially in Karakalpakia, with considerably reduced infant life expectancy. The worst data pertains to 1986, when 7.2 per cent of life-born infants died within a year in Karakalpakia, and 4.62 per cent in Uzbekistan as a whole. Data for 1990 shows some improvement, giving 4.92 per cent for Karakalpakia and 3.46 per cent for Uzbekistan (*Narodnoye ... Uzbekskoy* 1991:20).

Regional consequences: Economic decline and climatic change

Falling water levels and increasing salinity have nearly wiped out the fishing industry. Images of fishing boats lying idle on salty beaches have repeatedly appeared in the media over the last years. The fishing town of Muynak in Karakalpakia has meanwhile been cut off from the lake and lost its economic base.

The large surface of water has had a moderating influence on the winter temperatures of the cold steppes.

Compared to the period 1951-1960, relative humidity has dropped and the frost period has lengthened. It seems possible that the Amu Darya delta will loose its significance as a cotton-growing region. Because the waters of the Amu Darya do not pile up anymore during spring floods and the water table influenced by the Aral Sea has fallen, large tracts of the delta are desiccated and widespread desertification can be observed.

The water used for irrigation has also shown a marked increase in salinity of up to two grammes per litre, making it ever less suitable for cotton cultivation. Because of chemical contamination and high salinity, utilisation for drinking purposes is highly problematic and injurious to public health. Plans to expand the supply of potable water have been shelved because of general underdevelopment and lack of money. This is part of a vicious circle, for the consumption of contaminated water only adds to the health hazards caused by the atmospheric spread of salt and sand.

Can the situation be remedied?

Remedial proposals mainly suggest a more economical utilisation of water; Russian experts believe that savings of 31.5 cu.km by the year 2010 are possible, while Western observers estimate savings of only 10 to 20 cu.km. To stabilise the water level at about forty metres would need savings or an input of 35 cu.km per year, of which 15 cu.km could be saved by improved insulation and 20 cu.km by more careful utilisation. Such savings could be made by installing sprinkler systems or drop irrigation varying in intensity according to different crops, by a reduction in the size of plots together with overflow and furrow irrigation, by covering the open sections of canals and other methods of resource conservation. The estimated costs of such improvements were put at 45 to 59 billion roubles in 1991, i.e., before high inflation set in; after the demise of the Soviet Union the realisation of such projects appears even less likely.

A project abandoned in 1986 to the relief of many ecologists concerned the transfer of water from Siberia to Central Asia. (For the historical background of this project and the conflicting arguments, which were always partly politically motivated, see Radvanyi 1990:250) It has recently been revived by the Central Asian Research Institute for Irrigation (SANIIRI) with the aim of an annual transfer of twenty cu.km (the earlier project had envisaged 27.5 cu.km). Again prospects seem unpromising since the break-up of the Soviet Union. As before, the main stumbling block is the conflict between the Siberian and Central Asian lobbies - although now they represent independent states, which adds an eco-political aspect to the already complicated situation.

It is absolutely necessary that concomitant measures are taken within the social context, especially precautionary steps in health care and improvements in the welfare system. The present situation in Central Asia shows all the symptoms of the vicious circle characteristic of underdeveloped countries: A narrow economic base allows only limited investment, which restricts the national income, which then results in insufficient health care and severe supply deficiencies. Priorities are defined in purely economic terms, without any consideration of the social and ecological consequences. The results are deficiencies in food supplies, increasing impoverishment of the population, a decline in productivity and severe unemployment in the face of a rapid increase in population.

No short-term solution to the present crisis seems to offer itself, although the seriousness of the situation is not disputed and numerous national and international research projects have been set in place. If the present trends are allowed to go on, the surface of the lake will again be almost halved by the year 2000, while the water volume will have fallen to 102 cu.km - one tenth of the volume in 1960. If one could increase the annual discharge of the Amu Darya and Syr Darya to 27 cu.km, it should be possible to continue the present balance; otherwise in 2015 the water surface would be reduced to 8057 sq.km and the water volume to 66 cu.km (Dech and Ressl 1993).

Management of the environment vs. politics

So far the various parties involved cannot even agree on assessing individual factors. The main points of contention are the amount of savings in water that can be attained and the feasibility of water transfers from Siberia. For the moment a more efficient utilisation of the water reserves of Central Asia seems impossible, thus precluding any increase in the discharge of the Syr Darya and Amu Darya.

One cannot discount the possibility that water will be used for political leverage. Conflicting claims to sections of the Amu Darya put forward by Uzbekistan, Tajikistan and Turkmenistan are an ominous sign. Discussions about changes in global climates, the repercussions of military conflicts or of famine nowadays have a political slant. The new political situation in Central Asia calls for a new way of interpreting the ecological problems of the Aral Sea: By now there seems to be little point in blaming the catastrophe on the failure of certain regional policies of the defunct Soviet Union. Instead we have to address the potential supra-regional or even global consequences of this disaster. The flight of considerable numbers of the population cannot be ruled out. The consequence would be a shift of the problem to a different locality, which may in turn necessitate international intervention.

Bibliographies

Bibliography for the contributions by M. Pavaloi
Andersen, J., and V. Iversen. *Orientalische Reise-Beschreibung.* (1st publ. 1669) Ed. D. Lohmeier. Tübingen, 1980.
Balsinger, R.W., and E.J. Kläy. *Bei Schah, Emir und Khan: Henri Moser Charlottenfels, 1844-1923.* Schaffhausen, 1992.
Barthold, W. *Turkestan down to the Mongol Invasion.* 2nd ed. London, 1958.
Bergmann, B.F. *Nomadische Streifereien unter den Kalmücken in den Jahren 1802 und 1803.* 4 vols. Riga, 1804-5.
Blunt, W. *The Golden Road to Samarkand.* London, 1973.
Bosworth, C.E. *The Medieval History of Iran, Afghanistan and Central Asia.* London, 1977.
Boulger, D.C. *Central Asian Portraits: The Celebrities of the Khanates and the Neighbouring States.* London, 1880.
Boulnois, L. *Die Straßen der Seide.* Trans. J.A. Frank. Vienna, 1964.
Burnaby, F. *A Ride to Khiva: Travels and Adventures in Central Asia.* London, 1877.
Burnes, A. *Travels into Bukhara.* 3 vols. London, 1834.
Chaudhuri, K.N. *Trade and Civilization in the Indian Ocean: An Economic History from the Rise of Islam to 1750.* Cambridge, 1985.
Clavijo, R.G. *Narrative of the Embassy of Ruy Gonzales de Clavijo to the Court of Timur at Samarkand A.D. 1403-06.* Ed. C.R. Markham. Reprint New York, 1970.
Debout, M., D. Eeckaute-Bardery and V. Fourniau, eds. *Routes d'Asie: Marchands et voyageurs XVe-XVIIIe siècle.* Actes du Colloque organisé par la Bibliothèque Interuniversitaire des Langues Orientals, Paris, 11-12 décembre 1986. Istanbul and Paris, 1988.
Dupree, L. "From Whence Cometh Pasta?" In *Ethnologie und Geschichte. Festschrift für Karl Jettmar.* Ed. P. Snoy. Wiesbaden, 1983.
Franz, H.G., ed. *Kunst und Kultur der Seidenstraße.* Graz, 1986.
Fraser, G. "Alim Khan and the fall of the Bokharan emirate in 1920." *Central Asian Survey* 7 (1988).
Gabain, A. von. *Das uigurische Königreich von Chotscho 850-1250.* Vol. 5 of Sitzungsberichte der Deutschen Akademie der Wissenschaften zu Berlin, Klasse für Sprachen, Literatur und Kunst. Berlin, 1961.
Grousset, R. *The Empire of the Steppes: A History of Central Asia.* New Brunswick, N.J., 1970.
Grünwedel, A. *Altbuddhistische Kultstätten in Chinesisch-Turkistan.* Berlin, 1912.
Hamann, G. "Die wissenschaftsgeschichtliche Bedeutung der Gesandtschaftsreisen mittelalterlicher Mönche an die Höfe Inner- und Ostasiens." *In Kirche und Staat in Idee und Geschichte des Abendlandes. Festschrift zum 70. Geburtstag von Ferdinand Maass, S.J.* Ed. W. Baum. Vienna and Munich, 1973.
Hambly, G., ed. *Zentralasien.* Vol. 16 of Fischer Weltgeschichte. Frankfurt/Main, 1966.
Haussig, H.W. *Die Geschichte Zentralasiens und der Seidenstraße in islamischer Zeit.* Darmstadt, 1988.
Hedin, S. *Central Asia and Tibet.* 2 vols. London, 1903.
Herbst, H., trans. *Der Bericht des Franziskaners Wilhelm von Rubruk über seine Reise in das Innere Asiens in den Jahren 1253-1255.* Leipzig, 1925.
Hopkirk, P. *Foreign Devils on the Silk Road: The Search for the Lost Cities and Treasures of Central Asia.* Oxford, 1980.
Jettmar, K., et al. *Geschichte Mittelasiens.* Leiden and Cologne, 1966.
Krafft, H. *A travers le Turkestan russe.* Paris, 1902.
Le Coq, A. von. *Von Land und Leuten in Ostturkistan: Berichte und Abenteuer der 4. deutschen Turfanexpedition.* Leipzig, 1928
Le Coq, A. von. *Bilderatlas zur Kunst- und Kulturgeschichte Mittelasiens.* Berlin, 1925.
Lemercier-Quelquejay, C., G. Weinstein and S.E. Wimbush, eds. *Passé turco-tatar, présent soviétique. Etudes offertes à Alexandre Bennigsen.* Louvain and Paris, 1986.
Lentz, T.W., and G.D. Lowry, see Los Angeles 1989.
Lewis, R.A., ed. *Geographic Perspectives on Soviet Central Asia.* London and New York, 1992.
Los Angeles 1989, Lentz, T.W., and Glenn D. Lowry. *Timur and the Princely Vision. Persian Art and Culture in the Fifteeth Century.* Exh. cat. Los Angeles County Museum and Arthur M. Sackler Gallery, Washington, D.C. Los Angeles and Washington, D.C. 1989.
Moser, H. *A travers l'Asie central.* Paris, 1885.
Nagel, T. *Timur der Eroberer und die islamische Welt des späten Mittelalters.* Munich, 1993.
New York 1982. *Along the Ancient Silk Routes: Central Asian Art from the West Berlin State Museums.* Exh. cat. Metropolitan Museum of Art. New York, 1982.
Pelliot, P. *Les Grottes de Touen-houang.* 6 vols. Paris, 1922-24.
Rickmers, W.G.R. *Alai! Alai! Arbeiten und Erlebnisse der Deutsch-Russischen Alai-Pamir-Expedition.* Leipzig, 1930.
Shaw, R.B. *The History of the Khojas of Eastern Turkestan.* Suppl. of the *Journal of the Royal Asiatic Society of Bengal.* 1897.
Stein, M.A. *Ancient Khotan.* 2 vols. Oxford, 1907.
-. *Innermost Asia.* 4 vols. Oxford, 1928.
-. *On Ancient Central-Asian Tracks: Brief Narratives of Three Expeditions in Innermost Asia and North-Western China.* London, 1933.
Tadao, U. and T. Sugimura, eds. *The Significance of Silk Roads in the History of Human Civilizations.* Osaka, 1992.
Thackston, W.M., ed. *A Century of Princes: Sources on Timurid History and Art.* Cambridge, Mass., 1989.
Warner, L. *The Long Old Silk Road.* Arrowsmith, 1927.
Younghusband, F. *The Heart of the Continent.* London, 1896.
Yule, H., ed. *The Book of Ser Marco Polo, the Venetian, Concerning the Kingdoms and Marvels of the East.* 3rd ed., rev. H. Cordier. 2 vols. London, 1903.

Bibliography for contribution by H. Gaube
Altheim, F. *Geschichte der Hunnen.* 5 vols. Berlin, 1959-62.
Altheim, F., and J. Rehork, eds. *Der Hellenismus in Mittelasien.* Darmstadt, 1969.
Ammianus Marcellinus. *Rerum gestarum libri.* Trans. J.C. Rolfe. London, 1935-9.
Arrian (Flavius Arrianus). *Anabasis Alexandri.* Trans. E. Iliffe Robson. London, 1929.
Azarpay, G. *Sogdian Painting.* Berkeley, 1981.
Belenitzky, A.M. *Central Asia.* London, 1969.
Bernard, P., et al. *Fouilles d'Aï Khanoum.* 4 vols. Paris, 1973-87.
Bivar, A.D.H. "The History of Eastern Iran"In *The Cambridge History of Iran,* ed. E.Yarshater. *Vol. 3, pt. 1.* Cambridge, 1983.
Dandamaev, M.A. *A Political History of the Achaemenid Empire.* Leiden, 1989.
Freye, R.N. *Persien.* Munich, 1969.
Gabain, A. von. *Einführung in die Zentralasienkunde.* Darmstadt, 1979.
Göbl, R. *Dokumente zur Geschichte der iranischen Hunnen in Baktrien und Indien.* Wiesbaden, 1967.
Haussig, H.W. *Die Geschichte Zentralasiens und der Seidenstraße in vorislamischer Zeit.* Darmstadt, 1992.
Herodotus. *The Histories.* Trans. A. de Sélincourt. Harmondsworth, 1965.
Humbach, J. *Baktrische Sprachdenkmäler.* Wiesbaden, 1966-1967.
Maenchen-Helfen, O.J. *The World of the Huns.* Berkeley, 1973.
Masson, V.M. *Das Land der tausend Städte.* Munich, 1982.
Procopius. *Bella.* Trans. H.B. Dewing and G. Downey. London, 1914-40.
Schlumberger, D. *Der hellenisierte Orient.* Baden-Baden, 1969.
Stavisky, B.J. *Mittelasien: Kunst der Kuschan.* Leipzig, 1979.
-. *Die Völker Mittelasiens im Lichte ihrer Kulturdenkmäler.* Bonn, 1982.
Tarn, W.W. *The Greeks in Bactria and India.* Cambridge, 1951.
Tolstow, S.P. *Auf den Spuren der altchoresmischen Kultur.* Berlin, 1953.
Zeimal, E.V. "The Political History of Transoxiana". In *Cambridge History of Iran,* ed. E. Yarshater. Vol 3, pt. 1. Cambridge, 1983.

Bibliography for the contribution by K.J. Brandt
An, Jiayao. *Early Chinese Glassware.* Trans. M. Henderson. No. 12 of *Chinese Translations,* Oriental Ceramic Society. London, 1987.
Berlin 1993. M. Pjotrowskij, ed. *Die Schwarze Stadt an der Seidenstraße: Buddhistische Kunst aus Khara Khoto (10.-13. Jahrhundert).* Exh. cat. Museum für Indische Kunst. Berlin, 1993.
Berlin 1985. *Europa und die Kaiser von China.* Exh. cat. Martin-Gropius-Bau, Berlin. Frankfurt/Main, 1985.
Boulnois, L. *Die Straßen der Seide.* Vienna, 1964.
Cameron, N. *Barbarians and Mandarins: Thirteen Centuries of Western Travelers in China.* New York and Tokyo, 1970.
Dortmund 1993 . D. Kuhn, ed. *Chinas goldenes Zeitalter: Die Tang-Dynastie (618-907 n. Chr.) und das kulturelle Erbe der Seidenstraße.* Exh. cat. Museum für Kunst und Kulturgeschichte der Stadt Dortmund. Heidelberg, 1993.
Franke, H., and R. Trauzettel. *Das chinesische Kaiserreich.* Vol. 19 of *Fischer Weltgeschichte.* Frankfurt/Main, 1968.
Gernet, J. *Die chinesische Welt: Die Geschichte Chinas von den Anfängen bis zur Jetztzeit.* Frankfurt/Main, 1979.
Goepper, H., ed. Das alte China: Geschichte und Kultur des Reiches der Mitte. Munich, 1988.
Hildesheim 1994. A. Eggebrecht, ed. *China, eine Wiege der Weltkultur: 5000 Jahre Erfindungen und Entdeckungen.* Exh. cat. Roemer- und Pelizaeus-Museum, Hildesheim. Mainz, 1994.
Hopkirk, P. *Foreign Devils on the Silk Road: The Search for the Lost Treasures of Central Asia.* Oxford, 1980.
Kuhn, D. *Status und Ritus: Das China der Aristokraten von den Anfängen bis zum 10. Jahrhundert nach Christus.* Heidelberg, 1991.
Los Angeles 1994. A.T. Kessler, ed. *Empires beyond the Great Wall: The Heritage of Genghis Khan.* Exh. cat. Natural History Museum of Los Angeles County. Los Angeles, 1994.
Mackerras, C. *The Uighur Empire According to the T'ang Dynasty Histories: A Study in Sino-Uighur Relations 744-840.* Canberra, 1972.
Mahler, J.G. *The Westerners among the Figurines of the T'ang Dynasty of China.* Vol. 20 of *Orientale Roma.* Rome, 1959.
Nara 1988a. S. Nakanishi and S. Ueda, eds. *The Grand Exhibition of Silk Road Civilizations: The Oasis and Steppe Routes.* Exh. cat. Nara Prefectural Museum of Art. Nara, 1988.
Nara 1988b. K. Nishikawa and S. Ueda, eds. *The Grand Exhibition of Silk Road Civilizations: The Route of Buddhist Art.* Exh. cat. Nara Prefectural Museum of Art. Nara, 1988.
Schafer, E.H. *The Golden Peaches of Samarkand: A Study in T'ang Exotics.* Berkeley, 1963.
Singapore 1991. G. Wong et al. *The Silk Road: Treasures of Tang China.* Exh. cat. Empress Palace Museum. Singapore, 1991.

Bibliography for the contributions by J. Kalter
Abdullayev, T., D. Fakhretdinova and A. Khakimov. *A Song in Metal.* Tashkent, 1986.
Albrecht, M. *Russisch Centralasien.* Leipzig, 1883.
Allan, J.W. *Nishapur: Metalwork of the Early Islamic Period.* New York, 1982.
Anthony, D., D.Y. Telegin and D. Brown. "Die Anfänge des Reitens." *Spectrum der Wissenschaft* 2 (1992).
Balsinger, R.W., and E.J. Kläy. Bei Schah, Emir und Khan: Henri Moser Charlottenfels, 1844-1923. Schaffhausen, 1992.
Barret, D. *Islamic Metalwork in the British Museum.* London, 1949.
Barthold, W. *Turkestan down to the Mongol Invasion.* London, 1928.
Berlin 1981. *Islamische Kunst: Meisterwerke aus dem Metropolitan Museum of Art, New York.* Exh. cat. Berlin, 1981.
Bivar, A.D.H. "The Stirrup and Its Origins." *Oriental Art,* new series, vol. 1, no. 2 (1955).

Diem, C. Asiatische Reiterspiele: *Ein Beitrag zur Kulturgeschichte der Völker*. Berlin, 1941.
Düsseldorf 1973. *Islamische Keramik*. Exh. cat. Hetjensmuseum Düsseldorf, 1973.
Fakhretdinova, D.A. *Jevelirnoye iskusstvo Uzbekistana* (Ancient jewellery from Uzbekistan). Tashkent, 1988.
Fehérvári, G. *Islamic Metalwork of the Eighth to the Fifteenth Century in the Keir Collection*. London, 1976.
Folk Art of Uzbekistan. Tashkent, 1979.
Folsach, K. *Islamic Art: The David Collection*. Copenhagen, 1990.
Gabain, A. von. "Pferd und Reiter im mittelalterlichen Zentralasien." *Central Asian Journal* 10 (1965).
Hambly, G., ed. *Zentralasien*. Vol. 16 of *Fischer Weltgeschichte*. Frankfurt/Main, 1966.
Hasson, R. *Later Islamic Art*. Jerusalem, 1987.
Haussig, H.W. "Awaren, Shuan-Shuan und Hephthaliten." *In Handbuch der Orientalistik*. Pt. 1, sect. 5. Leiden, 1966.
Helmersen, G. von. *Alexander Lehmann's Reise nach Buchara und Samarkand in den Jahren 1841 und 1842*. (1852). Reprint Osnabrück, 1969.
Janata, A. *Schmuck aus Afghanistan*. Graz, 1981.
Jerusalem 1967/8. Goldmann-Schwartz. *Bokhara*. Exh. cat. Israel Museum.
Jettmar, K. "Die Entstehung der Reiternomaden." *Saeculum* 17 (1966).
-. Die frühen Steppenvölker. Baden-Baden, 1975.
Johannsen, U. "Der Reitsattel bei den altaischen Völkern." *Central Asian Journal* 10 (1965).
-. "Geschichte und moderne Entwicklung des Nomadismus in Mittelasien." (paper presented at the *Seminar über das Nomadentum*, Heidelberg, 1975.)
Kalter, J. *Aus Steppe und Oase*. Stuttgart, 1983.
Kußmaul, F. "Das Reiternomadentum als historisches Phänomen". In *Nomadismus als Entwicklungsproblem*. 1969.
Lane, A. *Early Islamic Pottery*. London 1947.
-. *Later Islamic Pottery*. London 1957.
Lansdell, H. *Russisch-Central-Asien*. Leipzig, 1885.
Leningrad 1988. Komleva, G. *Jewellery*. Exh. cat. Museum of the Ethnography of the Peoples of the USSR. Leningrad, 1988.
London, 1976. *The Arts of Islam*. Exh. cat. Hayward Gallery. London, 1976.
Meisterwerke aus dem Museum für Islamische Kunst, Berlin. Stuttgart and Zurich, 1980.
Milhofer, S.A. *Die Teppiche Zentralasiens*. Hanover, 1968.
Melikian-Chirvani, A.S. *Islamic Metalwork from the Iranian World: 8th to 18th centuries*. London, 1982.
Moscow 1984. Sykhova, N. *Traditional Jewellery from Soviet Central Asia and Kazakhstan: 19th and 20th Centuries from the Collection of the Museum of Oriental Art, Moscow*. Exh. cat. Museum of Oriental Art. Moscow, 1984.
Moser, H. *Durch Centralasien*. Leipzig, 1888.
New York 1973. Wilkinson, C.K. Nishapur: *Pottery of the Early Islamic Period*. Exh. cat. Metropolitan Museum of Art. New York, 1973.
Olufsen, O. *The Emir of Bokkara and His Country*. Copenhagen, 1911.
Otte, M. *Geschichte des Reitens von der Antike bis zur Neuzeit*. Warendorf, 1994.
Pander, K. *Sowjetischer Orient: Kunst und Kultur, Geschichte und Gegenwart der Völker Mittelasiens*. Cologne, 1982.
Paris 1992. *Terres secrètes de Samarcande: Céramiques du VIIIe au XIIIe siècle*. Exh. cat. Musée de l'Institut du Monde Arabe. Paris, 1992.
Pope, A., eds. *A Survey of Persian Art*. 14 vols. New ed. Tokyo 1964-77.
Schafer, E.H. *The Golden Peaches of Samarkand: A Study in T'ang Exotics*. Berkeley, 1963.
Schürmann, U. *Zentralasiatische Teppiche*. Frankfurt/Main, 1969.
Schwarz, F. von. *Turkestan*. Freiburg, 1900.
Schweinitz, H.H. Graf von. *Orientalische Wanderungen in Turkestan und im nordöstlichen Persien*. Berlin, 1910.
Spuler, B. "Geschichte Mittelasiens seit dem Auftreten der Türken." In *Handbuch der Orientalistik*. Sect. 1, vol. 5, pt. 5. Leiden, 1966.
Trippet, F. *Die ersten Reitervölker*. Hamburg, 1978.
Tshiyri, L.A. 'Tajik Jewellery' (in Russian). Academy of Sciences of the USSR, Institute for Oriental Research. Moscow, 1977.
Uzbek: The Textiles and Life of the Nomadic and Sedentary Uzbek Tribes of Central Asia. Exh. cat. Lörrach and Winterhur, 1979.
Westphal-Hellbusch, S., and J. Bruns. *Metallgefäße aus Buchara*. New series, vol. 29 of *Veröffentlichungen des Museums für Völkerkunde*. Berlin, 1974.
Wilkinson, C.K. *Iranian Ceramics*. New York, 1963.
Wissmann, H. von. "Bauer, Nomade und Stadt im islamischen Orient." In *Die Welt des Islam und die Gegenwart*. Stuttgart, 1961.
Zeller, R. "Dr. Henri Moser, 1844-1923." *Jahresbericht über die Enthnographische Sammlung in Bern*. Bern, 1923.

Bibliography for the contribution by A. von Gladiss
Allan, J.W. *Nishapur: Metalwork of the Early Islamic Period*. New York, 1982.
Atil, E., W.T. Chase and P. Jett. *Islamic Metalwork in the Freer Gallery of Art*. Washington D.C., 1985.
Balsinger, R.N., and E.J. Kläy. *Bei Schah, Emir und Khan: Henri Moser Charlottenfels, 1844-1923*. Schaffhausen, 1992.
Barret, D. *Islamic Metalwork in the British Museum*. London, 1949.
Barthold, W. *Turkestan down to the Twelfth Century*. 2nd ed. London, 1958.
Brisch, K., ed. *Islamische Kunst*. (Loose-leaf catalogue of unpublished objects in German museums). Mainz, 1981.
Bukhara: Caught in Time. Great Photographic Archives. Reading, 1993.
Chan Chun. *The Travels of an Alchemist: The Journey of the Taoist Chan Chun from China to the Hindukush at the Summons of Chingis Khan*. Trans. A. Waley. London, 1931.
Giuzalian, L.T. "The Bronze Qalamdan (pen-case) 542/1148 from the Hermitage Collection (1936-65)." *Ars Orientalis* 7 (1968).

Herzfeld, E. "A Bronze Pen-Case." *Ars Islamica* 3 (1936).
Komaroff, L. *The Golden Disk of Heaven: Metalwork of Timurid Iran*. Cosa Mesa, Calif., and New York, 1992.
Kondratieva, F.A. *"Keramika s zelenoy polivoy iz Paykenda"* (Green-glazed ceramics from Paykend). 6 (1971).
Kuwait 1990. A.A. Ivanov. *Masterpieces of Islamic Art in the Hermitage Museum*. Exh. cat. Dar al-Athar al-Islamiyyah. Kuwait, 1990.
Leningrad 1985. E.V. Zeimal. *Drevnosnu Tadzhikistana* (Antiquities from Tajikistan). Exh. cat. Leningrad. Dushanbe, 1985.
London 1976. *The Arts of Islam*. Exh. cat. Hayward Gallery. London, 1976
Marschak, B. *Silberschätze des Orients*. Leipzig, 1986.
Marshak, B. "Bronzovyi kuvshin iz Samarkanda" (A bronze ewer from Samarkand). In *Sredniya Aziya i Iran* (Central Asia and Iran). Eds. A.A. Ivanov and S.S. Sorokin. Leningrad, 1972.
Martin, F.R. *Kupferarbeiten aus dem Orient*. Stockholm, 1902.
Melikian-Chirvani, A.S. *Islamic Metalwork from the Iranian World: 8th-18th Centuries*. London, 1982.
Moscow 1991. K.A. Abdullaaev et al. *Kultura i iskusstvo drevnego Uzbekistana* (Culture and Art of Ancient Uzbekistan). Exh. cat. Moscow, 1991.
Paris 1992. *Terres secrètes de Samarcande: Céramiques du VIIIe au XIIIe siècle*. Exh. cat. Musée de l'Institut du Monde Arabe. Paris, 1992.
Pugachenkova, G., and L.I. Rempel. *Vidayushchiesya Pamyatniki Izobrazitelnogo iskusstva Uzbekistana* (Great Art Treasures of Uzbekistan). Tashkent, 1961.
-. *Istoriya iskusstva Uzbekistana* (Art History of Uzbekistan). Moscow, 1965.
Pugachenkova, G., and A. Khakimov. *The Art of Central Asia*. Leningrad, 1988.
Sarre, F. *Erzeugnisse islamischer Kunst: Metall*. Berlin, 1906.
Stuttgart 1993. H. Forkl et al., eds. *Die Gärten des Islam*. Exh. cat. Linden-Museum. Stuttgart, 1993.
Veselovsky, N.I. "Geratskiy bronzoviy kotelok 559 goda gijri (1163 g. po r.kh.)." (A bronze vessel from Herat dated AH 559/1163 A.D.). *Materiali po Arkheologii Rossii* (St Petersburg) 33 (1910)
Westphal-Hellbusch, S., and I. Bruns. *Metallgefäße aus Buchara*. New series, vol. 29 of *Veröffentlichungen des Museums für Völkerkunde*. Berlin, 1974.
Zurich 1989. *Oxus: Neue Funde aus der Sowjetrepublik Tadschikistan. 2000 Jahre Kunst am Oxus-Fluß in Mittelasien*. Exh. cat. Museum Rietberg. Zurich, 1989.

Bibliography for the contributions by G. Helmecke
Archeologicheskie raboty na novostroykach Uzbekistana (Archaeological work at building sites in Uzbekistan. Tashkent 1990.
Belinskaya, N.A. *Dekorativnoe iskusstvo gornogo Tadzhikistana*. Dushanbe, 1965.
Clavijo, R. G. *Embassy to Tamerlane 1403-1406*. Trans. Guy Le Strange. London, 1928.
Dzhanibekov, U. D. *Kul'tura kazakhskogo remezla*. 1892.
Franses, M., and R. Pinner. "Large Medallion Susani." *Hali* 1, no. 2 (1978).
Helmecke, G. "Die 'Buchara' – Stickereien im Islamischen Museum zu Berlin." Vol. 23 of *Forschungen und Berichte*. Staatliche Museen zu Berlin. Berlin, 1983.
Herrmann, E. *Asiatische Teppich- und Textilkunst*. 2 vols. Munich, 1990.
Isaeva-Yunusova, N. *Tazhikskaya vyshivka* (Tajik embroidery). Moscow, 1979.
The Kirghiz Pattern. Frunze, 1986.
Los Angeles 1989. Lentz, T.W., and Glenn D. Lowry. *Timur and the Princely Vision: Persian Art and Culture in the Fifteenth Century*. Exh. cat. Los Angeles County Museum and Arthur M. Sackler Gallery, Washington, D.C., 1989.
Mirzaakhmedov, D.K. K *historii khudozhestvennoy kul'tury Bukhary* (On the history of Bukhara's artistic culture). Tashkent, 1990.
Moscow 1991. *Kultura i iskusstvo drevnego Uzbekistana* (Culture and Art of Ancient Uzbekistan). 2 vols. Exh. cat. Moscow, 1991.
Mukanov, M.S. *Kazakhskie domashnie khudozhestvennye remezla*. Alma-Ata, 1979.
Snessarew, G. *Unter dem Himmel von Chwarezm*. Moscow, 1989.
Sucharewa, O.A. "Das Ornament der dekorativen Stickereien Samarkands in der 2. Hälfte des 19. bis Anfang des 20. Jahrhunderts." In *Susani Usbekistans*. Eds. G.L. Tschepelewezkaja and O.A. Sucharewa. Hamburg, 1991.
Taube, J. *Welt und Leben in Stickereien und Märchen mittelasiatischer Völker: Untersuchungen zur Geschichte von Weltsicht*. Wiesbaden, 1993.
Vok, I. Suzani: *Eine textile Kunst aus Zentralasien*. Munich, 1994.

Bibliography for the contribution by M. Zerrnickel
Akhbarov, A. *Sapalli-Tepe*. Tashkent, 1973.
Barthold, W. "Khlopkovodstvo v Srednej Azii s istoritsheskish vremen do prikhoda russkikh" (Cotton cultivation in Central Asia from the beginnings until Russian's penetration. *Sochinenya*., T. II, ch. 1. Moscow, 1963.
-. "Istoriya kult'turnoy zisni Turkestana" (The History of cultural life in Turkestan). *Sochinenya*, ch. 1. Moscow, 1963.
-. "Turkestan v epokhu mongol'skogo nashestviya" (Turkestan at the time of the Mongol invasion). *Sochinenya*. T.1. Moscow, 1963.
Belenizkij, A. "Iz istorii sredneaziatskogo shelkotskatshevestva (k identifikazii tkani zandanachi)" [On the history of silk weaving in Central Asia (on identifying *zandanechi* fabrics)]. *Sovetskaya arkheologiya*. 2 (1961)
Blackwel, B. *Ikats: Woven Silks from Central Asia*. Oxford, 1988.
Bosshard, W. *Durch Tibet und Turkestan*. Stuttgart, 1930.
Bruhn, W., and M. Tilke. *Das Kostümwerk*. Berlin, 1941.
Bühler, A. *Ikat, Batik, Plangi*. 3 vols. Basel, 1972.
Chepelevezkaya, G. *Susani Uzbekistana* (Suzanis from Uzbekistan). Tashkent, 1969.
Coll, C., I. Cuallado and T. Rosa. *Ikat*. Barcelona, 1990.
Fakhretdinova, D. *Dekorativno-prikladnoe iskusstvo uzbekistana* (The decorative applied arts in Uzbekistan). Tashkent, 1972.
Gontcharova, P. *Zolotoshvejnoe iskusstvo Bukhary* (The art of gold brocade embroidery in Bukhara). Tashkent, 1986.
Hopkirk, P. *Die Seidenstraße*. Munich, 1986.
Janata, A. "Ikat in Afghanistan." *Afghanistan Journal* 5, no. 4 (1978).

Jerusalimskaya, A. "O severo-kavkazskom schelkovom puti v rannen srednevekov'ye" (The north Caucasian silk route of the early Middle Ages). *Sovetskaya arkheologiya* 2 (1967).

-. "K slozeniyi shkoly khudozestvennogo shelkotkashestva v Sogde" (On the development of the artistic school of silk weaving at Sogd). In *V Knige Srednjaja Aziya i Iran*. Leningrad, 1972.

Kalter, J., M. Pavaloi and M. Zerrnickel. *The Arts and Crafts of Syria*. London, 1992.

Kennedy, A. *Central Asian Ikats*. Philadelphia, 1980.

Kirdök, M. *Ikat*. Vienna, 1993.

Kislyakov, N. *Semi'ya i brak u Tadzikov* (The family and marriage among the Tadjiks). Moscow and Leningrad, 1959.

-. *Patriarkhal'no-feodal'nye otnocheniya sredi osedlogo selskogo naseleniya bukharskogo Khanstva v konce XIX-natchale XX v* (The patriarchic-feudal relationships among the settled villagers in the Bukhara Khanate in the late 19th/early 20th century). Moscow and Leningrad, 1962.

-. *Zanyatiya i byt narodov Sredney Azii* (Work and life of the peoples of Central Asia). Leningrad, 1971.

Klein, W. *Inozemnye tkani bytovavzhie v Rosii do XVIII V. i ikh terminologiya* (Foreign fabrics and their terminology in Russia before the 18th century). Moscow, 1925.

Klyashtornyi, S. "Epokha Kutadgu bilig" (The epoch of the Kutadgu bilig). *Sovetskaya turkologiya* 4 (1970).

-. "Epokha Makhmuda Kashkarskogo" (The epoch of Mahmud of Kashgaria). *Sovetskaya turkologiya* 1 (1972).

Kostyum narodov Srednej Azii (The costume of the peoples of Central Asia). Moscow, 1979.

Krafft, J. *A travers le Turkestan russe*. Paris, 1902.

Krauze, J. "Zametki O krasil'nom iskusstve tuzemcev" (Notes on the native arts of dyeing). *Russkiy Turkestan*, 2nd ed. Moscow, 1872.

Kustarnye promysly v bytu narodov Uzbekistana XIX-XXX vv. (Cottage industries in the daily life of the Uzbekistan peoples during the 19th and 20th century) Tashkent, 1986.

Levushkina, S. "O Vozniknovenii shelkovodstva v antishnoy Baktrii" (On the evolution of silk production in ancient Bactria). *Obshestvennye nauki v Uzbekistane*. Tashkent, 1987.

Lyubo-Lestnizhenko, E. *Drevnije shelkovye tkani, i vyshivki V V. do n.e.-III V. n.e. v sobranii Gos Ermitaga* (Ancient silk fabrics and embroideries of the 5th century B.C. to the 3rd century A.D. in the collection of the State Hermitage). Exh. cat.. Leningrad, 1961.

Machkamova, S. *Uzbekskie abrovye tkani* (Uzbekistan ikats). Tashkent, 1963.

Machkamova, S., et al. *khudozestvennaja kul'tura Srednej Azii IX-XIII vv.* (The artistic culture of Central Asia of the 9th to 13th century). Tashkent, 1983.

Mell, R. *Der Seidenspinner*. Stuttgart.

Messeli, R. *Seide*. Zurich, 1985.

Moser, H. *Durch Central-Asien*. Leipzig, 1888.

Mukminova, R. *Ocherki po istorii remezla v Samarkande i Bukhre v XVI v.v.* (Notes on the history of crafts in Samarkand and Bukhara during the 16th century). Tashkent, 1976.

Needham, J. *Textile Technology: Spinning and Reeling*. Vol. 5, pt. 9 of *Science and Civilisation in China*. by D. Kuhn. Cambridge, 1988.

Pugachenkova, G. "K istrii parandzi" (On the history of the paranja). *Sovetskaya enziklop*, N. 3 (1952).

-. *K istorii kostyuma Sredney Azii i Irana XV pervoy poloviny XVI vv. po dannym miniatyur* (On the history of costume in Central Asia and Iran in the 15th and the first half of the 16th century as documented in miniatures). Tashkent, 1956.

-. *Khalchayan*. Tashkent, 1966.

Sadykova, N., et al. *Kustarnye promysly v narodov Uzbekistana XIX-XX vv.* (Cottage industries in the daily life of the Uzbekistan peoples during the 19th and 20th century). Tashkent, 1986.

Shirokova, Z., et al. "Dekorativnye vyschivki tadzikov verchovjev Zeravchana" (Decorative embroidery of the Tajiks from the upper region of the Zeravshan). In *Istoriya i etnografiya narodov Srednej Azii* (History and ethnography of the Central Asian Peoples). Dushanbe, 1981.

Shepherd, D., and W. Henning. "Zandaniji Identified? Aus der Welt der Islamischen Kunst." In *Festschrift für E. Kühnel*. Berlin, 1959.

Sidorenko, A., A. Artykov and R. Radzhabov. *Zolotoye shit'je Bukhary*. (Gold brocade embroidery in Bukhara). Tashkent, 1981.

Sukhareva, O. *History of artecraft in Uzbekistan*. Moscow, 1953.

-. *Bukhara XIX-nachala XX vv.: Pozdnefeodal'yj gorod i ego naselenie* (Bukhara in the 19th and early 20th century: a late feudal city and its population). Moscow, 1966.

-. *O tkatzkikh remezlakh v Samarkande* (The weavers' craft in Samarkand). Dushanbe, 1981.

-. *Istoriya sredneaziatskogo kostyuma* (History of Central Asian costume). Moscow, 1982.

Tolstov, S., and T. Zhdanko. *Sredneaziatskiy etnografichkiy* (Central Asian ethnography). 2 vols. Moscow, 1954, 1959.

Tursunaliev, K. *Katalog vyshivok Uzbekistana XIX-XX v.* (Catalogue of the 19th and 20th century embroideries from Uzbekistan). Tashkent, 1976.

-. *Chyubeteika-odin iz izljublennych golovnych uborov narodov Uzbekistana* (*Chyubeteika* – a popular cap among the peoples of Uzbekistan). Tashkent, 1990.

Weimarn, B. *Iskusstvo Sredney Azii* (Arts of Central Asia). Moscow and Leningrad, 1940.

Westphal-Hellbusch, S., and C. Soltkahn. *Mützen aus Zentralasien und Persien*. Berlin, 1976.

Whitfield, R., and A. Farrer. *Caves of the Thousand Buddhas*. London, 1990.

Zerrnickel, M. "Der karakalpakische Ksysyl Kijimeschek." *Tribus* (Stuttgart) 34 (1985).

Zhukovskij, P. *Kulturnye rasteniya i ikh sorodichi* (Cultivated plants and their relatives). Leningrad, 1964.

Bibliography for the contribution by G. Dombrowski

Black, D., and C. Loveless, eds. *Embroidered Flowers from Thrace to Tartary*. London, 1981.

Cadoux, A.M. "Asian Domestic Embroideries: The Burrell Collection." *Arts of Asia* 10, no. 3 (1990).

Cootner, C.M. "Gardens of Paradise." *Hali* 30 (1986)

Franses, M., and R. Pinner. "Large Medaillion Suzani." *Hali* 1, no. 2 (1978).

Helmecke, G. "Die 'Buchara'-Stickereien im Islamischen Museum zu Berlin." Vol. 23 of *Forschungen und Berichte*. Staatliche Museen zu Berlin. Berlin, 1983.

Isaeva-Yunusova, N. *Tadzhikskaya vyshivka* (Tajik embroidery). Moscow, 1979.

Lörrach 1975. Franses, M., and R. Pinner. "Suzani." In *Uzbek*. Eds. D. Lindahl and T. Knorr. Exh. cat. Lörrach, 1975.

Mannheim 1991. Besch, F. *Susani: Stickereien aus Mittelasien*. Exh. cat. Franz Bausback. Mannheim, 1991.

Shaffer, D. "History and Technique [of suzanis]." *Hali* 30 (1986)

Sucharewa, see Tschepelewezkaja

Taube, J. "Suzani-Stickereien aus Mittelasien". Vol. 12 of *Kleine Beiträge aus dem Staatlichen Museum für Völkerkunde Dresden*. Dresden, 1991.

-. *Welt und Leben in Stickereien und Märchen mittelasiatischer Völker*. Wiesbaden, 1993.

Taube 1994, see Vok

Tsareva, E. "Suzanis of Central Asia." *Eothen* (Munich) 2/3 (1994).

Tschepelewezkaja, G.L., and O.A. Sucharewa. *Susani Usbekistans: Ein Beitrag zur Technik, Ornamentik und Symbolik der usbekischen Seidenstickerei*. Hamburg, 1991.

Tursunaliyev, K. *Katalog vyshivok usbekistana XIX-XX vv* (Catalogue of Uzbekistan embroidery of 19th and 20th century). Tashkent, 1976.

Vok, I. *Suzani: Eine textile Kunst aus Zentralasien*. Munich, 1994.

Yanai, Y. *Suzani: Central Asian Embroideries*. Exh. cat. Haaretz Museum. Tel Aviv, 1986.

Bibliography for the contributions by J. Stadelbauer

Allworth, E.A. *The Modern Uzbeks: From the Fourteenth Century to the Present. A Cultural History*. Stanford, 1990.

The Aral Basin: A Man-Made Environmental Catastrophe. Special issue of *GeoJournal* (Dordrecht) 1 (1995).

Baldauf, I. "Some thoughts on the making of the Uzbek nation." *Cahiers du Monde Russe et Soviétique* 32 (1991).

-. "Identitätsmodelle, Nationenbildung und regionale Kooperation in Mittelasien." In *Nationalismus und regionale Kooperation in Asien*, ed. B. Staiger. Vol. 243 of *Mitteilungen des Instituts für Asienkunde Hamburg*. Hamburg, 1995.

Chislennost' i sostav naseleniya SSSR po dannym Vsesoyuznoy perepisi naseleniya 1979 goda (Population size and composition of the USSR based on the All-Russian census of 1979). Moscow, 1984.

Dech, S.W., and R. Ressl. "Die Verlandung des Aralsees: Eine Bestandsaufnahme durch Satellitenfernerkundung." *Geographische Rundschau* 45 (1993).

Fierman, W., ed. *Soviet Central Asia: The Failed Transformation*. Boulder, 1991.

Fragner, B. "Probleme der Nationswerdung der Usbeken und Tadshiken". In *Die Muslime in der Sowjetunion und in Jugoslawien*, eds. A. Kappeler, G. Simon and G. Brunner. Cologne 1989.

Glezer, O., et al. "Samaya politicheskaya karta SSSR" (The 'most political' map of the USSR). *Moskovskiye novosti* (Moscow News), 17 March 1991.

Gumpel, W. "Die politische und wirtschaftliche Entwicklung in den zentralasiatischen Turkrepubliken." *Osteuropa* 44 (1994).

Halbach, U. "Islam, Nation und politische Öffentlichkeit in den zentralasiatischen (Unions-) Republiken." *Berichte des Bundesinstituts für ostwissenschaftliche und internationale Studien* 57 (1991).

-. "Konfliktpotentiale in Zentralasien". In *Zeitgeschichtliche Hintergründe aktueller Konflikte III*, ed. K.R. Spillmann. Vol. 31 of *Zürcher Beiträge zur Sicherheitspolitik und Konfliktforschung*. Zurich, 1994.

Lewis, R.A., ed. *Geographic Perspectives on Soviet Central Asia*. London and New York, 1992.

Machatschek, F. *Landeskunde von Russisch-Turkestan*. Stuttgart, 1921.

Micklin, P. "The Aral Crisis: Introduction to the Special Issue." *Post-Soviet Geography* 33 (1992).

Murzayev, E.M. "Research on the Aral Sea and Aral Region." *Post-Soviet Geography* 33 (1992).

Natsional'nyy sostav naseleniya SSSR po dannym Vsesoyuznoy perepisi naseleniya 1989 g. (National composition of the population of the USSR based on the All-Russian census of 1989). Moscow, 1991.

Narodnoye khozyaystvo SSSR v 1990 g. Statisticheskiy ezhegodnik (The national economy of the USSR in 1990: Statistical handbook). Moscow, 1991.

Narodnoye khozyaystvo Uzbekskoy SSR v 1990 g. Statisticheskiy ezhegodnik (The national economy of the Uzbek SSR in 1990: Statistical handbook). Tashkent, 1991.

Nowikow, N. "Nationalitätenkonflikte im Kaukasus und in Mittelasien." *Aus Geschichte und Zeitgeschichte. Beilage zur Wochenzeitung Das Parlament* B52-53 (1991).

Radio Free Europe/Radio Liberty. *Research Report*. Munich, 1992-.

Radvanyi, J. *L'URSS: Regions et Nations*. Paris, 1990.

Simon, G., and N. Simon. *Verfall und Untergang des sowjetischen Imperiums*. Munich, 1993.

Stadelbauer, J. "Russische Eisenbahnen in Turkestan - Pionierleistung oder Hemmnis für eine autochthone Raumentwicklung?" In *Frühe Eisenbahnbauten als Pionierleistungen*, eds. W. Hütteroth and H. Hopfinger. Neustadt a.d.A., 1993.

-. "Politisch-geographische Aspekte der Systemtransformation in der ehemaligen Sowjetunion." *Geographische Rundschau* 45 (1993).

-. *Die Nachfolgestaaten der Sowjetunion*. Darmstadt, 1996.

Picture Credits

712
Belt-hook. Cast brass, engraved, eyes originally with inlay. The snake-head terminations are typical of Timurid belt-hooks.
Scale: c. 1:1
Northern Afghanistan or Central Asia, late 14th/early 15th century